SCOTTISH SOCIETY
1707–1830

MANCHESTER
UNIVERSITY PRESS

SCOTTISH SOCIETY
1707–1830

Beyond Jacobitism,
towards industrialisation

Christopher A. Whatley

Manchester University Press
Manchester and New York

distributed exclusively in the USA by St. Martin's Press

Published by Manchester University Press
Oxford Road, Manchester M13 9NR, UK
and Room 400, 175 Fifth Avenue, New York, NY 10010, USA
http://www.man.ac.uk/mup

Distributed exclusively in the USA by
St. Martin's Press, Inc., 175 Fifth Avenue, New York,
NY 10010, USA

Distributed exclusively in Canada by
UBC Press, University of British Columbia, 2029 West Mall,
Vancouver, BC, Canada V6T 1Z2

British Library Cataloguing-in-Publication Data
A catalogue record for this book is available from the British Library

Library of Congress Cataloging-in-Publication Data applied for

ISBN 0 7190 4540 1 *hardback*
     0 7190 4541 X *paperback*

First published 2000

09 08 07 05 04 03 02 01 00   10 9 8 7 6 5 4 3 2 1

Typeset in Sabon with Frutiger
by Action Publishing Technology Limited, Gloucester
Printed in Great Britain by
by Bell & Bain Ltd, Glasgow

For my father, H. Allan Whatley,
with love and gratitude

Contents

Maps and figures

Maps

Figures

Acknowledgements

On a very practical level I first wish to thank Dr Ian Graham-Bryce, Principal of the University of Dundee, for granting me additional sabbatical leave during which I was able to complete this book. It has been a long time in the making and without an extended period of leave it could not have been written. Dr David Gowland courageously took on the job of Head of the Department of History during my absence. The University of Dundee also provided me with a proportion of the financial resources with which I have been able to gather the material for the book. Many former students in the universities of Dundee and St Andrews have contributed, unconsciously, to the text by demanding jargon-free and straightforward answers to questions they have posed. My colleagues in the Department of History at Dundee have generated a climate of lively intellectual debate and enquiry that is highly conducive to productive research. During the early stages of the book's conception I was encouraged and assisted by my former colleagues in the Department of Scottish History at the University of St Andrews. In this regard I owe a special debt of thanks to Dr William Knox.

Research for this book has taken place in many archives and libraries in Scotland and elsewhere. Those whose staff have been especially generous in terms of their time and enthusiasm for the project are the City of Edinburgh Archives, where the Convention of Royal Burghs papers are held, Angus District Archives (in Montrose), City of Dundee Archives, Dumfries Archives (Marion Stewart has continued to send on copies of material since I visited some years ago), Perth and Kinross Council Archives (where Steve Connelly has provided sterling service), Devon Record Office, the Record Office in Carlisle, the Archives and Manuscripts Departments of the Universities of Dundee and St Andrews, and what until the latest round of local government reorganisation were Highland Regional Archives, Stirling Regional Archives and Strathclyde Regional Archives. I was assisted in Aberdeen by Judith Cripps. The library staff in the universities of Dundee, Glasgow, Strathclyde and St

Acknowledgements

Andrews, as well as the British Library, have also willingly responded to my requests for assistance. The National Library of Scotland is always a pleasure to work in, and remained so even during recent building work. I have also been ably assisted by the staff of the Advocates Library and the Signet Library. Curatorial staff at the National Archives of Scotland (formerly the Scottish Record Office) with whom I have had dealings have gone out of their way to provide help and guidance, sometimes enthusiastically. Unfortunately, in recent years, re-organisation and restrictions on the quantity of material which can be seen by readers during a visit, have seriously reduced the usefulness of this treasure trove of historical documentation for the serious academic researcher who is not Edinburgh-based.

I am grateful to the Duke of Buccleuch, the Clerks of Penicuik and many others who have deposited their family papers in the National Archives and allowed me to inspect and use them. The National Register of Archives (Scotland) made it possible for me to see several collections of family papers which remain in private hands. In particular, I wish to thank the Blair Charitable Trust and the Earls of Mansfield and Strathmore for granting permission for me to work on their muniments. The archivist at the castles of Blair and Glamis, Jane Anderson, greatly facilitated my researches there.

I have benefited greatly by trying out ideas informally with individuals whose opinions I value enormously. Into this category come Dr Bob Harris of the University of Dundee and Professor Christopher Smout of the University of St Andrews. Both have listened to my musings, read parts of the text, and then provided me with invaluable searching commentaries on what I have written. Absolutely no blame is attached to either for factual errors or mistaken or ill-judged interpretations on my part. On some issues we differ. Chris is a model scholar, not fearing but welcoming discussion and disagreement, conscious of the foolishness of adhering too strongly to positions which the evidence suggests but cannot confirm, and upon which shifting historical perspectives and new methodologies can shed new and very different light. David Alston, Paula Martin and Mary Young, three of my current postgraduate students, have provided useful leads. Dr Eric Graham was kind enough to present me with a copy of his fine Strathclyde doctoral thesis on the impact of mercantilism on the Scottish marine. Professor Charles McKean has willingly given of his time to discuss my elementary queries about Scottish architecture. Seminars to which I have contributed at the universities of Edinburgh, Stirling and Strathclyde have given me the opportunity to present my ideas and listen to cautionary voices of wisdom.

Mike Bartholomew, Anne Crowther, Roy Campbell, Ian Donnachie, Chris Bartlett, Murdo Macdonald, Rowy Mitchison, Sheena Andrew, Ken Simpson, Tom Devine, Hamish Fraser, Bob Morris, Daniel Szechi,

Harry Dickinson, Stana Nenadic, Lorraine Walsh, Jill Turnbull, John Robertson, Elaine Campbell and the late John Strawhorn all helped in various ways, either by listening, pointing to a source or sending a particularly useful book or off-print.

The original proposal for this book came from the late Francis Brooke of Manchester University Press. After a period during which little progress was made, it has been brought to fruition by the current editorial and production team, whose enthusiasm for the project has encouraged me to complete it when it looked as if competing pressures for time would leave it unfinished. With a great deal of patience and enormous skill, Sara Reid of the University of Dundee's department of history has prepared the entire text in accordance with the publisher's conventions. Carolyn Bain drew the maps with her customary precision.

Last and certainly not least, I would like to thank my wife Pat for her encouragement and support, and for her understanding on those evenings when on her return from work she was met with an empty table, a grim look and too little conversation. My children, Eilidh and Neil, wonder why I do it, but continue to appear genuinely interested. This I gathered from their frequent enquiries about when the book was to be finished.

Map 1 The Scottish counties in the eighteenth century (including proportions of Scottish population, 1755)

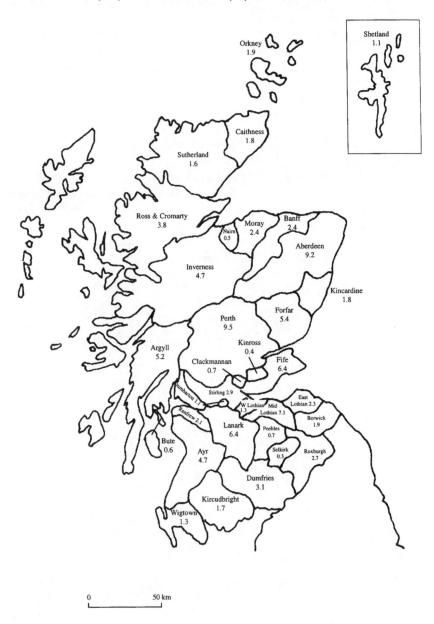

Source: derived from I. Whyte, *Scotland Before the Industrial Revolution* (London and New York, 1995), 116, 339.

Map 2 Relief map showing the main Scottish burghs, c. 1707

Source: derived from P. G. B. MacNeill and H. I. MacQueen (eds), *Atlas of Scottish History to 1707* (Edinburgh, 1996), 14, 228.

Introduction

This book encompasses a crucial period in Scottish history. At the turn of
the eighteenth century Scotland was beginning to recover from the 'ill
years' of the 1690s, when for three or four years (depending on region)
famine had ravaged the country. Somewhere between one and two people
out of ten perished. In some districts the loss was almost certainly
greater.[1] The surviving population stood at just over one million.

Most Scots lived in the countryside, in small settlements, with the
greater proportion in the north and Highlands. Aberdeen was the most
populous county, with Perth second. Lanarkshire had only half as many
people. Edinburgh had long been and still was the largest city, with some
54,000 inhabitants. An ambitious attempt to establish a Scottish trading
colony in the isthmus of Darien had foundered, again with the loss of life
and perhaps as much as a quarter of the nation's capital. Although
Scotland still had a Parliament of its own, and a Privy Council, under the
regal union neither was able to do much to resist English domination in
foreign affairs or even in British waters, where Scottish ships were periodically captured by English crews. The state apparatus in Scotland was
weak and the customs and excise systems notoriously corrupt. Apart
from linen cloth, Scotland's exports were either semi-manufactures or
agricultural products. Herring (which accounted for some 13.6 per cent
of the total value), wool and sheepskins vied for second place after linen.
Virtually all manufactured goods, including iron and copper, were
imported, as were luxuries, which included wine and coaches. Money
was scarce and, even in the best of times, living standards for the majority
were at rock bottom levels. There are indications that from the sixteenth
century the range of the typical diet in Scotland was narrowing, with
much less meat being consumed. Oatmeal had become the Scottish staple,
washed down with ale.

There were some bright spots however, such as the success of
merchants from Glasgow in establishing an illicit trade in tobacco with
England's North-American colonies. The significance of this and other

signs that suggest that the condition of Scotland was not as gloomy as this brief survey suggests are considered in more detail in chapter 1.

Not much more than a century later the picture had been transformed. There could still be short bouts of intense hunger but, while famine was still feared during the worst periods of shortage, there was sufficient surplus wealth to purchase grain or potatoes to feed the poor or unemployed. An improved transport infrastructure made distribution easier. From the 1820s steam-powered vessels could even ship foodstuffs into the seaward parts of the Highlands and to the Hebrides. The powerful British state could assist by banning the use of grain for distilling. So effective was such a ban, it was reported from Glasgow in October 1796, that a female bleachfield worker who for thirty-three years had been in the habit 'of appropriating two days in each week ... to the purposes of drinking', had not since the rise in the price of whisky, 'been once intoxicated, or one day absent from her work.'[2]

Most people lived longer too, with expectation of life at birth having risen from 33.5 years in the mid-eighteenth century to 39.4 in the 1790s, although the pattern would alter in the grimmer industrial towns in the nineteenth century. The death-rate too had fallen. By 1800 the population had risen to 1.6 million, and by 1831 stood at 2.3 million. Ireland's population however had grown at a faster rate during the eighteenth century, but what was striking about Scotland was not only the increased *per capita* incomes (in Ireland these had fallen), but also the mobility of the population. Great shifts had occurred. By 1821 almost half of the inhabitants of Scotland resided within the central belt, with manufacturing towns such as Paisley and Glasgow absorbing higher proportions of migrants than most. Lanarkshire had become the most populous county by 1801. By 1821 Glasgow had overtaken Edinburgh to become Scotland's biggest city (with a population of 151,000), and was second only to London in Britain. The rate of urban growth in Scotland in the second half of the century was faster than anywhere else in Europe except Poland (where the starting point had been exceptionally low).[3] Between 1801 and 1831 the growth rate in Scotland had reached unprecedented levels which would never be repeated. In terms of the proportion of population in towns of over ten thousand, by 1800 Scotland was fourth in the West-European league, and not far behind England and Wales. But of course rapid urban growth created unprecedented social problems and conflicts between the social classes.

Scottish-manufactured goods were well-known in North and South America, the West Indies and, nearer home, in England and Ireland. Agricultural practices in parts of Lowland Scotland were among the most advanced in Europe. The intellectual power-house of the Scottish Enlightenment, inextricably linked with the aspirations and demands of an ambitious social elite, provided the conditions in which entrepreneurial and inventive talents could flourish. So too did the challenges and opportunities which arose from Scotland's legal access (after 1 May 1707) to the British trading empire. Before the end of the eighteenth century, and increasingly so in the nineteenth, Scots – who had hitherto been drawing hard on English (and other) expertise – were making contributions to the industrialisation process in England and Ireland and on the continent of Europe. In the Highlands what had been the first stirrings of commercialisation in the late sixteenth century, consolidated in the seventeenth as the dismantling by Highland chiefs of the clan system began, had by the early nineteenth been turned into rampant estate capitalism. Heart-rending accounts of the worst social consequences of the programmes of land reform and clearance rever-berated through London and Edinburgh. The troubles of the post-Napoleonic War years were one of the factors which led to the orches-tration of a tartan-shrouded show of Scottish national unity for the visit of George IV to Scotland in 1822. Jacobitism, which had divided the country in 1715 and 1745–46, was now impotent, its romanticisation having begun within a few years of the defeat of Charles Edward Stuart at Culloden. But the lost cause served as a largely mythical pool of common memory which could be and was selectively plundered to serve the needs of the British state.[4] After Waterloo Highlandism was promoted by Tory counter-revolu-tionaries as a value system which 'took pride in military service [Scots had flocked to the British army during the wars with Revolutionary France] and which upheld traditional authority and associated values of religion, order, morality and patriotism'.[5]

The narrative in this book draws to a close around 1830. Scotland was not quite an industrial nation, but was well on the way. Steam power was being used on an ever-increasing scale, and iron and steel production, engineering and shipbuilding had all been established. But the era of their domination of world markets lay in the future.

Although by 1830 almost one-third of Scots lived in towns of five thousand-plus, two-thirds of the population still lived in the countryside or in towns and villages of less than five thousand people. Two-thirds of handloom weavers lived in such smaller towns, villages and settlements. But many of these were new and, in most, growth was rapid. As we will see, conditions were no better in smaller concentrations. In Caithness and elsewhere in the north-east, fishing villages grew roughly as fast as the industrial cities in the first half of the nineteenth century. It is important to recognise the diversity of Scottish society, even within the urban hier-archy, although historians know more about Edinburgh and the main industrial towns than the smaller, regional centres like Dumfries or Inverness, or how the older coal and salt burghs along the Forth fared in the age of transformation.[6]

But wherever they lived, the majority of Scots had become wage workers, proletarians. As will be seen in chapter 6 in particular, by the end of the 1820s the main lines of Scotland's economic development in the nineteenth century had been laid down. Before the end of that decade too, the struggle which had been waged between, on the one hand, a nakedly self-interested market system, and, on the other, those upon whose exploitation its success largely depended, had been won. As Professor Christopher Smout observed in his *Century of the Scottish People, 1830–1950* (1986), when accounting for Scotland's 'abiding poverty' in the nineteenth century, 'the upper classes held the whip hand over a divided and largely unorganised working class'. This had not always been so, although for the labouring classes the eighteenth century was not one of formal trade unions and political manifestos. It was however a century during which the common people acted in defence of what E. P. Thompson termed the moral economy of the poor. This book examines the constraints which labouring people imposed within the early modern workplace, and in their communities as they were confronted with a new economic system which was 'disinfested of intrusive moral imperatives'.[7] The breaking down of the forces of custom, organised labour and the restraints of community was a process which had begun prior to 1707 but reached new heights of intensity at various points through the eighteenth and early nineteenth centuries. Confrontation was concentrated into specific periods during which large parts of the country were affected. This was particularly so in the 1720s, the 1760s and 1770s, the 1810s and, above all, from around 1819 to 1825. Discussion of the conflicts which swept these years form substantial parts of chapters 2, 5, 7 and 8 respectively.

The book attempts comprehensiveness of a sort, although certain topics have necessarily been neglected. At the time of writing this introduction I am painfully aware of a growing pile of recently published books and articles at my side, the contents of which will not be incorporated here. At present there is no full-length economic and social history of Scotland in the period covered, although there are those which include these aspects of the eighteenth and early nineteenth centuries as elements in wider studies. The best-known, and still unsurpassed in its breadth and insight, is Christopher Smout's *A History of the Scottish People, 1560–1830* (1969). On the other hand, it is no longer the most accurate introduction to many of the topics with which it deals. This is inevitable given that in the thirty years since it first appeared, a sizeable contingent of graduate students and professional historians has been able to exploit previously inaccessible archival resources, uncover new ground and re-work the old with the help of modern methods and approaches.

Admirable studies of the economy have been written, along with the two classics by the late Professor Henry Hamilton, *The Industrial Revolution in Scotland* (1932) *and An Economic History of Scotland in the Eighteenth Century* (1963), and Professor Roy Campbell's enduring text, *Scotland Since 1707*, first published in 1965. Most of these are now hard to obtain.[8] In fact no new book-length study of the Scottish economy during the period has appeared since 1977, apart from the present author's short *The Industrial Revolution in Scotland* (1997).[9] Numerous studies of particular sectors of the economy have been published, on agriculture, banking and individual industries. Certain regions, notably the Highlands, have been extensively examined by professors Devine, Dodgshon, Macinnes and Richards, and written about with even greater passion by Jim Hunter. Social history too has blossomed north of the border since the 1970s. During the 1980s and 1990s whole new areas of enquiry were opened up. A great deal more is known than even twenty years ago about the social history of religion and sexuality, for example. Massive strides forward have been taken too in demographic studies, while, as the twentieth century drew to a close, the first fruits of explorations into the field of environmental history began to emerge. Readers will find references to large numbers of these publications in the extensive end-notes for each chapter.

It is with no small sense of indebtedness to the historians who have made such learned and invaluable contributions to our understanding of Scotland in the eighteenth and early nineteenth centuries that the writer of a book such as this draws on these riches. The trepidation that comes from the awareness of how much compression can deform an argument, or belittle years of scholarship, is relieved only during those parts of the book which are based on my own archive-based research. Some of the ideas have appeared in print before, although invariably at an earlier stage of their development, or without the broader economic, political and social context which the period covered by this book provides. Much material however is altogether fresh. For example, as in England until recently, relatively little was known about the economic and social history of the first half of the eighteenth century.[10] This book draws on little-used and in some instances hitherto untapped evidence (including papers of the Convention of Royal Burghs). It argues that far from being a somewhat inconsequential period lying between the momentous years leading up to the Union of 1707 and the onset of the early Industrial Revolution and large-scale agrarian change, the period was one which had a formative influence on subsequent Scottish development. The years between *c.* 1707 and *c.* 1750 are of as much interest and moment to economic and social historians as they are to the political historians who have tended to dominate coverage of the period.[11] Fear of Jacobitism played an enormously significant part in determining the character of these four or five decades and in explaining government attitudes to and actions in Scotland, but the successful integration of Scotland within the new British state required more than the elimination of the Stuart challenge to the Hanoverian dynasty.

The book then is not simply a neutral survey of recent research find-ings. It does have an interpretative framework and also qualifies and provides challenges to some accounts of Scottish historical development which are currently in the ascendant. A central issue is the explanation of Scotland's economic transformation. While there are various shades of opinion on this, most contain a large deterministic element, with Scotland being portrayed as a variant of a European pattern of industrialisation in which expanding world trade, ample mineral resources and comparative regional advantages – in Scotland's case in textile production – played the major roles. In a very broad sense all this is true, but what has to be explained is how Scotland came from so far behind to share with England the lead in European industrialisation by the early decades of the nine-teenth century. The burning question of what precisely produced the extraordinary 'lift off' in Scottish economic fortunes in the 1740s and 1750s has not yet been resolved.[12] Enormously stimulating and produc-tive analysis, with Ireland as the main comparator (but some Scandinavian countries too), has led to the conclusion that Scotland's economic success in the later eighteenth and nineteenth centuries lay in the 'texture' of Scottish society, which was favourable to growth.[13] In this regard, Scottish rural society is judged to have been of over-riding importance, in that it was improving prior to 1707, and was capable of creating agricultural surpluses and releasing a labour pool for urban manufacturing. Among other assumptions upon which this complex and compelling argument depends is that the problems of the 1690s were 'essentially temporary'. The decade represents therefore merely a 'dip' in what was otherwise a continuous trajectory of favourable forces which ran from the seventeenth century into the eighteenth. The Union of 1707 in this line of argument becomes 'more marginal to Scottish modernisa-tion than it had hitherto seemed'.[14]

It is not denied here that developments in eighteenth-century Scotland often had their pre-Union precursors. This however is very different from saying that one thing led directly to the other. After carefully weighing the evidence available, what I argue in chapter 1 of this book is that by the end of the seventeenth century Scotland's economy – and indeed Scottish society – had run into profoundly serious difficulties which could not be surmounted without the opportunities and protection which Union provided. With its minuscule navy (which in 1696 comprised three hulls borrowed from England and rigged out in London), Scotland was virtually defenceless at a time when aggressive European nation states were intent on carving up the world's trade on the basis of their ability to master the seas.

It is undoubtedly the case that in Scotland a dynamic governing class was committed to economic improvement before the Union. But the battery of policies they introduced was largely ineffective and, contrary to what has been argued elsewhere, this mattered enormously. Indeed, in part, Union can be interpreted as a necessary building block on the way to opulence and evidence of the acceptance of the economic realism which characterised the writings of several Scots on economic affairs in the 1690s and early 1700s. It presented risks too however. Ironically, it is also proposed that it was the failure of the Union in the short-term to provide the economic benefits which had been promised that produced the changes in state policy towards Scotland which are generally acknowledged to have been necessary to lift Scotland out of her post-Union malaise. But it is suggested that to a greater extent than has been understood hitherto, it was conditions in and around the towns and the availability of employment in manufacturing (which in the case of hand-spun flax and handloom weaving of linen was fairly widely dispersed into the countryside) that mattered, arguably, less than rural Scotland. What may not have been appreciated either is the range of ways in which Westminster aided the Scots or succumbed to special Scottish pleading. The political economy of Scottish development in the eighteenth century is an under-explored issue, and it deserves further investigation. The state is offered here as a potentially crucial piece in the jigsaw which explains Scotland's economic achievement by *c.* 1780 and which provided the basis for further spectacular advance. It should however be acknowledged that by a somewhat different route a similar conclusion was reached by Professor Roy Campbell when he remarked that when in the 1780s the Scottish economy was resting on a basis laid by achievements apparently its own, 'it was in reality resting on a foundation established through Union with England'. Even those who are inclined to emphasise the crucial role of structural factors do acknowledge the part played by the Union in facilitating economic advance. The debate is about balance and priorities.[15]

Another factor which has to be built into the equation regards the ongoing efforts of the Scottish landed classes to obtain for themselves the economic benefits which they had begun to secure as part of the mercantilist thrust of the Scottish Parliament and which were also enshrined in the Articles of the Treaty of Union. In this sense there was continuity, but of economic aggrandisement which the fragile Scottish economy could not sustain and which a suffering Scottish population would not tolerate. An uncomfortable reality incorporated into the reading of Scottish history which is presented in this volume, is that both directly and indirectly the Union shaped and overshadowed economic, social and political life in eighteenth-century Scotland in ways which simply cannot be ignored. It has been suggested that Scottish historians may have paid too much attention to the Union as a factor in the process of economic growth. If this has in the past encouraged parochialism and blinded practitioners to the similarities there were in the social structures of different parts of the British isles and other European regions, the observation is a sensible one. But while changing historiographical fashions and enthusiasms, new agendas and fresh insights are to be welcomed and adopted where appropriate, they cannot be permitted to write the facts out of the histories of states and nations.

In some accounts, natural resources have been relegated to a secondary role. Coal was judged not to have been essential to Scottish development prior to 1830.[16] It is now clear however that the existence of readily-exploitable coal in a particular locality, or nearby, had a powerful bearing on the pattern and pace of industrial development throughout Britain. Even more important at this stage, it made possible the urban growth referred to earlier. Without this plentiful and relatively cheap source of fuel for cooking and heating it is hard to see how this could have happened, even if in some parts of the country peat could act as a substitute.[17] Contemporaries certainly recognised that the absence of coal was a considerable hardship and cause of complaint in the western Highlands and Islands. Unlike Dundee, which bordered the coalfields of Fife, Aberdeen saw the early demise of large-scale textile production (c. 1840), partly as a result of the expense of imported coal. Evidence from Lancashire suggests that the availability of sources of running water which could be harnessed for the purpose of driving all sorts of mills comes into the same category. So too does the humid climate of the west of Scotland, which allegedly reduced the incidence of faults in weaving. Ample rainfall was even more important for spinners than weavers, as was the fact that the water was lime-free and soft enough for the finishing processes.[18]

The other major issue with which this book is concerned is power and the ways in which individuals and groups whose interests and means were very different co-existed. Overwhelmingly, the impression given in the literature is of a Scotland in which not only was the distribution of power enormously unequal (which it was), but also that it was exercised with remarkable ease. Tranquillity in the countryside, for example, was maintained partly through 'the delicate social ties of hierarchy and dependence'.[19] A social stability 'characteristic of feudalism', it has been claimed, was evident as late as the 1790s in a country in which a 'sense of hierarchy came naturally'. Patrician rulers glide calmly over the historical stage, able to swat away at will mildly irritating gestures of discontent arising from the cowed people below. Anything more energetic – the formation of a meal mob for example – is ascribed to the effects of hunger or alcohol; the 'Scots on the skite' as one patronising but self-confessed Tory writer puts it.[20] Political riots were raised by and on behalf of rulers who wished to bolster an argument or demand with a show of force. Thus the 'only significant actors' on the Scottish political stage in the early eighteenth century were the landowners, gentry and burgh councils.[21] Such indeed was the alleged timidity of the lower orders in Scotland that by and large the ruling classes were able to govern without recourse to the army, before whom the rabble invariably fled.

Social control was maintained too through the Kirk and parish schools, and the transmission by the former of an ideology which stressed humility, unworthiness and the need for moral and physical restraint. By means such as these, the Scots became and have been portrayed as an 'uninflammable' people, an image which has been underpinned by the couthy cap-touching portraits of social harmony painted by Dean Ramsay, Henry Gray Graham and their followers.[22] With a handful of exceptions, commercialisation, industrialisation and agrarian change were received with equanimity. The French Revolution posed no real threats to the authorities while in some accounts the 'Radical War' of 1820 has been treated almost contemptuously.[23]

A very different perspective is adopted here, with profound implications for our understanding of the direction of Scottish history in the period. For example, as has been suggested, in most histories of Scotland, the people are invariably relegated to a watching role. Most studies of the political circumstances in which the Union of 1707 was steered through the Scottish Parliament, have ignored the part played by popular opinion in determining the final shape of the Articles. Equally, and invariably in sweeping and unsubstantiated generalisations, its effect on the lives of ordinary Scots is deemed to have been marginal. It is argued here that neither of these propositions stands up to examination.[24] As has been noted already, the consequences of the Union were of the greatest importance on a day-to-day level. Without comprehending the marked impact the Union had in Scotland on people in all walks of life and in so many aspects of them, it is posited here that an understanding of the reasons for and nature of economic development in Scotland prior to *c.* 1780 will be partial at best. It was largely the post-1707 crisis in economic conditions and the consequent social tensions and political threats to the integrity of the new British state which was responsible for the resurgence of the Scottish economy from the 1740s. That Scottish urban society during parts of the period being examined here was more akin to a tightrope walker than has been suspected hitherto, may be gathered from the speed and apparent alacrity with which the authorities acted to tackle impending food shortages.

As has been observed by Douglas Hay and Nicholas Rogers in their examination of English society in the eighteenth century, 'coercion and the other forms that power takes do not overtly determine everything people can and cannot do'.[25] Chapters 4, 5 and 8 demonstrate that this observation applies equally well in Scotland. Perhaps the contrast between image and actuality is even more striking. Readers may be surprised by the frequency with which soldiers march across the Scottish historical stage, although not always with the result those who had called on their services hoped for. Certainly, the suggestion that coercion by military force prior to the later eighteenth century was confined to the Levellers Revolt in Galloway and suppression of the Jacobites will have to be revised. This however is another topic which requires closer scrutiny. We will discover too that the Kirk was a more fickle agent of social control than has usually been assumed. However, all but the most extreme dissenting sects set limits on political alternatives, beyond which believers discontented with their earthly lot would not dare to venture.

Hitherto, and with a few notable exceptions whose contributions will be referred to as we proceed, much Scottish history has been written 'from above', from the perspective of the powerful, those in whose hands it is implied that power was exercised without resistance or challenge.[26] Landowners are the prime example in Scotland, although as will be seen in chapters 2 and 4, there are grounds for qualifying the assumption of an all-powerful elite. By taking cognisance of the perspectives and responses of the common people and recreating a society in which the principal groups or classes interacted dynamically, a very different picture emerges, as it did of eighteenth-century England, largely as a result of E. P. Thompson's seminal reappraisal and other outstanding studies which followed.[27] Indeed, if built into the model is the possibility that in times of stress – dearth, anticipated dearth or political upheaval for instance – the outcomes are unpredictable, or were contemplated or envisaged as such by the authorities, the formal structures of power become somewhat unreliable guides to its *de facto* distribution. It is argued here that behind the walls of the classical Adam-designed mansion houses, 'new' castles, urban and semi-urban villas and the terraced dwellings of Edinburgh's New Town and Glasgow's Georgian squares, men and women periodically fretted and worried as they considered how best to proceed with what was in effect a programme of national social engineering while at the same time retaining the existing social structure. Just because the old ruling class in Scotland managed to survive the fundamental economic and social changes of the eighteenth and early nineteenth centuries, does not mean that the remarkable flexibility they demonstrated in order to maintain their position was undertaken on their own terms and of their own volition.

Yet it is not intended simply to offer a Scottish version of one of the Marxist-inspired 'stirring narratives of rural dispossession and urban proletarianisation' which have had their critics south of the border. (Although reflecting their importance in Scotland in the period under review, these 'narratives' do feature prominently.) Less thoroughly than is desirable perhaps, attention will also be paid to the rising middle classes and some of the areas of social co-operation and consensus which served to bind together communities of different classes.[28]

The Scottish coal miners and salters provide us with a telling example of how, by adopting a different perspective, we can transform our understanding of the nature of social relationships. By looking at the formal powers enjoyed by the landed coalmaster, who could also call on an oppressive set of laws passed by the Scottish Parliament designed to control the workers in the coal and salt industries, it seems perfectly reasonable to describe them as wretched serfs, their labour in the east exploited 'to a degree unparalleled elsewhere in the United Kingdom'.[29] Physically and socially isolated, they were easily supervised, a job made easier – the argument runs – because of the unskilled nature of their work. Yet careful examination of the residence patterns of coal and salt workers, and of the conditions in which they worked, produces little in the way of supporting evidence, as will be seen later. The proposition that they could be closely supervised 'under the eagle eye' of the nobleman's grieve is nothing more than creative historiographical fiction. Coal miners worked in gloomy, not to say dark, underground labyrinths of separate levels and 'rooms', each of which was worked by a single collier. To 'escape' was relatively easy, and frequently done, although more significant is the way in which coal workers were able to determine collectively – at least in part – their own pace of work. Negotiation within a power relationship which was not as unequal as it seems at first sight is the key theme here, and it runs through much of the book. Enclosed saltpans, enveloped in clouds of steam and smoke, producing salt in a process which continued over a twenty-four hour period, meant that it was virtually impossible to know what was going on inside. Both the occupation of collier and master salter required long training in what were craft skills. To let unskilled men loose in the former was to risk fire, collapsed roofs and, in short, the catastrophic loss of capital assets, while an untrained salt worker could easily damage and burn the valuable iron plates, imported from Sweden, which were bolted together to form the pan. As one more perceptive coalmaster asked rhetorically in 1774, when coal workers in some parts of the Scottish coalfield were proving enormously troublesome: who were the slaves, 'the Master or the Collier ... most people will be of opinion that the Masters are the Dupes and Slaves of their Colliers'.[30] Other relevant aspects of the revolutionised historiography of the Scottish coal workers are referred to later in the book.

No apologies are offered for writing a book on eighteenth- and early nineteenth-century Scotland in which the common people loom large. The eighteenth century of course was the period of the Enlightenment, which in Scotland saw the remarkable flourishing of Scottish science, philosophy and the visual arts in the persons of Henry Raeburn and David Wilkie. But sufficient attention has been paid to the relatively small numbers of individuals who were directly involved, even though new research has established that these were greater than was once thought and spread far beyond Edinburgh's High Street. Much is known about the cultural manifestations of the Enlightenment, civic humanism, the cultivation of the emotions, and the cult of sentimentality as exemplified by James MacPherson's *Poems of Ossian*.[31] But seen through such spectacles, eighteenth-century Scotland is something of a foreign country. These were the concerns of the minority, as too are most Enlightenment studies, which notwithstanding the awesome scholarship with which many have been conducted, 'exclude over 95 per cent of the population of Scotland who [it is argued] were not aware that an Enlightenment was under way during their ... own lifetimes'.[32] As we will see however, while the changes the Enlightenment in Scotland legitimised and reinforced may not have had a name, most of the four-fifths of Scots we can consider to have been members of the labouring classes around 1800 felt something of the effects of its rationalism. It impacted most acutely through the ordered use of labour either in the urban workplace or on the refashioned landed estate.

This book draws attention to another Scotland which would certainly have been more recognisable to most contemporaries, one which was less restrained, less deferential and more rumbustious. It was one upon which poets like Robert Fergusson and Robert Burns fed (although by no means exclusively in the case of this latter poet of multiple voices). It is the context in which so much of Burns' biting anti-authoritarian poetry is located. If we could hear the past, our ears would be assailed by the sound of a plebeian culture in which noise was enormously important: in 'rough music', rhythmic drum beating, bell ringing, rhyming doggerel, verse and song. By such means (which sometimes meant seizing the symbols of ruling class power – a towns's drum or pipes, or the town-house bells) solidarities were strengthened and hearts and spirits lifted, at work in the fields or the workshop, or on processions in protest against perceived ills and hated individuals. Little written evidence of this has survived, but as will be seen, enough can be done with scraps and incidental comments to add this element to our re-discovery of the far from quiescent – or quiet – Scot. To dismiss most Scots as being less interested in or having a lower participation rate in musical activity than their counterparts in the south and in Europe, as some historians have done, seems premature in the light of the paucity of intensive research on the subject. Popular culture, to which some space is also devoted, was different in that its repertoire was limited, but in terms of the energy expended in dancing, for example, it lacked nothing, nor was it necessarily ritually impoverished.[33]

In the English context, the late E. P. Thompson was criticised for omitting women and gender relations from his conceptualisation of class struggle. No Scottish historian has yet been bold enough to attempt to produce such a majestically comprehensive tome for Scotland.

Nevertheless, although it is in its infancy, work on women's history in eighteenth-century Scotland has begun, and it has been possible to incorporate females – and less often, children – into this narrative. The indications are that while women in Scotland shared much in common with their counterparts elsewhere in early modern Europe, there were aspects of their experience which were distinctive in Scotland, or at least sufficiently different to merit attention. Thus in the workplace they were proportionately more conspicuous than they were in England, and their capacity for violence in popular protest is at least worthy of notice and of further investigation. As has been suggested already, the labouring poor did contribute significantly to the shaping of Scottish history in the eighteenth century, notwithstanding their almost complete exclusion from the electoral process. Indeed, there is a sense in which it was the potential the working classes had to slow or divert the progress of Scottish capital which led to the bitter clash of class interests in the 1810s and 1820s. The outcome played a major part in determining how Scotland entered the Victorian era.

Notes

1 R. E. Tyson, 'Famine in Aberdeenshire, 1695–1699: anatomy of a crisis', in D. Stevenson (ed.), *From Lairds to Louns: Country and Burgh Life in Aberdeen, 1600–1800* (Aberdeen, 1986), 48–50.

2 *Glasgow Courier*, 18 October 1796.

3 R. A. Houston, 'The demographic regime', in T. M. Devine and R. Mitchison (eds), *People and Society in Scotland, Volume 1, 1760-1830* (Edinburgh, 1988), 22.

4 W. Donaldson, *The Jacobite Song: Political Myth and National Identity* (Aberdeen, 1988), 65, 93–4.

5 J. E. Cookson, 'The Napoleonic wars, military Scotland and tory highlandism in the early nineteenth century', *Scottish Historical Review*, LXXVIII (April 1999), 73.

6 Two postgraduate students at the University of Dundee, David Alston and Paula Martin, are working on Cromarty and Cupar respectively. Much can be expected from their theses.

7 See E. P. Thompson, 'The moral economy of the English crowd in the eighteenth century', *Past and Present*, L (1971), 90. Thompson's thesis has been the subject of lengthy debate and challenge. For Thompson's rebuttal of his critics, see 'The moral economy revisited', in E. P. Thompson, *Customs in Common* (London, 1991), 259–351.

8 H. Hamilton, *An Economic History of Scotland in the Eighteenth Century* (Oxford, 1963); H. Hamilton, *The Industrial Revolution in Scotland* (Oxford, 1932); R. H. Campbell, *Scotland Since 1707: The Rise of an Industrial Society* (Oxford, 1965).

9 B. Lenman, *An Economic History of Modern Scotland 1660–1976* (London, 1977).

10 For a recent contribution on Scotland, see I. D. Whyte, *Scotland Before the Industrial Revolution. An Economic & Social History, c. 1050–c. 1750* (London, 1995).

11 This is not a criticism. Some of their work has been outstanding, e.g. P. W. J. Riley, *The English Ministers and Scotland, 1707–1727* (London, 1964); J. S. Shaw, *The Management of Scottish Society, 1707–1764* (Edinburgh, 1983).

12 R. A. Houston, 'Eighteenth-century Scottish studies: out of the laager?', *Scottish Historical Review*, LXXIII (1994), 79.

13 T. M. Devine, 'The Union of 1707 and Scottish development', *Scottish Economic & Social History*, V (1985), 37.

14 C. Harvie, 'Scottish industrialisation, c. 1750–1880', in R. Schulze (ed.), *Industrial Regions in Transformation. Historical Roots and Patterns of Regional Structural Change: A European Comparison* (Essen, 1993), 180; for a study of the impact of the Union in the longer-run, see C. H. Lee, *Scotland and the United Kingdom: The Economy and the Union in the Twentieth Century* (Manchester, 1995).

15 For a short summary of Campbell's argument, see his *Scotland Since 1707*, 4–12.

16 T. M. Devine, 'The English connection and Irish–Scottish development in the eighteenth century', in T. M. Devine and D. Dickson (eds), *Ireland and Scotland, 1600–1850: Parallels and Contrasts in Economic and Social Development* (Edinburgh, 1983), 25.

17 C. A. Whatley, 'New light on Nef's numbers: coal mining and the first phase of Scottish industrialisation, c. 1700–1830', in A. J. G. Cummings and T. M. Devine (eds), *Industry, Business and Society in Scotland Since 1700: Essays presented to John Butt* (Edinburgh, 1994), 17–18.

18 D. A. Farnie, *The English Cotton Industry and the World Market, 1815–1896* (Oxford, 1979), 47–55.

19 T. M. Devine, 'Social stability and agrarian change in the eastern lowlands of Scotland, 1810–1840', in T. M. Devine, *Exploring the Scottish Past: Themes in the History of Scottish Society* (East Linton, 1995), 198.

20 M. Fry, *The Dundas Despotism* (Edinburgh, 1992), 163–5, 167. See too B. Lenman, *Integration, Enlightenment and Industrialisation: Scotland, 1746–1832* (London, 1981), 11.

21 B. Lenman, *The Jacobite Risings in Britain, 1689–1746* (London, 1980), 149.

22 H. G. Graham, *Social Life of Scotland in the Eighteenth Century* (London, 1899). See too C. A. Whatley, 'An uninflammable people?', in I. Donnachie and C. A. Whatley (eds), *The Manufacture of Scottish History* (Edinburgh, 1992), 52.

23 Lenman, *Integration, Enlightenment and Industrialisation*, 152.

24 On the first, see C. A. Whatley, *'Bought and Sold for English Gold?' Explaining the Union of 1707* (Glasgow, 1994), 43–4.

25 D. Hay and N. Rogers, *Eighteenth-Century English Society: Shuttles and Swords* (Oxford, 1997), vii.

26 Two important exceptions are K. J. Logue, *Popular Disturbances in Scotland, 1780–1815* (Edinburgh, 1979); W. H. Fraser, *Conflict and Class: Scottish Workers, 1700–1838* (Edinburgh, 1988). The first deals only with a

restricted period however, while the second is largely concerned with urban workers.

27 E. P. Thompson, 'Patrician society, plebeian culture', *Journal of Social History*, VII (1973–74), 382–405; e.g. P. Linebaugh, *The London Hanged: Crime and Civil Society in the Eighteenth Century* (London, 1991).

28 See R. Porter, 'The new eighteenth-century social history', in J. Black (ed.), *Culture and Society in Britain, 1660–1800* (Manchester, 1997), 30.

29 T. C. Smout, *A History of the Scottish People, 1560–1830* (1969), 433.

30 C. A. Whatley, '"The fettering bonds of brotherhood": combination and labour relations in the Scottish coal-mining industry *c.* 1690–1775', *Social History*, XII (1987), 149.

31 J. Dwyer and R. B. Sher (eds), *Sociability and Society in Eighteenth-Century Scotland* (Edinburgh, 1993); J. Dwyer, *Virtuous Discourse: Sensibility and Community in Late Eighteenth-Century Scotland* (Edinburgh, 1987); J. Dwyer, *The Age of Passions: An Interpretation of Adam Smith and Scottish Enlightenment Culture* (East Linton, 1998).

32 E. J. Cowan, 'Burns and superstition', in K. Simpson (ed.), *Love & Liberty. Robert Burns, A Bicentenary Celebration* (East Linton, 1997), 231.

33 For the more pessimistic assessment to which this is a response, see R. A. Houston and I. D. Whyte, 'Introduction', in Houston and Whyte (eds), *Scottish Society, 1500–1800* (Cambridge, 1989), 34–5.

1

The seventeenth-century legacy

Issues

There are several versions of Scotland's history in the seventeenth century, many of which have a bearing on the economic and social history of the period. At one extreme it has been portrayed as the 'dim twilight age before the black dark night of Union'. Viewed this way, parliamentary union in 1707 was the 'great betrayal' whereby Scotland surrendered its ancient sovereignty and independence in return for its place within a united British kingdom. In its various forms this is a venerable historiographical tradition which dates back to the first post-Union years, when Scottish politicians were once again accused of selling their nation for English gold – the first time was in 1701 when government supporters who had failed to vote for an act in support of the Darien colony were castigated for accepting favours beforehand.[1] Union in some variants of this interpretation is blamed for the failings of the Scottish economy in the first post-Union decades (and even up to *c.* 1750); as we will see, there are others for whom the Union played only a small part in achieving Scotland's eighteenth-century 'economic miracle'. Alternatively the century can be likened to the period of darkness which precedes dawn, with Union bringing archaic Scotland into a 'modern world of progress', wherein the Scottish people would experience stable government, economic improvement and Enlightenment.[2] There are of course intermediate positions between these extremes. To proceed with a book which focuses on the extent, causes and consequences of change in the eighteenth and early nineteenth centuries the historiographical conundrum outlined above clearly has to be resolved. We need to assess the condition of the Scottish economy at the turn of the eighteenth century.

For much of continental Europe, the seventeenth century was a period of prolonged crisis. One feature of this was a shift away from the formerly dominant Mediterranean countries of Italy and Spain towards the sea powers of the north. The Baltic and North Sea trades were the first to flourish. The Atlantic trade with the Americas and West Indies grew, with the flow westwards of manufactured goods and, increasingly, slaves being balanced by the importation into northern Europe of sugar cane and tobacco.[3] Scotland shared in this westwards movement. Like England, she had confronted the challenge of falling wool and woollen cloth sales in the mid-sixteenth century by exporting additional quantities of traditional goods, and from the 1570s by diversifying into new products or greatly increasing output of formerly unimportant commodities, such as salted herring, salt and coal.[4] Scotland's main trading partners, from where most manufactures, luxury goods and basic raw materials, such as iron, were purchased, lay around the eastern and southern edges of the North Sea.

Although later than either Holland or England (and in defiance of the English Navigation Acts), Scotland too managed to establish trans-Atlantic links from the Clyde and even from less well-located ports on the east coast, such as Montrose. Both sugar from the West Indies and tobacco from Virginia and Maryland were imported from the 1660s – occasionally Scottish ships took tobacco into the Baltic even earlier than this, while Scottish merchants and factors appear to have become established on the shores of the Chesapeake prior to 1700. Scattered settlements of Scots were also found throughout the English West Indian colonies, most notably on the sugar-growing Barbados, where Protestant, English-speaking Scots were particularly welcome (although there as elsewhere in the colonies, this was much less warm if they aspired to high government office).[5] Exports sent across the Atlantic included linen and woollen goods, coal and grindstones, as well as indentured servants, although much labour went westwards under duress, as prisoners of Oliver Cromwell's armies or of Charles II in the 1670s and 1680s, or as convicted vagabonds, thieves and other criminals.

Although bound by regal union to England since 1603, in terms of fiscal and commercial policy Scotland was in theory at least an independent north-European maritime nation. In terms of its location too, Scotland was well-placed. Although in one sense peripheral, proximity to the sea was an advantage, as too in the sixteenth, seventeenth and eighteenth centuries was the fact that Scotland lay closer to Scandinavia and the Baltic than most of England's eastern seaboard, thereby easing the importation of timber, Swedish bar iron and Russian flax. Her richer neighbour England lay overland to the south, while the Atlantic crossing round the north of Ireland was easily accessible from the Clyde, and quicker by some two or three weeks than for vessels from southern English ports. The Irish channel was narrow and relatively safe. Narrow too was Scotland's central waist, which made the transfer of human talent, capital and goods from east to west (and the reverse) relatively easy, even by road.[6]

Scotland however lagged some considerable way behind the other European states who fought for economic ascendancy during the seventeenth and eighteenth centuries. The early leader, the Dutch Republic, was a maritime state the population of which was not even double that of Scotland's estimated 1.2 million in 1700, but in 1670 boasted an awesome shipping capacity of over half a million tons.[7] By way of comparison, Leith, Scotland's leading port, could claim only twenty-nine vessels in 1692, and while the Clyde ports had sixty-six, the total burthen of both amounted to only 2,884 tons. The combined total of the Scottish mercantile marine (excluding coastal and fishing craft) is unlikely to have been more than 20,000 tons, and could well have been considerably less.[8] Most of these vessels were foreign-built – Holland and Norway made the best boats and had the lowest production costs. The major Scottish adventures overseas in the seventeenth century usually took place in vessels which were built and purchased from ports such as Amsterdam, Hamburg and London. Scottish vessels also tended to be smaller than those of their rivals; boats of 15 tons were more commonly found in Scottish waters than anything over 100 tons.[9] Of Dundee's twenty-three vessels, for example, only three were of 100 tons or above, while eight were under 15 tons, sailed by crews of one and two. Notwithstanding Scotland's proximity to the North Sea and her modest success in catching the herrings which swarmed through her coastal waters, as these figures show, the Scots could not match the highly-capitalised and brilliantly managed Dutch 'Great Fishery'. By contrast, most Fife fishing ports denied having any sizeable vessels (although Pittenweem had boats of 100 tons and 70 tons respectively). In 1709 the Fife fishing burgh of Earlsferry had only three open fishing boats and one yawl, while of the twenty-two fishing boats sailing from St Monance sixteen were used only seasonally, 'in tyme of the herring fishing', and manned by 'Country men of other Trades from other places'.[10]

Optimism and achievement

To explain Scotland's emergence as a significant economic player by the early nineteenth century, recent work by a number of historians has made possible the construction of a revised account of her earlier strengths and potential. This is radically different from the older view of Scotland at the close of the seventeenth century; a country described by Scotophobic English visitors as being wasted, barren and enormously poor, its stagnant towns and a 'lethargic, slovenly populace' obsessed with religious disputation.[11] It will be argued here however that while the research carried out by economic and social historians over the past two to three

decades has been of enormous importance in helping us to better understand later seventeenth-century Scotland and to counter the more extreme
of the older arguments, the conclusions which have been drawn from it
may have been over-optimistic.

The newer view rests largely on two main propositions: first, that
Scotland's economy and society was much more dynamic and conducive
to economic growth than had been assumed previously. Second, that
while there was much about Scotland which was distinctive, in 'several
important respects [Scotland] ... was similar both to England and other
more advanced parts of northern Europe'.[12] Scotland, it has been argued,
was 'the Sweden of the British Isles'.[13] At the forefront of the revisionist
perspective is the reassessment which has been made of Scotland's pre-
Improvement agriculture.

This crucial arena, the Scottish countryside, was far from static in the
seventeenth century. Rather, the sector was becoming commercialised
and responding to market opportunities. During the second half of the
seventeenth century landowners in the fertile, low-lying, cereal-growing
coastal lands in the east of Scotland, the Moray Firth, Angus and the
Lothians in particular, not only sent grain coastwise and inland – inadequate roads and high transport costs meant that this could only be to
consumers who were not much more than twelve miles distant – but also
managed in some seasons to export it. Even Orkney, in the far north,
frequently sent grain to Norway, Scotland's main foreign buyer.
Edinburgh, probably the largest city in Britain after London, was the
single most important internal consumer but rapidly-rising Glasgow
exerted increasing pressure on producers, even encouraging the shipping
of grain from Caithness and other east coast counties through the
Pentland Firth and the Minch as the lower Clyde region suppliers and
(illegal) imports from Ireland proved insufficient by the later part of the
century.

The 'dramatic' rise in the numbers of weekly and annual market
centres authorised by Parliament between 1660 and 1707 – 346,
compared to 143 between 1550 and 1660 – further helped to activate the
home market by extending trade at district and regional level, as opposed
simply to local, estate transactions, many in the form of barter, which
had prevailed at the beginning of the century. Thus a smaller royal burgh
like Brechin, with its parish of some 2,100 souls in 1691, was holding a
series of regular markets and fairs: a weekly market on Tuesdays, which
was supplemented by a 'Calsey' market which began on the first Tuesday
of Lent, and another market on Martinmas Tuesday; there was also an
annual Palm Tuesday market and a Trinity Fair. A weekly craft market
was held on Tuesdays between Michaelmas and Christmas. Markets held
in the burghs of barony and regality which also lay within Brechin parish
added to the number: the laird of Edzell held a weekly market on

Wednesdays and an annual 'St Laurence Fair', while serious competition was created by 'Falconer of Newtown and his Tutors' who in the early 1690s had established a market on 'North water bridge within four myles of Brechin', which as it was held on Mondays, interfered with the Sabbath but also allegedly damaged Brechin's market, 'by intercepting ... goods which are coming to their Tuesdays Mercat'.[14] Further away, Kirriemuir, a small burgh of regality, not only had sixteen merchants but also held 'several' yearly fairs and a weekly market. Although to what extent is unknown, the new market centres had the effect of reducing dependence on subsistence farming and assisted too in drawing the Highlands into the market economy, with commercial centres at Campbeltown, Stornoway and Gordonsburgh (later Fort William) from the early seventeenth century. By 1707 only 18 per cent of mainland Scotland was more than 20km from such a centre.[15]

The cash incomes which black cattle generated for clan elites (*fine*) in the western Highlands encouraged an increase in the numbers driven south from the 1630s (and earlier in some cases) to markets for meat, leather and tallow in the Lowlands, England and the Continent. Meal was sent in return to those parts of the Highlands where grain could not be easily grown. English markets however, easier to enter as the Borders were pacified, and legalised sometime after 1607, were initially supplied by cattle from Galloway and the Borders; Highland drovers sought sales in the Scottish Lowland towns. Market conditions improved in the post-Restoration decades. Naval and imperial demand for salt beef from London, Europe's largest city, grew to new heights. With Irish cattle to England banned from 1666, further expansion of the Scottish trade was encouraged, with droves of more than one thousand head of cattle leaving from the Highlands by the 1680s, two and three times greater than in the first half of the century.[16]

The impact of commercialisation and market centres is seen too in the beginning of the process of commuting rents in kind (including 'kain' – livestock – rents and labour services), to money payments, which appear to have been more common in the west Highlands (where cash was paid for black cattle) than the Lowlands. In the north and further west rents in kind predominated, although the proportion paid in cash was rising as far north and west as Skye and Harris in the 1670s and 1680s respectively.

Greater efficiencies were sought and achieved through a reduction in the numbers of multiple tenancies, where tenant holdings were fragmented by the runrig system, and the more common use of longer, written leases. Incomplete poll tax evidence from the 1690s suggests that in the south-eastern Lowlands but also in lowland Aberdeenshire, a more stratified rural society was emerging, at the top of which were landowners but beneath them fewer tenants in larger holdings and, probably, a bigger landless population than there was in most of rural Scotland.[17] By contrast, but driven by similar although not identical forces and directed towards the same end of raising estate income (and above all of reducing high levels of indebtedness), in Highland Argyll the *fine* of Clan Campbell led while others followed in the use of shorter leases of between five and nineteen years, in order to ensure more regular accountability on the part of tenants.[18] Cosmopolitanism, closer links with the Lowlands, including assimilation into the Scottish landed classes, not only caused many more Highland chiefs to re-define customary expectations but also drew them towards more legalistic forms of estate management, which was becoming increasingly exploitative.[19]

The area of land under cultivation was also extended, by the draining of mosses and burning or removal of turf and peat, while the improvement of yields and the cultivation of former waste lands and some upland slopes and plateau country were achieved by liming and manuring. Although the use of lime had begun in the sixteenth century, it was not until the middle of the seventeenth that its application became more extensive, leading to spectacular rent increases of several hundred per cent in some parishes.[20] Agricultural productivity was increased too through the introduction, not only in the Lothians but also elsewhere, of three and four-crop rotations which included legumes (normally peas) and, less often, a fallow year. Although the evidence is slight, it has been argued that at its best, Scottish arable farming by the end of the seventeenth century was capable of matching better English practice, and of surpassing those of 'considerable parts of continental Europe'.[21]

Examination of Scotland's urban sector also appears to support a favourable judgement on the seventeenth century. Estimates of the populations of the larger European towns (i.e. ten thousand-plus) reveal that Scotland experienced a continuous increase after 1550. This compares with the urban population of the Mediterranean region, which fell between 1600 and 1700. It is true that only two Scottish towns – Edinburgh and Glasgow, with estimated populations of between forty thousand and forty-seven thousand (for 'greater' Edinburgh) and about eighteen thousand respectively in 1691 – come into the category of large town and that Ireland, for example, had three (and none in 1600). Nevertheless, the proportion of Scotland's population living in large towns, 5.3 per cent (which new estimates suggest might have been matched by Ireland), was greater than that of Scandinavia, similarly situated on the northern fringes of Europe.[22] If smaller towns of 2,500 and above are included, Scotland's urban population in the 1690s may have been as much as 11.9 per cent. Furthermore, recent heroic calculations on the basis of hearth tax returns, and including parishes of one thousand or even fewer inhabitants, indicate that urbanisation levels in the Forth basin were unusually high and may even have been on a par with those of the Netherlands (where 45 per cent of the population lived in towns), which were the highest in Europe.[23] It was thus at the top and the lower levels of the urban hierarchy, rather than in second and third rank provincial centres such as Aberdeen and Dundee and Ayr and Dumfries respectively, that growth occurred during the seventeenth century. Much of this took place in the burghs of barony, fifty-one of which were founded between 1660 and 1707.

As in England the smaller towns within the economic orbits of major centres such as Edinburgh and Glasgow did best, as did marketing towns located in prosperous agricultural regions such as Strathmore in Angus (of which Brechin was part), and a handful of places which were emerging as specialist industrial centres, indicating that functional specialisation was becoming a feature of Scotland's urban life. Hence textile manufacture was especially prominent in Paisley and featured to a greater than average extent in a town such as Musselburgh.[24] Within the larger burghs at least, an identifiable 'middling sort' was emerging from the ranks of the merchants, manufacturers and professions, 'establishing solid middle-grade foundations' for future economic development. In Edinburgh, over 50 per cent of the urban labour force comprised domestic servants, with the thickest concentrations being found in those parishes where the most affluent residents lived.[25]

Accommodating only 4.7 per cent of Scotland's estimated population of around one million at the end of the century, Edinburgh could not act as the powerful 'engine of [economic] growth' which London – with almost 10 per cent of the population – did in England. Even so, with a socio-economic profile which was similar to London's but with a higher proportion of professionals, and much better off than its size relative to the total population indicates, the Scottish capital did exercise a considerable pull on the surrounding countryside. It is no coincidence that the Lothians were at the forefront of agricultural improvement, and notable that the orbit of Edinburgh's demand for foodstuffs stretched far up Scotland's east coast before but particularly after c. 1660, encompassing first the grain-growing estates of Strathmore and the Moray Firth, and, later, Caithness and Orkney. Almost wholly dependent upon coal for their fuel, the inhabitants of Edinburgh – 'Auld Reekie' – comprised the single largest non-industrial market for Scottish coal, while the strength of domestic demand for salt provided an outlet for several of the saltworks which lined the southern bank of the Forth, as at Joppa and Prestonpans.[26] Glasgow too, which was also growing rapidly, exerted a favourable pull both in its immediate hinterland and further afield, and while along with other medium-sized Scottish towns Aberdeen and Dundee experienced population losses between 1639 and the 1690s, both were important regional centres. It may be that by exerting favourable pressures on employment and wages such towns contributed to the creation of the more homogenous economy which has been observed in contrast to that of Ireland where the greater gulf between high real wages in Dublin and low rates for the unskilled in the countryside may be a symptom of relative underdevelopment.[27]

The change in the direction of Scottish trade which would be crucial in the long term has already been noted. There were other shifts too, although the pattern which had been established earlier, with strong links with the Low Countries, France, Scandinavia and the Baltic, remained broadly the same until the last two decades of the century. Increasing numbers of small Scottish ships from west coast ports from Glasgow south to Portpatrick embarked on what was a relatively secure sea route to Ireland, encouraged by the settlement in Ulster of west-country, Presbyterian Scots, who emigrated in a series of intermittent streams during the seventeenth century. This westward movement was to be the first stage in a process which would ultimately lead growing numbers of Scots to cross the Atlantic as Ireland became less attractive after c. 1660 while the West Indies and the mainland of North America promised more in the way of work and other opportunities for gain. Estimates of the numbers leaving for Ireland vary – one contemporary referred somewhat ungenerously to 'swarmes' of Scots – but a total of as many as 130,000 over the course of the century is not inconceivable. This compares to the estimated six thousand or so who went to the New World prior to 1700.[28] The demand for consumer goods generated by the Scots in Ulster – who prior to the 1690s were mainly small tenant farmers – has been credited with giving Glasgow merchants a solid income base which allowed them to engage in more dangerous ventures to Iberia and across the Atlantic. Coal too began to be shipped from Ayrshire. Shipments in the other direction consisted mainly of the products of pastoral agriculture, cheese, butter, tanned leather and grain, imports of which were of enormous importance to the west of Scotland during famine years. Other essential commodities, such as Norwegian timber and tar and Swedish iron, continued to be shipped from Scotland's traditional trading partners in nearby Scandinavia and the Baltic.[29]

Further evidence that Scotland's economy was developing comes from looking at the changing composition of trade. At the end of the sixteenth-century Scottish exports had been overwhelmingly (but not exclusively) those of an underdeveloped economy: raw materials and foodstuffs – with hides and skins, fish, wool and coal predominating. A century later however linen topped the list. Linen was looked on almost universally as the Scottish manufactured product most likely to improve Scotland's prosperity, and the suggestion that exports to England (the main external market) rose some thirty-six-fold between c. 1600 and the end of the seventeenth century when at least 650,000 ells of Scottish linen were going south, indicates that considerable expansion had taken place.[30]

Contemporaries were well aware of its importance as an employer of 'poor people' and as a factor which enabled tenants to pay their rents.[31] While woollens did less well after the Restoration (peaking as early as 1639), there were periods when Aberdeen's plaiding and fingrams (a coarse serge) industry flourished once more – in the 1670s for instance; Galloway's woollen cloth trade was marked by similar fluctuations. More promising was the bonnet-making trade in north Ayrshire, and in Aberdeenshire the commencement of the manufacture of hand-knitted stockings. Growth occurred too in the extractive industries, especially in coal mining, to the extent that Scotland could number a handful of collieries which ranked alongside the biggest in Britain.[32] Lead smelting in Scotland also expanded. Other new industries which were established included glass-making, and more important, paper-making, although both were on a small scale.

Development and change can be seen in the organisation of production and distribution. The linen industry for example, had long been scattered through the country, with small independent producers aiming mainly to serve local consumers. By the end of the seventeenth century it was largely concentrated in five counties, Lanarkshire and Renfrewshire in the west and Angus, Perth and Fife in the east. Parts of the woollen industry too were organised along proto-industrial lines. Organisation, financing and marketing was mainly in the hands of urban merchants based in the royal burghs.[33] Urban merchants were also heavily involved in the establishment of large manufactures, a high proportion of which were located in the burghs. As many as 106 such concerns may have been either proposed or established between 1587 and 1707, with some three-quarters appearing (in the written records at least) after 1660. It was not only merchants, or even all merchants, who were the market innovators. They were a heterogeneous group, both in terms of income and outlook.[34] Distinctions can be made however between merchants in the royal burghs and the growing numbers of those 'trafficking' in the burghs of barony and regality. Within four miles of the struggling royal burgh of Dysart on the Fife coast in 1691 it was estimated that another thirty-one persons were importing and exporting goods, while a further thirty merchants and shopkeepers were also trading primarily in the home market.[35] Pressure for change came too from within the ranks of the burgh's craft incorporations, with some sections of the same trade calling for an easing of rules governing apprenticeship or the employment of unfreemen, for example, while traditionalists fought against economic liberalisation and in defence of their legal privileges.[36] The search for low labour costs and efforts from within to curtail the powers of guilds provide a marked contrast to the economies of Italy and Spain where failures in these regards in the face of lower-cost competition from England and the Netherlands, had a devastating impact on their textile industries.

With limited opportunities for more than modest commercial success from serving a home market which was weak and virtually non-existent over large tracts of self-sufficient countryside, substantial income-enhancement could best be achieved by exploiting opportunities overseas. Poverty, lack of employment and thwarted ambition had encouraged thousands of Scots to go overseas to seek livelihoods and advancement from the later sixteenth century and, utilising their martial skills in the seventeenth century, large numbers fought as mercenaries on European soil, as in the case of the ten thousand men who were reputed to have been under the command of Gustavus Adolphus of Sweden during the Thirty Years' War, while almost as many may have enlisted under the French flag. After 1660 the Dutch armies were the main receptacle for Scottish soldiers. Such outlets also attracted members of the Scots nobility, some of whom reached the senior ranks. For those anxious to prosper by more peaceful means Ulster was a common destination, although some of these emigrants became 'fighting farmers', with a proposed settlement of Scots in Monaghan being designed to form a wall between the English and 'the wild Irish'.[37] Poland, described by one contemporary Scot as 'the Mother of our Commons', probably took more Scots than anywhere else prior to 1650 – as many as forty thousand, some of whom were recruited as soldiers.[38] Scandinavia was next, not only for soldiers but also traders.

Significantly, at all levels, Scotland's merchants included men with acutely sensitive commercial antennae, whose intelligence networks and business acumen were sufficiently well-developed to ensure that they both knew about and could seize new trading opportunities virtually anywhere in Europe. Occasional forays had been made further afield, to the Portuguese Azores in the later sixteenth century, and to the West Indies and the Americas in the early seventeenth. In 1634 a Scottish Guinea Company had been founded, in an attempt to break into the African trade, although this was largely a London-based venture.[39] Transatlantic colonial ventures however were constrained by the lack of resources – human and financial – available to the Scots, owing to high levels of emigration to Europe and the credit-stretching cost of settlement in Ulster.[40]

Scottish merchants imported a vast range of goods, but were more restricted in the variety of commodities they could export.[41] Merchant enterprise underpinned by new business methods and arrangements such as partnerships and credit facilities was evident in Scotland from the later sixteenth century at least – although only a quarter or a third of the merchant communities of the larger burghs were involved in overseas ventures.[42]

A telling instance of mercantile opportunism comes from the salt trade, with the first Spanish embargo on Biscay salt bound for the salt-hungry

North Netherlands in 1572. By 1574 exports of Scots salt had risen a remarkable eight times above their 1570 level, as merchants strove to exploit the gap in supply and the higher prices this had created. In the 1620s and 1630s too, another period of determined Spanish economic warfare against the Dutch, the Scottish salt industry boomed, with a massive expansion in Scottish saltpan construction taking place.[43] Similarly, in 1663, the imposition of higher duties on English coal led to an almost simultaneous 'surge in exports' to the Continent, as Scots coal temporarily supplanted its more expensive rival.[44] A different kind of example is a sudden sizeable influx of Scots into Gothenburg in the 1620s, explained by the granting of fifteen years of tax freedom for burghers of the recently established (1621) town.[45] Scots were particularly heavily involved in opening up the Norwegian timber trade north of Stavanger, the 'Scotterhandel'.[46] And although they were barred from trading directly with England's colonies from 1671, Glasgow merchants continued to trade in tobacco by freighting Whitehaven ships.[47] Significantly, it was merchants from Glasgow who were the most articulate and outspoken critics of what many increasingly saw as the straightjacket of the older Scottish staple port at Campveere, once the main point of entry into Europe for Scotland's goods, but by the 1690s 'ane great grivance to the merchants of this Country [rather] than any advantage' – an irritating legal hindrance to the trade they wished to pursue with ports such as Rotterdam and Amsterdam.[48] From the west Highlands, Cameron of Lochiel was associated with some Bristol merchants in the New Jersey land market.[49] As has already been noted, Scottish enterprise abroad was by no means confined to wealthy merchants. Scots settlers in Poland in the later sixteenth and earlier seventeenth centuries were mainly lesser merchants and pedlars (as well as tradesmen), dealers in cheap, low-grade goods, notable above all for their ability to respond to market needs. Similarly, the Glasgow pioneers of the tobacco trade who became established in Virginia in the later seventeenth century and who laid the basis of the Scottish store system, were small-scale operators who had insufficient resources to act as commission merchants.[50]

Although most opportunistic ventures were supported by merchant capital – Edinburgh merchants for instance were conspicuous investors in coal, salt and lead in the early seventeenth century – schemes such as these required at least the tacit support of landowners and often their active involvement. The positive and important role played by Scottish landowners in the country's economic development from the 1660s has long been recognised.[51] Most of the rural changes outlined above were landowner-led. Where their estates contained coal and there was a reasonable market within easy reach, they would usually work it, albeit through grieves or factors. But increasingly in the later decades of the seventeenth century, and in contrast to Ireland where such initiatives were fewer and came later, landowners could be found in other extractive and manufacturing enterprises, motivated to seek additional revenues by the failure of grain prices to rise after *c.* 1660. Such schemes were also a means of recovering some of the losses of the Covenanting and Civil Wars, when their political power too had been reduced.[52] Examples of landed diversification are not confined to the Lowlands. Cameron of Lochiel initiated iron smelting at Achnacarry on Loch Arkaig, while members of the House of Argyll were involved in coal and salt, fishing and lime and slate quarrying. Iron smelting, using native wood and imported ores, began even earlier – around 1610, at Gairloch – thereby establishing a pattern of mainly short-lived Highland iron-making ventures which would continue into the following century.[53]

The desire of the landed classes to assert their dominance and status in Scotland, and also their ambitions within British society, are exemplified by the 'reforming' of castellated dynastic dwellings by adding wings, turrets and pavilions to produce 'uniformitie', or symmetrical structures, as proprietors and Scottish architects such as Sir William Bruce and James Smith embraced European classicism.[54] The most prominent example, achieving a 'new standard of austere architectural grandeur', was the ducal Hamilton Palace, carefully modelled along the lines of the most fashionable French houses, and with some advice from Sir Christopher Wren.[55] Others less well-endowed – or unburdened by the past (rising lesser lairds, for example) – built new, smaller compact villas, again inspired by recent continental and English designs. Many of the new constructions were embellished by the work of artists and craftsmen imported from mainland Europe, mainly Holland, from whence came Jacob de Wet in 1673, a figure of lasting influence in Scottish art, to work first on Holyroodhouse, and later for the earl of Strathmore at Glamis, although he also carried out commissions for many other Scottish families.[56] Dutch paintings were imported in bulk. Demand was such that Brussels-born Sir John de Medina was able to make a living in Scotland as a portrait painter until his death in 1710, after he had been persuaded, reluctantly, to come north in 1694. The clothes of the elite and an English education (compulsory for the sons of Highland chiefs under the terms of the Statutes of Iona, 1609), further confirmed the process of anglicisation, as to some degree did the adoption by the landed classes of more formal modes of behaviour and demands for outward shows of deference from their inferiors.[57] The extent to which the Scots aristocrats were assimilated however, as measured by noble marriages, language (as well as education) and presence at court, can be greatly exaggerated.[58] Substantial numbers of the Scottish elite – and not simply the landed classes – through their education in increasing numbers after the Restoration in leading European universities such as Leiden, posts abroad and travel, had absorbed the culture and the cutting edge of the new intellectual climate of the Continent. The roots of the Scottish

Enlightenment of the following century were being copiously nourished. By the 1680s much that had been learned was being copied; nowhere was emulation more in vogue than in the area of economic improvement.[59]

Scottish landed society at its highest levels was not easy to penetrate. Compared to Ireland and other parts of Europe, it was remarkably stable. The transition from feudalism from the later sixteenth century had been relatively smooth in the Lowlands, while the 'unusually narrow' band of tenure lengths was one of a number of factors which favoured the Lowland as well as the Highland landlord and enabled estates to be run on commercial lines.[60] All this, it has been argued, made it easier to embark on economic and social innovation. Scottish landowners were also enormously powerful, and becoming more so in the seventeenth (and eighteenth) centuries. Arguably they were the most absolute in Britain, although as will be seen later in this book, there were constraints on their behaviour. Peasants were more secure in countries such as Norway, Sweden and Denmark, where they were protected from landlord power, whereas in Scotland landowners were able to exercise their authority through the jurisdictions of regality and barony courts, of which there were just under two hundred and one thousand respectively.[61] The regality courts had greater powers and could try cases of robbery, rape, murder and arson, and also regulated prices, wages and markets. In the areas under their jurisdiction, some of which in the Highlands in particular were extensive, they were 'effectively petty kingdoms'. Although the full powers of the smaller and less powerful barony courts tended not to be used in the seventeenth century, they may well have helped to maintain good relations in rural communities and to sustain the established social order.[62] In the final decades of the seventeenth century the numbers of landowners (of which there were about five thousand) in most regions fell, with the proportion of land held by the magnates and the lairds or smaller landowners increasing at the expense of 'bonnet lairds', the smaller landed proprietors.

There were however no hard and fast lines between land and commerce, and entry into both was feasible, if not near the top of the respective ladders. Such fluidity and evidence of social ambition were important, and in this respect Scotland was not unlike England. Far from being a static caste, the ranks of the merchant guildry were constantly being refreshed by the end of the seventeenth century. Much to the irritation of the royal burghs, numerous individuals outwith their boundaries and controls were adding themselves to the country's pool of entrepreneurial activity. Merchants' sons formed the largest category of new entrants to the guilds, but much of the new blood came in the form of male offspring of the landed classes. Their engagement with commerce was encouraged in the case of the first-born by a wish to improve their financial standing, and by primogeniture in the case of younger sons, who often aspired to re-enter the land market on their own account. Numbers of the more successful, socially aspiring merchants also sought estate ownership.[63] In Aberdeenshire in the later seventeenth century it was wealthy merchants who headed the lists of new landowners, who also included lawyers, soldiers and administrators.[64] If mercantile land purchase was limited – land was more often held in wadset in this period – merchant investment in projects such as the New Mills manufactory and the Bank of Scotland (established in 1695) was of immense importance. Not long after 1695, Scotland had a working paper currency; by the end of 1700 a banknote for £1 Scots had been issued – an innovation of no small significance in an economy in which silver coin was becoming scarce and of a poor quality – while before the Union of 1707 bank lending was spread across Scotland 'from Inverness to the Borders'.[65]

Reflecting its wealth as well as one of the main functions of the expanding capital city was the extent to which Edinburgh's investors also included professionals such as surgeons and lawyers, whose contribution to enterprises not directly related to their primary professional function was almost the same as the merchants.[66] Yet moneylending, whether on bond or by unsecured loan, was not confined to the upper echelons of Scottish society: recent investigations have revealed the existence of creditors at the level of urban domestic servant, and in the countryside, among small tenants, smallholders and even cottars.[67]

Taking stock: the state, Darien and Scottish limitations

Clearly, late-seventeenth-century Scotland was by no means as backward as was once assumed, and to the catalogue of achievement compiled here can be added other factors which support a more optimistic assessment of the country's economic strengths at the end of the seventeenth century. Arguably one of the most important in the long-run was the willingness of large numbers of Scots to move, more often temporarily but also permanently, from their place of birth in search of employment, an apprenticeship, higher living standards, or for marriage. The point has already been partially made in relation to emigration, but even more striking is the extent to which migration took place within Scotland, with Edinburgh attracting migrants from a wider geographical area than anywhere else. Longer distances were travelled by apprentices, and in particular by young women from sixteen upwards, who especially if they were the daughters of cottar households were also more likely than males to move the shorter distances required to find work as domestic or agricultural servants.

There were marked regional differences in mobility patterns, the most notable being the relatively small (but growing) proportion of temporary migrants from the Highlands searching for harvest work in the seventeenth century. Destitution in their native parishes too could drive Highlanders south. Nevertheless, bearing in mind the sizeable proportion of the population which remained stationary, what is certain is that the scale of permanent migration in Scotland was a crucial factor in the rapid urban growth of the early modern period. While in many respects these aspects of Scotland's demographic history are similar to those in England and elsewhere in northern Europe in the later seventeenth century as the 'old order' was transformed, differences are revealed by comparison with Ireland, where population mobility was more limited.[68] On the other hand, no matter how positively the emigrant Scot is portrayed, the plain fact is that most emigrants were fleeing from a country which could not support them adequately, and probably going at a faster rate in the seventeenth century than anywhere else in Europe.[69] The Scottish state too became increasingly involved in economic development. Early on, hopes that the Highlands and Western Islands would adopt new economic values were given legal basis in the Statutes of Iona (of 1609, and re-stated in 1616). These were designed to bring clan chiefs under the civilising influences of the state and the kirk, which was to be effected by rooting out feasting and feuding, practices which provided the ideological and practical basis of the clan system. A society where food production was governed by the requirements of local consumption was to be converted into one which responded to the needs of the market. With the revival in 1681 of the Council of Trade under the chairmanship of James, duke of York (soon to be King James VII), Lord High Admiral of Scotland, was initiated the first ever high-level investigation into the condition of Scotland's economy and launched a 'drive to full membership of the European mercantilist system'.[70] Scotland's trading deficit was to be eliminated by the classic means of reducing imports by heavy customs tariffs and embarking on an aggressive policy of increasing exports. The claim has been made that the Revolution of 1688–89 marked a sharper turning point and inaugurated an era of 'economic politics'. Whether or not this is valid, what is clear is that the accession of William and Mary added impetus to an emerging programme of national economic regeneration in the forefront of which was a Scottish landed class anxious to reduce estate indebtedness.[71] In 1692 the Convention of Royal Burghs, meeting in Dundee, was urged by King William to turn their meetings 'for the use they were Designed: to fall upon effectual measures for the improvement of the trade and manufactures of the Kingdome'.[72] Home-based industries were encouraged by a series of liberties and inducements which were intended to reduce dependence upon foreign manufactures. Agriculture too was supported – not surprisingly given the domination of Scotland's Parliament by landowners. This was effected through the Corn Bounty Act of 1695 which freed exports of all duties and offered drawbacks when prices were low, and the Commonty Act of the same year which succeeded a more restricted act of 1647, and in the long run had the effect (unlike England) of removing all common pasture in Scotland outside the crofting districts. This was the last of a series of eleven improving statutes which were passed in Scotland after 1660.[73]

Growing Scottish ambition in the aftermath of the Williamite Revolution and an awakening sense of national self-confidence manifested themselves in the Darien scheme, which was known to contemporaries by several names in Scotland and in England as the Scotch East India Company.[74] Its legal basis was the incorporation in 1695 of the Company of Scotland Trading to Africa and the Indies. Its immediate foundations lay in the hopes of a group of London and Edinburgh merchants of breaking the monopoly of the English East India Company. The Company was initially led by William Paterson (founder of the Bank of England), who for at least ten years had been attempting to drum up support for some sort of trading post on the isthmus of Panama, thereby creating a bridge linking the Atlantic and Pacific oceans, and indeed the Scots had made several earlier efforts to establish a foothold in the Americas, but never south of the tropics. English success in the West Indies provided an enviable model which some Scots believed they could emulate: one remarkably optimistic proposal in 1693 argued that 'Scotland is weell and better furnished with all things necessar for plantations than England, Holland or any oyr place in Europe', and urged the Scottish Parliament to apply to King William for a 'patent for some one of the Caribee Islands'.[75] By the 1690s there was general agreement among influential Scots that overseas trade was the 'Golden Ball' or the 'great Designe' to which European nations aspired, and this venture, 'an emporium without empire', was to provide Scotland with a fast track to economic prosperity.[76] Darien attracted enormous interest and support from within Scotland, with subscribers coming 'in Shoals from all Corners of the Kingdom to Edinburgh, Rich, Poor, Blind and Lame', and committing themselves to the tune of £400,000 sterling.[77] Darien however was more than an ambitious scheme for national economic salvation; it was in part too a spiritual mission the work of which 'Blinded Pagans' would gratefully acknowledge, according to the author of one broadsheet poem written on the eve of the departure of the first expedition. With this, alongside the linen, woollen cloth, periwigs and other goods to be traded, went 1,500 English bibles and two zealous Scottish ministers.[78]

This is an impressive array of evidence and, as will be seen, several of the factors noted here did indeed play their part in the process of change which occurred later in the eighteenth century. Yet the identification of structural strengths and social characteristics which would, in certain circumstances, be of long-term economic benefit, should not conceal major difficulties which pressed heavily on the country's undoubted potential. The improvements which were taking place in the Scottish economy in the second half of the seventeenth century should also be put in perspective; Scotland at the time of Darien was still underdeveloped in comparison to England and at the time, lagged behind Ireland. The value of Irish exports, for example, has been calculated at 6s. (30 pence) *per capita*, while the Scottish figure was around 4s. (20 pence).[79] Indeed as was suggested by the figures noted earlier comparing Scottish and Dutch shipping, pre-Union Scotland's share of world trade was 'trifling'; and 'slight' even when using more realistic comparators such as Norway, Sweden and Hamburg.[80] Supporting statistics are few but telling: when exports of Scottish salt rose to their new peak in the early 1570s the average quantity of salt shipped from Scotland into the Baltic amounted, at most, to less than 1 per cent of a poor year for shipments to the same destination of Portuguese 'Bay' salt; in the same period, woollen cloth exports from Scotland were only 2 per cent of those from England, and fell during the following century.[81] One recent count of Scottish shipping at the end of the seventeenth century indicates that Scotland had 1 ton of shipping for every 100 of England's.[82]

It is true that Scottish agriculture was able, in normal circumstances, to feed the Scottish population, including those in the towns and villages. Yet the increase in grain for sale may partly be accounted for by greater landlord exploitation of the tenant class through demands for a greater proportion of their produce and consequently, a reduction in the latter's living standards.[83] These seem to have been falling anyway since the sixteenth century if, as seems reasonable, these are measured by food consumption: over time Scots were able to eat less meat, and were forced instead to consume greater quantities of oats.[84] Both factors are likely to have added to the pressure to emigrate. Undoubtedly the area under culti-vation rose but enclosures and instances of tree planting were rare beyond the policies of the landowners and gentry. Research from the perspective of environmental history has suggested that nitrogen levels were low in Scottish soils, which were suffering from long-term degrada-tion,a process which was only arrested in privileged localities where, for instance, liming was practised. Paring and burning, a method used in the seventeenth century to bring waste ground under cultivation produced only temporary benefits and was of little or no lasting benefit, rather the reverse.[85] Although largely of localised significance, there is some evidence that towards the end of the seventeenth century there may have been a greater incidence of damage done by wind-blown sand, with subsequent land-loss on Bernera (1697) and on Shetland from the 1670s. Although these disasters were by no means confined to this period, the reduction in cultivable land in Shetland was in addition to severe and lasting financial dislocation which had resulted from the dearth of 1693–96 and a serious outbreak of smallpox on the islands in 1700.[86]

Cottars were still to be found in substantial numbers in the majority of Lowland Scottish parishes for which poll tax data for the 1690s have recently been analysed. In many parts of the Lowlands a peasant social structure still prevailed, with most farming beyond the Borders and Lothians being concerned with 'scarcity and survival rather than surplus and profit'.[87] The point has been made that advances in agriculture had tended to occur *within* the existing rural social framework, where 'the forces of continuity were more powerful than the forces of change'.[88]

Scotland too remained overwhelmingly rural, 'a peripheral, marginal, largely upland country with a mainly pastoral economy'. The urban population was growing, but of the estimated 1.2 million people resident in Scotland in 1691 almost nine out of ten still lived in a countryside which was characterised by dispersed farmsteads, cottages and hamlet clusters, with few nucleated villages.[89] It is readily admitted that the figures upon which the heavier than expected levels of urbanisation in the Forth basin parishes are derived, are 'suspect', in that they do not distinguish rural from burgh dwellers.[90] England's urban population was 18.7 per cent in 1700, while her total population was five times as large. However, the larger landowners and more prosperous merchants were ardent consumers of fashionable high-quality and luxury goods such as Chinese and black lacquered Japanese furniture, china and Delftware, much of which was brought from London or imported, although quantities of good furniture and other household items were made by Scottish craftsmen.[91] Scottish gunsmiths and silversmiths were capable of putting out work of the highest quality. Even so, an estimated £30,000 was being spent on imports of furniture, mirrors and clocks in 1704, 8.4 per cent of the total, and a larger sum than for any group of exports other than linen cloth. At the same time, such was the level of demand for better-quality linen, muslins and cotton that domestic purchases of imports of these goods were greater than the value of Scottish linen exports.[92]

The effect of spending on imported 'luxuries' thus created additional pressure on Scotland's already-strained balance of payments. However, that the Restoration habit of wig-wearing and hence the occupation of wig-making had flourished in late seventeenth-century Edinburgh, but apparently nowhere else in Scotland, suggests that the consumption of fashionable items may have been fairly limited outside of the capital, although Glasgow was rapidly increasing in wealth in the later seventeenth century. As Highland chiefs and landlords became increasingly integrated with Lowland society and travelled to the Continent their appetite for imported luxuries was also awoken.[93] Scotland however was a net exporter of human hair, for London wig-makers; it was reputedly with the hair of Highlanders that the periwigs sent to Darien were made. Lower down the social scale, even although household size, structure and function in parts of the Lowlands were not unlike England, Scottish houses were smaller and less well-furnished. Tenant farmers for instance lacked household goods such as crockery and cutlery of the standard which was becoming commonplace in many parts of England.[94] As has been observed, home demand was slight: annual *per capita* consumption of iron for example was roughly a quarter of England's 15 lbs. Wage levels in both town and country remained more or less constant – and, in real terms, low – from the middle decades of the seventeenth century until the 1760s, thereby restricting consumer demand for anything beyond subsistence needs.[95]

The awarding of patent rights and monopolies to sponsors of the array of grandiose manufacturing schemes by the Scottish Privy Council, under the terms of the 1681 Act 'For Encouraging Trade and Manufactures', provides evidence of Scottish ambition, but also highlights the difficulties of establishing new kinds of enterprise where the necessary social and economic infrastructure – and secure markets – were absent. There was not always agreement on what the national interest was, as when in 1694 Whitefield Hayton and his partners, from London, who wished to – and did – establish a leather manufacturing works, encountered bitter opposition from the Skinners of Edinburgh. The Skinners contested the Londoners' claims for the uniqueness of their project and the quality of their products, including glue, arguing strongly but somewhat complacently and without pointing to any hard evidence, that 'it is nottourly known, that there is as good Glue made here in Edinburgh, as in any place of Britain, or as comes from abroad'.[96]

Even when such ventures materialised, and this was by no means always the case, they rarely survived long, in spite of the extremely generous (and in some respects very modern) terms of the 1661 and 1681 Acts to encourage manufactures. There were a couple of exceptions, sugar refining especially, and the textile venture at New Mills, near Haddington, which struggled on until 1713.[97] There were large undertakings, such as a Glasgow woollen manufactory (established 1699) which employed 1,400 people, but most were much smaller. Although not universally so, rural manufacturing was underdeveloped and proto-industry was still in its infancy: it was not until the middle of the eighteenth century for instance that most stocking knitters in Aberdeenshire became rural proletarians.[98] Slow economic growth and sharp short-term fluctuations in demand for most commodities militated against changes in organisation and technology in urban production.[99]

Even the undoubted growth which took place in the Scottish coal industry, along with its coal-fuel dependent partner, sea salt, seems to have been more modest than has been assumed by historians since the appearance of Professor J. U. Nef's estimates in 1932. Re-worked figures suggest that output from this 'major' growth industry in the seventeenth century should be halved, to some 225,000 tons, while exports of both coal and salt were minimal by the end of the century.[100] There are signs too that at some of the more heavily mined coastal collieries, the techno-logical limits of water draining methods were being reached and the most accessible seams had been worked out. 'It is evident as Sun Shine', urged one alarmed contemporary who demanded that a survey into the coal industries of England as well as Scotland be undertaken, 'that ffour parts of ffive of all the Coals of Scotland (which hath Communication with the Sea) is exhausted'.[101] The same writer represented a widespread sense of frustration coupled with impotence when he condemned the Dutch who, 'catch their ffishes in our Sease without the least Acknowledgement And give the French, Spanish and Portuguese the Benefite of the Salt Trade'.

With very few exceptions the components of Scotland's small manu-facturing sector were struggling by the turn of the eighteenth century, and would almost certainly have continued to do so even if markets had not been cut off by war and tariff barriers. Deep-seated weaknesses remained, mainly the poor quality of manufactures, the result in large part of a chronic shortage of indigenous technical and business know-how, notwithstanding periodic efforts to deal with the former by importing skilled workers from England and elsewhere. Such labour however was expensive and if brought from the Continent could cost as much as 50 per cent more than from England. Imported workers were also difficult to retain in what was an alien and sometimes hostile environment.[102] There were doubts in some quarters as to the extent which their skills were disseminated among the Scottish population. In order to solve their labour problems landed coal and salt masters had instituted in 1606 a form of labour coercion not unlike the 'new serfdom' of Eastern Europe. Despite the oppressive legal framework which the Scottish Parliament had created however, coal workers continued to exercise considerable independence (see chapter 3).

Although there is a frustrating lack of precision about contemporary trade figures, there is a reasonable case for regarding black cattle as Scotland's second most valuable export.[103] Scottish cattle were certainly hardy – they had to be to travel the hundreds of miles of drove routes into England – but the trade suffered from two weaknesses. First, cattle from Scotland were periodically subject to restrictions in the form of export duties as well as an import levy once they reached England. Secondly, despite evidence of improved rearing and cattle management practices in Galloway, for example, only an estimated twenty to thirty thousand head of cattle were going south in the early eighteenth century. This was considerably less than the figure of around sixty-one thousand cattle which appear to have been entering England from Ireland prior to the Irish Cattle Act of 1667, which banned Irish cattle from the English

market, thereby – in theory at least – opening the door for the Scots' inferior beasts. With export and import taxes falling over the course of the
seventeenth century, the number of Scottish-bred cattle entering England
should have risen, but apart from single years, this appears not to have
happened, which points to a failure on the part of Highland landowners
to respond to market opportunities there.[104] Instead, quite rationally, as
was noted earlier, they seem to have preferred to supply the growing
towns of southern Scotland, to obtain higher profits.[105] Generally speaking, sheep, largely bred in the Borders, did better and in some years went
in bigger numbers than cattle, although their value per head was considerably less.

There are three other qualifications of the more optimistic assessments
of Scotland's economic condition at the end of the seventeenth century.
The first concerns Scotland's overseas trade. Discussion thus far has been
designed to identify long-term shifts in the composition and direction of
trade. Yet if we adopt a shorter perspective, there are compelling reasons
for believing that the Scottish economy was slipping into deep recession
from 1688, in which condition it would remain until some years after
1707, notwithstanding the first faint signs of an upturn in 1705. There
were other bright spots, in the Baltic trade for example between
1698–1700 and 1701–6, when the shipping figures returned to their best
levels of the 1670s and 1680s respectively.[106] Baltic markets however
were simply compensating (in part) for trading losses in France and the
Low Countries. From 1689 France banned the importation of foreign salt
herrings and, at a stroke, cut Scotland off from her main market for this
commodity, although a significant number of ships from Glasgow, for
example, continued to take herrings to Stockholm. In the Low Countries,
Scottish coal and salt were forced out by cheaper and superior rivals.
Elsewhere the picture looked gloomy, not least in relation to England,
where Scottish export levels were halved between 1698–1700 and
1704–6. Tariffs, which had been rising from the 1680s, were imposed by
Scotland's main customers on virtually every Scottish export of any
consequence. England even increased linen duties in 1698, thereby
contributing substantially to the downturn noted above. By tightening
the Navigation Acts in 1696 England also made it more difficult for the
Scots to trade with the Americas. The irony was however that as
Scotland's economic position worsened, she found herself increasingly
dependent upon England for her survival.[107]

Short-term shocks pushed the economy even closer to the point where
it would cease to be viable: the indications are that over time, Scotland's
balance of payments position was worsening. In 1704 the deficit on
'visible' trade appeared to be more than £2 million Scots (£171,700 sterling), and even if this is exaggerated there is no evidence to suggest
anything other than a trade imbalance.[108] The wars with France between

1688 and 1697 and 1701 and 1713, which cut off direct trade, led to new demands from the Royal Navy for manpower and hence conscription of Scottish sailors. Not until 1696 was Scottish shipping adequately enough protected by armed merchantmen to reduce at least some of the havoc created by French privateers.[109] (A minor compensation was that home sales of Scottish sea salt rose as imports of Bay salt from France and Spain were interrupted by the hostilities.) A series of poor harvests between 1695 and 1698 created four years of famine conditions during which between 5 and 15 per cent of the population perished, perhaps 25 per cent in the north-east, but also led to a 'dearth of monies' and a further downturn in economic activity, adding to the numbers of poor and complaints about vagabonds, both of which had been rising before-hand.[110] Merchants, lairds, victuallers and brewers were all hit. Of forty-seven joint-stock companies formed between 1690 and 1695 only twelve appear to have survived to 1700.[111] After a short period of recovery a further cash crisis led to the suspension of payments by the Bank of Scotland in December 1704. It was 'ye cheapness of victuall' which caused the value of Dundee's petty customs (paid on goods bought and sold in the town's market) to fall by half between 1700 and 1707. Burghal impoverishment was real enough in the case of Dundee, which in 1704 was burdened by debts amounting to £120,000 Scots.[112] State finances too were in a parlous condition, with the cost of funding the civil list, the military and government being estimated to be some £14,311 sterling more than Scotland's total annual revenues of around £113,194 at the time of the Union.[113] Payments were also several years in arrears. The tax yield from customs and excise in Scotland was 2.8 per cent of the English figure, equivalent to around 14 per cent *per capita*.[114]

Rampant economic nationalism abroad put a small and weak maritime nation like Scotland at a grave disadvantage. The inadequacies of the Scottish merchant marine have already been noted. The Scots did erect protectionist barriers against Irish grain, victuals and cattle, but elsewhere retaliation was at best futile and at worst self-defeating. The principal rivals for the 'empire of the seas' were England and the Dutch, both of whose mercantile marines far outstripped Scotland's. A Scottish navy of three vessels was formed, but with hulls borrowed from England. Co-operation on this matter however was deceptive. Deteriorating political relations between the two countries resulting from incidents such as the premeditated massacre of Glencoe in 1692 were accompanied and inflamed by attacks on Scottish ships by English privateers, and even naval vessels, within Scotland's coastal waters.

Fears that the Darien scheme might succeed and damage the interests of both England and Spain had drawn hostile responses, bolstered for the Spaniards by financial support from Pope Innocent XII who was concerned about the potential damage which Scottish Presbyterians could do to the Catholic faith in the region.[115] Apparently reluctantly (although in fact we know little for sure about regal motives), King William sided with English merchant interests, thus precipitating the withdrawal of English capital from the Company, and blocking anticipated merchant investment from Amsterdam and Hamburg. Two expeditions left from Scotland, in 1698 and 1699 respectively, but Spanish military and naval action, allied to disease, bad luck and poor management, brought the Darien adventure to an ignominious end, although the Company of Scotland continued to trade on a piecemeal basis for a further six years.[116]

The failure of Darien was a profoundly important event in Scottish history, seared into the nation's memory. Suggestions that the Scots had been deluded – even 'bewich'd', by the 'Golden Dreams of Paterson the Pedlar, Tub-preacher, and ... Whimsical Projector' in support of a doomed colony which had been settled 'in the very Bosom and Centre of the three chief Cities of the Spanish-Indies, to wit, Carthagena, Portobello and Panama', and even closer to Spanish silver mines, could be heard only with difficulty above the din of the popular clamour of support for 'Caledonia', and public grief at its dismal end. Historians too have failed to appreciate the strength of a Spanish empire which, although in decline, was far from being militarily impotent.[117] Rather, it was urged by the author of a broadsheet which listed those who had perished at sea *en route* for Darien, or after landing, that the names of those lost should 'stand upon Record as being among the first Brave Adventurers that went upon the most Noble, most Honourable, and most Promising Undertaking that Scotland ever took in Hand'.

England's part in the scheme's collapse was condemned by snarling Scots. There were more sober responses however. Bad enough was the estimated capital loss of some £153,000, a sum which may have represented a quarter of the nation's liquid assets. This brought home to contemporaries more forcefully than any other blow to her trading ambitions the realities of Scotland's economic (and geo-political) situation: in an age of muscular mercantilism Scotland would find it hard to prosper independently. Scotland's range of options was 'drastically' reduced.[118] To conduct overseas trade successfully, Scotland probably needed English acquiescence. The failure of Darien appears to have precipitated a further flurry of pamphlets on the condition and future of the Scottish economy, as well as Scotland's future relationship with England, which was clearly unsatisfactory. The ambitions of the French monarch Louis XIV and the threat of a French Universal Monarchy, heightened by fears that France would succeed to the Habsburg empire on the death of Charles II, strengthened the case for a reconstituted union with England. Various options were aired in a debate led by Andrew Fletcher of Saltoun. These included federalism and complete separation from England – a solution favoured by Jacobites – but with world conditions as they were and not as they might be wished, the most persuasive was that survival depended on the accomplishment of an aim which had been articulated periodically during the seventeenth century: 'a union of trade' with England.[119] This was called for even in Glasgow which had managed to establish an Atlantic trade in spite of the Navigation Acts, but which felt the adverse effects of an improved English customs service after 1696.[120]

Darien however was symptomatic of wider and deeper problems which confronted the Scottish economy in the years which preceded the Union of 1707 and which led to despair in some quarters. It is surely significant that the author of the 1693 'Overture for a Plantation' felt that the main advantage of such a scheme was that Scotland had 'plentie of men and women to plant', and that the principal benefit would be that 'It would ease the Kingdome of many thousands of idle profligate begging people', a number of whom would be taken compulsorily from each parish.[121]

If crisis is an over-used term then the notion of a severe check to Scottish development in the later seventeenth and early eighteenth centuries is not overly dramatic. The Angus burgh of Brechin, the population of which had grown by several hundred during the course of the century, had raised enough money to build a bridge over the river Southesk around 1685, but a description of its condition a few years later, in 1691, is not unlike those of many other burghs, other than it is more detailed. Inland trade, 'very mean and small', had 'altogether failed' over the previous two or three years, with the result, it was claimed, that more than a third of the merchants and inhabitants had either gone bankrupt or left the burgh. Imports, brought overland from Montrose, comprised only 'Soap Starch Salt Iron potts pans and other small wairs', while the trade done by the town's eight or ten grain dealers was 'extraordinarily Inconsiderable'; consumption of drink was confined to a little sack and brandy, while demand for ale had fallen so far that 'the brewars have none or little seall for ale but from Strangers and at the Common fairs'.[122]

Fifteen years later similarly dismal accounts were still common. Thus in 1705 the royal burgh of Bo'ness – through which the bulk of Glasgow's trade was shipped, carried east and west overland – complained about not only ships and men which had been lost in 'Caledonia' (the colony at Darien), but also of the dire effects of privateering and war, which reduced the number of voyages each ship could make each year. Whereas there had been thirty ships sailing out of Bo'ness in 1698, it was claimed that only ten were left by 1705, while of the town's 557 families, 205 were those of widows; unemployed seamen were being forced to leave and find work with Newcastle colliers. Similar accounts – which owing to their status as petitions from royal burghs, many of whom were anxious to reduce their burden of taxation, may contain an element of exaggeration – came from numerous places in Scotland, including Glasgow, whose merchants claimed to have lost seventeen ships to seizures (fourteen) and bad weather (three) in the year to June 1707.[123] Evidence which is untainted by special pleading – customs dues at Leith and tolls on goods brought for sale into Edinburgh – tell a similar story.[124] Notwithstanding the efforts of individuals, the Convention of Royal Burghs, and an increasingly interventionist Scottish state, Scotland's economy still lagged far behind those of England, France and the Low Countries, and in the early years of the eighteenth century there was little to suggest to those who sought to emulate them that the gap in living standards would be closed.

Darien had also highlighted the tensions which existed under the dual monarchy. Faced with a choice, King William had favoured his English subjects, a possibility which proponents of such schemes had hardly considered, if indeed they had not been persuaded that their monarch would willingly support them. A further blow to Scottish aspirations came in February 1703 with the breakdown of negotiations over a possible union between England and Scotland which had been instigated by the recently-crowned Queen Anne and her ministers, largely owing to English unwillingness to compensate the Scots for the larger tax burden which they would have to carry. Scotland would be required to comply with English terms. As relations between the two countries worsened there was a determined show of Scottish independence by a new Scottish Parliament in 1703 and 1704, with the passing of the Act of Security, the essence of which was that Scotland would not be bound to support England's nomination for a successor to Queen Anne, and the Act Anent Peace and War which reserved to the Scottish Parliament the right after Anne's demise to declare war and conclude peace. Economic warfare was declared with the Wine Act and another act in 1704 which forbade the importation of but allowed the export of wool, steps which were judged by English woollen interests to be hostile. Reaction in England, both in the country and in the Houses of Commons and Lords, was angry and decisive. Locked into the War of the Spanish Succession, England feared the withdrawal of Scots regiments from the north European theatre of war and the possibility of Scotland's support of France. England's response was to pass the Aliens Act of March 1705 which declared that unless there was agreement on the succession to the throne by Christmas, as well as progress on the question of union, there would be an embargo on Scottish linen, coal and black cattle. A 'formidable economic bludgeon', if implemented the Scottish economy would have been crippled.[125] On the eve of the Union of 1707, England was Scotland's single most important export market for the threatened commodities. On occasion, linen, Scotland's single most valuable export, represented as much as two-thirds of the value of Scottish exports to England, yet even this, it was argued in 1704, was sold furth of Scotland in considerably smaller quantities and at half the price than formerly.[126]

At the turn of the eighteenth century, although the main lines of eighteenth-century development were visible, Scotland was still an economy and society of considerable but unrealised potential. Abundant natural resources such as fertile land, coal and other minerals had begun to be developed and, not unlike England, marked her off from European rivals which were less favourably endowed.[127] As in England's case too, textiles dominated Scotland's export trade, amounting to 68 per cent of the 1703–4 total, even though the list still included primary produce. It could hardly be said of Scotland however that the country's greatest comparative advantage lay in 'the steady accumulation of skilled labour capable of manufacturing commodities that might be profitably traded on world markets for imports desired by ... consumers'. More perceptive travellers recognised that Scotland was by no means alone in Europe in its poverty and under-development, and that there were some reasons for optimism. Yet when John Farrington left Holland and entered Germany in 1710 it is striking that he felt the best way of conveying the difference between the two countries to a British readership was to call on the example of Scotland: 'No more pleasant villages, fine plantations, nor more signs of plenty, but it is almost incredible, Sir, how soon Scotland in its worst dress began to appear'.[128] There was some elasticity in the supply of labour in Scotland, but not of skilled workers, whose numbers dwindled further following the dearth of the 1690s. The range of tradeable goods was also more restricted. As has just been seen, the market for Scotland's linen was limited too, and she also had an effective rival, in terms of both quality, price and political clout in England – Ireland, which had been permitted by the English Parliament in 1705 to export Irish linen directly to the American colonies.[129]

Notes

1 For a brief discussion of the eighteenth-century background to this theme, better known in the poetry of Robert Burns, see C. A. Whatley, 'Burns and the Union of 1707', in K. G. Simpson (ed.), Love & Liberty. Robert Burns: A Bicentenary Celebration (Edinburgh, 1997), 184–5.

2 D. Stevenson, 'Twilight before night or darkness before dawn? Interpreting seventeenth-century Scotland', in R. Mitchison (ed.), Why Scottish History Matters? (Edinburgh, 1991), 37–47.

3 P. Kriedte, Peasants, Landlords and Merchant Capitalists: Europe and the World Economy, 1500–1800 (Oxford, 1990 ed.), 61–100.

4 I. Guy, 'The Scottish export trade, 1460–1599', in T. C. Smout (ed.), Scotland and Europe, 1200–1850 (Edinburgh, 1986), 62–81.

5 D. Dobson, *Scottish Emigration to Colonial America, 1607–1785* (Athens, Georgia, 1994), 57, 69–72.

6 L. M. Cullen, 'Scotland and Ireland, 1600–1800: their role in the evolution of British society', in Houston and Whyte, *Scottish Society*, 227–8; C. A. Whatley, *The Industrial Revolution in Scotland* (Cambridge, 1997), 50.

7 J. I. Israel, *The Dutch Republic: Its Rise, Greatness, and Fall, 1477–1806* (Oxford, 1998 ed.), 998–1018; J. de Vries and A. van der Woude, *The First Modern Economy: Success, Failure and Perseverance of the Dutch Economy, 1500–1815* (Cambridge, 1997), 673–87.

8 E. J. Graham, 'In defence of the Scottish maritime interest, 1681–1713', *Scottish Historical Review*, LXXI, (1992), 101; Graham, 'The impact of mercantilism and war on the Scottish marine, 1651–1791' (unpublished Ph.D. thesis, University of Strathclyde, 1998), 50–2.

9 T. C. Smout, *Scottish Trade on the Eve of the Union, 1660–1707* (Edinburgh, 1963), 47–57.

10 Edinburgh City Archives (ECA), Convention of Royal Burghs (CRB), Moses Collection, SL 30/226, 'Lists of ships etc. belonging to the various ports of Scotland', June 1709.

11 H. G. Graham, *The Social Life of Scotland in the Eighteenth Century* (1909 ed.), x; P. Hume Brown, *Early Travellers in Scotland* (Edinburgh, 1973 ed.), 251–65.

12 Whatley, *Industrial Revolution*, 10.

13 Cullen, 'Scotland and Ireland', 229.

14 ECA, CRB, Moses Collection, SL30/217, 'Accompt of the condition of the burgh of Brechin', 1691; SL30/215, 'Memoir for the town of Brechin', 1693.

15 I. D. Whyte, *Agriculture and Society in Seventeenth Century Scotland* (Edinburgh, 1979), 178–92, 222–34.

16 R. A. Dodgshon, *From Chiefs to Landlords: Social and Economic Change in the Western Highlands and Islands, c. 1493–1820* (Edinburgh, 1998), 113–14; A. I. Macinnes, *Clanship, Commerce and the House of Stuart, 1603–1788* (East Linton, 1996), 142–3; Whyte, *Agriculture and Society*, 234–45; A. Gibson and T. C. Smout, 'Scottish food and Scottish history, 1500–1800', in Houston and Whyte, *Scottish Society*, 77.

17 I. D. Whyte and K. A. Whyte, 'Some aspects of the structure of rural society in seventeenth-century Lowland Scotland', in Devine and Dickson, *Ireland and Scotland*, 38–9.

18 Macinnes, *Clanship*, 122–58.

19 A. I. Macinnes, 'Gaelic culture in the seventeenth century: polarisation and assimilation', in S. G. Ellis and S. Barber (eds), *Conquest and Union: Fashioning a British State, 1485–1725* (London, 1995), 162–94; Gibson and Smout, 'Scottish food', 82; see too Dodgshon, *From Chiefs to Landlords*, 102–22.

20 Whyte, *Agriculture and Society*, 207–8.

21 *Ibid.*, 217.

22 J. de Vries, *European Urbanisation, 1500–1800* (London, 1984), 28–48; I. D. Whyte, 'Scottish and Irish urbanisation in the seventeenth and eighteenth centuries: a comparative perspective', in S. J. Connolly, R. A. Houston and R. J. Morris (eds), *Conflict, Identity and Economic Development: Ireland*

and Scotland, 1600–1939 (Preston, 1995), 16–18.

23 M. Lynch, 'Urbanisation and urban networks in seventeenth century Scotland: some further thoughts', *Scottish Economic & Social History*, XII (1992), 35.

24 I. D. Whyte, 'The Occupational structures of Scottish burghs in the late seventeenth century', in M. Lynch (ed.), *The Early Modern Town in Scotland* (London, 1987), 231.

25 H. M. Dingwall, *Late 17th-Century Edinburgh: A Demographic Study* (Aldershot, 1994), 144, 275.

26 C. A. Whatley, *The Scottish Salt Industry: An Economic and Social History* (Aberdeen, 1987), 12, 42–3.

27 L. M. Cullen, T. C. Smout and A. Gibson, 'Wages and comparative development in Ireland and Scotland, 1565–1780', in R. Mitchison and P. Roebuck (eds), *Economy and Society in Scotland and Ireland, 1500–1939* (Edinburgh, 1988), 113.

28 T. C. Smout, N. C. Landsman, and T. M. Devine, 'Scottish emigration in the seventeenth and eighteenth centuries', in N. Canny (ed.), *Europeans on the Move: Studies in European Migration, 1500–1800* (Oxford, 1994), 76–90; R. A. Houston, *The Population History of Britain and Ireland, 1500–1700* (London, 1992), 62.

29 Smout, *Scottish Trade*, 152–66, 175–82.

30 *Ibid.*, 233.

31 CEA, CRB, Moses Collection, SL30/213, 'Scroll of a letter to Master of Stair from the Convention of Royal Burghs', 1691.

32 J. Hatcher, *The History of the British Coal Industry, Volume 1, Before 1700: Towards the Age of Coal* (Oxford, 1993), 108–9.

33 I. D. Whyte, 'Proto-industrialisation in Scotland', in P. Hudson (ed.), *Regions and Industries: A Perspective on the Industrial Revolutionin Britain* (Cambridge, 1989), 232.

34 R. A. Houston, *Social Change in the Age of the Enlightenment: Edinburgh, 1660–1760* (Oxford, 1994), 345–6.

35 ECA, CRB, Moses Collection, SL30/231, 'A list of the trafficking merchants living within four miles of Dysart', 1691.

36 Houston, *Social Change*, 351–7.

37 Smout, Landsman and Devine, 'Scottish emigration', 80.

38 G. Donaldson, *The Scots Overseas* (London, 1966), 30–1.

39 R. Law, 'The first Scottish Guinea Company, 1634–39', *Scottish Historical Review*, LXXVI (October 1997), 189.

40 N. Canny, 'The origins of empire: an introduction', in N. Canny (ed.), *The Oxford History of the British Empire, Volume I: The Origins of Empire. British Overseas Enterprise to the Close of the Seventeenth Century* (Oxford, 1998), 13–15, 17.

41 See Dingwall, *Late 17th-Century Edinburgh*, 171–7.

42 J. J. Brown, 'Merchant princes and mercantile investment in early seventeenth century Scotland', in M. Lynch (ed.), *The Early Modern Town in Scotland* (London, 1987), 127.

43 Whatley, *Scottish Salt*, 38–40.

44 Hatcher, *History of the British Coal Industry*, 103–4.

45 E-B. Grage, 'Scottish merchants in Gothenburg, 1621–1850', in Smout, *Scotland and Europe, 1200–1850*, 112.

46 T. C. Smout, 'The culture of migration: Scots as Europeans 1500–1800', in R. Jackson and S. Wood (eds), *Images of Scotland* (Dundee, 1997), 22.

47 J. V. Beckett, *Coal and Tobacco: The Lowthers and the Economic Development of West Cumberland, 1660–1760* (Cambridge, 1981), 104.

48 ECA, CRB, Moses Collection, SL30/221, 'Petition for the merchants of Glasgow and others', 1703.

49 Macinnes, *Clanship*, 77.

50 A. Bieganska, 'A note on the Scots in Poland', in Smout, *Scotland and Europe*, 157–63; T. M. Devine, 'The golden age of tobacco', in T. M. Devine and G. Jackson (eds), *Glasgow, Volume I: Beginnings to 1830* (Manchester, 1995), 147.

51 T. C. Smout, 'Scottish landowners and economic growth, 1650–1850', *Scottish Journal of Political Economy*, XI (1964).

52 R. Mitchison, *Lordship to Patronage: Scotland, 1603–1745* (London, 1983), 94–9; I. D. Whyte, *Scotland's Society and Economy in Transition, c. 1500–c. 1760* (London, 1997), 3–27.

53 J. Lindsay, 'The iron industry in the Highlands: charcoal blast furnaces', *Scottish Historical Review*, LVI (April 1977), 49–63.

54 M. Glendinning, R. Macinnes and A. Mackenzie, *A History of Scottish Architecture From the Renaissance to the Present Day* (Edinburgh, 1996), 72–90.

55 *Ibid.*, 88; R. Marshall, *The Days of Duchess Anne: Life in the Household of the Duchess of Hamilton, 1656–1716* (London, 1973), 189–208.

56 J. Holloway, *Patrons and Painters: Art in Scotland, 1650–1760* (Edinburgh, 1989), 13–32; D. MacMillan, *Scottish Art, 1460–1990* (Edinburgh, 1990), 79–80.

57 Whyte, *Scotland's Society*, 16–17.

58 K. Brown, 'The origins of a British aristocracy: integration and its limitations before the treaty of union', in Ellis and Barber, *Conquest & Union*, 222–49.

59 R. L. Emerson, 'Scottish cultural change 1660–1710 and the Union of 1707', in J. Robertson (ed.), *A Union for Empire: Political Thought and the Union of 1707* (Cambridge, 1995), 121–44; see too R. H. Campbell and A. S. Skinner (eds), *The Origins and Nature of the Scottish Enlightenment* (Edinburgh, 1982).

60 P. Roebuck, 'The economic situation and functions of substantial landowners, 1660–1815: Ulster and Lowland Scotland compared', in Mitchison and Roebuck, *Economy and Society*, 81–92.

61 Gibson and Smout, 'Scottish food', 82–3.

62 I. D. Whyte, *Scotland Before the Industrial Revolution. An Economic & Social History, c. 1050–c. 1750* (London, 1995), 210–12.

63 T. M. Devine, 'The Scottish merchant community, 1680–1740', in Campbell and Skinner, *Origins and Nature of the Scottish Enlightenment*, 35–6.

64 R. Callander, 'The pattern of landownership in Aberdeenshire in the seventeenth and eighteenth centuries', in D. Stevenson (ed.), *From Lairds to Louns: Country and Burgh Life in Aberdeen, 1600–1800* (Aberdeen, 1986), 7.

65 R. Saville, 'Scottish modernisation prior to the industrial revolution, 1688–1763', in T. M. Devine and J. R. Young (eds), *Eighteenth-Century Scotland: New Perspectives* (East Linton, 1999), 12; R. Saville, *Bank of Scotland: A History, 1695–1995* (Edinburgh, 1996), 58, 72.

66 Dingwall, *Late 17th-Century Edinburgh*, 100–6.

67 I. D. Whyte and K. A. Whyte, 'Debt and credit, poverty and prosperity in a seventeenth-century Scottish rural community', in Mitchison and Roebuck, *Economy and Society*, 70–80.

68 Houston, *Population History*, 58–65; R. A. Houston, 'Geographical mobility in Scotland, 1652–1811: the evidence of testimonials', *Journal of Historical Geography*, XI (1985); I. D. Whyte and K. A. Whyte, 'The geographical mobility of women in early modern Scotland', in L. Leneman (ed.), *Perspectives in Scottish Social History: Essays in Honour of Rosalind Mitchison* (Aberdeen, 1988), 83–106; C. W. J. Withers, *Urban Highlanders: Highland–Lowland Migration and Urban Gaelic Culture, 1700–1900* (East Linton, 1999), 3–4, 62–6.

69 T. C. Smout, 'The Improvers and the Scottish environment: soils, bogs and woods', in Devine and Young, *Eighteenth-Century Scotland*, 211.

70 Dodgshon, *From Chiefs to Landlords*, 102–7; Graham, 'Scottish maritime interest', 89.

71 See Saville, 'Scottish modernisation', 7–9.

72 ECA, CRB, Moses Collection, SL30/214, Letter, John Dalrymple (on behalf of the King) to the Royal Burghs of Scotland, 11 July 1692.

73 Whyte, *Agriculture and Society*, 99–100.

74 See G. P. Insh, *The Company of Scotland* (London, 1932).

75 ECA, CRB, Moses Collection, SL30/215, 'Overture for a Plantation', 1693.

76 D. Armitage, 'The British empire and the civic tradition, 1656–1742' (unpublished Ph.D., University of Cambridge, 1991), 136.

77 W. Herries, *A Defence of the Scots Abdicating Darien* (Edinburgh, 1700), 8.

78 *Ibid.*; ECA, CRB, Moses Supplementary Bundles, 2/91, Darien Company Papers, 'Scotland's wish for a prosperous voyage to her African and Indian fleet', n.d., *c.* 1699.

79 L. M. Cullen and T. C. Smout, 'Economic growth in Scotland and Ireland', in L. M. Cullen and T. C. Smout (eds), *Comparative Aspects of Scottish & Irish Economic and Social History, 1600–1900* (Edinburgh, 1977), 4; Saville, 'Scottish modernisation', 11–12.

80 Smout, *Scottish Trade*, 27–9.

81 Whatley, *Scottish Salt*, 36; Whatley, *Industrial Revolution*, 17.

82 Graham, 'Mercantilism and war', 52.

83 Gibson and Smout, 'Scottish food', 82.

84 Smout, 'The Improvers', 210–11.

85 *Ibid.*, 213–14, 217.

86 Dodgshon, *Chiefs to Landlords*, 24, 195; H. D. Smith, *Shetland Life and Trade, 1550–1914* (Edinburgh, 1984), 41.

87 R. A. Dodgshon, *Land and Society in Early Scotland* (Oxford, 1981), 272.

88 T. M. Devine, *The Transformation of Rural Scotland: Social Change and the Agrarian Economy, 1600–1815* (Edinburgh, 1994), 16.

89 Whyte, 'Proto-industrialisation', 230.

90 Lynch, 'Urbanisation', 35; see too I. D. Whyte, 'Urbanisation in eighteenth-century Scotland', in Devine and Young, *Eighteenth-Century Scotland*, 177.

91 See, for example, M. Clough, *Two Houses: New Tarbat, Easter Ross; Royston House, Edinburgh* (Aberdeen, 1990).

92 Saville, *Bank of Scotland*, 60.

93 Dingwall, *Late 17th-Century Edinburgh*, 137–8; Dodgshon, *From Chiefs to Landlords*, 115.

94 L. Weatherill, *Consumer Behaviour and Material Culture in Britain, 1660–1760* (London, 1988), 60.

95 See A. J. S. Gibson and T. C. Smout, *Prices, food and wages in Scotland, 1550–1780* (Cambridge, 1995), chapter 8.

96 ECA, CRB, Moses Collection, SL30/216, 'Petition for Whitefield Hayton, citizen in London, to the Privy Council', 1694; 'Petition by the Skinners of Edinburgh', 1694.

97 Mitchison, *Lordship*, 106; C. Gulvin, *The Scottish Hosiery and Knitwear Industry, 1680–1980* (Edinburgh, 1983), 7–11.

98 R. E. Tyson, 'The rise and fall of manufacturing in rural Aberdeenshire', in J. S. Smith and D. Stevenson (eds), *Fermfolk & Fisherfolk: Rural Life in Northern Scotland in the Eighteenth and Nineteenth Centuries* (Aberdeen, 1989), 66–7.

99 Houston, *Social Change*, 349.

100 Whatley, 'New light on Nef's numbers', 4–7.

101 National Archives of Scotland (NAS), Hamilton MSS, GD 406/1/4975, 'Memorandum concerning coal and salt, 1702'; see too C. A. Whatley, 'Salt, coal and the Union of 1707: a revision article', *Scottish Historical Review*, LXVI (April 1987), 26–45.

102 C. Gulvin, *The Tweedmakers: A History of the Scottish Fancy Woollen Industry, 1600–1914* (Newton Abbot, 1973), 27–8.

103 Saville, *Bank of Scotland*, 62, 68.

104 D. Woodward, 'A comparative study of the Irish and Scottish livestock trades in the seventeenth century', in Cullen and Smout, *Comparative Aspects*, 156–7.

105 Whyte, *Agriculture and Society*, 235.

106 Smout, *Scottish Trade*, 254–5.

107 See T. C. Smout, 'Scotland and England: is dependency a symptom or a cause of underdevelopment?', *Review*, III, IV (1980), 607–11.

108 Saville, 'Scottish modernisation', 12.

109 Graham, 'Maritime interest', 98–100.

110 R. Mitchison, 'North and south: the development of the gulf in Poor Law practice', in Houston and Whyte, *Scottish Society*, 208–214; Tyson, 'Famine in Aberdeenshire', 32–52.

111 Saville, *Bank of Scotland*, 40.

112 C. A. Whatley, 'Economic causes and consequences of the Union of 1707: a survey', *Scottish Historical Review*, LXVIII (October 1989), 168; ECA, CRB, Moses Collection, SL30/221, 'Petition to Convention of the Royal Burghs from Dundee', 1704.

113 British Library, Portland Papers, Add. 70047, Appendix No. 1, 'Concerning the revenue & charge of the government of Scotland before the Union', 1712.

114 Smout, 'Scotland and England', 605.
115 C. Storrs, 'Disaster at Darien (1698–1700)? The persistence of Spanish imperial power on the eve of the demise of the Spanish Habsburgs', *European History Quarterly*, XXIX, 1 (1999), 22–3.
116 G. P. Insh, *The Darien Scheme* (London, 1947), 22.
117 Storrs, 'Disaster at Darien', 27.
118 D. Armitage, 'Making the empire British: Scotland in the Atlantic world, 1542–1717', *Past & Present*, CLV (May 1997), 58.
119 J. Robertson, 'Union, state and empire: the Britain of 1707 in its European setting', in L. Stone (ed.), *An Imperial State at War: Britain from 1689 to 1815* (London, 1994), 239–40; Armitage, 'British Empire', 160.
120 G. Jackson, 'Glasgow in transition, *c.* 1660–*c.* 1740', in Devine and Jackson, *Glasgow*, 74. How strong this vein of support was is open to question, given the anti-Union petitioning which emanated from the city, whose MP, Hugh Montgomerie, also voted against the ratification of the incorporating union. See J. R. Young, 'The parliamentary incorporating union of 1707: political management, anti-unionism and foreign policy', in Devine and Young, *Eighteenth-Century Scotland*, 32.
121 ECA, CRB, Moses Collection, SL30/215, 'Overture for a plantation', 1693.
122 ECA, CRB, Moses Collection, SL 30/217, 'Accompt of ye condition of the burgh of Brechin', 1691; see too SL30/215, 'Memoir for the town of Brechin', 1693.
123 ECA, CRB, Moses Collection, SL 30: see in particular bundles 222 and 224.
124 R. A. Houston, 'The economy of Edinburgh, 1694–1763: the evidence of the common good', in Connolly, Houston and Morris, *Conflict*.
125 Lenman, *The Jacobite Risings in Britain*, 81; the best narrative account of the prelude to Union is W. Ferguson, *Scotland's Relations with England: A Survey to 1707* (1994 ed.), chapters 10–13.
126 Smout, *Scottish Trade*, 23–34; Anon, *Scotland's Interest: Or, The Great Benefit of a Communication of Trade with England* (London, 1704), 5.
127 P. K. O'Brien, 'Inseparable connections: trade, economy, fiscal state, and the expansion of empire, 1688–1815', in P. J. Marshall (ed.), *The Oxford History of the British Empire, Volume II: The Eighteenth Century* (Oxford, 1998), 56.
128 Quoted in C. D. van Strien, *British Travellers in Holland During the Stuart Period* (Leiden, 1993), 234.
129 J. M. Price, 'The imperial economy, 1700–1776', in Marshall, *Oxford History of the British Empire*, 88.

2

The Union and the
first economic transition,
c. 1707–c. 1778

The Union of 1707: causes and consequences to c. 1727

There has been intense debate among historians about the causes of the Union of 1707.[1] During the 1970s and 1980s older arguments – that incorporating union had been a bargain in which the Scots obtained free trade in return for the loss of political independence – were cast aside in favour of those which emphasised the seamier side of British politics in the reign of Queen Anne. At their most extreme, historians of this more cynical persuasion attributed Union almost entirely to political management and bribery. Indeed the notion that the Union was the outcome of 'the politics of the closet' has become the new orthodoxy, widely believed and authoritatively disseminated, sometimes less than scrupulously in the case of those anxious to assert the case for Scottish independence at the end of the twentieth century on the basis of the 'treachery' of 1707.[2] Notwithstanding the plethora of pamphlets which were published in the immediate pre-Union years, the suggestion that argument and principles played any part in the making of the Union is brusquely dismissed. Clearly machinations of the sort outlined eased the process, and there can be little doubt that the failures at crucial moments of the nominal leader of the Country Party, the fourth duke of Hamilton, to oppose Court initiatives and lead opposition to union, weakened the divided opposition camp, but evidence that promises of pensions and sinecures actually altered the voting intentions of more than a handful of members of the Scottish Estates is hard to find.[3]

It is not intended here to provide a rounded explanation for the Union of 1707. Such texts can be found elsewhere. The best of them are multi-factoral, adopt a broad perspective, and account for the British union of 1707 in its European context. They also acknowledge that whatever its real or supposed benefits for Scotland, the impetus on this occasion came from an expansive English state whose forces had occupied Gibraltar in 1704 and under the duke of Marlborough had experienced a resounding military triumph at Blenheim.[4] They might have well have been turned on a tardy Scotland.[5]

To suggest however that economic considerations did not play any part in persuading a majority of the members of the Scottish Estates to vote in favour of incorporating union – an argument invented by Victorian historians according to one ill-informed critic – seems a somewhat perverse denial of the overwhelming evidence there is to the contrary, including the speeches and writings of contemporaries such as John Arbuthnot and George Mackenzie, earl of Cromartie. At least one observant Scot in early Hanoverian Scotland believed that notwithstanding the anti-Union sentiments of the 'Generality of the People', 'the only popular Topick produced for rendering it palatable was the great Advantage that must accrue to Scotland from the Communication of trade', a 'weighty' consideration. Indeed if there was one thing which united supporters and opponents of the Union, it was the fact of Scotland's economic condition and poverty. The disputes were about how to improve matters.[6] To imply, as some historians have recently, that because Union failed to deliver immediate economic success it could not have been inspired by economic motives, is to overlook entirely the deep sense of grievance many Scots felt in the immediate post-1707 decades that pro-Union promises about the economy had been broken.[7] It was the threat to Scottish trade posed by the English Alien Act of 1705 that brought the Scots to the negotiating table, but there were those who were convinced anyway about the advantages a union would bring. The 'Hony Lys in the Trade', reflected one anonymous but cynically self-interested Scot who was realistic enough to recognise that as far as trade was concerned 'ane Union' would be 'as Seeds Sown or Stones laid for a foundatione, which time only can raise to Maturity'. Nevertheless, he reasoned that the Union

> may bring us into the way and knowledge of these Places and Things which they [the English] have Laboured to Conceal from us, And having once got in a foot we may possibly scrue into the bowels of the hive.[8]

It is probably true that there were some who supported union not simply because Scotland was poor and they could see no other way of riches, but 'because they were poor and rapidly getting poorer'.[9] Yet the prospect of economic gain was also a positive pro-union inducement, notably for those members of the Scottish Parliament who formed the Squadrone, whose votes in favour of the Union were of crucial importance.[10] In fact it can be argued that in its economic provisions the union settlement which was hammered out during the closing months of 1706 created a trading environment which achieved in large measure what many commercially-minded Scots had sought for several decades, access to and participation in a maritime empire. (Not all traders were persuaded of course: in the burghs, for example, there were fears about the consequences of higher taxation.) There were even those who argued that union with England would lead to a weakening of the grip of a tyrannic Scottish nobility; prosperity achieved thereby, and freedom, went together.[11]

What the proposed union promised was unhindered access to markets in England and protected trade with her colonies. This was precisely what was advocated by William Seton of Pitmedden, who may have accepted a pension from the Court but whose argument that 'without Force to protect its commerce' Scotland would continue to languish economically was a brutally clear analysis of Scotland's situation which was consistently propagated by its author.[12] As has been seen, there must be serious doubts about the extent to which Scotland could act autonomously in the pre-Union period, notwithstanding the reassertion of Scottish parliamentary power after the Revolution of 1689–90.[13] Scotland's sovereignty existed only 'within her own confines', and independence, according to the contemporary John Clerk, a Scottish patriot and reluctant Scottish Commissioner for union, was illusory, 'a meer shadow and an empty name'.[14] Clerk, like others, suffered considerable personal anguish during 1706 and indeed throughout the rest of his life, his conscience tormenting him about the enormity and consequences of voting for incorporating union. For reflective Scots, including patriots, the decision whether or not to support an incorporating union was rarely an easy one.

As far as the economic case for Union is concerned, it is important that during the autumn and early winter of 1706 the Scottish Parliament managed to squeeze further concessions from England for those Scots who had come to recognise that free trade cuts both ways and that Scottish goods might suffer from English competition in the home market. Fifteen of the twenty-five Articles of the Union concerned economic matters, a crude if unambiguous measure of their importance to contemporary politicians. It was these which often generated the most heated debates among the Scottish commissioners and produced the closest votes – apart from the IVth Article, which granted free trade and was even supported by twenty-six members who were generally opponents of union.[15] By conceding to Scottish demands the amended Articles assuaged fears and gave further benefits to specific Scottish interest groups, including grain exporters, dealers in pork and beef, and proprietors of coal and salt works.[16] To the twentieth-century eye some of these might look like comparatively minor concerns, and the financial benefits insignificant, but it is important to understand the issues in their early eighteenth-century context, which includes the Scots' interest in and need for small money windfalls. Daniel Defoe described the debate and vote on the VIIIth Article, which dealt with the salt trade, as the 'Grand

Affair'. Saltworks made massive contributions to the economics of many coastal collieries in Scotland. Purchases of salt for domestic purposes, for which demand was relatively inelastic, were made in return for cash, and the development of banking and the spread of the bill of exchange notwithstanding, coin was still scarce but essential for day-to-day transactions. Saltwork income from the Dysart works of the St Clair family for example was used to pay for services such as razor-sharpening, pot-tinning, wig-dressing and clock-making, as well as various servants' wages.[17]

If few Scottish politicians were enthusiastic advocates of incorporating union in 1707, sufficient numbers of them were attached to party groupings whose leaders were persuaded that in the circumstances this constitutional model provided the only possible avenue if Scotland's economic ambitions were to be realised. The vexed matter of the succession to the throne was also settled at English insistence in favour of Protestant claimants (a matter of no little concern to Scottish Presbyterians, although the most extreme of them, the Covenanters, remained 'hostile to ... engagement with an uncovenanted state'), while parliamentary union might resolve the unenviable dilemmas a succession of the monarchs of the two nations had faced.[18] It was not the ideal solution but it was probably the only realistic one available at the time, given England's demands and Scottish needs. Seen in the context of developments in the rest of Europe, where the number of independent states was falling as dynastic unions and other forms of closer alliance between states created great fiscal and military entities, most notably those of Austria, France and Spain, the British 'problem' of peacefully accommodating a composite monarchy seems much less of an aberration.[19] That the XVth Article also created the so-called Equivalent further sweetened the pill for contemporaries, by allocating to the Scots £398,085 10s. for undertaking to repay part of England's national debt and as compensation to the shareholders of the Company of Scotland for losses incurred by Darien, with an additional 5 per cent interest. Monies from the Equivalent were also to be used to provide much-needed support for woollen manufacturing in the wool-producing counties, and to encourage the fisheries and other manufactures in Scotland.

The impact of the Union is another hotly-contested issue. Opinion is divided between those who have attributed all or much of the growth which occurred in the Scottish economy over the course of the eighteenth century to the Union of 1707, and those who argue that its effects were much less substantial. The emphasis of the former is on the Union as the creator of a common market, the largest free trade area in Europe. Scotland now had unhindered access to Britain's north-American colonies, whose European population grew at 3 per cent *per annum* after 1700 (considerably faster than England or Scotland), creating a market of over 2.1 million people in 1770. Jamaica's population was 340,000 in 1800, and had grown at 2 per cent *per annum* during the eighteenth century. Through the century, too, Britain's overseas territory expanded in a series of leaps at the peace treaties, such as those which ended the War of the Spanish Succession in 1713 and the Seven Years War in 1763.[20] Other benefits claimed for the Union were political stability and closer association of the Scots and English, with a flow of capital, labour and ideas from south to north. Indirect benefits to Scotland may have been the disappearance of the Scottish Parliament from Edinburgh, which meant that more energy could be devoted to economic matters, and the civilising effects of English society and subsequent Scottish attempts to emulate their southern superiors.[21]

The recent tendency has been to downgrade the significance of 1707, to suggest that the crisis conditions at the end of the seventeenth century were temporary and that in the longer-run certain of those structural factors which were noted in the previous chapter mattered more. These were, primarily, a rural social structure which was conducive to change and the process of agrarian improvement which had begun in the seventeenth century, but also the existence of a political and social elite which was committed to economic improvement, a dynamic business class and a legal and banking system which helped sustain it, favourable geological resources, and Scottish scientific and technical ingenuity. Where there is disagreement, it is about the relative importance of these factors. The Union, it has been argued, was 'relevant but not in itself decisive ... the structures of society were more decisive than key political events'. The fundamental causes of modernisation 'lay ... within the texture of society'. Pre-Union policies of Scotland's governing class were perpetuated, widened and adapted after 1707.[22] It will be argued here that all of these factors are indeed relevant and that the Scots' own responses to the risks and opportunities provided by Union were important. Trends established in the later seventeenth century can be found manifesting themselves more robustly in the eighteenth. On the other hand it will be suggested that this model of economic advance places insufficient emphasis on the Union and the English connection. It also overlooks the consequent critical features of the political economy of Scottish economic development in the first half of the eighteenth century.

There has been something of a consensus among historians that the short-term effects of the Union of 1707 were broadly neutral, and that any damage done was slight. This judgement however is based on relatively little hard evidence; the first three post-Union decades have attracted little interest from economic and social historians. It is also difficult to distinguish long-term trends, favourable as well as damaging, from what may appear at first sight to be the effects of the Union. Thus the number of voyages made by Leith skippers plummeted between 1703 and 1704 but began to rise again thereafter, prior to 1707. The number of vessels at the port appears to have risen too, to thirty-three ships in 1709, a modest increase since 1692.[23] Nor is there much sign that the Union made a difference to the number of voyages being made by Scottish ships sailing into the Baltic between 1690 and 1720. Similarly, the drive by landowners to enclose common ground had begun before the Union, and continued in the immediate post-Union decades. In Ayrshire the opening up and expansion of the collieries in Stevenston, which had grown from a 'small clachan of two [or] three Houses' into a 'consider-able village' by 1719, owed little or nothing to union. The surge in exports of Ayrshire coal to Ireland during the 1720s, is largely accounted for by aggressive landed leadership on the part of the Cunninghames of Auchenharvie and some short-lived enterprise on the part of a handful of English mining adventurers led by Daniel Peck.[24]

Closer examination of the evidence however shows that the Union did have short-term effects but that these were enormously varied and complex. Some small but significant changes in trading patterns produced temporary dislocation. Being bound by British commercial policy meant that long-standing trade links with France and the Low Countries were weakened. Imports of popular French claret, for example, had to be replaced by *legal* traders with heavier, sweeter wine from England's ally, Portugal, and indeed the largest single contribution to the post-1707 increase in shipping activity recorded by Trinity House came from voyages to and from Spain and Portugal. The number of ships from England rose too, as did other forms of coastal trading.[25]

According to contemporaries, but overlooked by most historians, the immediate beneficiaries of Union were the landowners and merchants who engaged in the seaborne grain trade. The impact is striking, with grain and oatmeal shipments from Scotland more than doubling to an annual average of over 57,000 quarters between the two five-year periods 1707–12 and 1717–22, when they reached their eighteenth-century peak (although there were single years when more was shipped out). During the Union negotiations Scottish landowners had been able to obtain an additional drawback on oats, oatmeal and bere exported from Scotland, over and above the allowances payable by the Corn Bounty Act of 1695. (The same clause *guaranteed* that Scots cattle entering England should be subject to no more duties than were payable on English cattle. Black cattle had apparently ceased to be exported to England after 1703.) The value of grain debentures rose from an average of £45 16s. in 1703 and 1704 to over £319 in 1708 and £7,374 12s. in 1712, a remarkable 161-fold increase which as will be seen in chapter 4, had profound social repercussions. Bank of Scotland lending in the five years after 1709 further encouraged agrarian innovation.[26] It may be inferred from the outbreak of strongly-supported and widespread anti-enclosure riots in

Galloway in 1724 that the Union had encouraged landowners in the
south-west to extend their cattle rearing activities and further commer-
cialise their pastoral farming methods in order to benefit from the
newly-secured English market and higher prices. More commercially-
oriented cattle rearing was also evident in Argyll from the early 1700s.[27]
In part however this was a continuation of the pre-1707 trend, as are
indications that the sheep trade was prospering between 1695 and
1725.[28]

Other beneficiaries in the short-term were certain categories of coastal
and overseas merchants, whose vessels were now able – in theory at least
– to seek protection from naval cruisers or sail in 'strong Convoys' under
the protection of the Royal Navy. Most prominent among the merchants
were the Glasgow men who dealt in sugar and tobacco, and who from
1 May 1707 could participate freely – and legally – in colonial trade. For
the first one and a half decades after 1707 however much of their success
was based on their ability to evade on a massive scale and bend to their
own advantage the new customs regulations. In the 1710s and up to
1722 between 62 and 47 per cent of Scotland's tobacco imports, some 90
per cent of which came into the Clyde, are estimated to have been smuggled.[29] In addition, with their lower wage and provisioning costs during
peacetime the Glasgow merchants were able to make sizeable inroads
into the market shares of Bristol and Whitehaven tobacco importers, the
last-named suffering a fall in imports of tobacco from an average 1.5
million pounds between 1698 and 1702 to 1.2 million pounds between
1722 and 1726.[30] Between 1698 and 1707 and 1722–31 average annual
imports of tobacco to Scotland rose from 1.5 million pounds to 5.6
million.[31]

The Union too opened up the Irish market for certain 'enumerated'
commodities, mainly tobacco and muscovado sugar, which Irish merchants
were barred from importing directly by the Navigation Laws. Although an
illicit re-export trade from Scotland in these and other goods had been run
prior to 1707 the quantities of tobacco recorded as going over the Irish Sea
from Scotland after the Union are spectacular, rising from an annual
average between 1700 and 1704 of 542 pounds to 637,613 pounds ten
years later.[32] The rise of the Glasgow tobacco trade in the years immediately
following the Union was in this sense much more significant than is
suggested by reference to a 'relative malaise' up to the 1720s.[33] Whereas the
British tobacco trade stagnated in the first quarter of the eighteenth century,
by 1714–17 Glasgow, through her outports of Greenock and Port Glasgow,
had pushed ahead of all of the other British tobacco ports except London.[34]
Indeed Glasgow stood out as the only sizeable place in Scotland that was
thriving in the politically sensitive year of 1715, much to the relief of
anxious Hanoverians who noted that 'we hear less of Jacobitism from the
west country than from all other places'.[35]

Presumably this localised buoyancy also owed something to the success of other trade-related ventures, sugar houses and soapworks (whose pre-Union privileges were continued), rum distilling and glass-works, although some craftsmen were soon to follow the merchants in launching capital-intensive enterprises. Some Glasgow (and Montrose) merchants too became involved in the slave trade, but to nothing like the extent of Liverpool, London or Bristol, at least as far as direct trading was concerned.[36] Contemporary observations that overseas merchants catering for the better-off continued to be active in the immediate post-Union decades are confirmed by a more or less continuous rise in Edinburgh's fruit market customs from 1694 to 1763.[37] Demand for commodities which fall into the category of luxuries may have been made firmer by another consequence of Union – the regular payment of the salaries of state and government officials, the result of introducing the more efficient English revenue system to North Britain. Payment was also made of most – but not all – of the 'publick debts' in Scotland, from the Equivalent fund, greatly to the benefit of the Bank of Scotland which also became the depository for certain government monies and the revenues from taxation.[38] French wine too continued to be imported, smuggled on a massive scale to avoid new higher duties.

In other respects the short-term economic impact of Union appears to have been either neutral or negative, although care has to be taken not to exaggerate the degree of damage done to what was already a struggling domestic economy. As has been seen, many of the royal burghs had been complaining about falling revenues and decaying public buildings prior to 1707. Another complicating factor was the War of the Spanish Succession, which continued until 1713. Privateers caused havoc for Scottish vessels, even those which were fishing in coastal waters and many of the east-coast burghs complained of the severe depredations done to their shipping. From Elgin it was protested in 1708 that all of their vessels had been lost and that no foreign trade had been carried on for two years.[39] The Scottish sea salt industry, which continued to be protected under the terms of the VIIIth Article of Union, appears to have carried on in a more or less steady state through the second decade of the eighteenth century. A steep rise in exports during the 1720s was against the long-term downwards trend and is explained by the interruption in the export of 'Bay' salt into the Baltic due to the outbreak of plague in Marseilles in 1720 and the renewal of war between Britain and Spain.[40]

There is evidence from many parts of Scotland however that the condition of both manufacturing and fishing were worsening in the wake of the Union. This was given as the main reason, along with higher taxes and threats of more to come, by the earl of Findlater in June 1713 when he moved a motion in the House of Lords which, if slightly better supported, would have led to the dissolution of the Union.[41] A report from 1711 on the condition of the burgh of Kilrenny on Fife's east coast is fairly typical of the sort which were received by the Convention of Royal Burghs throughout the 1710s and 1720s. It was claimed that:

> The whole subsistence of our little Towne is by fishing and linen manufacture both which branches of trade are now under such sad decay that we are daily made to lament the necessities of people who are most willing to ply industry and virtue but want encouragement.[42]

It is true that pro-Jacobite propagandists exploited and exaggerated the ill effects of the Union (see chapter 5) but cries about 'our poor decay'd nation' also came from traders such as George Yeaman of Dundee, who, notwithstanding his Jacobite sympathies, was painfully aware of the damaging effects which the new economic environment was having on certain Scottish commodities. Among his main concerns was linen, already Scotland's 'staple' and, as has been noted, seen by many as the trade most likely to bring prosperity and employment to Scotland. Scottish linen was proving extremely hard to sell in London however, and by 1723 becoming more so, not least because of its poor quality: bleaching with lime – 'Hott pernicious stuff' – caused the cloth to rot, while merchants too were disinclined to accept bales which were under-length or where the cloth was too narrow.[43] In addition, linen suffered from the imposition in 1711 and 1715 by Westminster of duties on exported and printed linens respectively.

In 1714, a successful bid for a drawback of the duty on soap, made on behalf of the English woollen interest, was followed by failure to get equivalent relief for Scottish linen, by which means, forecast George Lockhart, 'the Irish must and will undersell us and our linnen become a meer drug.'[44] Over time finer Scottish-made cloth was even replaced in Scotland by Irish and Dutch imports. In woollens, Scottish producers were forced out of the trade in finer goods and indeed it was at this end of the market where a number of Scottish manufactures had the greatest difficulty in surviving the brunt of English competition.[45] So too did paper-making and candle-making, both of which were subject to new excise duties. Recorded output from the paper-makers fell from 100,000 pounds to 40,000 pounds between 1712 and 1720. Charles Gray, a comb-maker in Dundee, petitioned the town council for the post of the town's jailer on the grounds that whereas before 1707 he had had 'a very good livelihood' from his trade, this had been 'effectually broke' by the Union. Shoe-making in Forfar, the town's only manufacture, was 'much decayed' since the imposition of a leather duty, it was protested in 1730. Wool and woollen cloth exports from Dundee and elsewhere to the Netherlands were evidently severely reduced, sacrificed in the interests of English manufacturers. Brewing also appears to have suffered, both immediately and in the longer-term, with growth being slowed by the imposition of excise duties. Glass-makers too found it harder to survive. Complaints were made by the Convention of Royal Burghs on at least three separate occasions before the matter was resolved temporarily in 1718, that customs officers in Scotland were charging higher fees than those agreed at the time of the Union, which were to be based on the table approved by the House of Commons in 1662.[46]

Fishing was more variable. New taxes on imported salt imposed from 1707, the restrictions on the use of Scottish sea salt for curing fish for export, and 'Pirats & Privateers', were but three burdens under which the formerly prosperous Fife fishing industry complained that it now laboured. The unpredictability of the herring shoals was another, albeit unrelated to the Union, although the ramifications of declining catches spread inland, it was argued from Cupar in 1734, where allegedly, many fisher people, 'particularly of the poorer Sort', had swollen the burgh's poor roll. At Peterhead it was complained in 1709 that the number of seafarers and 'whytfishers' had been more than halved, many of them having left to serve in 'the Inglis fleetes', although it is not clear if this had all happened since 1707. Inverness reported in 1721 that the herring fishing had been 'quite sunk' for the past three years. A further blow in the east was felt on 19 January 1724 when an unusually fierce storm severely damaged several piers and harbours. Cromarty fishing on the other hand prospered until c. 1730, Aberdeen had a sizeable trade in salmon, and boats fishing for 'Glasgow herring' in the western sea lochs within easy reach of the Clyde also seem to have done reasonably well.[47]

It was not only new and higher levels of taxation – approximately five-fold overall – which had a deleterious effect on economic activity. So too did the new and complicated procedures which were introduced to collect customs and excise duties.[48] The notoriously inefficient Scottish customs had been farmed to private individuals prior to 1707, and in the localities officers had been less than scrupulous either in collecting taxes or implementing Privy Council restrictions on certain imported goods. After 1707 complaints abounded at the expense of and time lost in satisfying the demands of the customs officers, with the skippers of small vessels which carried coal on the firth of Forth, for example, being required to collect a warrant from the custom house to load and then obtain clearance to sail. These and other bureaucratic irritations, along with the fees which were charged, resulted in 'an expense which these small loadings are not able to bear', by doubling the cost of navigation but also by preventing skippers sailing at the 'first fair Wind', which caused the selling price to rise. The loudest complaints were made about the Salt Laws, a cumbersome set of regulations whose impact fell particularly harshly on the small-scale, open-boat operations which characterised the Scottish fishing industry.[49]

Paradoxically, it may be proposed that it was the debilitating effects of the Union – real and imagined – which partly helped create the conditions by which the Scottish economy was lifted to an unprecedentedly buoyant condition by the 1770s. These however were generally indirect rather than direct results. The argument that the Union presented the Scots with risks as well as opportunities is sound, but the full range of tactics which the Scots had to adopt in order to minimise these risks and to enhance their opportunities has not been recognised hitherto. Almost everything had to be fought for, hard. The point will be developed further in chapter 3.

One measure which has been used to demonstrate Westminster disinterest has been the fact that between 1727 and 1745 only nine Acts of Parliament dealt specifically with Scotland.[50] Yet this excludes private bills and ignores altogether the lobbying that was done on behalf of Scottish interests almost immediately after the Union took effect on 1 May 1707. Although they rarely acted in concert, Scotland's representatives were a formidable grouping when they combined to vote together on an issue, as in 1713 when the House of Lords came within four votes of approving a motion to bring in a bill to dissolve the Union.[51] Scottish Whigs could be grasping and avaricious. Supporters of Argyll and their 'deadly' rivals the Squadrone often lacked political principle.[52] Yet to write off the Scots at Westminster for having failed to represent Scottish grievances owing to their fear of causing offence is probably unfair.

Contemporaries, concerned with the immediate past and the short-term future, and much more conscious therefore than most modern historians of the impact of legislation on economic affairs, were aware from the outset of the importance of ensuring that the Westminster Parliament was not allowed to harm – even inadvertently – Scottish interests. Yet more positive results were anticipated too. 'Our longing Eyes', wrote one pro-Hanoverian pamphleteer in 1727, as King George II acceded to the throne, 'are now fixed upon the Parliament for Relief', with 'the whole Country' being in a 'kind of Suspense, waiting the Event of His Majesty's most Gracious Resolutions'. If Scotland's trade and manufactures prospered following an act of a *'British'* Parliament, discontent would be diminished and the 'Flame of Sedition ... must be extinguished for want of proper Fewel'.[53]

The Convention of Royal Burghs not only maintained contacts with MPs they felt would represent their views, but also periodically paid for an agent in London to lobby on their behalf. Initially their priority was damage limitation, and in the early post-Union years the Scots presented eight petitions opposing an extension of the English Royal African Company's monopoly, their efforts to expose a breach of the VIth Article of Union motivated by fears for the triangular tobacco and slave trade.[54] In 1709 Scots successfully petitioned for an extension of the XIIth Article of Union, which relieved Scottish coalmasters from paying duty on water-borne coal within the estuarial limits of the Forth, defined as running from St Abb's head in the south to the Red Head near Arbroath in the north. Frantic petitioning on behalf of the inhabitants of the burghs of Arbroath, Dundee and Perth ensured that in an area within which lay two of Scotland's three most dense concentrations of population, coal could be purchased free of coal duty (until 1793). Aberdeen's more substantial use of peat allegedly caused less pain than in Montrose, where even 'men of Substance' found it hard to afford fuel owing to their greater dependence on coal, and where the coal tax applied, because, the burgh was convinced, they had been temporarily without a representative in Parliament.[55] Of much greater significance nationally was the Convention of Royal Burghs' success in 1720 in blocking an attempt by London woollen and silk manufacturers to effect a ban on the wearing of printed calicoes and linens, a step which it was argued would have had devastating social and political consequences in Scotland by creating widespread unemployment in the Lowlands. So desperate was the country's condition that in the opinion of one petitioner, linen was 'the only manufacture ... left to maintain the poor'.[56] Indeed from early in the eighteenth century (and perhaps earlier) the payment of rents on the Atholl estates in Highland Perthshire depended more on the success and timing of linen sales than agricultural produce.[57]

Reference has already been made to the tobacco trade and its progress to 1722, which was achieved partly through customs evasion. However, that between 1716 and 1722 only £1,351 had been paid on tobacco carried coastwise from Scotland to England, whereas the duty should have been at *least* sixty-one times greater, suggests that this may be an understatement.[58] The vigour with which this illicit trade was conducted may also in part have been born of passionate anti-Union sentiment. Growth slowed after the reorganisation of the customs service in 1723, which included the abolition of the separate Scottish customs board. The remaining duty on re-exported tobacco was also lifted, thereby removing from the Scots some part of the price advantage they had secured through customs evasion. A period of lower prices and stricter application of customs regulations eliminated several weaker Glasgow firms, which meant – fortuitously and as an indirect result of Union – that in the longer run the legislation of 1723 helped create 'a stronger and more viable merchant community in Glasgow'.[59] The benefits in capital accumulation that smuggling on such a grandiose scale generated should be judged in similar terms.

Pain of elimination motivated merchant-manufactures in the west of Scotland to diversify into new and finer branches of the linen trade. A new linen works was established in Ayrshire in 1718. Dunfermline too adapted and by 1720 had turned to the production of damasks. In the east, appeals were made from London for better-quality coarse linen, and sporadic but largely unsuccessful attempts were made to improve the manufacture as well as to better regulate the trade through the appointment of burgh stampmasters.

The economic landscape in Scotland then was not uniformly bleak. The reports of the Swedish industrial spy Henry Kalmeter, made in 1719 and 1720, portray considerable buoyancy at the coal, salt, silver, lead and other works he visited. Bank of Scotland lending too increased rapidly between 1722 and 1726. Nonetheless as will be revealed in greater detail in chapters 4 and 5 there are grounds for arguing that during the 1720s Scotland was faced with grave economic difficulties at what was a critical time in the process of British political integration. The roots of the problem were poverty and the weakness of domestic manufacturing. Expansion was essential to provide full- and part-time employment not only for the growing numbers of village and town dwellers but also in order to sustain rural communities, as well as to provide, by stimulating demand, the means by which agricultural reform could advance further.

Central government was made fully aware of the connection between underemployment, any worsening in the economic situation and national security. In the Jacobite rising of 1715, led by the earl of Mar, dissatisfaction with the Union had been a highly effective recruiting agent.[60] It was only four years later when renewed demands were made on behalf of the disgruntled remaining 'Creditors of the Publick in Scotland', who had still not been fully recompensed from the Equivalent. Nor had the monies allocated in the Articles of the Union for the encouragement of fisheries and manufactures in Scotland been put to the purpose for which they had been designed. Such failures on the part of the government to honour the agreements made in 1706 it was argued were not only widely known in Scotland, but also 'sower[ing] the spirits of your Majestys most dutyfull and Loyall subjects'.[61]

Such was the severity and nature of the malt tax riots, interpreted by the government as an outrageous and unprecedented 'rebellion against the law', that action was required which would both mollify stunned and vengeful ministers such as the Secretary of State the duke of Newcastle and remove the root cause of Scottish dissatisfaction. Without 'proper laws and suitable Encouragements' declared one gloom-filled pamphleteer, 'our Circumstances must daily grow worse', and Scotland would become a burden, 'an open Back-door for the enemies of our happy Constitution to enter by'. 'The people', he went on, 'when oppress'd with Poverty and Want, and are idle and uneasy in their Affairs, are ready upon the slightest Ground of Complaint, to murmur and mutiny'.[62]

After lengthy wrangling at the highest governmental level, as well as discussion among Scottish representatives in Parliament, the decision was taken in 1726, with the strong support of the Prime Minister, Sir Robert

Walpole, to divert any surplus from the malt tax to 'provoke our country [Scotland] to industry'. More regular funding was to come from the Equivalent. The outcome was the establishment, in 1727, of the Board of Trustees for Fisheries and Manufactures, with legislation initiated at Westminster but which was to operate along lines which had been advocated by the Convention of Royal Burghs, as well as the patriotic Honourable Society of Improvers in the Knowledge of Agriculture, founded in June 1723.[63] Also founded in 1727 was the Royal Bank of Scotland, again funded from the Equivalent and which, notwithstanding the private and political motives of some of its shareholders and supporters, was also established as an agency for national economic improvement, under the Governorship of the earl of Ilay.[64] Hopes for the future then were higher at the end of the 1720s than they had been earlier. Little however had been achieved and in 1730 Sir John Clerk was still struck by Scotland's poverty, the want of manufactures and the lack of encouragement to the poor to work.[65] For some years the desire for political ascendancy on the part of Ilay and his agent Lord Milton diverted Whigs from their declared aim of national economic renewal, as they skirmished for example in the 'bank war', the short-lived and unsuccessful attempt by the Royal Bank to bring down the Squadrone-backed Bank of Scotland.[66]

Tracking economic developments to c. 1778

The impact of the Board of Trustees was almost immediate. Stampmasters, whose main tasks were to examine and approve the quality and measure of woven cloth, were appointed throughout the Scottish weaving districts, mainly Angus, Fife, the Lothians, Renfrewshire and Lanarkshire. Several spinning schools were established in order to improve the quality of the spun yarn, while Dutch, French and Irish weavers were brought in to pass on their skills in a sector of the industry which was characterised by seasonal, customary work. The effect of the Board was arguably greatest in bleaching, which had been 'lamentably deficient' prior to 1727. It was with the support of the Board of Trustees that – slowly at first – Scotland acquired a commercial bleaching industry, with full-time specialist bleachers being imported from Ireland and Holland.[67] Lint mills too were altogether new. Indeed in numerous processes associated with textile production the Board was instrumental in introducing either new or improved techniques and disseminating them. While the supply of skilled labour provided by the Board was insufficient to satisfy Scottish needs, and there were some disastrous failures, it was in this area that it made its greatest, and essential, contribution. With the assistance of monies provided by the Board, the

British Linen Company's bleachfield at Saltoun trained twenty-seven apprentices between 1751 and 1762, of whom about three-quarters went on to run their own bleachfields.[68]

The Board had little immediate effect on the output of cloth however, and the 1730s constituted a period of learning, experiment and adaptation. (The apparent upturn after 1728 revealed in Figure 1 is more likely to represent improving methods of recording cloth suitable for sale by stampmasters.) Samples of foreign-made cloth were examined, and copied by Scots weavers. Merchants such as William Sandeman of Perth proposed and implemented schemes for teaching boys how to weave and then encourage them 'to settle in the different parts of the Country', supported by premiums and prizes from the Trustees. Networks of hecklers and spinners were extended into the smaller settlements in Perthshire.

Slowly, the industry began to develop from one characterised by small, capital-starved, independent weavers into one in which manufacturers who owned a number of looms or who supplied weavers with webs and credit predominated. A few weaving factories were also established, but these were unusual. The trend was neither steady nor unidirectional however. In 1759 the directors of the British Linen Company were being advised to reduce their dependence on 'factory' weavers and instead to make more use of 'common weavers' who, once trained, could produce cloth much more cheaply than the former, and without the disadvantage to the Company of accumulating quantities of unsold goods.[69]

Spinning seems to have done better than weaving, both in terms of quality and output, with demand from England and Ireland creating shortages for Scottish cloth manufacturers. Spinning spread geographically too, with central Scotland yarn merchants and urban manufacturers putting out flax to females located in the countryside further north and west into Argyll. Flax-growing in Scotland was encouraged by premiums offered by the Board of Trustees, but it was a long time before there was any marked rise in the acreage sown, and even then most flax used in Scotland was imported from the Baltic and the Low Countries.[70]

Overall, the 1730s appear to have been years of modest but patchy growth. That the serious harvest failure of 1740 did not threaten a mortality crisis like that of 1695–99 has been interpreted as evidence that progress had been made in the Scottish economy during the first four decades of the eighteenth century. In Ireland by contrast there was severe suffering in 1740 and 1741, as there was in parts of mainland Europe. Subsidiary explanations for the relative ease with which Scotland managed to avert another demographic catastrophe have included an assumption of somewhat greater wealth on the part of lairds and burgesses, thereby making it easier for them to make charitable contributions for the support of the poor, as well as improvements in the organisation, transportation and distribution of grain.[71] (Superior organisation of emergency relief however is given as the main difference, and is an issue to which we will return in chapter 5.)

Contemporary opinion was often guarded. Despite the 'fresh Vigour' and improvements which he had seen in the linen industry, a man such as the Edinburgh merchant Patrick Lindsay was still conscious in 1735 that whatever its undoubted potential (along with the fisheries) to become one of the foundation stones of Scottish prosperity and the route to fuller employment, it required further state support, of the sort provided in Ireland.[72] Linen output overall rose only slowly, although there were sharper increases of the finer kinds such as Bengals. Woollen manufacture was carried on in several places, and appeared to be more than holding its own in Musselburgh and Galashiels. In and around Glasgow too there were signs of more concentrated mercantile involvement in industry, with the establishment *c*. 1734, for instance, of the Smithfield Iron Company, initially established as a smithy and nail works but which diversified into the manufacture of other goods such as axes, hoes and spades for which there was strong colonial demand.[73] As has been noted, this was a flat decade for the Scottish tobacco trade. Any optimism about the overall condition of the Scottish economy at this stage must surely be qualified.

Hopes for some earlier promising economic ventures were dashed – in coal and iron for instance, as well as other, more precious minerals, for which searches were made throughout Scotland by determined but often deluded adventurers. Some – the Zetland Company of London, for instance, who had undertaken to supply the earl of Cromartie with fishing busses, large decked vessels, for Loch Broom and Gairloch – were simply fraudulent.[74]

Shipments of Ayrshire coal, the only Scottish export to Ireland which had grown markedly in the first three decades of the eighteenth century, dropped sharply from a peak of around 25,000 tons in the later 1720s (16 per cent of the Irish market for coal), a level which was not reached again until the mid-1760s.[75] With rising iron prices in the 1720s, speculators and adventurers from England recognised the potential there was for making low-cost charcoal in the woodlands of the Scottish Highlands, a region the economic potential of which was being advertised by landowners, many of whom were overly optimistic about the ease with which their resources could be exploited. However, Montrose estate wood as well as the birchwoods near Loch Katrine were utilised for iron-ore smelting by two partnerships led by John Smith, from Donegal, in 1718. Another Irish partnership began smelting at Glenkinglass in Argyll around 1722. The woods of Speyside had first attracted the attention of the London-based York Buildings Company in 1727, who had hoped to produce ships' masts (for which there was a government premium of 20*s*. each) and water pipes, but the Company also began to smelt iron ore at Abernethy, in 1730, and was involved in another two Highlands ironworks. In 1727 the Backbarrow Company, from Cumberland, established an ironworks at Invergarry, also using imported iron ore. None however could withstand the revival of imports of the superior Swedish iron, while the York Buildings Company itself crashed in 1733. Lead mining too proved a fatal attraction for the Company, but others too were drawn to Scotland from England to search for lead and other minerals, sometimes in partnership with Scots, but with little lasting success – although there were some which survived longer, such as the Scotch Mines Company, which obtained its initial inspiration and funding (its nominal capital was £100,000) from London Scots.[76]

It was during the 1740s and into the third quarter of the eighteenth century that the pace of economic activity began to quicken, suggesting that Scotland's economic trajectory may have followed that identified by Deane and Cole in their study of British economic growth.[77] 'Osnaburgs' (termed 'Edinburgs' by the patriotic Board of Trustees), a loosely woven, coarse lint or tow-based linen cloth made in imitation of a German import began to be woven in the later 1730s and ultimately became the most important variety made in east-central Scotland. Sales quadrupled, from 0.5 million yards in 1747 to 2.2 million in 1758. Higher-priced fine linen production soared too, with the value of cambrics and lawns made in Scotland tripling to over one million yards in the ten years from the end of the 1750s.[78] By the 1760s the linen trade was employing in the region of twenty thousand handloom weavers and, at the very least, one female spinner from every second or third family in Scotland. In many places, it was expected that women would be drawn into spinning. On the Grants of Monymusk estate on Speyside, for example, male tenants were obliged to have 'at least two Spinners', who were required to spin a predetermined quantity of yarn each day when they were not employed at agricultural work, while similar requirements were made of the third duke of Argyll's tenants on Tiree in 1756, where over 100 female spinners were employed.[79]

Particularly rapid expansion occurred during the Seven Years War, with continental production of cloth and yarn being slashed: this, according to Henry Home, provided 'a favourable opportunity for diffusing widely the art of spinning, and for making our spinners more and more dexterous'. It also presented the Scottish producers with an unprecedented opportunity to replace their formal rivals in London, 'the greatest market in Europe'. Huge orders for Scots-made soldiers' shirtings and navy linen provided a further boost.[80] The estimated value of linen stamped in Scotland by the period 1773–77 was £573,400, more than four times the figure for 1728–32. Linen accounted for a massive three-quarters of Scotland's exports of textiles, which in their turn provided some 40–50 per cent of all Scotland's home-produced exports. Although there is some uncertainty about the precise proportion, it appears that around half of Scotland's linen output was exported, either to England or the colonies overseas (where the coarser but cheaper light linen cloth made in the east of Scotland was in great demand), as well as to the increasingly important Irish market. From around 1760 until the mid-1770s there was a steady but sure rise in the value of Scottish domestic exports to Ireland, with a peak during the years of the American War of Independence.[81]

In the west, Paisley followed Glasgow and began to establish a reputation for fine threads, linen and lawns. In 1759 silk gauze weaving began and, supported by a substantial capital injection from Spitalfields, managed to undercut the London makers. In woollens, native enterprise combined with Board of Trustees' expertise and funds and imported English waulking (fulling) mill technology. The quality of Scottish tarred and inadequately sorted wool however continued to be a subject of complaint into the 1770s. On the other hand, the Scottish woollen industry survived English competition in Scotland, and there is some evidence that some coarse woollen products continued to be exported to traditional markets in Holland and that a trade across the Atlantic was established.[82] There was an increase too in exports of hand-knitted stockings made by part-time workers who were also sub-tenants in rural Aberdeenshire. Another traditional product, *uisge beatha* (whisky), which had largely been produced on a small but wide scale, began to be made in a number of larger distilleries which were constructed in the later 1740s and early 1750s.[83]

Higher pig-iron prices at the end of the 1740s encouraged a second foray of ironmasters into the Highlands, this time entirely led by Englishmen. The Lorn Furnace Company settled on Duncan Campbell of Lochiel's woods in 1752 and erected works at Bonawe in Argyll. The Duddon Company of Lancashire settled at Craleckan (now Furnace), near Inverary. Sea connections for both importing ore and shipping off their products were crucial in both cases, the cheapness of fuel enabling them to survive into the nineteenth century. Even so, Scottish charcoal-fuelled iron smelting accounted for only a small proportion of British output.[84] This was to change later, during the coke-fuel phase of the British iron industry which was heralded in Scotland with the formation in 1759 of Carron Iron Works, by a partnership of Dr John Roebuck from Sheffield, Samuel Garbett of Birmingham and William Cadell of Cockenzie. The three men had first become manufacturers in Scotland in 1749, with the Prestonpans Vitriol Company.

What this all points to is a thickening and widening of economic activity. Much of this was concentrated in and around Glasgow, where even more striking than the growth of linen sales was the sharp upwards trajectory of the re-export trade in tobacco. This however had not been immediate nor was it inevitable. During the 1720s and 1730s Glasgow had been outpaced by Whitehaven, where tobacco imports rose from an annual average of 1.8 million pounds between 1726 and 1730 (when most tobacco was sold to the Dutch) to over 10 million in 1748 and 1749. By the 1750s however Glasgow had not only overtaken Whitehaven – which, like Glasgow, had begun to supply large quantities of tobacco to France – but was also rivalling London. In 1762 52 per cent of the country's exports were of tobacco, virtually all of which was re-exported. In 1769 Scotland – mainly Greenock, Port Glasgow and Glasgow – had captured 52 per cent of the British tobacco trade, import-ing in the peak year of 1771 47 million pounds.[85] More often than not the same merchants also traded in sugar and the provision trade of the Caribbean islands. The multiplier effect was of 'considerable' importance in the west-central region. This was so not only in the more obvious outlets for mercantile investment such as sugar refining, but also in coal-bearing estates and a range of manufacturing enterprises, the number of which increased in the middle decades of the century, while older estab-lished enterprises such as leather works, ropeworks, soapworks and sugar refineries grew. Edinburgh and Leith also experienced a great upturn in trade, from the 1740s.[86] Yet there were losers too. Ayr, Dumfries and Kirkcudbright suffered as French buyers of tobacco turned increasingly to Glasgow for their purchases and severed their connection with the lesser Scottish ports which had accounted for 25 per cent of their Scottish business in 1747. During the 1730s Dumfries had some ten or twelve ships engaged in the tobacco trade, but had lost all of this by 1772. The value of customs duties paid on goods imported and exported at Dumfries also collapsed, from an annual average of £27,959 between 1745–46 and 1749–50 to £558 between 1773–74 and 1778–79.[87]

While their incomes were smaller than those of the great landowners and London businessmen, Glasgow's 'tobacco lords' were 'easily the most opulent group to have emerged in Scotland before the nineteenth century'. Entire manufacturing sectors – leather and boot- and shoe-making – were dominated by colonial merchants, while in others, such as malleable ironworks and glassworks, they played a major role. Between 1730 and 1750 colonial traders had funded some eighteen manufactures, double the number in which they had become involved in the previous eight decades. Numerically their impact was greatest in units related to textiles, which comprised 52 per cent of their investments between c. 1700 and 1815.[88] Their role was particularly important in the finishing processes, for these – bleachfields and printworks – required large quanti-ties of capital to get going.

The indirect effects of such mercantile endeavour should also be recog-nised, in the formation for example of Carron Iron Works, which owed much to the demand of Glasgow merchants for its products. Early work on the Forth and Clyde canal was similarly inspired. The initial need was to link Glasgow with European markets which were more easily reached from the east coast. The financial infrastructure of the west of Scotland benefited too from the promotion of banking, in the form of the Glasgow-based Ship, Arms and Thistle Banks. Thereby the relatively small and close-knit concentration of colonial merchants contributed to one of the fastest-growing sectors in mid-century, there being a fifteen-fold increase in the circulation of banknotes between 1744 and 1772. Bank assets rose from £329,000 to £3.1 million. Between these dates thirteen provincial banking companies were launched, thereby generating additional lines of credit in and around other regional centres such as Aberdeen and Dundee.[89]

Parts of the Highlands too reaped gains from and responded to the rise of Glasgow, Scotland's 'imperial entrepot'. Argyll was best-placed, and saw the development of inshore fishing, tobacco spinning and various textile-related operations during the first half of the eighteenth century. From 1748, with the assistance of the Board of Trustees, the earl of Ilay, aided by Andrew Fletcher, Lord Milton, his Scottish 'manager', ambitious plans were implemented to expand linen manufacturing in Argyll, which for a short period during the 1750s accounted for more than half of the stamped linen made in the Highlands. Commercial endeavour was also evident, in the formation, first of the Inveresregan Trading Company in 1706, and a series of co-partneries which traded in a variety of commodities, and reached out not only to other parts of Scotland but also Dublin and, from the 1730s, the West Indies and the American colonies. Clan consumerism was also facilitated by contact with the Glasgow merchant importers.[90] In towns such as Cromarty and Inverness, which bordered the eastern Highlands, large proto-factories opened in 1765 and 1772 respectively, for linen and hemp production for bagging used for colonial goods shipped between London and the West Indies. They sucked in and employed several hundred workers between them during a short period in the economic development of Scotland when the more peripheral parts of the country could exploit their comparative advantage of low labour costs. These were mainly previously under-employed boys and women from the surrounding Highlands, employed to work within the factories and as out-workers.[91]

Manufacturing clearly played a major part in Scotland's great economic leap forward in the eighteenth century. Much of the employment this generated was located in the countryside, although opportunities for work grew in the towns too, not least in the building trades, increased activity in which is indicated by a surge in timber imports into Leith in the 1740s and elsewhere from 1755.[92] Although the degree of expansion in the smaller Scottish towns during the first half of the century may have been exaggerated, the total urban population in Scotland rose from 11.9 per cent in the 1690s to 17.3 per cent in 1755, with the numbers in the four largest towns with populations of over 10,000 more than doubling, to 119,000, over roughly the same period. This 124 per cent increase represents a faster rate of growth than similar sized towns in either England and Wales (42 per cent) or Ireland (68 per cent).[93]

Largely permissive rather than causal in the case of early urbanisation, the progress of agricultural improvement in Scotland during the first half of the eighteenth century appears to have been variable rather than steady or spectacular. Crucially however, agricultural performance was strong enough to feed the Scottish population, including the inhabitants of the rapidly growing towns, although the fact that the population total had not risen much above its level of the early 1690s by mid-century qualifies the achievement somewhat.[94] In part, so too does the fact that large quantities of grain were being imported (illegally) into Scotland from Ireland during the first three decades of the eighteenth century, although it may be that such imports into the west coast were compensating for high levels of bounty-led exports from the east.[95] Albeit slowly, grain and meal prices rose in Scotland during the first half of the eighteenth century, by 50 per cent between 1705 and the early 1760s, when there had been a further increase. This was in contrast to England, where prices tended to fall during the same half-century.[96] The Scottish increase has been attributed to better economic performance post-1707. The evidence for this – surveyed above – is slight, although heightened economic activity almost certainly caused the sharper price increases of the 1760s and 1770s. Irish imports dropped off from 1725, and until 1752 Scotland appears to have been more or less self-sufficient, with supplies from England making up most of the shortfall during occasional crises such as that caused by the poverty of the harvest throughout most of Europe in 1740.

To a large extent, Lowland agriculture developed along lines established in the seventeenth century. Thus longer, nineteen-year, written leases became increasingly common. The move to single as opposed to multiple tenancies accelerated too, with marked falls in the proportion of the latter on most estates which have been examined by historians. By mid-century the vast majority of tenancies over large swathes of Lowland Scotland were single, thereby making it easier to institute later improvements and reduce the size of the tenant class. The growth of single tenancies also increased the numbers who were or would be forced to leave the land. More striking was the extent to which rural society became commercialised, with conversion on a large-scale of payments of rent in kind to monetary transactions, a move which replaced a system of customary structures and obligations by one in which market forces predominated.[97] The efforts of some ambitious landowners notwithstanding (and while as will be seen in chapter 4 many adopted aggressive policies to enlarge their holdings), the period prior to 1760 was not one of significant rural reorganisation, and changes in farming systems proceeded slowly.[98] 'Improvers', landowners such as John Cockburn of Ormiston, and progressive lairds who included urban merchants and lawyers, were common enough, and, as has been seen, in 1723 the Society for Improving the Knowledge of Agriculture was formed. Yet several over-reached themselves and, like Cockburn, suffered bankruptcy. Enclosure tended to be restricted to the mains farms, while estate maps indicate little in the way of structural change. Until mid-century the rural landscape remained much as it had been in the previous century, with irregular, undivided fields, runrig cultivation and the retention of the infield-outfield system. The laying out and construction of planned villages, an important and integral part of the process of economic and social reconstruction in the Scottish countryside was similarly delayed. Of one published list of 126 planned villages established in the century after 1730 only ten (7.9 per cent) seem to have been founded before 1760. Of another more comprehensive survey only 13.9 per cent were founded between 1725 and 1769.[99] However, contemporary descriptions of the new towns as 'colonies', for which only suitable tenants were accepted, shows that a process of social selection – which could be political as well as economic – was well under way in Scotland by the 1760s.[100]

Most of the planned villages were in the Lowlands; in the Highlands and Islands only five were developed between 1725 and 1769. One of these was at Inverary (1742), the ducal and administrative heart of the revolutionary campaign of political and economic and cultural transformation waged by successive dukes of Argyll and their chamberlains from around 1710. Change had been evident in the seventeenth century, with clan Campbell being among the earliest Scottish landowners to 'acclimatise' to the new British political situation created by the Union of the Crowns in 1603. Further 'civilising' moves followed, including the elimination of the mercenary *buannachan* (redshanks) as a military caste, as part of the process of state-led reformation of the Highland region. Within the clan system, which valued armed men rather than sheep, cattle, or land mass, the tacksman – *daoine uaisle* – had been an intermediary between chief and tenant, responsible for raising men and dependent in turn on the labour services sub-tenants provided. The traditional concept of heritable trusteeship, *duthchas*, was replaced, among the elite, by the legalistic concept of landownership, *oighreachd*, which enabled the *fine* to manage their estates along commercial lines and in many cases abandon their roles as patrons and defenders of their clansmen.[101] Commercial competitive bidding for farms, systematically applied on Argyll lands from 1737, had the effect of undermining the tacksmen and replacing the customary relationships of the traditional townships with rental payments made directly to the landlord through the chamberlain or factor. The effects of commercial landlordism were felt at the lower levels of Highland society too, as rights such as woodleave and free access to seaware were restricted and given a cash value, although on some estates tenants had become accustomed to paying for timber they cut from their lords' forests. In Argyll, on the Uists and elsewhere the use of hand querns was forbidden, tenants instead being required to take grain to estate mills for grinding, with the result that mill rents could be raised.[102]

With rising prices in the 1760s however there was a marked acceleration in the pace of change in Scottish agriculture in both this and the subsequent decade, which in turn, produced substantial social dislocation. This was the first of two periods of dramatic development in the countryside of Lowland Scotland during the second half of the eighteenth century. The speed of the process was unprecedented, and contrasts with the slower pace of agrarian change in England. In the European context too it is quite remarkable. Recent detailed investigations into Scottish Lowland rural society have revealed several key indicators of change, although this did not occur at the same speed throughout the Lowlands. Enclosure, for example, was well-advanced in the Lothians by 1750. In the north-east, adaptation was slower, but there could even be enormous variations in the pattern of improvement on neighbouring estates. Lord Auchinleck, James Boswell's father, had begun the process of improving the family estate in Ayrshire during the 1750s, starting with the construction of Auchinleck House, levelling and beautifying the grounds, tree planting, road building and enclosing and exchanging land with neighbours in order to consolidate his holding. His neighbours however had made further progress by 1777, and much remained for Boswell to do when he succeeded to the estate in 1782.[103]

Virtually everywhere however was affected by the impact of market penetration, with most rents in kind finally being commuted to cash, and much movement of agricultural produce outside its place of production to numerous local markets as well as, more predictably, the larger towns. Industrial works in the countryside, numbers of which were increasing as mills and mines were established or extended, also provided valuable outlets, as did clusters of handloom weavers. In 48 per cent of Fife parishes, for example, there was an industrial presence of some kind.[104]

In 68 per cent of the sixty parishes where information on the timing of improvements is available, these occurred in the 1760s and 1770s rather than earlier. Enclosure was widespread, altering the appearance of the landscape by the creation of neat fields, and compact single farms separated by hedge, ditch and dyke. By the time the *Statistical Accounts* were compiled in the 1790s, significant advances had been made in the Lowland counties in central Scotland. A concentration of division of commonty cases has also been identified in the period 1760–1815. Improving leases, which were lengthy, detailed and prescriptive, were used in increasing numbers, thereby ensuring that tenants adopted new crop rotations which included sown grasses, root crops, such as turnips, and cereals. Tenants were considerably more likely to be evicted for rent arrears after *c.* 1760 than they were at the turn of the century. Landed expenditure on estate infrastructure rose to new heights, as on Strathmore estate in Angus, where over £22,000 was spent on agricultural improvement – enclosing, draining, road and bridge building and house construction – between 1771 and 1776.[105]

New farming techniques too began to be used, with the introduction in the 1760s of James Small's smaller plough, 'the most notable innovation in farm implements in the eighteenth century', not least as it was drawn by two horses instead of the team of oxen required to move the cumbersome old Scots plough.[106] The quarrying and burning, in kilns, of limestone, the use of which dated back in Scotland to the sixteenth century at least, intensified with enclosure, newly-enclosed land commonly being spread at the rate of between 400 and 600 bushels per acre. Landed investment and efforts to effect a rural revolution were rewarded with higher rents which were demanded from the 1760s. These, along with extensive bank lending, enabled major and minor landowners and lairds to build, improve, extend or embellish their increasingly grand houses, the priority for many. Fine furnishings and walls decorated with the paintings, prints and sculptures readily available from the more numerous painters and art dealers now resident in Edinburgh, enabled them to enjoy in splendour the economic and political power and social status which contemporary values prescribed for owners of landed property.[107]

Another outcome of the intensifying culture of commercialisation in the countryside was a more sharply defined pattern of regional specialisation, with farmers more determinedly exploiting their comparative advantages. Dairy and fruit farming for instance became increasingly common in Ayrshire, Renfrewshire and Clydesdale, which were within striking distance of industrial Glasgow and its crowding satellites and hinterland. The Lothians, Fife and Angus confirmed their role as barley producers, supplying important centres of malting and brewing, while further north, in Aberdeenshire and Buchan, 'bigg' (or 'bear') supplied nearby breweries although here and to the north and west they also provided for the needs of distillers.[108] In the southern part of Lanarkshire, the higher ground in Ayrshire and the highland parishes of Angus, sheep and some cattle farming became prevalent.[109] The clearance of small tenants and cottars which accompanied this movement echoed the better-known displacements of the Highland straths.

The degree to which Highland enterprise and indigenous commercial forces were in evidence has already been noted. Other profit-making uses of land included an increase in cattle rearing and droving, numbers of which crossing the border into England may have risen from some forty thousand around 1740 to sixty thousand in 1780.[110] The price of cattle rose too, but not at the three-fold rate claimed by Adam Smith. Kelp manufacture along the coasts of Fife and southwards into England was begun in the 1720s, if not earlier, partly in response to the needs of the weak but tenacious Scottish glass industry. Dulse gathering and burning was a seasonal activity which was carried on most successfully on Orkney (Britain's main kelp-producing location in the eighteenth century) and in the Outer Hebrides from mid-century, along with certain sea lochs on Mull and Skye, as well as on rocky parts of the mainland coastline around Ardnamurchan.[111] More notoriously, from the 1750s, the rearing of the Linton breed of black-faced sheep, an activity which was long established in Tweeddale and the Southern Uplands, was introduced into the Highlands, first into Argyll and Morvern, while by 1763 they had reached eastern Ross and Cromarty.[112]

The foundations of economic growth at this stage were still insecure and unevenly spread. What can be interpreted as balance of payments difficulties checked progress in 1762. The withdrawal of perhaps £500,000 of English capital, retrenchment on the part of the Scottish banks following a substantial increase in the circulation of notes on the part of the Glasgow banks in the mid-1750s, and a steep upturn in Bank of Scotland credits between 1759 and 1764, created difficult conditions. In 1765 the Scottish Bank Act was passed, in spite of the opposition of the Arms, Ship and Thistle Banks of Glasgow, which curtailed the issuing of unbacked notes, while notes under twenty shillings were abolished. Recovery was well under way by the end of 1767 but in June 1772 the Ayr Bank of Douglas, Heron & Co. crashed spectacularly, at the heart of a banking crisis which reverberated throughout Scotland as most building work in the towns ceased, as did work on the Forth and Clyde and Monkland canals. The result of the failure was to concentrate banking in Scotland in Edinburgh, with the Royal, the Bank of Scotland and the Linen Bank predominating, and to ensure henceforth the close scrutiny of the Scottish banking system by leading members of the government, the legal profession and the nobility. The system however was thereby made secure, operated more consciously in the 'national' economic interest, and provided a robust basis for the first phase of Scottish industrialisation.[113] That rural day-labourers' wages had begun to rise in the 1760s and move closer to English levels was another positive sign that the Scottish economy was catching up, as too was the reduction in the Lowlands of the differential between unskilled and skilled workers in the building trades.[114]

At this stage however the *per capita* value of home-produced goods in

Scotland was probably still four or five times less than England, although Ireland's previous lead was being rapidly reduced.[115] Linen was the only manufactured product of national importance, while a range of manufactures was imported from the south. Even linen was vulnerable however, and while the industry had boomed during the Seven Years War, it suffered from German and other foreign competition within Britain after the conflict had ended. Ongoing Scottish attempts to imitate cloths made in England and from the continent were of variable success: in September 1760, for example, Thomas Junor in Kirkcaldy was informed by the British Linen Company that, 'In place of imitating these patterns [from Manchester] the weavers you employ have debased this fabric to a mere rag'. No more would be ordered.[116] Coarse linen producers felt insecure, convinced that their hold on the market was due to state support, in the form of export bounties and import duties which, frequently in concert with the Irish linen interest, and less often with English linen manufacturers, they sought to adjust in their favour.[117] Scotland's trade overseas was still conducted on a relatively small scale, principally with Europe. Deficiencies in Scottish manufacturing meant that between 1740–44 and 1770–74 Scotland's share of British exports to Virginia and Maryland, increased only marginally.[118] Although Glasgow and her outports were flourishing and the small coal ports of Fife and along the Forth had grown rapidly, trade elsewhere grew slowly in the 1750s, 1760s and the first half of the 1770s, with only seven ports clearing more than 5,000 tons outwards in 1775. The importing picture was little better, although serving Edinburgh, Leith did well.[119]

Constraints

In chapter 1 some attention was paid to those factors which had hindered Scottish development in the decades prior to 1707. It is time now to consider some of these constraints in more detail and to explain in what ways they continued to operate before the Scottish economy began to grow more strongly in the 1760s. The short-term effects of the Union of 1707 have already been reviewed. Occasionally its longer-term impact has been misunderstood, as, for example, in the case of the 'burden' of the tax on coastal coal shipments on the east coast, which is alleged to have been one of the factors which some historians believe hampered the Scottish coal industry, and therefore slowed the process of industrialisation.[120]

In fact, as has been seen, Scottish coalmasters had agitated in 1709 to preserve for themselves a tax-free zone within the estuarial limits of the Forth, which prevented what became much more expensive Newcastle coal from getting into east-central Scotland. An earlier generation of

historians also blamed the Union for the alleged demise of the salt industry, 'adversely hit by ... the new fiscal system'. Actually the industry's
fortunes improved over time, and it managed to survive by several
decades the disappearance of salt manufacturing on Tyneside and in
Cumberland, protected by both a lighter tax than was payable on English
rock salt, and its geography.[121] Nevertheless, despite the agreement with
the Customs Commissioners in 1718 that fees would be charged in accordance with the 1662 Book of Rates (which held until *c.* 1745), lawful
Scottish traders outside the main Clyde ports and Leith complained that
they were subject to steeper fees than those imposed by customs officers
in England. By 1781 according to the Convention of Royal Burghs, the
situation – a clear breach of the Union – had become 'quite intolerable'.
Coal and corn in particular, it was alleged, were being charged with
customs fees which were as much as twenty times higher than those listed
in the Table of Fees, an imposition which amounted to the 'greatest bar'
to manufacture and improvement in Scotland's colder climate.[122]

Just what impact such arbitrary charges had on Scotland's coastal
trade is hard to measure – although there is pretty convincing evidence
that rates three and four times those agreed in 1718 were being
demanded by 1774. The general buoyancy of coastal trade however
suggests that the fees were more of an irritant than anything else, the
effects of which may have been felt more sharply as the operation of
customs regulations became tighter from the 1760s. Customs evasion no
longer provided a feasible aid to business success.

The focus here is on deeper-seated difficulties. Some of these are fairly
obvious and need little elaboration. Inland transportation has been relatively little-researched in Scotland. It is clear however that this was poor
(although not entirely inadequate) in the first half of the eighteenth
century, even though some stone bridges had been built over the deeper,
faster-flowing rivers in the Lowlands in the previous century and even
earlier – replacing some ferries, fords and wooden structures. In the
Highlands, where between 1726 and 1738 General Wade had been
responsible for building some forty of them (as well as some 250 miles of
road), sturdy bridges over unfordable rivers were even more important
than road carriageways. Ascertaining the condition of bridges in the
Highlands was one of the first tasks undertaken by the Commissioners
for the Annexed Estates in 1755.[123] Although progress was made in some
parts of the country under the auspices of the Commissioners of Supply,
it was only from the 1740s and into the 1750s that JPs began to act
consistently in maintaining and improving roads in the Lowlands. Scarce
resources and recalcitrant providers of statute labour, tenants, cottars
and farm servants and labourers, were the main obstacles to development
prior to the introduction of the first private road bill in 1766. Legislation
of this sort enabled the counties to raise taxation in place of statute

labour for road works. Turnpike development lagged behind that of England and Wales. Although they were much-discussed, less than a handful of canal schemes came to fruition, and then much later in the century.[124]

The first stretch of the earliest canal in Scotland approved by Parliament, the Forth and Clyde, opened in 1775 but was not completed from Grangemouth over to Stockingfield, on the river Kelvin, near Glasgow, until 1790. Colliery waggonways were rarely constructed: the two-and-a-quarter-mile long wooden tracks laid down by the York Buildings Company between Tranent and Cockenzie in 1722 stand out because this was probably the sole Scottish example until around 1760.[125] Export and coastal shipping was constrained by the existence of too many small and often exposed piers and harbours, which restricted the size and numbers of vessels which could load or disembark. Judging by the frequency of complaints from the royal burghs about the crumbling condition of their harbours in the early eighteenth century it would appear that the economic difficulties of the preceding decades had halted work on their repair and upkeep. Scottish ships continued to be relatively small, a factor which disadvantaged them in the Irish coal trade, for example, with the average burden of ships belonging to Saltcoats being one-third less than their custom-built, shallow-draughted Workington rivals. Low agricultural productivity slowed development too: during the 1720s, for example, colliery expansion in Ayrshire was inhibited by, among other things, the difficulty there was in procuring enough food for the pit ponies.[126] In turn, agricultural reform was slowed by widespread resentment of and some open outbursts of resistance to enclosure and other innovations in the countryside (see chapter 4). But a crucial incentive for widespread improvement was missing: buoyant market demand.

Markets and living standards

Notwithstanding efforts to extend it in the seventeenth century, the home market in Scotland remained relatively restricted until the 1750s. Care has to be taken however when interpreting official figures for consumption derived from customs and excise returns. Thus Edinburgh's annual income from its ale tax averaged £7,383 in the five years to 1728, but fell to an average of £4,905 between 1739 and 1744. Ale consumption had indeed fallen but, it was alleged, this had been more than compensated for by an increase in tea and punch drinking, made from smuggled tea (and sugar) and spirits. Tea, wrote one alarmed contemporary, had become the 'common Breakfast of *Bluegowns* and the *Fish-carriers* of *Musselburgh*', while footmen and porters got drunk on punch as freely and almost as cheaply as they had formerly done on ale.[127] Demand for ale recovered sufficiently however to encourage the emergence of some larger breweries and, albeit with difficulty, bottle-making survived the Union. Paper-making recovered from its post-Union decline, with new mills being opened near Edinburgh and Glasgow, thereby reflecting their respective roles as centres for law, printing and education, and business and commerce. Snuff- and wig-making too were encouraged in and around some of the larger towns. In Edinburgh the number of journey-men tailors seems to have risen substantially from the 1690s in response to the needs of visitors and the growing numbers of professionals resident there.[128] Until 1725 women in Perth (and one presumes, in other middle-ranking towns) 'whose riches or circumstances intitled them to Cloathes tolerably decent or genteel' sent to Edinburgh to have them made, while others made and mended their own.[129] For certain commodities however it was fairly clear that demand was slack – window glass, for example, was hard to sell in Scotland during the 1730s, although the fact that imports continued to be brought from Newcastle suggests that the problem (as with many other commodities) was also likely to have been compounded by the poor quality and high price of the Scottish-made article.[130]

As has been seen, Scotland's population failed to recover to its c. 1690 level until around the middle of the eighteenth century. Living standards too were low for the bulk of the population, more so in the country than the towns, although regional and local variations as well as enormous differ-ences between the circumstances of one household and another confound confident generalisations. Poverty, resulting from old age, illness, unem-ployment, or other personal disasters, including debts, rent arrears, a midwife's fee or funeral expenses, was crippling whether located in town or in a rural township. Uncertainty prevailed at all levels, although despera-tion was most strongly felt among the landless and itinerant poor who flitted from town to town in search of a livelihood, frequently at the insis-tence of urban authorities who zealously reserved scant resources for their own parish poor. The weight and geographical range of instances of oppo-sition to attempts by landowners in the vicinity of towns to reclaim common ground in the later seventeenth and early eighteenth centuries (see chapter 4) is indicative of the precariousness of the lives of the labouring poor in the burghs. These stretches of land, the 'liberties of the poor', described by the magistrates of Forres in 1725 as 'absolutlie necessarie', had customarily provided free grazing land, some supplementary arable ground or peat and turf.[131] It was not until the second half of the century, and then strongly only in especially favoured areas in the central Lowlands, that living standards began to rise (see chapter 3). Much more striking – and for contemporaries, crisis-inducing – were sharp and sometimes severe annual fluctuations in prices and earnings, with harvests and wars being the princi-pal causes of dislocation, although small scale disasters such as the flooding of or fire in a town's coal pit could cause localised suffering. Wage rates remained more or less flat until the 1750s and 1760s. Until then wages in Scotland were no more than half of those paid in England and there was also a wide differential between skilled and unskilled levels, another sign of an underdeveloped economy; on the other hand, the Scottish differential was less than that for Ireland, suggesting that such growth as was occurring in Scotland, was more widely spread.[132]

Oatmeal, of which around 30 ounces a day were necessary to feed the typical adult male, accounted for at least half of the total expenditure of a labouring family; two-thirds in the case of the poorest.[133] This was eaten in the form of porridge, brose, oatcakes or sowens, and taken hot and cold. Potatoes only became widely used from the 1750s, although as late as 1774 the Convention of Royal Burghs attempted to have the price of imported oatmeal reduced on the grounds that it was still 'the capital article of food among the lower people of Scotland especially labourers and manufacturers'. Recent calculations suggest that the families of rural labourers in the first half of the eighteenth century must have struggled even to attain subsistence levels, while unskilled workers in the urban areas can hardly have fared much better. Household survival was a struggle which was achieved by supplementing inadequate and irregular wage payments with the waged and non-wage contributions of other family members. It was critical therefore that such households had access to land from which they could wrest some fuel and additional foodstuffs such as milk and greens, mainly in the shape of kale. Animal flesh was eaten rarely and generally in small quantities, with the exception of those who lived in close proximity to the sea, who had fish – herring, haddock, saithe and various types of shellfish.

'Perquisites' from the workplace, as well as waste materials – small quantities of coal, wool, timber – were taken for the family's own use or to sell. Women and children grasped what opportunities there were to supplement what was literally a hand-to-mouth existence, whether or not they were household members or living independently. Common types of employment for poorer women in Edinburgh, for example, were as clothes and blanket washers and seamstresses, as well as service and ale-selling.[134] Pawning and pledging too were used as means of raising cash in the short-term, as also on a localised basis was rag gathering, for paper mills, although payment depended on the quality (as well as the quantity) of the rags gathered. Petty theft was rife, as in the Aberdeenshire parish of Nigg, where it was complained in 1764 that 'stealing Peats is so common that many [of those involved] seem not to be ashamed of it'. The same could be said of wood. In towns, clothes, particularly fashionable items, were frequently stolen and re-sold. Prostitution was another way of keeping going. To be caught however usually meant banishment, as happened to Isobel Armstrong who was drummed out of Aberdeen in

December 1735 on the grounds that she was a 'lewd woman' and for taking up with soldiers and 'poxing them'.[135] Apart from the better-off – landowners, coastal and overseas merchants and the like – only the families of skilled craftsmen in the towns and single youths and adults in either farm or domestic service, where free board was provided, can have had much disposal income. We should not overlook however the earned contributions of the wives of craftsmen, merchants and others from the 'middling sort', notably in Edinburgh, such as writers, ministers and professors. Such women worked on their own as shopkeepers or mantua-makers, for instance, or joined their husbands in family businesses, or carried these on after the death of their spouses.[136]

Consumption of high quality manufactured goods such as china, pewter, drinking glass, mirrors, silk gloves, fine leather goods, shoes and luxuries like lemons therefore tended to be restricted to the middling and upper ranks, and such goods were usually (but not always) imported from England or abroad. An exception was salt, which was the single commodity which brought virtually every inhabitant of early modern Scotland within the orbit of the market economy, although ale, brewed in the main by a myriad of small producers, must have been similar, while there was a fairly active market too for iron goods and other 'staple commodities'. Home demand for timber, for logs, housebuilding and so forth, was more important in areas such as Loch Arkaig and Rothiemurchus than hoped-for sales to England and elsewhere.[137]

Salt and iron were the only imports in otherwise virtually self-sufficient communities such as the island of Iona as late as the 1770s.[138] Salt – which was used to preserve food and sharpen what would otherwise have been a dull, largely farinaceous, diet – was essential for every household. It was produced in commercial quantities in Scotland in salt-pans which were clustered thickly along the Forth, and in smaller numbers in Ayrshire, the south-west and periodically on other coastal sites as far north as Orkney where cheap coal or peat were present. Roughly speaking, home consumption in the eighteenth century seems to have followed Scotland's main demographic fluctuations for most of the century.[139]

Some of the consequences of weak demand in Scotland have already been noted, and are revealed too in the enthusiasm with which landowners and grain dealers in the east exported bounty-supported oats and oatmeal. Yet other types of enterprise too could suffer, particularly during periods when cash or credit were particularly hard to obtain. That he was not getting money 'regularly out of Customers hands' was one of the main reasons why Patrick Grant was persuaded to temporarily close the glassworks at Port Seton in 1734, and 'let the hands disperse', even though demand for glasses and bottles in Scotland seems to have been steady enough.[140] Unless they were paid regularly, and for their 'play days' when no work was available, workforces were inclined to disappear in search of alternative ways of making a living.

The main spurts of economic activity before *c.* 1760 were inspired by opportunities for sales outside Scotland. Thus on the demand side the dramatic rise in coal shipments from Ayrshire from a possible 1,400 tons in 1691 to 25,000 tons by 1729 is accounted for by the fuel requirements of Dublin and other towns along Ireland's eastern and northern coasts. The construction of five steam pumping engines on this part of the Ayrshire coalfield between 1719 and 1734 – by far the thickest cluster in Scotland – is similarly explained. Beyond the larger towns domestic demand for coal in Scotland was too dispersed to justify large-scale investment in coal working. In Ayrshire, for example, inland from the coastal towns and excluding Kilmarnock, demand was generally slight until the 1790s. At Muirkirk, prior to the establishment of an ironworks in 1786, coal was 'picked out of the crop by one collier, who was employed one month of the year without the aid of any machinery'.[141] It is this which explains why so many coastal colliery concerns in Scotland needed saltworks to burn otherwise unsaleable 'small' coal, although demand from limeworks and other industrial users was growing, albeit slowly before *c.* 1760. It was the high prices for iron goods internationally which explain the timing of the establishment of charcoal-fired ironworks in the Highlands in the first half of the century (where, in normal circumstances, transport costs would have proved an insuperable barrier), while wars further heightened entrepreneurs' market awareness. It is no coincidence that Carron was founded during the Seven Years War, and Craleckan (1775) and Wilsontown (1779) during the American War of Independence.[142]

Quality control

As has been suggested above, the poor quality of most Scottish goods would have inhibited their sale even if the home market had been stronger. This was both a further symptom and cause of underdevelopment. Weavers, for example, usually worked on their own account, with inadequate capital, thus forcing them to work on a piecemeal basis, taking what orders they could obtain. Accordingly, they rarely developed specialist skills, while buyers were unable to secure long production runs.[143] From before the Union and until the Atlantic trade in linens was established, much if not most Scottish-made linen was bought at summer markets in small batches by the estimated two to three thousand 'Hawkers, Pedlars & Petty Chapmen' who conducted a regular cross-border, two-way cash trade with England.[144]

Partly, though, inferior quality was a matter of bad luck. For example, while geological conditions varied across the Scottish coalfields, on the whole Scotland was less well placed than the leading mining districts in England. Little could be done about the coal which was available from many of the pits at coastal collieries in the east of Scotland. 'Great' coal, preferred by domestic consumers in Edinburgh, was mined, but much of the coal brought up tended to be of the largely unsaleable 'small' variety. Scottish coal was less economic to burn than its Newcastle counterpart, which by comparison was a 'rich, fat Caking Coal'. The company which had leased Kinneil colliery on the Hamilton estate complained in 1758 that they had tried to export coal but that its quality was 'universally Complained off'.[145] Throughout the century, Ayrshire coal fetched a lower price in Ireland than that from Cumberland, principally because it was not the 'caking' coal sought by distillers and other industrial users. As was noted earlier, by the end of the seventeenth century, there are signs that some of the best and most easily-accessible coal along the banks of the Forth had been worked out. Weak markets discouraged investment in both transport and the new but expensive water pumping technology developed by Richard Savery (1698) and Thomas Newcomen (1712), and consequently coal seams which were more than three or four miles from the coast or larger urban markets lay untouched, whereas in the north-east of England lateral development occurred as a network of waggonways was constructed and thereby facilitated the working of thicker coal seams.[146] Highland forest proprietors faced problems getting timber to the coasts, and found it difficult to compete with the Norwegians in terms of both price and quality.[147]

Yet in an important respect the shortcomings in Scotland's products were the result of human deficiencies. Skill shortages blighted Scottish manufacturing for decades. For the lower end of the home market this was of little consequence, and in the woollens industry, for example, 'very nastily made' coarse cloth woven from local tarred wool and by native labour was perfectly adequate, cost little, and continued unaffected by the Union. It had even sold abroad during the seventeenth century until war and protective policies on the part of former customers in countries such as France drove the trade down.[148] For the upper end of the market however, and in order to satisfy buyers from abroad on a larger scale, better quality yarns and cloths were required. A 'general fault' of Scottish woollen yarns it was asserted in 1749, was 'that they are unevenly spun' and 'too hard twisted'. What was wanted were spinners who could use the 'Yorkshire wheel'.[149]

Similar difficulties were faced in other commodities, even where apparently simple operations were involved. As late as 1770, for example, the workmanship of nail-makers in Stirlingshire was described as 'scandalous', and sufficient 'to ruin the character of any Business'. A close inspection of Prestonpans Pottery in 1786, whose proprietors had hopes of displacing Staffordshire ware in Scotland, concluded with a critical report in which it was remarked that the 'Enamling ... Man would do as well with a Mop'.[150] Attempts had been made before 1707 to entice skilled workers to Scotland from elsewhere, even though, as has been noted, the costs of this strategy were high. More often than not however such efforts had brought little lasting benefit. Glassworks still required foreign workers in the early nineteenth century.[151] The practice was necessarily continued however, and problems remained to be overcome. There were language difficulties and culture clashes which discouraged foreigners from staying long.[152] Englishmen bore the brunt of the Scots' xenophobia. Thus while they were used by the partners at Carron to get the works off the ground, care was taken to keep their numbers to a minimum and to return them south as soon as was expedient.

Rightly, economic historians have pointed to the difficulties in financing large-scale enterprises.[153] Significantly however, an investigation into the operation of Carron in 1769 concluded that the Company's early difficulties lay elsewhere, and not in its location, which was good in terms of water (for the blast furnaces), raw materials and London sales. Rather, it was an 'unwieldy machine' (that is the company and its component parts, collieries, ironworks, naileries etc.) and had been established in a 'Country of Idleness'.[154] Two serious and interconnected problems are highlighted here. The first was managing sizeable organisations. The second concerned the characteristics of labour and the labour market in Scotland. Although neither of these difficulties was unique to Carron, or Scotland, proportionately, in their extent they were almost certainly greater than in England in mid-century, where industrial capitalism was further advanced. Problems of labour recruitment and control confronted entrepreneurs everywhere as they attempted to create in 'traditional' societies profitable business organisations which were capable of competing in the market economy.[155] Hitherto historians in Scotland have tended to pay little attention to this subject, the significance of which has not been fully recognised.

Labour market conditions in Scotland have been favourably compared with Ireland, where the relative ease with which land could be subdivided encouraged rural dwellers to remain in the countryside on fragmented holdings, increasingly dependent upon part-time textile production for their livelihoods. While a similar system of small landholding, propped up by by-employments and the returns from temporary work in the south, developed in the western Highlands in Scotland and as far south as Breadalbane in Perthshire, in the Lowland districts small tenants, sub-tenants and cottars who no longer had a place in the capitalist farm structure left the countryside for the towns and villages to engage in industrial work.[156] Apart from the burghs and their suburbs and some random isolated developments – in mining, for example – this was also undertaken in the sheds, workshops and small factories which were erected in landowner-sponsored planned villages, thereby giving landowners the best of both worlds by retaining their former dependents as rent-payers and creating local markets for the produce of their farms. On the macro-economic level this model has much to commend it and there is evidence of such population shifts having taken place at the local level. At the newly laid-out village of Kenmore in Breadalbane in 1758, for example, the factor could boast to the Board of Trustees that the people had 'become ... [as] tractable as any in the Highlands ... ready to be let into any kind of Industry that may be thought for their Advantage'.[157] What is more, as will be seen in chapter 4, it has been argued that labour in Scotland was admirably suited to the demands of regular supervised work.

Yet care must be taken not to over-simplify what is a complicated issue. Labour which is 'stable, reliable, and disciplined' is 'extremely scarce' in backward or underdeveloped economies; international studies have shown that the creation of such a labour force is a 'difficult and protracted process', which requires 'the fiercest wrench from the past'.[158] The labour market in Scotland in the early, middling and even later decades in the eighteenth century was far from perfect. Oft-cited advantages with which the Scots are credited, such as a relatively high literacy level, prove, on close inspection, to have made little difference, at least not before the middle of the eighteenth century when the new, vocational subjects began to be introduced into the burgh and then the rural parochial schools.[159] Complaints about the numbers of the poor and hard evidence there is about extensive underemployment notwithstanding, this did not necessarily easily convert into the sort of labour force which was required. This is one reason why seventeenth-century legislation (in 1605, 1621, 1649 and 1692) which permitted the proprietors of manufactures such as saltpans and mines to sweep up beggars and vagabonds and put them to work was of only limited value.[160] There was a concern in some quarters that such was the 'languishing, nasty, slothful and useless' condition of the common people, used to lives of 'Idleness, picking and thieving', that even the young would be 'rendered ever after unfit for honest Labour and Industry', serving only to stock this and future generations with thieves and 'lazy idle Beggars'.[161] There were some tasks, even those for which little formal skill was required, for which their attitude and lack of experience – and their unfamiliarity with the 'knacks' of the trade – made them unsuitable, thus serving to create a paradox whereby labour shortages existed alongside widespread under-employment.

Nor were dispossessed rural dwellers, particularly if they were adult males, easily re-employed. 'Time discipline', the concept of a regular working day extending to a set number of hours, was understood by urban tradesmen. From the seventeenth century the hours of work and rest were announced to town dwellers by the ringing of bells, a burgh piper, trumpeter, or more usually, a drummer. So disadvantaged did the inhabitants of the Gallowgate in Aberdeen feel, owing to their 'remoteness' from the kirk and tolbooth, that in 1727 they requested that consideration be given to the re-use of the old tolbooth bell in their district.[162]

Such a regime however was alien to adult migrants from the countryside, although the increase in temporary migration would limit this problem in the longer run. Their age and tight restrictions on entry exercised by the craft incorporations in the royal burghs prevented them from serving apprenticeships and becoming journeymen. The crafts too seem to have had considerable success in restricting the inflow of certain time-served men into the burghs, although the vigour with which they tried to retain their privileges varied according to the prevailing economic climate. The frustrations such practices caused were felt most acutely by exporters. Thus in 1755 the incorporation of cordiners in Glasgow was accused by the merchant James Dunlop and his partners of hindering their efforts to sell saddlery, boots and shoes in the plantations. The lack of tradesmen, it was argued, 'became a matter of great Difficulty', as 'the Quantity of Goods required could not be furnished upon a Suddenty'. If they could not employ more local people, their only alternative was to send for goods from England.[163]

There is not much evidence of anything other than temporary and localised labour shortages in the first half of the century, although these could frustrate efforts at economic diversification. In 1703, for instance, the duchess of Hamilton was advised that the exploitation of coal on the island of Arran might be delayed as it would be 'very difficult in the whole west of Scotland to get workers who understand an edgecoal'. In addition the island had no smiths.[164] When the coal and saltworks was established on the island it was with the assistance of workers from Bo'ness. Contrary to received opinion, coal mining was not an unskilled occupation, but necessitated instead life-long familiarity with underground work on the part of boys whose fathers or uncles were coal miners and who passed on to them the 'art' of hewing. There is no evidence to suggest that adults from non-mining backgrounds were recruited into the industry other than occasionally.

From the 1740s and beyond more serious bottlenecks did appear, not only in coal mining, but also in what seem to have been less arduous or risky occupations such as dyeing and glass-making. There was an unprecedentedly acute shortage around the time of the establishment of Carron Iron Works in 1759, and in Glasgow during the 1750s and 1760s disputes broke out between ambitious merchant exporters and the town's vested interests in several trades. By the early 1770s wages at some collieries in Scotland had risen far above those paid to colliers around Newcastle and in north-west England (although this was partly the result of labour combinations in Scotland).[165] Costs had been high at Port Seton glassworks too in the 1730s, because the proprietors had been forced to employ English workers at English wages, a factor which was not compensated for by cheaper raw materials – kelp and (inferior) coal.

As might be inferred from the previous paragraphs, economic growth in Scotland in the 1760s led initially to a tightening of the labour market. Scotland's rate of population increase in the second half of the eighteenth century averaged only 0.6 per cent *per annum*, compared to an Irish rate which was three times faster, and an English one which was roughly twice as fast, although within Scotland there were variations, with the western Lowlands growing at 1.3 per cent *per annum*.[166] Even so, there was greater competition between employers for scarce labour throughout the Lowlands than there had been previously, and after *c.* 1760 the first signs of a period of rising wages (which lasted until the early 1790s) began to appear both for skilled workers such as masons, and even more so for the unskilled, with harvest earnings for males, for example, doubling by the 1770s.[167] As will be seen later however, the benefits for the economy of rising real wages were substantial.

In spite of hopes to the contrary on the part of employers whose planning assumptions had included low Scottish labour costs, the workforce in Scotland was not noticeably more 'docile' than its English or Irish counterparts (see chapter 4). In addition to their inferior quality, the price of many Scottish goods was too high for mass markets overseas owing to poor productivity, either in the entire sector or in part of the production process. Thus in 1761 it was noted that while partly due to lower rents, heating and yarn costs, the prices for *weaving* chequered linen were lower in Kirkcaldy than Manchester, the small scale of dyeing and bleaching was pushing the overall price of Scottish goods too high for them to attract London and colonial buyers.[168]

Combinations and other instances of collective action such as strikes were much more common in Scotland in the eighteenth century than was once believed. Instances of groups of workers taking advantage of favourable market conditions are well-documented. Effectively organised craft unions date from the 1720s at least, condemned by the woollen manufactures of Aberdeen in 1762 on the grounds not only that 'Caballs or Societys' tended to raise wages but also because they encouraged men to become 'lazy and indolent & indifferent about their work'.[169] Combinations of Scottish colliers have been discovered in the seventeenth century, but not, as yet, in England where collective action in the coal industry seems to have been taken first by the keelmen (a significant proportion of whom were migrant workers from Scotland).[170] Paradoxically, coal workers (and, with them, salters), long considered by some historians to have been the most servile and oppressed workers in Scottish labour history, now provide us with some of the most convincing evidence we have of the existence of early combinations and of the difficulties employers faced in inculcating good behaviour, religion and regular habits of work.[171] If the historiography of the Scottish collier serfs can now be turned upon its head, it follows that there may be reasonable grounds for looking more critically at older portrayals of other aspects of Scottish labour history of the period.

Largely because so much work was seasonal and opportunities for employment were intermittent, but also because they chose to exercise a 'leisure preference' (or preferred not to work longer than was absolutely essential if the rewards were meagre), labouring people had become accustomed to a broken pattern of work. Opportunities for material gain were balanced against the effort required. Thus, notwithstanding the efforts of the British Linen Company to introduce spinning into the Highlands and Islands, there was an exasperated report in 1760 that the 'poor people ... decline working for more than what will barely subsist them', so that when food prices were low 'little is manufactured'.[172] With many retaining a foothold on the land, workers in a wide variety of trades absented themselves during sowing and harvest and continued to do so into the nineteenth century. For most building workers the pattern was seasonal and therefore fairly regular, although fluctuations in demand and periods of excessively bad weather were difficult to forecast. Tailors too could reckon on being busy during the late spring and early summer when seasonal demand was high. Day labourers on the other hand could experience enormous differences in their employment pattern – and therefore earnings – from year to year, although one heroic estimate proposes that they are unlikely to have obtained work for more than around two hundred days *per annum* in the early eighteenth century.[173] Where the data exist to enable the historian to recreate work patterns in the early eighteenth century, as they do for coal and salt workers in a few locations, these reveal a mix of both predictable and unpredictable breaks in work.

Fewer breaks in work than those enforced by events such as running into geological difficulties (in coal mines) or saltpan repairs were 'voluntary' absences determined by workers in these as well as some urban trades. These were more likely to occur on Mondays or on the days following fairs, while days were sometimes taken off for weddings, births and funerals. Fast days on the other hand could involve whole communities. Interestingly, given the legal requirement for coal and salt workers to labour for six days a week, throughout the year, salters at Winton saltworks, Cockenzie, seem to have worked on average for only twenty-nine weeks in what seem to have been the fairly typical years 1716–17 and 1717–18, although the number of weeks worked by individual salters could range from thirteen to thirty-nine. By the 1770s colliers at pits where demand was intense were working three, four and at most five days rather than six.[174]

In the countryside after *c.* 1760 much of the responsibility for implementing change at the level of the individual farm was taken by the tenant farmers, in accordance with plans laid by landowners and their factors and set out in detail in the terms of their leases. This small but large enough cadre of men committed to the ideals and practice of improved capitalist agriculture had partly been created during the first half of the eighteenth century as the process of thinning out multiple tenancies had proceeded. Many of these more individualistic, often educated, tenant farmers who remained in possession of farms played a crucial role in effecting and easing the process of rural transition which culminated in the new ordered agrarian regime.[175] The situation was very different in industry and manufacturing, which was often being introduced where no previous tradition existed and therefore working knowledge was absent, or where the scale of operation had been very small.

Below the level of proprietor or partner there was a shortfall in the availability of 'middle management' who could supervise and control labour, or who had the necessary expertise to direct what could be technically complicated operations. Thus when Largoward colliery changed hands around 1753 the new proprietor had to call his colliers together for several 'Long Conferences' where they gave their opinions on the condition of the coal and laid plans for 'puting my Coalworks again upon a profitable footing for both me and they'.[176] At Lochgelly colliery in 1767 an exasperated estate factor, anxious to dismiss an unsuitable coal grieve, declared that 'it is next to a miracle to get one to that office that is honest'.[177] 'Close attendance' was required, it was remarked some years earlier at the same colliery, in order to manage 'our misbred pack of Coalliers'. Similarly, Sir Archibald Grant of Monymusk, in the process of establishing textile manufacturing in his planned village of Archiestown in 1765, was advised not to set up a bleachfield on the grounds that 'the whole success of an undertaking of this kind depends upon a proper person to manage ye business & such are not easie to be had'. At Carron in 1767 Samuel Garbett despaired that the works had so many 'insufficient' overseers. Specifically, he reckoned the reason for the poor quality of the guns currently being cast was the 'inaccuracy & slovenliness' of the man appointed to supervise the furnace.[178]

Notes

1 For recent surveys, see Whatley, *'Bought and Sold for English Gold'?*; C. A. Whatley, 'The Union of 1707', in A. Cooke, I. Donnachie, A. MacSween and C. A. Whatley (eds), *Modern Scottish History, 1707 to the Present, Volume I: The Transformation of Scotland, 1707–1850* (East Linton, 1998), 1–22. A classic account is that of T. C. Smout, 'The road to Union', in G. Holmes (ed.), *Britain after the Glorious Revolution, 1689–1714* (London, 1969).

2 C. Kidd, *Subverting Scotland's Past: Scottish Whig Historians and the Creation of an Anglo-British Identity, 1689–c. 1830* (Cambridge, 1993), 36–50. For a nationalist account which omits key economic evidence in favour of the Union, see P. H. Scott, *Andrew Fletcher and the Treaty of Union* (Edinburgh, 1992).

3 Whatley, *'Bought and Sold for English Gold'?*, 19–20.

4 Not comprehensive but of this high quality is J. Robertson, 'Empire and union: two concepts of the early modern European political order', in Robertson, *A Union for Empire*, 3–36.

5 J. R. Young, 'The Parliamentary incorporating union of 1717: Political Management, anti-Unionism and foreign policy', in Devine and Young, *Eighteenth Century Scotland*, 39–46.

6 D. Forbes, *Some Considerations On the Present State of Scotland in a Letter to the Commissioners and Trustees for improving the Fisheries and Manufactures* (London, 1744), 4; Phillipson, 'Culture and Society', 417.

7 A recent example is R. J. Finlay, 'Caledonia or North Britain? Scottish identity in the eighteenth century', in D. Brown, R. J. Finlay and M. Lynch (eds), *Image and Identity: The Making and Re-making of Scotland through the Ages* (Edinburgh, 1998), 145.

8 NAS, Hamilton MSS, GD 406/1/4976, 'Memorandum regarding Union', n.d., *c.* 1702.

9 R. Mitchison, *A History of Scotland* (London, 1982 ed.), 311.

10 P. W. J. Riley, *The Union of England and Scotland: A Study in Anglo-Scottish Politics in the Eighteenth Century* (Manchester, 1978), 271–2.

11 Kidd, *Subverting Scotland's Past*, 38.

12 W. Seton of Pitmedden, *A Speech in Parliament on the First Article of the Treaty of Union* (Edinburgh, 1706).

13 J. R. Young, 'The Scottish Parliament and national identity from the Union of the Crowns to the Union of the Parliaments, 1603–1707', in Brown, Finlay and Lynch, *Image and Identity*, 122–3.

14 D. Duncan (ed.), *History of the Union of Scotland and England by Sir John Clerk* (Edinburgh, 1993), 199–200.

15 See A. I. Macinnes, 'Studying the Scottish Estates and the Treaty of Union', *History Microcomputer Review*, VI (Fall 1990), 11–25.

16 Whatley, 'Economic Causes', 162–5.

17 Whatley, 'Salt, coal and the Union', 36.

18 On Scottish Presbyterians and the Union, see C. Kidd, 'Religious realignment between the Restoration and Union', in Robertson, *Union for Empire*, 145–68.

19 J. H. Elliot, 'A Europe of composite monarchies', *Past & Present*, CXXXVII

(November 1992), 48–71; Whatley, 'Union of 1707', 9–10.

20 D. Hancock, *Citizens of the World: London Merchants and the Integration of the British Atlantic Community, 1735–1785* (Cambridge, 1997 ed.), 26–27.

21 For a summary of these arguments see Devine, 'The Union of 1707 and Scottish development', 23–40.

22 *Ibid.*, 28, 37; see too Saville, 'Scottish modernisation', 14–23.

23 Whatley, 'Economic causes', 170; ECA, CRB, Moses Collection, SL30/226, 'Lists of ships etc. belonging to the various ports of Scotland', June 1709.

24 C. A. Whatley, 'The process of industrialisation in Ayrshire, 1707–1871' (unpublished Ph.D. thesis, University of Strathclyde, 1975), 116–31.

25 Whatley, 'Economic causes', 170.

26 Historical Manuscripts Commission, *Report on the Manuscripts of the Duke of Portland, X* (London, 1931), 172–7; British Library, Portland Papers, Add. MSS 70047, 'An Account of the Premiums and Debentures paid out of Her Majestie's Revenues and Customs and Excise in Scotland since the Commencement of the Union ... to the 25th Decmbr. 1712'; Saville, *Bank of Scotland*, 81.

27 Whatley, 'Economic causes', 169; Withers, *Urban Highlanders*, 39.

28 Houston, 'Economy of Edinburgh', 56.

29 R. C. Nash, 'The English and Scottish tobacco trades in the seventeenth and eighteenth centuries: legal and illegal trade', *Economic History Review*, XXXV (1982), 364; T. C. Barker, 'Smuggling in the eighteenth century: the evidence of the Scottish tobacco trade', *The Virginia Magazine of History and Biography*, LXII (October 1984), 393–7.

30 Beckett, *Coal and Tobacco*, 106.

31 Nash, 'English and Scottish tobacco trades', 363.

32 L. E. Cochran, *Scottish Trade with Ireland in the Eighteenth Century* (Edinburgh, 1985), 8–11, 76.

33 Devine, 'Golden age of tobacco', 140.

34 J. M. Price, *France and the Chesapeake* (Ann Arbor, 1973), Volume I, 604.

35 NAS, Montrose MSS, GD 220/5/468/19, Charles Cockburn to John Cockburn, 9 July 1715.

36 G. Jackson, 'Glasgow in transition', 79–80; N. Tattersfield, *The Forgotten Trade* (London, 1991), 349; D. G. Adams, 'Trade in the eighteenth and nineteenth centuries', in G. Jackson and S. G. E. Lythe (eds), *The Port of Montrose: A History of its harbour, trade and shipping* (Tayport, 1993), 125–6. The involvement of Scots in the slave trade is a topic which might repay deeper investigation.

37 Houston, 'Economy of Edinburgh', 59.

38 A. Murray, 'Administration and law', in T. I. Rae (ed.), *The Union of 1707: Its Impact on Scotland* (Glasgow, 1974), 33–5; Saville, *Bank of Scotland*, 75–7.

39 ECA, CRB, Moses Collection, SL30/225, 'Petition for the Burgh of Elgin', 1708.

40 C. A. Whatley, 'Sales of Scottish marine salt, 1714–1832', *Scottish Economic & Social History*, VI (1986), 8.

41 G. Holmes, 'Trade, the Scots and the parliamentary crisis of 1713',

Parliamentary History: A Yearbook, I (1982), 56.

42 ECA, CRB, Moses Collection, SL 30/227, 'Report on the State of the Burgh of Kilrenny', 26 March 1711.

43 ECA, CRB, Moses Collection, SL30/238, 'Representation, the Scots Factors in London Anent Linen Cloath', 30 March 1723.

44 D Szechi (ed.), *Letters of George Lockhart of Carnwath, 1698–1732* (Edinburgh, 1989), 103.

45 Saville, *Bank of Scotland*, 83; Anon, *Reasons for Improving the Fisheries and Linen Manufacture of Scotland* (London, 1727), 20.

46 City of Dundee Archives (CDA), General Petitions to Town Council, Petition of Charles Gray, *c.* 1717; ECA, CRB, Moses Collection, SL30/242, 'Representation of the Burgh of Forfar', 1730; Moses Supplementary Bundles, SL 30/4/6, 'State of Facts & Evidents relating to the Fees Exacted by Customhouse Officers as transmitted to the Board of Customs', 6 March 1781; J. Shaw, *Water Power in Scotland, 1550–1870* (Edinburgh, 1984), 59; Whatley, 'Economic causes', 173.

47 ECA, CRB, Moses Collection, SL 30, bundles 227, 239 and 243; T. C. Smout (ed.), 'Journal of Henry Kalmeter's travels in Scotland, 1719–20', in *Scottish Industrial History: A Miscellany* (Edinburgh, 1978), 15; Cochran, *Scottish Trade*, 41–3.

48 See Riley, *The English Ministers and Scotland*; J. Price, 'Glasgow, the tobacco trade, and the Scottish customs, 1707–1730', *Scottish Historical Review*, LXIII (April 1984), 1.

49 ECA, CRB, SL 30/238, Petition, 'The Coal Masters To the Royal Burghs', 10 July 1724; SL 30/227, 'Report on the State of the Burgh of Kilrenny', 1711; 'State of the Fishery Trade Drawn up by and given in by Anster Easter', 24 March 1711.

50 Shaw, *The Management of Scottish Society*, 125–6; Devine, 'Union of 1707', 30.

51 Riley, *English Ministers*, 122, 243.

52 B. Lenman, 'A client society: Scotland between the '15 and the '45', in J. Black (ed.), *Britain in the Age of Walpole* (London, 1994 ed.), 85–90.

53 Anon., *Reasons for Improving the Fisheries*, 28.

54 Riley, *English Ministers*, 120–2; Tattersfield, *Forgotten Trade*, 348–9.

55 Whatley, 'Salt, coal and the Union', 41; ECA, CRB, Moses Collection, SL 30/228, 'Petition for the Town of Montrose', 14 July 1713.

56 Perth and Kinross Council Archives (PKCA), Perth Town Council Minutes, B59/16/13, 5 Dec. 1719; A. J. Durie, *The Scottish Linen Industry in the Eighteenth Century* (Edinburgh, 1979), 8–11.

57 L. Leneman, *Living in Atholl: A Social History of the Estates, 1685–1785* (Edinburgh, 1986), 30.

58 Barker, 'Smuggling in the eighteenth century', 397.

59 Price, *France*, Volume I, 664; Price, 'Glasgow, the Tobacco Trade', 1–36.

60 Lenman, *Jacobite Risings*, 99–102.

61 Royal Bank of Scotland Archives, Equivalent Papers, EQ 23/1, 'Petition of the Commissioners for disposing of the Equivalent and ors.', 1719.

62 Anon., *Reasons for Improving the Fisheries*, 16.

63 Durie, *Scottish Linen Industry*, 13–21; Shaw, *Management*, 124; ECA, CRB,

SL 30/242, Provost Drummond to Archibald McAulay, 1 March 1726; Drummond to Annual Committee of the Royal Burghs of Scotland, 19 March 1726.

64 Royal Bank of Scotland Archives, Equivalent Papers, EQ/68, Letter Book, Daniel Campbell, 1725–28, Patrick Campbell to Court of Directors of the Equivalent Co., 8 July 1727; Shaw, *Management*, 118–23.

65 T. C. Smout, 'Sir John Clerk's observations on the present circumstances of Scotland, 1730', in *Miscellany, X* (Scottish History Society, Edinburgh, 1965), 206–8.

66 Saville, *Bank of Scotland*, chapter 6,

67 Durie, *Scottish Linen Industry*, 55–64.

68 Shaw, *Water Power in Scotland*, 22, 171–220, 229.

69 National Library of Scotland (NLS), Saltoun Papers, MS 17595, fo. 205, 'Some Observations on the British Linen Co.'s affairs', 1759.

70 Durie, *Scottish Linen Industry*, 38–43, 72–4.

71 T. C. Smout, 'Famine and famine-relief in Scotland', in Cullen and Smout, *Comparative Aspects*, 25–26; M. W. Flinn (ed.), *Scottish Population History from the Seventeenth Century to the 1930s* (Cambridge, 1977), 216–23.

72 Lindsay, *Reasons for Encouraging the Linen Manufacture*, 9, 45–6.

73 Gulvin, *Tweedmakers*, 32; Shaw, *Water Power in Scotland*, 424.

74 M. Clough, 'Early fishery and forestry developments on the Cromartie estate of Coigach: 1660–1746', in J. R. Baldwin (ed.), *Peoples & Settlement in North-West Ross* (Edinburgh, 1994), 234.

75 Whatley, 'Process of industrialisation', 42–3; Cochran, *Scottish Trade*, 27–43.

76 Clough, 'Early fishery and forestry developments', 235–42; Lindsay, 'Iron industry', 56–7; A. J. G. Cummings, 'Industry and investment in the eighteenth century Highlands: the York Buildings Company of London', in Cummings and Devine, *Industry, Business and Society*, 24–42; T. C. Smout, 'Lead-mining in Scotland, 1650–1850', in P. L. Payne (ed.), *Studies in Scottish Business History* (London, 1967), 118–20.

77 See P. Deane and W. A. Cole, *British Economic Growth 1688–1959: Trends and Structure* (Cambridge, 1962), chapter II.

78 Durie, *Scottish Linen Industry*, 28.

79 NAS, Grant of Monymusk MSS, GD 345/1025, Scrap notes regarding tenants, 1748; E. Cregeen, 'The changing role of the house of Argyll in the Scottish Highlands', in N.T. Phillipson and R. Mitchison (eds), *Scotland in the Age of Improvement* (Edinburgh, 1996 ed.), 11.

80 H. Home (Lord Kames), *Sketches of the History of Man* (Glasgow, 1819 ed.), Volume II, 150; A. Durie (ed.), *The British Linen Company* (Edinburgh, 1996), 123–4, 132, 159.

81 Cochran, *Scottish Trade*, 14–15.

82 Gulvin, *Tweedmakers*, 31–7; Tyson, 'Rise and fall', 64–8.

83 M. Moss and J. R. Hume, *A History of the Scottish Whisky Industry* (Edinburgh, 1981), 35–6.

84 Lindsay, 'Iron industry', 60–2.

85 T. M. Devine (ed.), *A Scottish Firm in Virginia 1767–1777: W. Cunninghame & Co.* (Edinburgh, 1984), ix.

86 R. H. Campbell, 'The making of the industrial city', in Devine and Jackson, *Glasgow*, 190; 'Houston, 'Economy of Edinburgh', 54.
87 Price, *France*, Volume I, 612; ECA, CRB, Moses Collection, SL 30/8/1, Misc., 'Account of the Total Amount of HM Duties of Customs Paid by the Inhabitants of Dumfries upon all goods and merchandise imported and exported from and to Foreign Parts, 1745–46 – 1778–79'; Certificate, W. Maxwell, Collector of Customs, 28 June 1780.
88 Devine, 'Golden age of tobacco', 164, 166–7.
89 T. C. Smout, 'Where had the Scottish economy got to by the third quarter of the eighteenth century?', in I. Hont and M. Ignatieff (eds), *Wealth and Virtue* (Cambridge, 1983), 56, 69–70; see too C. W. Munn, *The Scottish Provincial Banking Companies, 1747–1864* (Edinburgh, 1981).
90 Shaw, *Management*, 135–46; Macinnes, *Clanship*, 225–6.
91 I am indebted to David Alston, a history postgraduate student at the University of Dundee, for this information.
92 Houston, 'Economy of Edinburgh', 52; Saville, *Bank of Scotland*, 270; see too Smout, 'Where had the Scottish economy got to?', 58–9.
93 Calculated from Whyte, 'Scottish and Irish urbanisation', 18; T. M. Devine, 'Urbanisation', in T. M. Devine and R. Mitchison (eds), *People and Society in Scotland, Volume I, 1760–1830* (Edinburgh, 1988), 27–52.
94 R. E. Tyson, 'Contrasting regimes: population growth in Ireland and Scotland during the eighteenth century', in Connolly, Houston and Morris, *Conflict*, 66–7.
95 Cochran, *Scottish Trade*, 102–7; C. A. Whatley, 'The Union of 1707, integration and the Scottish burghs: The case of the 1720 food riots', *Scottish Historical Review*, LXXVIII (October 1999), 201–2.
96 Gibson and Smout, *Prices, Food and Wages*, 164–7.
97 Devine, *Transformation*, 22–4; see too M. Gray, 'The social impact of agrarian change in the rural Lowlands', in Devine and Mitchison, *People and Society*, 53–69.
98 I. D. Whyte, 'Rural transformation and Lowland society', in Cooke, Donnachie, MacSween and Whatley, *Modern Scottish History*, 94.
99 T. C. Smout, 'The landowner and the planned village in Scotland, 1730–1930', in Phillipson and Mitchison, *Scotland in the Age of Improvement*, 103–6; D. G. Lockhart, 'Planned village development in Scotland and Ireland, 1700–1850', in Devine and Dickson, *Ireland and Scotland*, 133.
100 Although John Maclean had successfully improved his farm, drained Iona's peat moss and introduced commercial linen spinning to the island, it appears that his involvement with the Jacobite cause led the third duke of Argyll to refuse to renew his tenancy in 1757: E. M. MacArthur, *Iona: The Living Memory of a Crofting Community, 1750–1914* (Edinburgh, 1990), 18–21.
101 Macinnes, *Clanship*, 60; 'Scottish Gaeldom: the first phase of clearance', in Devine and Mitchison, *People and Society*, 70–2, 82–5.
102 Dodgshon, *Chiefs to Landlords*, 116–18, 239–40; F. Watson, 'Rights and responsibilities: wood-management as seen through the baron court records', in T. C. Smout (ed.), *Scottish Woodland History* (Edinburgh, 1997), 101–14.

103 N. P. Hankins and J. Strawhorn (eds), *The Correspondence of James Boswell with James Bruce and Andrew Gibb, Overseers of the Auchinleck Estate* (Edinburgh, 1998), xxxix, 11, 14, 16.

104 Devine, *Transformation*, 44–5.

105 *Ibid.*, 46–8, 50–2.

106 R. H. Campbell, *Scotland Since 1707: The Rise of an Industrial Society* (Edinburgh, 1985 ed.), 25.

107 See, for example, T. Barry and D. Hall, *Spottiswoode: Life and Labour on a Berwickshire Estate, 1753–1793* (East Linton, 1997); Holloway, *Patrons and Painters*, 112; R. H. Campbell, 'The landed classes', in Devine and Mitchison, *People and Society*, 99–103.

108 I. L. Donnachie, *A History of the Brewing Industry in Scotland* (Edinburgh, 1979), 38–61.

109 Devine, *Transformation*, 50.

110 Smout, 'How far had the Scottish economy got to', 56.

111 On this little-explored industry see W. P. L. Thomson, *Kelp-Making in Orkney* (Orkney, 1983).

112 A. R. B. Haldane, *The Drove Roads of Scotland* (Newton Abbot, 1973 ed.), 192–4; C. W. J. Withers, *Urban Highlanders*, 39.

113 Saville, *Bank of Scotland*, 137–48, 166–94; although with good reason, Saville argues that Scotland had a 'memorable' banking system earlier, at the end of the Seven Years' War, 'Scottish modernisation', 19.

114 Gibson and Smout, *Prices, Food and Wages*, 276, 279.

115 Smout, 'Where had the Scottish economy got to?', 66.

116 Durie, *British Linen Company*, 136–7.

117 ECA, CRB, Moses Collection, SL 30/244, Alex Dundas to CRB 'Anent Duty on Foreign Linen Exported', 1 December 1737; SL 30/4/6, box of financial papers concerning linen, 1724–1821, includes John Coutts, 'Report Anent the Linen', 1744; 'Memorial for the Linen Dealers in the Town of Perth', 27 July 1778; George Ross to Walter Hamilton, Lord Provost of Edinburgh, 28 January 1779; see too *Glasgow Journal*, 29 October 1772.

118 J. M. Price, 'New time series for Scotland's and Britain's trade with the thirteen colonies and states, 1740 to 1791', *William and Mary Quarterly*, XXXII (1975), 310–14.

119 G. Jackson, 'Scottish Shipping, 1775–1805', in P. L. Cottrell and D. H. Aldcroft (eds), *Shipping, Trade and Commerce* (Leicester, 1981), 118–19.

120 For fuller discussion of this issue see Whatley, 'New light on Nef's numbers', 3, 7–8.

121 Whatley, *Scottish Salt*, 49.

122 ECA, CRB, Moses Collection, SL30/4/6, 'State of Facts & Evidents relating to the Fees Exacted by Customhouse Officers as transmitted to the Board of Customs', 6 March 1781.

123 A. M. Smith, *Jacobite Estates of the Forty-Five* (Edinburgh, 1982), 183–6.

124 A. Gordon, *To Move with the Times: The Story of Transport and Travel in Scotland* (Aberdeen, 1988), 5–7; A. R. B. Haldane, *New Ways Through the Glens: Highland Road, Bridge and Canal Makers of the Early Nineteenth Century* (Newton Abbot, 1973 ed.), 1–14; I. Donnachie, *Industrial Archaeology of Galloway* (Newton Abbot, 1971), 153–67; J. R. Hume, *The*

Industrial Archaeology of Scotland 1. The Lowlands and Borders (London, 1976), 3–32; A. Whetstone, *Scottish County Government in the Eighteenth and Nineteenth Centuries* (Edinburgh, 1981), 80–9.

125 J. Lindsay, *The Canals of Scotland* (Newton Abbot, 1968); C. J. A. Robertson, *The Origins of the Scottish Railway System 1722–1844* (Edinburgh, 1983), 7.

126 Whatley, 'Process of industrialisation', 8.

127 Forbes, *Some Considerations on the Present State of Scotland*, 7–11.

128 Donnachie, *Brewing Industry*, 6–7; Shaw, *Water Power*, 363–64, 464; W. H. Fraser, *Conflict and Class: Scottish Workers, 1700–1838* (Edinburgh, 1988), 23–4; for an informative study of glass in this period, see J. Turnbull, 'The Scottish glass industry, 1610–1750' (unpublished Ph.D. thesis, University of Edinburgh, 1999).

129 NAS, West Register House, Court of Session Papers, CSP 234/P3/8, Answers, Mary Lyon, Rachel Currie and other Mantuamakers in Perth, 1756.

130 NAS, Grant of Monymusk MSS, GD 345/765/7, P. Grant to Sir Archibald Grant, 9 August 1733.

131 D. A. Symonds, *Weep Not for Me: Women, Ballads and Infanticide in Early Modern Scotland* (Pennsylvania, 1987), 132–3; ECA, CRB, Moses Collection, SL 30/239, Petition for the Magistrats of the Burgh of Forres, 1725.

132 L. M. Cullen, T. C. Smout and A. Gibson, 'Wages and comparative development in Ireland and Scotland, 1565–1780', in Mitchison and Roebuck, *Economy and Society*, 105–16.

133 Gibson and Smout, *Prices, Food and Wages*, 231–2; 343–56.

134 E. C. Sanderson, *Women and Work in Eighteenth-Century Edinburgh* (London, 1996), 138.

135 *Ibid.*, 152–4; City of Aberdeen Archives (CAA), Enactment Books, 1730–41, 17 December 1735; Press 19, Parcel T, Torry Estate Papers, Bundle D/33, 'Petition to the Magistrates of Aberdeen from Tenants in the Parish of Nigg', 1764.

136 Sanderson, *Women and Work*, 108–35,

137 T. C. Smout, 'Cutting into the pine: Loch Arkaig and Rothiemurchus in the eighteenth century', in Smout, *Scottish Woodland History*, 118–23.

138 MacArthur, *Iona*, 27.

139 Whatley, 'Sales of Scottish marine salt', 10.

140 NAS, Grant of Monymusk MSS, GD 345/765/9, Patrick Grant to Sir Archibald Grant, 31 October 1734.

141 C. A. Whatley, 'The introduction of the Newcomen engine to Ayrshire', *Industrial Archaeology Review*, II, 1 (Autumn 1977), 69–77; Whatley, 'Process of industrialisation', 58.

142 J. Butt, 'The Scottish iron and steel industry before the hot-blast', *Journal of the West of Scotland Iron and Steel Institute*, LXXIII (1966), 202.

143 NLS, Saltoun Papers, MS 17594, British Linen Company, 'Copy or Scroll to Mr Goodchild October 1744, Anent the Grand Manufactory'.

144 PKCA, B59/24/8/10–11, Magistrates of Glasgow to Magistrates of Perth, 25 February 1730; Linen Dealers of Glasgow to Provost Brown (Perth), 27

February 1730.

145 Whatley, 'Salt, coal and the Union', 33, n. 3; NAS, Hamilton MSS, Lennoxlove, 57/2136, 'Memorial for George Hoar & Co.', 1758.

146 Hatcher, *Coal Industry*, 88–96

147 Smout, 'Cutting into the pine', 123.

148 Gulvin, *Tweedmakers*, 29–37.

149 NLS, Erskine Murray Papers, MS 5127, fo. 64, 'Observations upon the Woolen Manufactory in the South of Scotland', 12 June 1749.

150 NLS, Cadell MSS, Acc. 5381, Box 28 (2), 'Remarks on the Quantity ... of the Nails', October 1770; 53/1, William Cadell to John Cadell, 6 December 1772; Box 39 (3), Richard Adams to William Cadell, 27 March 1786.

151 J. L. Carvel, *The Alloa Glassworks: An Account of Its Development since 1750* (Edinburgh, 1953), 13–14.

152 Gulvin, *Tweedmakers*, 22; R. H. Campbell, *Carron Company* (1961), 65; B. F. Duckham, 'English influences in the Scottish coal industry 1700–1815', in J. Butt and J. T. Ward (eds), *Scottish Themes: Essays in Honour of S. G. E. Lythe* (Edinburgh, 1976), 41.

153 See, for example, Campbell, *Carron Company*, 129–32; C. W. Munn, *The Scottish Provincial Banking Companies, 1747–1864* (Edinburgh, 1981), 211–16; 'The Financing of Carron Company', *Business History*, I (1958), 21–34; J. Butt, 'Capital and enterprise in the Scottish iron industry, 1780–1840', in Butt and Ward, *Scottish Themes*, 67–79; S. G. Checkland, *Scottish Banking: A History, 1695–1973* (London, 1975).

154 NAS, Carron Company Records, GD 58/4/1/1, Anonymous Report on the Affairs of Carron Co., 28 January 1769, 1.

155 The classic studies in Britain are S. Pollard, *The Genesis of Modern Management: A Study of the Industrial Revolution in Britain* (London, 1968 ed.), and E. P. Thompson, 'Time, work-discipline and industrial capitalism', *Past & Present*, XXXVIII (December 1967); more recent examples are R. E. Pahl (ed.), *On Work: Historical, Comparative & Theoretical Approaches* (London, 1988); and M. Berg, *The Age of Manufactures, 1700–1820: Industry, Innovation and Work in Britain* (London, 1994).

156 T. M. Devine, 'The English connection and Irish and Scottish development in the eighteenth century', in Devine and Dickson, *Ireland and Scotland*, 19–20.

157 NAS, Breadalbane MSS, GD112/39/308/1, J. Campbell to Mr Flint, Secretary to the Trustees for Encouraging Manufactures, 22 December 1758.

158 A. Gerschenkron, *Economic Backwardness in Historical Perspective* (Cambridge, Massachusetts, 1962), 9; Pollard, *Genesis*, 189.

159 For discussion of the unresolved issue of literacy levels (and schools provision) in early modern Scotland, see R. A. Houston, *Scottish Literacy and the Scottish Identity* (Cambridge, 1985); and D. Withrington, 'Schooling, literacy and society', in Devine and Mitchison, *People and Society*, 163–87.

160 Whatley, *Scottish Salt Industry*, 100.

161 Anon., *The Present State of Scotland Considered* (Edinburgh, 1745), 18–20.

162 CAA, D 18/65, 'Petition, Burgers and Gentlemen in the Gallowgate', 1727.

163 Fraser, *Conflict and Class*, 19–20; Signet Library, Edinburgh, Court of

Session Papers, CSP 20:10, James Dunlop and ors. v. Incorporation of Cordiners, Glasgow, 1755.

164 NAS, Hamilton MSS, Lennoxlove, 57/2922, 'Memorandum To Her Grace the Duchess of Hamilton from Matthew Frew Concerning the Coall in Arran', 3 May 1703.

165 C. A. Whatley, '"The fettering bonds of brotherhood": combination and labour relations in the Scottish coal-mining industry c. 1690–1775', *Social History*, XII (May 1987), 149.

166 Tyson, 'Contrasting regimes', 68.

167 Gibson and Smout, *Prices, Food and Wages*, 273–80.

168 NLS, Saltoun Papers, MS 17595, fo. 32, Memorial, British Linen Company's Office, 1761.

169 Fraser, *Conflict and Class*, 3–5, 39–52; Whatley, '"Fettering bonds of brotherhood"', 143–5; *Scottish Salt Industry*, 111; CAA, Press 18/Bundle 9, 'Memorial for the Woolen Manufacturers of Aberdeen', 10 July 1762.

170 J. Lucassen, 'The other proletarians: seasonal labourers, mercenaries and miners', *International Review of Social History*, XXX1X (1994), Supplement 2, 189–90.

171 Compare, for example, Smout, *History of the Scottish People*, 178–83, 430–40, with C. A. Whatley, 'The dark side of the Enlightenment: sorting out serfdom', in Devine and Young, *Eighteenth Century Scotland*, 259–74; and *Whatley, Scottish Salt Industry*, 98–125.

172 Durie, *British Linen Company*, 141.

173 Gibson and Smout, *Prices, Food and Wages*, 284.

174 Whatley, *Scottish Salt*, 15–26; Whatley, 'Scottish "collier serfs" in the 17th and 18th centuries: a new perspective', in E. Westermann (ed.), *Vom Bergbau-Zum Industrierevier* (Stuttgart, 1995), 247–9.

175 Devine, *Transformation*, 25–9, 68–70.

176 National Register of Archives (Scotland), Survey 3246, Dundas of Arniston, Largo Papers, Bundle 24, 'Mr Durham's Notes about Largoward and Lathen (?) Coal', c. 1773.

177 NLS, Minto Papers, MS 13257, fo. 53, Robert Beatson to Sir Gilbert Elliot, 15 April 1767.

178 NAS, Grant of Monymusk MSS, GD 345/1015/142, William Sanderson to Sir Archibald Grant, 12 April 1765; NLS, Cadell Papers, Acc. 5381, Box 28 (1), Samuel Garbett to William Cadell, 18 July 1767.

3

Political economy
and Scottish development

Models of change

Attention has already been drawn to the disagreements between historians about the impact of the Union of 1707 on Scottish economic
development in the eighteenth century. This discussion will be taken
further in this and subsequent chapters. Various other attempts have been
made to explain Scotland's economic development in the eighteenth
century and the onset of early industrialisation. The aim here is to outline
briefly the main explanations which have been given to account for the
growth of the Scottish economy up to *c.* 1778, when, in spite of continuing weaknesses, it is clear that Scotland's position relative to Ireland had
improved, while the gap between Scotland and England had visibly
narrowed. There are three main indicators of the former: first, the
resilience and greater reserves of Scottish rural society, where 'food shortage, not crisis, was experienced in 1756, 1776, 1782–83 and 1799';
second, the greater extent of urban growth in Scotland; and third, the
balance of population to resources whereby in Scotland population
growth (slower than in Ireland) and increased linen production did not
lead to the sub-division of the land into smaller units of part-time
weavers; instead, over time, rural society and manufacturing de-coupled.[1]
That the yawning gulf in living standards between England and Scotland
was being reduced is indicated not in the closing of the differential
between the wages of craftsmen in the respective countries (which for the
Scots remained at 40 or 45 per cent of their London equivalent, and
began to close only after 1760), but rather in the narrowing of the gap in
rates between skilled and unskilled workers in the Lowlands, a reduction
of which (from two to one to 60 per cent by *c.* 1780) is judged by economists to be a telling indicator of relative economic growth.[2]

Scottish economic success in the eighteenth century has been linked
with the notion of complementary development. As before the Union,
Scotland continued to copy many of the economic methods of her south-

ern neighbour, but unlike the pre-Union period of independent but impotent Scottish mercantilism, success was to be achieved in areas of
economic activity which did not compete with those of England.[3]
Although at first sight persuasive, and not without foundation in that this
was the direction free market competition forced the Scots to take, closer
examination suggests that the concept should be applied cautiously. At
one level, the model seems to portray a synergetic pattern of economic
development wherein England concentrated on woollens and Scotland on
linen. In reality, Scottish linen manufacturers and merchants were
involved in frequent disputes at parliamentary level with English dealers
who imported linen from the Continent, one of the most damaging occasions being in the second half of the 1770s, when the 'languishing' state
of the industry was almost entirely blamed by manufacturers in Scotland
on the ability of English linen importers to keep import duties low.[4]
England also had a coarse linen industry (in defence of which Scottish
and English – and Irish – interests did periodically combine), while
competition with Manchester in some of the finer grades of linen was
intense. In Scotland, woollens were manufactured; indeed, as has been
noted, it was as a result of post-1707 competition with England that
Scottish fine woollens had suffered, along with some other commodities
which were made in both countries. Silk weaving in Paisley was begun in
1759, partly with the aim of undercutting the wage costs of the
Spitalfields weavers in London. Later on, Scottish and Lancashire cotton
interests would partly collide, as would the two countries' leather and
shawl industries, although Scots producers did attempt to find sanctuary
in niche markets, as in the pottery trade where Scottish producers learned
to concentrate on making (mainly, but not exclusively) low-quality earth-
enware rather than china and tableware.[5] In glass-making, the fierce
cross-border competition of the seventeenth century carried on well into
the eighteenth.[6] As has been seen, competition in the tobacco trade was
intense, while Ayrshire and Lanarkshire coalmasters competed with
Cumberland for the Irish market for coal, and in the east their counterparts in the Lothians, Stirlingshire and Fife did their best to hold off
imports from the Newcastle area. From the outset the partners at Carron
were intent on rivalling English ironmasters, as well as English nails and
other iron products both in home and overseas markets by matching
quality with lower costs.[7]

   Proto-industrialisation is a model of economic development which has
been widely applied by historians who have been anxious to ascertain the
causes of industrialisation proper. Briefly, what it represents is a domestic
system of manufacture located in the countryside carried on by full- or
part-time rural dwellers, typically in family or household groups, for
distant markets, usually overseas.[8] This system of production, it has been
argued, will lead eventually to the centralised or factory form of produc-

tion, by enriching urban capitalists who recognised the disadvantages of the putting-out system but who would be able to call on a labour force which had grown rapidly in response to income opportunities in the rural setting. Such attempts as there have been to explain Scottish development in the eighteenth century by reference to the proto-industrial model have concluded that it can only have limited application; when applied to Britain as a whole it has even less explanatory value.[9] In that industrialisation in Scotland was 'preceded by widespread rural manufacturing, particularly of textiles for distant as well as local markets', it is useful, and from a broader European perspective it has some merit.[10] Yet examined more closely, on a regional basis, there are too many exceptions, as in the cases of the Southern Uplands or the Highlands where for social and cultural reasons concentrations of industrial activity of the sort which were found in the Pennines or the Alps did not materialise. Although there were sizeable areas of proto-industrial production in Scotland, these were rarely in regions where pastoral farming was carried on or where land holdings were small. Heavy industrialisation (as elsewhere in Europe) on Clydeside by-passed the domestic system, which never operated in coal mining or iron production. Furthermore, it has been argued that largely owing to the prominence and legal rights of the burghs, commercial production of textiles and many other goods 'was more urban in Scotland than in most west European countries.'[11] On the other hand, although one of the least-researched aspects of proto-industrialisation, attention is now being paid to the part played in its progress by the state. State attempts to set up proto-industries, and the effects states had, often indirectly, on economic development in early modern Europe through warfare, for example, or the weakening (or strengthening) of local social institutions, are considered to be worthy of serious investigation.[12] The role of the British state in Scotland's economic history in the eighteenth century will form a key component of this chapter.

In many respects, the late Alexander Gershenkron's observations on the characteristics of economically backward countries which later industrialised provide the most useful model for Scottish development, even though in this chapter we are only concerned with the earliest stages of industrialisation, and Gershenkron's focus was nineteenth-century Europe. Scotland's technological deficiencies have been noted already, and these had to be imported and imitated on a large scale; labour was cheap, but the 'umbilical cord' connecting it with the land had only partly been cut, and the habits, attributes and attitudes of the workforce required to be extensively re-fashioned. In its favour Scotland was wellendowed with natural resources such as water and coal, and such was the enormity of the challenge of development that sufficient 'tension' existed to generate a purposeful response. This came in part from the state and the banks, but also – and this is crucial – a belief 'that the golden age lies not behind but ahead of mankind'; that is, there was a more powerful stimulus for improvement than simply the prospect of economic gain.[13] It was such a vision which had at least in part inspired Darien, and also underpinned much of the economic and social thinking of the Scottish Enlightenment. Economic improvement and 'virtue' were interdependent.[14] Yet the model is wanting as far as Scotland is concerned, in that Gershenkron's definition of a backward country included a lack of entrepreneurial talent. It is true that English enterprise ventured northwards during the eighteenth century, but as was observed earlier, a striking feature of Scottish society, and one which stood out prior to 1707, was the ability of its multi-layered merchant class.

Mercantile as well as landed endeavour may well have benefited from two features of Calvinism in a society which was staunchly Presbyterian. In 1790 only 2.5 per cent of the population lay outside the Presbyterian fold. It has been strenuously argued on the basis of case studies such as that of the landowner-coalmaster John Clerk of Loanhead that there was in seventeenth-century Scotland evidence of an 'elective affinity' between the Calvinist ethic and Weber's 'spirit of modern capitalism'; that is, devotion to capital accumulation as an end in itself, profit maximisation and frugality in personal consumption.[15] In the eighteenth century, it has been proposed, the elevated position of individual conscience in Scottish Calvinism resulted in constant self-criticism and a need to do better. Predestination demanded that God's earthly 'elect' provide evidence of their salvation to their fellows. Together, these 'implanted in the individual a high motivation towards achievement', and certainly it was characteristics of this kind which impressed British visitors to Holland in the seventeenth and early eighteenth centuries. The case however can be overstated, and weakened upon examination of the career of a man such as William Adam, the architect, who also managed several industrial concerns during his lifetime. Scots such as Ramsay, Raeburn and Burns were creative men of the first rank whose 'businesses' were in the arts. There is limited merit therefore in the proposition that wordly success was achieved in ascetic economic action rather than the creative arts in eighteenth century Scotland.[16]

The Union, the British imperial state and the English connection

There is broad agreement among most historians that the period *c.* 1730–78 was when Scotland derived most benefit from the Union, measured in large part by the rising fortunes of the black cattle, tobacco and linen trades. The growing numbers of black cattle driven from Scotland were all destined for the English market, with London being the principal purchaser. Around one-third of Scottish linen cloth appears to have been sold in England, and as much as half of the yarn, mostly to fustian manufacturers in the Manchester district. An even higher proportion of Scottish-made thread may have gone south.[17] An historiographical tendency in the 1980s and 1990s however has been to attribute Scottish economic success largely or even solely to the initiative and enterprise of Scots. While the adoption of such a stance – 'the Scottish economy boomed because the Scots made it boom' – rightly counters inferiorist interpretations of Scottish development which emphasise new market opportunities at the expense of Scottish endeavour, stated baldly assertions of this sort may be interpreted as a form of nationalist rhetoric.[18] Arguably one of the critical internal factors which strengthened the Scottish economy from the 1740s was the quality of the entrepreneurial response, in part a consequence of Scotland's greater social mobility (in comparison to, say, Ireland). The concentration of landownership both offered and demanded a move away from the land on the part of younger sons towards more lucrative avenues to wealth and status, such as careers in law.[19] Such a judgement however must be tempered by the fact that in Scotland, as in England, much more is known of the commercial successes than the failures, of which there were many, and by an awareness of the existence among other ethnic groups of positive entrepreneurial characteristics which were by no means unique to the Scots.[20] The argument which posits the importance of entrepreneurial action in economic growth holds true in the Scottish case because there were also other favourable factors at work.

Insufficient attention has been paid to the role of the state in Scottish economic development in the eighteenth century. In the sense that the British state helped to create an ordered trading environment in Scotland, England and Wales, and overseas through military and naval might in establishing and maintaining colonial and other foreign markets, Scotland benefited no more and no less than the other parts of mainland Britain, although in terms of the dislocating potential of high politics Scotland appears to have been much calmer than Ireland.[21] On the other hand, lacking this sheltered market environment prior to 1707, we should expect the Scots to have experienced a noticeable difference once the imperial system began to operate in its interest. It was as early as 1709 that on behalf of the Lord High Admiral (the earl of Pembroke and Montgomery), the earl of Wemyss ('Vice Admiral of that Part of Brittain formerly called Scotland') carried out a comprehensive survey of Scottish shipping and related activities so that the former would be in a better position to judge the necessity of providing convoys for Scottish traders.[22]

The first half of the eighteenth century has been portrayed as a period in which the 'essentially reactive' British government acted to promote economic growth and social welfare following initiatives from outside its own ranks, from 'interest groups, voluntary societies, and local government'.[23] With its acute needs for support of this kind, this was particularly fortuitous for Scotland. In each of these guises the Scots missed few opportunities to reap the benefits this relative openness on the part of the British state offered them.

Even before the end of the War of the Spanish Succession Scots shippers on the Atlantic routes to southern Europe and in the North Sea had begun to appreciate the improvements in security on the high seas effected by the London-based Lords of the Admiralty. Coastal shipping too was better protected by the twelve cruisers which were allocated to 'North Britain' under the terms of the Cruiser and Convoy Act of 1708, inaugurated in 1710. Although far from invincible, notably between 1715 and 1720 when British and Dutch ships were subject to attack by Sweden, this was an expensive system and a deployment of naval resources to a degree which would have been 'quite beyond' an independent Scotland.[24] Mercantilism, however defined, requires enormous state and naval power if it is to succeed. It is not simply a commercial system. Threats from the Dutch, France and Spain loomed large. For the next half century Scottish Atlantic traders, as well as those working the Baltic routes, enjoyed the protection of a powerful Royal Navy and an effective system of treasury and naval administration – the 'sinews of power' of the English fiscal-military state which developed between 1650 and the beginning of the eighteenth century, during which time 'aggressively active' government policies had served to create England's Atlantic maritime empire. So secure was the British navy's hold in Caribbean and American waters that, with piracy being greatly suppressed after 1714, by the later 1720s 'most transatlantic trading ships were able to dispense with deck guns', and peacetime insurance rates were cut.[25]

Frequently acknowledged in passing by historians, the importance of the sheltered position Scotland acquired within the British imperial state in the eighteenth century requires to be emphasised.[26] Contemporaries with trading interests and ambitions overseas were in no doubt about the value of this, with the Royal Burghs, for example, expressing their gratitude to the dying King George II for military and naval success during the Seven Years War. Not only had the Royal Navy curtailed the French privateering Commodore Thurot's depredations of Scottish shipping which had led to a sharp reduction in overseas trading in 1759, but by the end of 1760 the British had captured Quebec (Canada was ceded to Britain under the terms of the Treaty of Fontainbleau in 1763) and made further territorial gains – thereby enhancing opportunities for Scottish exporters – in the West Indies.[27]

Of significance too was the extent to which the system of government and Scotland's 'semi-independent' status – rather than government policy towards Scotland, which hardly existed other than in *ad hoc* responses to immediate crises – provided the Scots with additional leverage which assisted the Scottish economy in making considerable advances in the decades which preceded the appearance of the country's first cotton mill in 1778 and the subsequent march towards industrialisation. In stressing the difficulties which some historians have argued that the Scots faced in obtaining favourable legislation from Westminster, and in influencing ministers, care has to be taken that very real Scottish achievements in prising favourable treatment from the centre are not overlooked. London wanted to retain the support of Scottish peers and MPs in order to maintain the Hanoverian regime. Significantly, the pacification and prosperity of Scotland, including the crushing of Jacobitism, which would in part be achieved through the implantation of 'industry' north of the border, were recognised by Sir Robert Walpole (effectively British Prime Minister between 1721 and 1742), to be in the interests of Great Britain and not of Scotland alone. The British state was committed to the attainment of economic growth and prosperity through the creation and preservation of employment generated by the export of manufactures. The fourth duke of Newcastle, Secretary of State from 1724 and then First Lord of the Treasury for most of the period from 1754 to 1762, had similar aims in relation to Scotland.[28]

In the wider British historiographical context attention has recently been drawn to the part played by government as part of an assault on what have been described as the 'Ashtonian and Mancunian traditions in the writing of British economic history', where economic growth is attributed almost wholly to private initiatives.[29] Scotland's economic history in the eighteenth and early nineteenth centuries has been similarly characterised and, as has been seen, considerable emphasis in the past twenty years has quite properly been placed on Scotland's favourable social structure and business capability, as well as its geographical advantages.[30] Even so, there have been some straws in the wind which have hinted that this omits an important variable, described some years ago as the 'peculiar connection which existed between the Treasury bench and the Scottish patronage system'.[31] The inference here is that the Scots may have secured favourable ministerial treatment in the conduct of their commercial affairs, and indeed modern research has confirmed that they did, most notably as a result of the political power garnered by the second duke of Argyll and his brother Archibald Campbell, earl of Ilay (and after 1743 third duke of Argyll), and the influence they managed to exert over government decisions relating to Scotland between 1725 and 1761.[32]

There were certainly deep suspicions that notwithstanding the superior organisational qualities of the Glasgow tobacco trade (although a similar system, including the direct purchase of tobacco, was used in

Whitehaven), and quickly-negotiated, relatively low-priced cash sales of large quantities of tobacco to resident French buyers, the Clyde-based Scots were pulling ahead of Whitehaven at the end of the 1740s by devious means. These included their alleged 'understanding' with the customs officers, which, for example, enabled them to continue to send large (but unrecorded) quantities of tobacco into England without paying duty.[33] It is certainly the case that the Tobacco Act of 1723 was much less severe in its impact on Scottish tobacco traders than had been hoped by some in England. Indeed in its concessions to Scottish interests (which were defended by Walpole), it has been described as 'rather generous', with lower duties for example going a long way towards compensating for the loss of an allowance for 'damaged' tobacco, which had previously been exploited to the full by the Scots.[34] Whitehaven's perception that a grave injustice and no little harm were being done would continue according to Sir James Lowther, the town's MP and the leading local businessman, as he doubted whether ministers would either interfere with something which the Scots would protest was a breach of the Union, or do anything about those outports which sent Members of Parliament who 'Influence[d] ye Electors in favour of the Creatures of the Ministry'.[35]

This suggestion – which requires to be more fully investigated – is somewhat at odds with the explanation for the rise of the Scottish tobacco trade which is currently favoured by historians, which emphasises the importance of the direct purchase of tobacco by shrewd Glasgow merchants through the store system and their strong and long links with the tobacco growing regions of Virginia and Maryland.[36] Whereas most tobacco houses in Bristol, Liverpool and London bought and sold on commission – a system which worked best when tobacco prices were high – Glasgow traders purchased tobacco directly from planters in return for goods or credit. Over time too the Scots also developed efficient commercial and shipping methods which reduced the turn-around time of their ships and cut freight costs.[37]

But these factors do not provide a complete explanation for the 'golden age' of the Scottish tobacco trade, when Glasgow and her Clyde outports reigned supreme in Britain. In Whitehaven as well as Glasgow, sales of tobacco soared in the 1740s, largely destined for France, while the English town could also boast a 'very enterprising breed of merchants'.[38] Indeed the role of the French is crucial. It was from around 1740, precisely when the French United General Farms, sole purchasers of tobacco for the French industry from 1730 and therefore a major force in the European market, began through their London agents to buy massive quantities of tobacco from William Alexander, an Edinburgh merchant and director of the Royal Bank of Scotland. Glasgow firms, most notably Andrew Buchanan & Co. through their London agent and kinsman James Buchanan, had been dealing in Virginia tobacco for the French prior to this, but in much smaller quantities. 1740 however is the significant date. The Clyde was ideally located for ships sailing from the Chesapeake by the safer route round the north of Ireland during the War of Jenkins's Ear which had begun in 1739, and the War of Austrian Succession (1740). The price differential was considerable.

Whitehaven however was equally well-placed and French purchases on a similar scale commenced there the following year, a system of passes ensuring that the trade in tobacco was continued during the war with France. Whitehaven had similar advantages to Glasgow, where, as has been noted, there was a shake-out of smaller firms after 1723. By the turn of the 1740s there were in both places firms trading on their own account which were 'large enough to make big sales [and therefore attractive to French bulk purchasers] but not strong enough to be extortionate at the bargaining table'.[39] That the French buyers paid promptly in cash was a major attraction for the northern merchant partnerships with their narrow capital bases. Profits from tobacco sales were low as a result, but more than compensated for by the profitability of the goods sold from the expanding chains of stores along the James River and the Potomac established by Glasgow firms to supply credit-hungry planters.

Better performance from Glasgow in the later 1740s, however, led to a doubling of legal imports between 1722–31 and 1739–48. By 1747 Glasgow was providing 50 per cent of British tobacco exports to France, 60 per cent four years later.[40] Whether owing to sharp practices by Glasgow men or not, Whitehaven could not keep up and eventually lost the battle. The demise of the Whitehaven tobacco trade was precipitated by the failures of two of its leading participants, in 1759 and 1763 respectively. The influential Sir James Lowther of Whitehaven had died in 1755. By the early 1760s Whitehaven lacked Glasgow's depth of capitalisation and business infrastructure. Further expansion largely depended on the Glasgow merchants' ability to draw on the credit of the new banks (referred to in chapter 2) and more importantly by ploughing back profits and mobilising, through high-yielding bonded loans, the funds of the middling classes in and around the city.[41]

If smuggling and sharp practices were not in the long run the 'decisive' factor which explains the Clyde's ascendancy in the British tobacco trade, it was almost certainly an important one in enabling the Scots to establish their lead over most of the rest prior to 1750. It is hard to see how this would have happened otherwise. Within the union such infringements could be overlooked by benign British rulers, but outside it they would not have been tolerated. Exploiting Scottish (and particularly Argathelian) resentment at the appointment by the duke of Newcastle of Englishmen to Scottish offices in the Customs and Excise Boards, Argyll and his dependents successfully resisted Treasury attempts to remove corrupt officers from the Customs and the Excise departments in Scotland and thereby continued to provide the Scots with a useful commercial advantage until George Grenville (Prime Minister 1763–65) 'began the long process of making the Customs system work in Scotland'.[42]

The present author has demonstrated the extent to which state policy towards the salt industry in Scotland protected it from imports from England and elsewhere in the second half of the seventeenth century until the abolition of the Salt Laws in 1825. In chapter 2, reference was made to the campaign which was waged to ensure that coal shipped within the estuarial limits of the Forth remained free of the duties on coal shipped coastwise from 1710. As was noted, initially at least it served to protect east coast coalmasters, whose export trade had declined dramatically, from encroachments from Newcastle. Defended publicly on the grounds that to remove the tax would be a breach of the Union, but in reality clung on to because the coalmasters alongside the river Forth and the estuary enjoyed the benefits of the monopoly it gave them over coal sales from St Abb's Head in the south to Montrose in the north, it was eventually removed at the instigation of Henry Dundas in 1793, in the interests of his Midlothian constituents, consumers of coal north of the Tay, and also because its disappearance might 'silence in some measure, the present discontent among the lower orders', a theme which will be explored in greater detail in chapters 4 and 7.[43]

The circumstances in which those representing certain Scottish economic interests in the immediate post-Union decades and in which the Board of Trustees and the Royal Bank of Scotland were founded have already been described, and will be further explored later. At this juncture however it is worth adding that the legislation campaigned for by English woollen and silk interests in 1719–20 to ban the importation of Asian silks and calicoes (as well as Scottish and Irish linens), was passed and came into effect from 1722, but linens were excluded, largely because of fears of political instability and disaffection in Scotland. Irish and Scottish linens could freely enter England.[44] Public disorder however continued into the 1730s, most spectacularly in the shape of the Porteous Riot in Edinburgh in 1736. And while there were no outbreaks of militant Jacobitism between 1719 and 1745, Jacobite propagandists continued to press the connection between the Act of Union and the nation's ills.[45] Ilay and Milton, and indeed all Scottish politicians who were intent on maintaining favour at court, the fountainhead of the system of patronage, were acutely aware of the onus there was on them to deliver a contented Scotland which was committed to the Union and loyal to Hanover.[46] As before, the importance of employment creation as a means of securing popular quiescence continued to be recognised. John Cockburn of Ormiston, MP, for example, 'sensible of the advantage to all

Ranks from their thriving', declared his complete support for any measures which would encourage the linen trade or indeed any other manufactures. The observant Patrick Lindsay too, in his survey of Scotland's economic and social condition in the mid-1730s, was acutely aware of the extent and dangers of underdevelopment: 'every thing that renders a Nation despicable', he wrote, 'may be said to flow from Idleness'.[47] That employment and social and political order were inextricably linked is seen in a proposal made in 1744 for establishing textile manufactories in Inverary and Campbeltown, which were both to be 'under the direction of the Justices of the Peace'.[48] The Board of Trustees' efforts notwithstanding, a further boost was required for linen, and campaigned for by the Irish linen trade, along with London-based Scottish linen merchants and the Convention of Royal Burghs. State support for mechanisms which would induce quiescence in the population through employment were not confined to the Lowlands. The Board of Trustees and the British Linen Company, as well as the Annexed Estates Commission, set up in 1755 to manage and improve thirteen Highland estates which their Jacobite proprietors had had to forfeit in 1747 in the wake of Culloden, embarked on a series of measures designed to establish textile manufacturing from Perthshire northwards.[49]

Contemporaries were certainly convinced that the sharp increase in linen exports to the Plantations – which had formerly been supplied with foreign cloth – was directly attributable to the linen bounty, a 'low cost' to the government which had first been paid in 1743, when bounty payments amounted to £294, then increased (following petitions from Scotland and Ireland) to support even lower-priced cloth in 1745.[50] Some years before the bounty was introduced the advantages which could accrue to Scotland if the drawbacks on re-exports of foreign linen were removed were stressed, as too was the importance of even a small price difference: 'With such an Encouragement', one London-based advocate of the Scottish industry wrote in 1737, 'how soon should we outdo other Nations ... in coarse Linens ... to the British plantations'.[51] Just under forty years later, Walter Biggar, an Edinburgh linen manufacturer, conceded that no Scottish linen cloth had succeeded, 'except when the same Foreign Fabrick has been subject to an high Duty on Importation'.[52]

The impact of partial protection and the linen bounties can be clearly seen in Figure 1, which shows marked rises in the quantity of linen stamped for sale after 1742. In the three years prior to 1743 almost 13.9 million yards of Scots-made linen had been stamped for sale, in the equivalent period up to 1 November 1751 the quantity had risen to 22.8 million yards. In the nine bounty-supported years 'great numbers' of young people had been taken on as spinners and weavers, who otherwise, it was argued, would have been 'rendered destitute of Bread', a condition

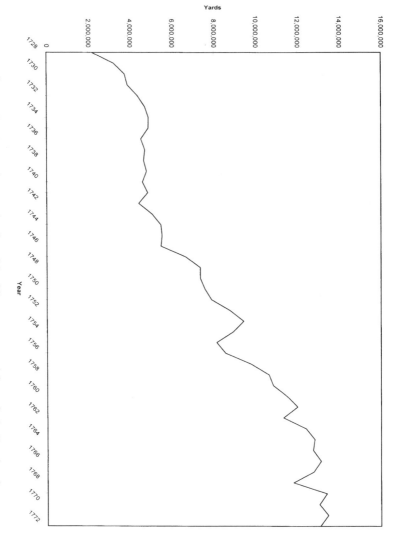

Figure 1   Annual quantity (yards) of linen stamped for sale in Scotland, 1728–72

to which they would return if the bounty was withdrawn.[53] When it was, temporarily, in 1754, the effects were severe in the east of Scotland, which specialised in the manufacture of coarse linens like Osnaburgs, which could simply not be sold abroad (although this is not reflected in Figure 1, which measures output rather than sales. Spinning and weaving were continued by the British Linen Company at first, for 'national' reasons). Perhaps as many as two-thirds of the country's looms were thrown idle. Firms – like the British Linen Company, founded in 1745, and the biggest linen concern in Scotland in mid-century – were eventually forced to stop production. Indeed the value of the Company's sales crashed from £37,000 in the year ending in May 1754 to £12,000 in 1756. It was only when the bounty was restored from June 1756, the result of skilful political manoeuvring by the duke of Argyll, that exports recovered, although the Company's survival also owed much to the favourable conditions created by the Seven Years War, described earlier.[54] In the five years ending Christmas 1765, with the help of the bounty, the average annual quantity of linen stamped for sale in Scotland was just over twelve million yards, compared to eight million in the five years up to Christmas 1755. Between them Scottish and Irish producers claimed they were able to substitute seven million yards of foreign imports into Britain.[55]

The effect of what was a small subsidy therefore seems to have been substantial. Britain had exported virtually no linens to America or Africa at the turn of the century, but by 1772–74 these were worth some £681,000.[56] There is a frustrating lack of precision about the quantities of linen sent to London for on-shipment and subsequent export, but there is enough evidence to suggest that at least half of the bounty-supported linen exported from England was manufactured in Scotland. Exports of all kinds of linen from Scotland grew four-fold between the 1740s and the early 1770s. Not all of this was subsidised however, and apart from a rocky period which coincided with the '45, between 1730 and 1750 the yardage of finer, higher-priced linen stamped for sale rose from 11,000 to 444,000, a forty-fold increase over twenty years.[57] What is easily overlooked however is the extent to which this remarkable growth was due to the degree of protection afforded to the fine linen trade. Scots were at the forefront of repeated campaigns to persuade government to raise the level of import duties on fine linens, and while French cambrics and Holland lawns continued to be smuggled in, there is a clear link between raised duties and the level of activity in the Scottish fine linen trade. These, according to the industry's leading historian, were 'essential', with government intervention creating as many as a hundred thousand jobs (albeit that many were part-time) in the three decades after the 1730s. Less well-known is a deal evidently struck between the Glasgow manufacturers and the government in 1766, when in return for a stiffening of the rules for the importation of French cambrics and lawns, the Glasgow men undertook to supply half the London market in two or three years, and the whole of it sometime later.[58]

With or without subsidies, the West Indies, principally Jamaica, along with North America, mainly Virginia, were crucial areas as far as the establishment of the Scottish economy on surer foundations was concerned – a 'vast Acquisition' flowing from the Union, according to 'A Friend of Great Britain'.[59] In the second half of the eighteenth century nine-tenths of all linen exported from Scotland was destined for customers in these markets, brightly coloured for the West Indies and buff for the tobacco plantations.[60] Indeed there is a suggestion that it was an alliance of planters and London merchants led by Sir John Dalrymple, who offered to lend money at 4 per cent, which was directly responsible for the introduction and extension of Osnaburg production in the vicinity of Perth in 1742.[61] The background to the British Linen Company, 'one of the most conspicuous fruits of the early British Empire', is complicated. Yet the extension of the manufacture of coarse linens which would take advantage of the export subsidies was almost certainly one of the motives behind its formation and almost certainly accounts for the scale of investment (58.6 per cent of the total) from London-based Scots as well as some English merchants.[62] Woollens too benefited, with the Scots having begun to produce lighter fabrics in the previous century 'in response to the growing colonial market', an outlet which grew further in the eighteenth century, and encouraged the establishment of hose manufacture in Glasgow. By 1743 Aberdeenshire woollen-stocking knitters were sending some two hundred thousand pairs abroad, and although most went to northern Europe, some were sent to North America.[63] Beer and ale began to be sent to the same destination in growing quantities after mid-century, to the extent that by 1755 62 per cent of Scottish beer exports were going to North America, encouraged by Scottish merchants living overseas. The total value of Scottish domestic exports to North America and the West Indies rose strongly, from 42 per cent in 1755 to 72 per cent in 1799.[64]

Reference has already been made to Glasgow's tobacco merchants, comprising thirty to forty partnerships which narrowed to some two dozen dynasties dominated by four families, the Dunlops, Bogles, Oswalds and McCalls. Most were from merchant families and several could trace their mercantile lineage back to the seventeenth century, but it was their colonial adventures in the eighteenth century which produced their 'overwhelming' material ascendancy and enabled them to provide massive capital injections for the domestic economy. Not only is it important that the colonial merchants invested in a total of eighty-eight industrial units between 1700 and 1815, but so too was the nature of that investment, which was often in larger-scale manufacturing – factory-type concerns – rather than the much more common smaller domestic workshop.[65] By the second half of the eighteenth century the bulk of goods sent out to the colonies appear to have been Scottish-made, many of them – soap, beer, nails, shoes, saddles and a long list of others – manufactured in the works in which the tobacco merchants had made their sizeable investments.[66]

Land was another outlet for merchant capital derived from empire dealings, bringing with it 'social distinction and security'. Between 1770 and 1815 some sixty-two American and West India merchants purchased landed estates, mainly in Glasgow and the counties immediately surrounding it.[67] Although most merchant investment was in Glasgow and west-central Scotland, some turned their attentions further afield and managed to find other ways of gaining from the British connection. Richard Oswald, a cousin and partner of the Oswald brothers of Glasgow, left for London and became a major tobacco trader there as well as dealing in slaves and acquiring, through marriage, a Jamaican estate. By 1754 a quarter of Jamaica's landholdings were in Scottish hands, more by 1771–75. Scots owned even higher proportions of some other West Indian islands.[68] Throughout the course of the rest of his life Oswald added to his land holdings, in Virginia and West Africa, while in Scotland he purchased Auchincruive estate, in Ayrshire, in 1764. This followed Oswald's success in making 'stupendous' profits as a government contractor during the Seven Years War, mainly supplying British and allied troops with bread (five million loaves between 1759 and 1763), for which he earned over £112,000. Sir Lawrence Dundas, the son of 'an impoverished Edinburgh draper', but from 1768 and into the 1770s the most influential Scottish MP in the House of Commons, also owed the greatest part of his fortune to supplying the British army in Germany.[69]

The opportunities presented by the imperial colonies were exploited through connections made by Highland as well as Lowland entrepreneurs. Landowners from Argyll were active in Jamaica during the first half of the eighteenth century, in the sugar and rum plantations and in the slave trade, from which they built up reserves of capital for use in Britain. Prominent among them were the Malcolms of Poltalloch, who by the 1770s were yearly 'repatriating profits in excess of £40,000'.[70] Several Scots of substance, including the earl of Cassillis, Sir Archibald Grant of Monymusk and Lord Adam Gordon, were involved in establishing colonial schemes in North America prior to 1775, following in the footsteps of Scotsmen who had attempted to found establishments in Newfoundland and Nova Scotia in the early seventeenth century.[71] It was not only those at the top of the social hierarchy in the Highlands and Western Islands who sought to exploit Britain's imperial opportunities over the Atlantic. One consequence of the effects of the commercialisation of Highland agriculture and the growing pressures imposed upon the *bailtean* – the basic socio-economic unit of the Highlands and Hebrides, multi-tenanted townships either managed by tacksmen or set directly to multiple tenants – was a 'rage for emigration'. Between 1768 and 1775 around ten thousand Highlanders may have left for the British colonies in North America.[72] Although large, this was not the first wave of migration outwards (significant numbers had left – first from Argyll and Inverness – in the 1730s and 1740s), nor of course would it be the last. Neither should the greater total which left from the Lowlands be ignored: an estimated sixty thousand people in the eight decades between 1701 and 1780.[73] Highland out-movement in the later 1760s and early 1770s however did represent the highest rate of emigration in Britain, and was supplemented by a rise in emigration from Galloway and Ayrshire from 1773, in the wake of the financial crisis of 1772, and later those of 1782 and 1783.[74]

Prominent among those leaving the Highlands were many of the former but now redundant tacksmen, driven off by high rents and loss of prestige, leading parties of families of their sub-tenants on voyages of hope – that they could establish secure Gaelic communities in what were then the Highlanders' favoured destinations in the Carolinas, New York and Nova Scotia.[75] Earlier, others from lower down the social scale, as well as former Jacobites, had been drawn by military service into regiments such as Simon Fraser's 78th, formed in 1756 for duty in the British Hanoverian cause in America (a cruel irony, given that Fraser's father Lord Lovat had been beheaded for his part in the '45), and later settled near Montreal and Quebec and in the Mohawk Valley.[76] The military skills of the Highlanders, and their usefulness in protecting the southern frontier of the infant colony of Georgia from French and Spanish insurgents, was the main reason why the Trustees for Establishing the Colony of Georgia in America recruited in Sutherland and Caithness in 1735.[77] The enforced enlistment of men into the Highland regiments of the British army formed an integral part of the business of estate improvement, although later in the century and in the early nineteenth demands for land from returning soldiers led to some larger farms being sub-divided into crofts. Large numbers of men were involved, especially during the French Revolutionary and Napoleonic wars, although as many as twelve thousand Highlanders may have served during the Seven Years War. Some 42,700 Scots fought for the British army and navy during this conflict, many of whom were forcibly conscripted. As most of the Highland military recruits were drawn from the ranks of the landless and cottars, and deliberately included social undesirables, so the empire aided the weeding-out process (noted in the previous chapter) which continued to ensure that the best and trouble-free tenants were retained, and encouraged those remaining to adopt the work ethic and to satisfy their landlords by providing them with a population better suited to the needs of commercial farming.[78]

In the early 1770s 'Drink, Pipers and Fiddles' were alleged to have been utilised by 'disappointed' tacksmen to entice 'poor people ... to follow their fortunes ... [and] rouse their Spirits to the Expedition[s]', supplemented by inflated promises above all of land, but also a warmer, drier climate and opportunities to become prosperous. Those who could afford it – it is often argued that this was 'no flight of the ... poor' – needed little persuasion to go.[79] On the other hand, new research is beginning to uncover tacksmen who prior to the arrival on a large scale of sheep flocks, did adapt to the demands of commercial farming and who turned to black-cattle management, a move which pressured smaller tenants, led to inter-tenant rivalry and competitive bidding for farms and the subsequent removal – and emigration – of those who lost out, the subtenants. Displeasing to many but not all landlords (especially in the south-east Highlands), alarming to Scotland's Lord Advocate Henry Dundas who feared -wrongly – that armed emigrants might support the rebel cause in North America, and in the longer-run a tragic loss of entre-preneurial talent of tenant-farmer status from the region, in the short-term the out-movement of the displaced and economically-strait-ened may have dissipated what might otherwise have become a simmering cauldron of unrest.[80]

British imperialist ventures in the east were also attractive and benefi-cial to Scotsmen who, as has been seen, had long looked overseas for the prospect of gain. Unlike Highlanders who crossed the Atlantic, most Scots who went to India hoped to return home, although the likelihood of those from the lower classes (who found themselves in the army *en route* for or serving in India) doing so were considerably less than those from the upper classes. London and the English East India Company attracted growing interest in the years following the Union, and by mid-century Scotsmen had established themselves as directors and shipowners for the Company, as well as having secured positions in its service. Approximately one in five of the Company's employees were Scots in 1772. That is proportionate to the numbers of Scots in Britain, although they were better represented among the officer ranks in the army, and of fourteen royal regiments which served in India between 1754 and 1784, seven were raised in Scotland. Able to trade on their own accounts, or if the Company's lines of patronage worked for them, to secure an ancillary appointment or a victualling or building contract, disproportionately large numbers of titled Scots or the younger sons of landed families sought and obtained appointments in India. Roughly one-third of these were going to Scots by 1750, thereby securing a route both to better fortune and social connections which may not have been made in the Scotophobic England of the mid-eighteenth century. Although not all amassed the wealth they may have hoped for – two of Henry Dundas's brothers died in India without having much to show for their efforts, considerable numbers of the 'nabobs' returned to Scotland to purchase and develop estates. Highland landlords too were involved. Not unusual is the case of Sir Alexander Campbell of Inverneil, who by the 1780s was accumulating something like ten times as much income from his East India Company dealings, along with other stocks and shares, as he managed to raise from his estates.[81]

The other important market which the British union kept open for the Scots was Ireland, imports of grain from which began in the 1760s to play a key role in keeping the price of oats and oatmeal lower during years of relative scarcity; the inhabitants of the ports and industrial towns of west-central Scotland appear to have gained most from this additional source of supply.[82] Poor and often in direct competition in the late seventeenth and early eighteenth centuries, little trade was conducted between the two countries. As has been seen however the Union turned the balance very much in Scotland's favour. The volume of Scottish trade with Ireland during the second half of the eighteenth century was dispro-portionately large, rising from 12 to 20 per cent of the total value of Scotland's overseas trade (although compared to England, Scotland accounted for only a very small share of Irish exports). The share of Scottish domestic exports taken by Holland, Scotland's main market outside the imperial zone in 1755, had fallen to 10 per cent by the early 1790s. Scottish exports to Ireland utilised some 36 per cent of Scotland's overseas shipping capacity in 1771–75 and 1781–85. At a low and fluctu-ating level during the early decades of the century, Scottish trade with Ireland grew more strongly from the later 1740s and early 1750s, and again during the 1760s and 1770s, until threats of war with the American colonies caused a sharp fall in Scottish re-exports to Ireland. At this stage Scottish exports to Ireland were dominated by re-exports, mainly of tobacco, although trade dislocation during the Seven Years War encour-aged Irish importers to turn to Scots and English merchants for their supplies of muscovado sugar. The linen trade between the countries also blossomed in the same conditions, in both directions.

During the American War of Independence, Ireland provided a useful alternative outlet for domestic exports – including plain linen – which could no longer be sent to America. Between 1777 and 1782 Ireland took virtually all of the tobacco which the Scots managed to re-export during the conflict.[83] On the other hand, the same war led to some contraction in the Scottish herring fleet (although less regular payment of bounties has also been blamed), which had grown and increased its exports to both Ireland and America from mid-century, with expansion being linked with the availability of a raised bounty on fishing busses in 1757, peace in 1763, as well as fortuitous movements of fish on Scotland's west coast.[84] Similarly, the American War appears to have been the turning point for the Scottish whaling fleet, which had grown from virtually nothing in the 1740s to some fifteen or sixteen vessels ten years later, directly as a result of the bounty of 1749. Nationally of little importance, for the east-coast ports involved, mainly Dunbar, Dundee and Aberdeen, the multiplier effects of bounty payments which totalled £301,746 between 1750 and 1799 were a major localised boon.[85]

Although not linked directly with the Union of 1707, technology transfers from England to Scotland played a crucial part from the 1720s to the 1770s in raising the standard of Scottish manufactures to a level at which they could compete in both the home and export markets. While the strategy of importing technologies and attracting skilled workers into an area was by no means confined to Scotland in the early modern period, and pre-dated the eighteenth century, close examination makes it clear that there was hardly an industrial process of any importance in Scotland which to some extent or other was not improved with know-how from England, or less often, from other countries which had greater expertise in a particular process. Irish 'tuke mills' (washing mills) and rubbing mills, used in the process of bleaching coarse linens, were intro-duced into Scotland from the 1730s, while Irish enterprise and knowledge of iron smelting were involved in the setting up of two of the early Highland ironworks. Holland provided models for various forms of water-powered technology, including flax-dressing machinery (1728–29) and bleaching machinery (c. 1728).[86] France was the source of some dyeing and bleaching techniques. Pottery, brick-making, lead mining and smelting, certain kinds of mason work such as furnace and kiln construc-tion, glass-making, and framework knitting are just some of the processes for which the Scots sought English advice and technical expertise, although the presence of Anthony Stobach, a German glass engraver at the Glasgow Glasswork Company, not only extended a long-standing tradition in that industry of using continental labour but also serves to emphasise the international horizons of the Scots' search for skills.

Without these inputs, some ventures would have had the greatest diffi-culty in getting off the ground. The proprietors of the recently laid-out Pollockshaws printfield boasted to their customers that they had acquired the services of a calico printer from London and, for bleaching, 'proper hands from Manchester'. Prior to c. 1743, the Aberdeenshire woollen-stocking industry was largely in the hands of small independent producers who made up their own low-grade materials, including badly combed wool. It was argued on behalf of the woollen merchant-manufac-turers of Aberdeen in 1762 that the industry only began to flourish, rising to over twice its previous value, after one of their number had been to London to be 'instructed in wool combing by one of the most eminent masters there'; journeymen combers had also been brought north to instruct apprentices in Aberdeen in their art.[87] Virtually every aspect of Scottish coal mining was dependent upon exemplars from England, from steam-pumping machinery through coal cutting by the 'longwall' method to the erection of horse-drawn waggonways which were much more widely used in Scotland from the 1750s.[88] This example is significant, for, as was indicated in the previous chapter, the perception of the place of coal in the modernisation of the Scottish economy and the first decades of industrialisation has recently been radically altered. Once seen as slow-growing and impeding the early stages of economic growth, re-calculated output figures for the coal industry reveal a respectable eight- or ten-fold rate of growth over the course of the eighteenth century. The crucial importance of coal mining to the twin processes of rapid urbanisation (even during the first half of the century) and early industrialisation has now been recognised, not only as a facilitating factor in that it responded promptly to sharply rising demand in the 1760s, but also as a stimulus to other sectors of the economy such as agriculture and transport.[89]

At the level of the firm, the most telling instance of the importance for Scotland of England's earlier lead in industrial development is Carron, symbol of Scotland's first phase of industrialisation. English involvement in the iron industry in Scotland, whether defined by place of birth or source of capital, continued to be 'substantial' until 1806, after which only the Coltness Iron Company originated south of the border.[90]

In its operation, layout and the general conduct of the works, Carron Iron Works was closely modelled on Coalbrookdale, while the more productive longwall method working of coal (as opposed to the traditional 'stoop and room' or 'pillar and stall' method) at the firm's Kinneil colliery was supervised by a Derby man, working with coal miners brought north from Shropshire.[91] Close familiarity with the trade concerned was an enormously valuable asset, especially where the intention was to compete directly with England. Again the attitudes and actions of the partners at Carron Iron Works provide the necessary confirmation. From the outset Samuel Garbett insisted on and often arranged for skilled men from all the main trades related to iron-making and foundry work to come north, as did John Roebuck, the other English partner in the concern. William Cadell's proposal that the first furnaces should be built by men from the ironworks at Inverary was described by Garbett as 'gregarious folly', and instead the company used masons, bricklayers, millwrights, furnacemen, a coke burner, an engine man and others who had either been employed at Coalbrookdale or in other English ironworks.[92] Not only would men such as these bring their expertise and enable Carron to cast goods which equalled in quality those from the best English works. They would also know where to hire the most capable assistants and perhaps, if they found the work congenial, persuade others to come who presently found the prospect of working in Scotland a 'strange notion' for which they demanded and were paid premium wages. A slitter in Yorkshire, for example, was paid around £30 a year in 1766, but required £50 or a guinea a week to persuade him to come to Carron. As has been noted above, such men were expensive. The objective was to replace them with Scots at lower wages as soon as possible, or to squeeze down the rates paid to English workers in Scotland, and to cut costs further by demanding rent for housing which had initially been provided free of charge to entice them to the works. Although the importance of imported skills and technologies lessened towards the end of the century, when a reverse flow led by men like James Watt began to correct the balance, crucially important inventions from England continued to be introduced (see chapter 6).

The Scots were quick to adopt and incorporate what they needed from elsewhere. But they contributed to the process of technical improvement too, as in the case of John Smeaton, an engineer whose work in the later 1760s and the 1770s in increasing the efficiency of water wheels was of national and international significance. Less well-known but enormously influential were James Meikle and his sons Andrew and Robert, millwrights and early engineers.[93] Mainly involved in textiles, setting up and improving machinery for lint mills, flax mills and bleachfields, their expertise was also used in dry dock and river engineering, while Andrew Meikle invented the ultimately ubiquitous labour-saving threshing mill in 1776. Scotland, a country of imitators in the early and middle years of the eighteenth century, would within a few decades become an enterprising society in its own right which in the world context was able to produce a disproportionate number of major innovators.

Emulation, Enlightenment and economic development

Most ambitious agronomists, manufacturers and to a lesser extent, merchants either recognised the deficiencies in their respective spheres of interest themselves or were made aware of them in the voluminous letters, pamphlets and reports which were written about the condition of Scotland and its industries. Attention has already been drawn to the searching enquiries and bold and varying solutions for Scotland's economic ills which appeared in growing numbers from the end of the seventeenth century. That the benefits of Union were slow to materialise, and uneven and even damaging and socially disruptive when they did, ensured that pre-Union concerns about how to alleviate the country's economic difficulties remained high on the agendas of thoughtful Scots. Better-known contributions to the debate are William Mackintosh of Borlum's *Essay on the Ways and Means for Inclosing* (1729), Sir John Clerk's *Observations on the Present Circumstances of Scotland* (1730) and Patrick Lindsay's *The Interest of Scotland Considered* (1733), but, as has been suggested, these were but a fraction of the total. Many writers, including Mackintosh, adopted a comparative approach, and contrasted Scottish weaknesses with English, Dutch and even Irish strengths. No holds were barred in denigrating the poor quality and relatively high costs of Scottish goods, but most were convinced of Scotland's long-term economic potential. 'Is there one Spot of Earth *more improveable* than *Scotland*, and yet so *barren and unfruitful?*', asked one pamphleteer in 1745, who blamed smuggling, but more particularly unpatriotic 'landed Gentlemen and [the] leading Inhabitants', who consumed run goods and other imported products, and failed to support Scottish manufacturing.[94] This was a common charge, and a source of disappointment to observers who held to the notion of the Scottish nation as a moral community.[95]

Although impossible to measure, and hard for the historian not equipped with the skills of the social psychologist to describe and explain satisfactorily, emulation and ambition on a national scale seem to have been crucially important characteristics of and contributors to Scotland's catching-up process in the middle decades of the eighteenth century. The ideology upon which it was founded had been apparent in the 1690s, but it re-emerged again in the 1730s. Self-critical, anti-feudal and patently patriotic despite its modelling of a reformed Scotland on English institutions and liberties, it was more noble in its aims than simply economic. As with the Darien venture, the endeavour had a quasi-religious quality.[96] It was real enough to contemporaries, with Lord Minto commenting in 1752 on the universality of 'a truly public and national spirit' devoted to the improvement and prosperity of Scotland.[97] Paying less attention than he should have to the pre-1707 era, Henry Home remarked that once Scots had begun to appreciate the opportunities provided by union with England, 'the national spirit was roused to emulate and excel', and 'latent talent' was released.[98]

In part it was exemplified by changed attitudes to country-house building; later seventeenth-century attempts to combine old and new were dropped in favour of exclusively classical designs, some in the style of Palladio. Classical houses of course had been built in Scotland before 1707, and provided architects of the eighteenth century with a distinctively Scottish inheritance, but what was striking now was the confidence and extent of the new building. An early example was the Glasgow merchant Daniel Campbell's Shawfield Mansion (1712), another Sir John Clerk's villa at Mavisbank, deliberately sited near to his Loanhead colliery but described by a visitor in 1739 as like being 'in a valley near Tivoli'.[99] An instance of patriotic building was Edinburgh's Royal Infirmary, inspired by the medical school at Leiden. Building began in 1740 to a design by William Adam, with the scheme being led by George Drummond and supported by subscriptions from throughout Scotland and from Scots abroad; the inspiration for Edinburgh's New Town was partly economic regeneration, but was envisaged too as a North-British equivalent of London's socially exclusive Mayfair and a fitting monument to Scotland's rightful place in Hanoverian Britain. Hence the street names (George, Frederick, etc.) and the original plan of its layout, proposed to be in the form of a Union Jack. Other Scottish towns too laid out imposing George Streets and, in smaller numbers, Union Streets.[100]

The patriotic spirit was something which was also noted by outside observers such as Sir James Lowther, the leading Cumberland coalowner, who observed, after anxiously scanning conditions in the Irish coal market in 1750, that 'they [the Irish] & the Scotch are both more national than the English'.[101] The goal of national economic improvement diluted divisions between Scotland's leadership class and united them in supporting, for example, the more grandiose proposals for the Forth and Clyde canal (Glasgow merchants had backed a plan for a shallower canal).[102]

That Scotland was more sharply focused than England in this respect and adopted a somewhat more unified approach to economic success is manifested in representative institutions such as the Convention of Royal Burghs, annual meetings of which had been held from 1578, and which continued both to regulate and, where possible, assist in the affairs of its constituent burghs and to agitate at parliamentary level in their interest in the eighteenth century. In 1772 the Convention was accused of inaction by Scotland's linen manufacturers and dealers, in spite of the willingness of Irish and English linen-manufacturing interests to demand additional duties on imported cloth.[103] In January 1779 however, following a period of extensive campaigning on the part of burghs involved in the linen trade, which was struggling to compete with linen imports and the efforts of English linen merchants to retain the current low duties on foreign linen, the London agent appointed by the Convention, George Ross, attended a 'respectable meeting of our Countrymen' at the House of Commons. A memorial on behalf of the Scottish burghs was read, considered and supported by Scottish MPs, some of whom, such as Adam Ferguson, lord provost of Edinburgh, had already made clear their determination to 'promote either at the Treasury or in Parliament a Matter [the future of the linen industry] of so essential consequence' to Scotland.[104] As was noted earlier, large sums of money were expended by the Convention on such campaigns, as in 1755–56 when £426 was spent in seeking to raise linen bounties and reduce the duties on imported yarn. This was only a proportion of the total bill, the rest – a bigger sum – being paid by the Irish linen interest. The costs of travel, entertaining in taverns and coffee houses, numerous handwritten copies of documents, bills and amendments, all had to be paid for, including £105 which was spent by the agent's 'attendance upon several Members, the Treasury and the parties at the House and other places which ... were almost daily from the latter end of October last to the 23rd of March [1756] ...

frequently my sole Employ[ment] for many Days together'.[105]

The Board of Trustees for Fisheries and Manufactures was another such body, charged with the task of achieving national economic regeneration. The British Linen Company, 'the only chartered bank in the United Kingdom that had as its purpose industrial development', had a similar if more specific objective, which was achieved in the first instance by expanding the putting-out system by extending credit and issuing its own notes.[106] With these and other forums such as the General Assembly being held in Edinburgh, where too were located the Scottish Board of Customs, Board of Excise, Post Office and other official bodies, the city remained a major centre of government, and an important channel – and buffer – between North and South Britain.[107]

The desire for emulation noted above is entwined with the individual or dynastic ambitions of leading Scots. The driving force this represents has been best expressed in relation to the dukes of Argyll, leading estate improvers whose pioneering and extensive programmes of economic and social reform were inspired by their determination as aspirant members of London's political and social spheres, 'not to appear down at heel among the Russels, the Stanhopes and the Pelhams.'[108] The quest was not solely for financial gain, although this was a necessary prerequisite for the social acceptance which ambitious Scots craved. Thus Winchester and Eton were the preferred schools, while Oxford provided the means of becoming an 'English Divine'; otherwise one anxious father despaired of his son that 'wee must putt up with Breeding him att home a dull Scots Presbiterian [sic] the poorest of all Trades'. Few perhaps were as tormented in their desires as James Boswell of Auchinleck, immensely proud of and in one sense deeply contented with his role as an Ayrshire laird, yet unable for long to stay away from London or discard his hopes of becoming, 'one of the brightest Wits in the court of George the Third'.[109] It is significant that of a cadre of twenty-three London-based merchants loosely linked by their interests in trans-Atlantic trade between 1735 and 1784, Scotland was the birthplace or supplied the parentage of the largest number (ten). Scots were prominent 'outsiders' in London, and actively sought the status of 'gentlemen', an accolade which by the middle of the eighteenth century was attainable by, among other things, suitable deportment, appropriate forms of consumption and cultural display and a commitment to 'improvement'.[110]

Yet it is arguable that in some individuals the patriotic impulse was at least as strong as the desire for personal advancement. This may only have been partly true of Ilay, even though the Board of Trustees and the Royal Bank were established during the period of his ascendancy.[111] More 'national' in his approach (but by no means averse to private gain) was Ilay's Scottish manager, Lord Milton, who as has been seen, was one of the forces behind the establishment of the British Linen Company (which in its ultimate form also required London involvement), a venture which it was anticipated would harness the self-interest of the partners for the public good. Even Milton's main scheme for pacifying the Highlands in the wake of the Jacobite Rising of 1745, the Annexed Estates Commission, included among its aims the utilisation of the labour of Highlanders in the economic interest of Scotland.[112]

George Drummond, another Whig and six times lord provost of Edinburgh, provides another example. Drummond was a staunch Presbyterian, deeply religious, as well as being a supporter of Hanover and the Union. A Commissioner of Customs and later an Excise Commissioner, and a leading light in the instigation of plans for Edinburgh's New Town, Drummond also acted as an agent for the Convention of Royal Burghs in 1726 in the aftermath of the malt tax disturbances. In this capacity he was partly instrumental in ensuring that the government response was 'to the solid good of the country', as opposed either to retribution or a solution which might benefit only the landed interest. But even so it is interesting to note that while Scottish opinion at Westminster was divided on this occasion, as it would be again, Drummond was convinced that those 'who think differently from us, think with as much sincere integrity for the good of their country as we do.'[113] Westminster politics, patronage and Scotland's economic interests continued to be interwoven, although the impression is not to be given that there was a consensus about the last of these. The appeal from Glasgow's merchants in 1756 that fine linen should also be supported by a bounty was rejected, while Lord Deskford's opposition to the proposed removal in the same bill of the duty on imported yarns on grounds that Highland spinning would be hurt, was also ignored.[114] Looking forward to the later eighteenth century, Henry Dundas, Scotland's second great political manager at Westminster in the eighteenth century, and the first Scot (other than the earl of Bute) to become a leading British politician, also involved himself in improvement schemes for Edinburgh, and in the 1780s and 1790s was active in economic reform in the Highlands and responsible for instigating freer trade and improving the efficiency of government.[115]

Men like Milton and Drummond rubbed shoulders and shared ideas with leading figures of the Scottish Enlightenment. Notwithstanding the diversity of the interests and views of its adherents, at its core the Scottish Enlightenment was intensely practical – and patriotic, built on intellectual foundations which preceded the Union, its concerns shaped by the economic and social context in which it came to fruition.[116] In essence this was, according to one Marxist historian, the problem of making the transition from 'feudalism' to capitalism and in particular the means by which agriculture could be transformed.[117] The argument may be overstated and the progress Scottish agriculture had made by mid-century overlooked (understandably given that virtually all of the revisionist writing on Scottish agriculture has appeared since the essay referred to here was written), but its emphasis on the pragmatism of Enlightenment economic thought is soundly based, although equally there were among its adherents some reservations about the compatibility of the 'corrupting' effects of early modern capitalism and virtuous manners and morals.[118]

Once again the subject of the impact of the Union arises, in that by depriving the leadership class in Scotland of its traditional political role (Westminster allowed for only forty-five Scottish MPs, and sixteen representatives of the Scottish peerage in the House of Lords), it has been argued that Union led to a process of 'inversion' whereby political energy was redirected into intellectual pursuits which in part recalled pre-1707 interest in national and personal wealth creation.[119] To acknowledge the pre-1707 intellectual roots of the Scottish Enlightenment as well as the European connections and universal concerns of many of its participants need not detract from its economic and social pragmatism, nor indeed its patriotic edge within the orbit of 'English-oriented North Britishness' which had become such a firm part of Scottish patrician culture by the 1750s.[120] Scotland's 'literati' tended to be drawn from the institutions which were 'at the centre of Scottish public life' – the universities, the Church (of Scotland) and the law (practitioners in which were largely the sons of landed gentlemen) – and were conscious therefore of pressing contemporary issues, including the need for agrarian reform. The sweeping changes made in the countryside owed much to the rationalism of the Enlightenment, at war with rude nature and customary structures and practices.[121] Newtonian principles of order and simplicity and the ideal of social progress were widely diffused through the pulpits of Moderate ministers, lecture-rooms and parish and burgh schools. The fruits of empirical observation were to be found in the improvements made in the utilisation of water power by three generations of the Meikle family, referred to above, and in the many minor, mostly unheralded but cumulatively significant incremental gains made through modifications to textile machinery.[122]

Henry Home, Lord Kames, was atypical only in the magnitude of the mark he made on his age as a patron and publicist of Enlightenment ideas. Born in 1696, son of a Berwickshire landowner, a gifted advocate and legal scholar, subsequently a Court of Session and later a High Court judge, Kames was also a moral philosopher and a prolific author who mingled at dinners, dances and in learned clubs like the Philosophical Society and the Select Society with the cream of the Scottish Enlightenment. These included men such as his close friend David Hume, or William Robertson, Hugh Blair, Adam Smith and others, several of whom wrestled with the problems of Scotland's economic backwardness and wealth creation in a civil society. Long interested in teaching Scots how to pronounce a form of English acceptable in southern England, Kames was also committed to Scottish economic prosperity, and urged upon the medical educator and scientist William Cullen the importance of the practical application of science in agriculture and manufactures.[123] A Jacobite earlier in his life, but adopting Whig principles and support for the Union from some time in the 1730s, as well as sharing in the growing admiration in Scotland for the liberties created by the English constitution, Kames (who for patriotic reasons favoured port over French brandy) joined in the strengthening criticism of Scotland's feudal laws and played an active part – through his attack on the 'pernicious' law of entail, for example – in adapting the Scottish legal system to the needs of a commercial society.[124] Like Lord Milton, Kames was a believer in the motivating power of self-interest, and as a commissioner for both the Forfeited Estates and the Board of Trustees attempted to tap this feature of human behaviour for the public good and generate a climate of self-reproducing 'opulence'.[125] This he furthered by commissioning agricultural surveys such as those made by the Rev. John Walker in 1764 and Andrew Wight during the 1770s, one purpose of which was to record and disseminate best agricultural practice, and backing ventures for improving roads and bridges (an 'addiction' for Kames) and cutting canals.[126] In his own right, Kames was a noted improving landowner, and drained over 330 acres of moss land on his Blair Drummond estate, hailed by one near contemporary as 'the most singular and considerable improvement in Scotland'.[127]

The extent to which Enlightenment thinking impacted upon the Scottish economy and how far its influence was felt in wider society can in part be seen in the case of the 'emancipation' of the Scottish coal workers from serfdom. This had developed in accordance with estate custom and with the encouragement of Court of Session decisions in the eighteenth century, and had become more onerous in the 1760s.[128] The first of two Acts which abolished serfdom was passed by Parliament in 1775. Various reasons have been given to explain the pressure for this legislation, ranging from humanitarianism, through attempts by the coal-masters to cut wages and attract fresh labour into the industry by removing the 'stigma' of serfdom, to a desire, again on the part of the colliery proprietors, to outlaw combinations among the coal and salt workers. Each of these provides a partial explanation of a change in the law which is likely to have happened anyway, but omitted is the part played by Enlightenment economic and social ideology.

Scottish serfdom itself was not a major issue in Enlightenment circles. Indirectly of far greater importance was the 'rich country–poor country' debate in which David Hume was a seminal participant, as too was the methodology of systematic rational enquiry. The question of the means of achieving national economic success was the subject of passionate discussion in Edinburgh clubs in the years leading up to 1774, which, coincidentally or otherwise, was when the employers' campaign to alter the labour laws in the coal and salt industry, marshalled in the first instance by Walter Scott, the novelist's father, began to gather momentum. Central to the prognostications of Hume, as well as the influential Sir James Steuart, was the importance for poor countries of low wages in their struggles to emulate their more opulent rivals.[129] This consideration featured prominently in the thinking of some of the reforming coalmasters. Men such as George Glasgow in Irvine and William Alexander in Ayr were trying to compete with Cumberland in the Irish coal market using colliers who were organised into tight-knit combinations, and, as the observations of Professor John Millar had demonstrated, were paid twice what their English counterparts earned. The 'slave system' which had given rise to this situation was another remnant of 'feudalism' – anathema to Enlightenment theorists whose objective was to 'embrace the commercial system, i.e. to effect a transition from feudalism to capitalism'.[130] Objectionable too was the delight some landed coalmasters took in 'the Sound that ... Coalliers are ... [their] Slaves'; it was 'contrary to reason & common sense', absurd and contradictory, with little or no foundation in law. It was harmful not only to the interests of individual coalmasters but also to the community at large and the 'Trade Commerce & Manufactories of the Country'. Low wages, it was pointed out, had attracted London manufacturers to what was now the thriving silk-manufacturing town of Paisley, and had given the leather- and saddle-makers of Glasgow and Kilmarnock the advantage over England in the North-American and West-Indian markets.[131]

As this suggests, the reformers' arguments were not confined to coal, but developed in the broader context of how Scotland might become a great manufacturing nation. Coal rather than corn, George Glasgow argued, had been the key locational factor in the establishment of textile manufacturing in Lancashire and the North and West Riding. Its absence in Ireland, Adam Smith concluded three years later, would delay the progress of 'Great Manufactures' there.[132] If the cost of coal in Scotland could be cut, goods currently sold in Scotland but brought from England and the Continent could be made along the banks of the Forth and Clyde canal in central Scotland instead. Yet in public the reformers had to be careful not to arouse English fears and hostility to the measure in Parliament; their aim, they declared, was not to 'underwork' coal miners' wages in England, rather it was to 'come as near them as possible'. Servitude however was also contrary to the rights of individuals established under the British constitution: it had been 'imposed upon a set of men, members of the community who have ane Equall right with ourselves to the benefits of living in a free Country', wrote Scott.

Enlightenment concern with moral improvement may have formed part of the reformers' agenda too, seen in the disapproving references to the way excessively well-paid colliers' families were blighted by drink.

Radical in its origins, the Act of 1775 was a conservative measure, a fudge which represented the splits that existed among the Scottish coalmasters, some of whom worried that they would lose all or most of their colliers, and the ending of legal servitude was only slowly accomplished.[133] The campaign and the Act however encapsulated a struggle between the monopolising landed proprietors of established coal mines and an emergent group of capitalist entrepreneurs whose leaders articulated – and anticipated – the doctrine of a custom-free market in labour which in due course would better serve the needs of the Scottish economy.

The example reveals too that the concerns of the Scottish Enlightenment were not confined to the vicinity of Edinburgh's High Street. Aberdeen and Glasgow too felt the effects of Enlightenment culture and thought. With its bustling vitality and colonial and European links, Glasgow in the mid-eighteenth century was a hive of intellectual as well as commercial and industrial activity, although philistinism and a strong strand of evangelical Presbyterianism combined to slow and limit the course of the Enlightenment in the city, and also to make definition more complicated.[134] At least 22 per cent of the city's tobacco merchants had also matriculated at Glasgow University, around which the Enlightenment's adherents in mid-eighteenth century Glasgow clustered, feeding off and in turn feeding the city's commercial buoyancy (although a smaller proportion of the sons of merchants followed in their fathers' footsteps than attended the University).[135] James Watt's experiments as a university technician with steam engines in the 1760s were to herald the emergence in the Glasgow region of skilled engineering, while William Cullen and James Black, also of the University, were pioneers in applied chemistry. Growing tensions from the 1760s between the commercial sector and a university which became increasingly committed to 'academic notions of enlightened learning' were to some extent resolved by the work of John Anderson and his followers in teaching 'useful' subjects: following his death, and with the assistance of his will, this was institutionalised in the form of 'Anderson's Institution' in 1796, with its closer ties to commerce, industry and the applied sciences.[136]

Labour, gender and markets

Along with endeavours to improve the quality of Scottish products, determined efforts were made to address what in some respects was the more deeply-rooted problem of high production costs which resulted from low productivity, despite lower wage rates in Scotland. Much had to be done, the partners at Carron noted early on, 'by Oeconomy and steady atten-tion to reduce the price of Labour at our Works', sentiments which were shared by many of their contemporaries in business.[137] Overcoming the cost hurdle was essential if Scottish manufacturers and merchants were to make substantial inroads into markets either at home or overseas. Agriculture was subject to the same strictures: 'To make the greatest Improvement at the Smalest Expense is the great Secret of Farming', wrote Sir Gilbert Elliot's factor in 1767, before reporting measures he had taken to reduce the number of harvest shearers and binders.[138] At different times and in a far from uniform manner the consequences for cost and quality of 'idleness' and 'indolence' were tackled. Proletarianisation had occurred in a few trades such as coal mining or tailoring, where in Edinburgh by the 1730s there were three to four hundred journeymen working in their masters' workshops, but for most employers, if the market opportunities they visualised were to be exploited, a new kind of worker was required.[139]

In weaving and other skilled occupations where expansion beyond the reach of the urban incorporations was anticipated, the preferred new recruits were largely boys or youths, who were to be taught the requisite skills as well as the necessity for regular working. But this was a slow process which took decades rather than years to produce significant results and so resort was had to men from other trades. Yet if such recruits were to be taken on by improving landlords such as Grant of Monymusk they had to be 'good' and 'not Sloathful'. Some workers could be recruited from the 'Country', especially at casual labouring and other unskilled work, but the flow of suitable recruits into manufacturing was far from steady or certain.

Such was the severity of the bottleneck in linen weaving by mid-century, with handloom weavers' wages rising in extreme cases to 14s. a week, that resort was had to legislation, and decisively, in 1751, the weaving incorporations were stripped of their powers to restrict the entry of weavers of linen and hemp into the trade.[140] Even before this some employers had begun to make use of formerly independent 'country' weavers, while others were employed in weaving factories and sheds, a departure pioneered by the British Linen Company who equipped their works with looms and other essential equipment.[141] In certain occupa-tions, as has been noted, boys rather than adult males were sought. An example is provided by nail-making, where, owing to labour shortages and inadequacies in Scotland, nails cost more to make than in Staffordshire, Carron's main competitor. The partners constantly scoured the political and economic skylines, searching for opportunities to lessen their labour costs in this and other parts of the business. The end of the Seven Years War in 1763 was one such occasion, with demobilisation causing 'numbers of young Fellows' to be 'destitute of employment'; it might also allow the company to cut labourers' wages by 25 per cent and reduce their dependence upon highly paid Shropshire colliers. Yet of the twenty-five apprentice nail-makers employed by Carron Company in the later 1760s, sixteen were from the 'Charity House, Edinburgh', while fifteen of the original twenty-five were also reported to have 'gone away'.[142]

Where adult males were employed, efforts were made to instil new habits and eliminate costly customary practices such as embezzlement of raw materials (hard labour and whipping were potential punishments), although the pace with which this process progressed was slow and uneven. Indeed the embezzling of webs by weavers appears to have been an even more serious problem in and around Glasgow at the end of the century than it was earlier.[143] Where and when the competitive edge was sharper, the intensity of interest in reform was often strongest. Thus Carron was in the vanguard and has been credited with its comparatively early efforts to break the 'cake of custom'.[144] Physically striking and highly effective in maintaining 'the Order and Respect of the Works ... the safety of the Goods, and Sobriety of the Workmen' were the enclosing wall and gates which were constructed in 1764. Two porters too were appointed at 8s. per week to keep an account of the men working in the company's time, 'to preserve order, prevent Embezzlement, admitt people into the Works and keep a Register of Workmen, Strangers & a daily Journal'.[145] At collieries too, working methods and arrangements came under increasingly close scrutiny, through the appointment of more effective grieves who were expected to stamp out long-established customs such as the colliers' right to sell coal on their own behalf and impose a more formal set of rules and regulations, including written contracts of employment, through which tighter control of output and costs could be exercised.[146]

Demand intensified among employers for more regular labour (employees in better-paid work continued to exercise a preference for leisure over what was judged to be excessive work). Yet for most cottars, for instance, weaving was necessarily a part-time occupation, engaged in along with the farming duties they carried out for the tenant farmers from whom they held accommodation and a small plot of land.[147] Payment by the piece at rates set low was one way employers could ensure greater or more sustained periods of effort. More common however was the employment of workers such as day labourers, building and agricultural workers for longer periods of the year, as, for example, on the Buchanan estate in Stirlingshire, where by the 1770s day labourers were working for an average of no less than 276 days *per annum*; that is some 25 per cent or more than they would have worked half a century earlier.[148] There were considerable fluctuations however, according to the weather, seasons, state of the trade over time, and district by district.

Insecurity of employment remained the norm; for most, the era of steady five- and six-day working lay in the future.

For 'unskilled' work (a problematic term which can mean dull, repetitive, arduous and above all, badly-paid) or those employments where it was judged that certain assumed gender-specific attributes such as manual dexterity were called for, females were recruited, sometimes in place of males.[149] Although there were regional variations, with females in the Highlands generally being paid less for all kinds of work than in the Lowlands, generally speaking women could be hired for wages which were one-third to half the level of those obtainable by males, although for harvest work the differential was considerably less.[150] Thus at Saltoun bleachfield in 1762, where the proprietors were anxious to improve the quality of their finishing and cut costs, the master bleacher was instructed that, 'no Men should be employed upon what a woman can perform. Four men have always been employed on every Bittling [beetling] machine. Three women and one man may do the business equally well'.[151]

It was not only for their skills and cheapness that women were employed, however, in processes in which there was a clear sexual division of labour. The prospect of entering colonial and export markets acted as a particularly sharp spur to producers to break down former restrictions in the labour market.[152] In 1762, Robert White, a hosiery manufacturer in Glasgow, was accused by the city's Incorporation of Tailors of employing women who, 'because of their sex', could be paid less than men to sew up the plaid he cut for them. White admitted the charge, defending his actions not only on the grounds that rival English manufacturers were employing women and children, thereby enabling them to 'undersell and carry away the Market where such labour cannot so easily be had', but also because they could perform tasks such as stitching and sewing with 'Exactness' and 'more Expedition' than journeymen. In addition, women could be readily employed during periods of intense demand. Without this benefit, White argued, his production of plaiding hose would be halved.[153]

It is true that new insights into work commonly done by females have revealed that for some urban occupations such as shop-keeping, mantua-making and millinery, which it has been assumed were simply an extension of women's domestic roles, formal education and training was required.[154] Such women however, who were periodically driven to defend their right to work in what had formerly been male preserves, were in a minority.[155] So too were female coal bearers, long portrayed in the historical literature as bow-backed appendages of their husbands and menfolk who cut the coal, and like them, victims of the system of serfdom. Female coal hewers were certainly exceptional in British coal mining and in Scotland largely confined to the eastern districts of the

Scottish coalfields. Yet evidence from local studies in Fife – from whence the bleakest accounts of coal working conditions in Scotland are derived – is beginning to point to a separate labour market for at least some female coal bearers, who signed annual contracts and received entry money and drink money in their own right, and who were paid by their hewers, husbands or not, at rates determined by the coalmaster. Rather than feudal labour laws, there are grounds for suggesting that it was an extension of the custom in rural society in east-central counties of Scotland whereby male farm workers (hinds) were expected to provide a female partner to assist them which drew the wives of coal workers into the pits, a tendency which was further encouraged by the relative scarcity of female coal bearers.[156]

Otherwise in Scotland, supply-side conditions in the female labour market were at least as favourable as those in England, if not more so. The male-female sex ratio was low in both countries, especially in the towns, where females consistently outnumbered males. Two distinct advantages Scotland had were the higher rate of first marriage – twenty-six to twenty-seven during the later eighteenth century, as opposed to an English range of twenty-three to twenty-seven – and a level of celibacy among the female population which may have been as much as twice as high as that for England. Even though life expectancy was shorter in Scotland in mid-century – perhaps by five years – both of these factors would have increased the number of single women in Scotland searching for employment. To this should be added females on the parish poor rolls, twice as many as men, which included widows (and their dependents) who had outlived their menfolk, and wives who were either separated or had been deserted.[157] An example is Stonehaven-born Jean Wood who, prior to her banishment from Perth for vagrancy in December 1777, had worked in Thomas Paterson's brewery for ten or eleven weeks, gone to the harvest with a David Thomson for 'about seven weeks', and then engaged 'by the day to anyone who employs her'.[158] Her circumstances can be multiplied many times over.

The Scottish Poor Laws played a crucial part in creating the conditions just described. Regional and local variations complicate the picture, but what can reasonably be concluded is that while the Poor Laws kept potential workers alive, parish support was disbursed at a level and on conditions which normally made it necessary for recipients to find paid employment if they were to live at anything above bare subsistence level. Those without testimonials and who after enquiry were found to belong to another parish were moved on, like Elizabeth Clerk, the daughter of a Glasgow coal miner, who was banished from Aberdeen in 1740 on the grounds that she was a vagabond and fortune teller.[159] By encouraging vagrancy, which continued to be a feature of Scottish society longer than in England, the Poor Laws also ensured that this segment of the casual labour pool was mobile. The officially recognised begging and needy poor only accounted for around 2 or 3 per cent of the typical parish population. The able-bodied poor normally had to fend for themselves.

The ubiquity of low-level household incomes in Scotland has already been noted. Unlike Ireland and England, living standards appear not to have risen in the later seventeenth century, and there was no discernible improvement in real wages in Scotland until after *c.* 1760. Thus in Scotland, as in much of the rest of Europe, the principal factor which drove females and children into the labour market in eighteenth-century Scotland was the imperative of family or household subsistence, as well as the need for individuals to make a living.[160] A comprehensive study of real wages in Scotland has demonstrated the stark reality that throughout the country the wives (and children) of the labouring classes (including some craftsmen), regardless of pregnancy and the demands of childcare, simply had to obtain some form of paid employment, which was often different from that of their husbands in the case of married women in towns such as Edinburgh, if even a bare level of subsistence with the most frugal of diets was to be achieved.[161]

Nowhere is this seen more clearly than in rural Aberdeenshire, where the quality of arable land was poor, the climate unfavourable and topography difficult, and the process of agricultural improvement began later than in most of the rest of Lowland Scotland. The county's large but impoverished population provided a vast pool of cheap labour for Aberdeen's merchants from the seventeenth century until the end of the eighteenth. The putting-out system they developed from the mid-eighteenth century employed as many as thirty thousand mainly part-time weavers and knitters, the last-named being predominantly women, the wives and womenfolk of cottars, whose labours could also include dulse-gathering, kelp-making, fish-selling, peat-digging, harvesting and household duties.[162] Without female earnings, such households could not have survived. There was more mutuality however about contributions towards family budgets than is suggested by the usual description of females' contributions as 'supplementary'.[163]

The pressure on females to find some form of employment however was not confined to Aberdeenshire. It was the fact that there were some four hundred families in the mining town of Leadhills where the women were 'quite idle' and dependent wholly on the wages of their menfolk which persuaded the British Linen Company to introduce spinning there in 1747, which, it was hoped, would enable the females employed to earn between 1*s.* 4*d.* (7 pence) and 2*s.* 4*d.* (12 pence) a week.[164]

Arguably, it was the degree of household poverty which persuaded females in Scotland to move more readily than their counterparts in, say, Normandy, and travel long distances in the search for work, as well as for marriage partners. Emphasising the connection between agricultural improvement and the shaking out of female labour from the countryside is the example of East Lothian, from whence females had been leaving since the early seventeenth century. The fall in size of landholdings in the Highlands in the seventeenth and eighteenth centuries seems to have increased poverty and is likely to have accounted for at least part of the increase in the proportion of females migrating to Edinburgh prior to marriage. This rose from 1.2 per cent between 1701–10 to 7 per cent between 1771–80.[165] Rapid population increases added to demographic pressures in the later eighteenth century, thereby encouraging further seasonal migration of females (although, as has been seen, Highland migration to the Lowlands for the harvest had been in evidence from the seventeenth century).[166] Short distance migration was more common however and females in farming and household service moved at least as frequently as males from an early date. A period of employment in either of these occupations was for adolescent and young adult females the normal experience in Scottish rural society during the seventeenth and eighteenth centuries. Females were much more numerous than males in the towns, to the extent that in the 1690s they accounted for almost one in four of the pollable population in Aberdeen (where they comprised 75 per cent of the servant population), slightly less in Edinburgh and Perth. Between them, the four main Scottish towns may have employed one in ten Scottish females between the ages of fifteen and twenty-four.[167]

Although impossible to date precisely and by no means unique to Scotland, females from the middling and upper ranks were being persuaded to withdraw from the formal world of work in which they had participated in greater numbers – in Edinburgh at least, which has been studied in greater depth than the other Scottish towns – than were suspected formerly. The ideology of domesticity, with its emphasis on 'softness' and sensibility and also the importance of women within the home environment as 'affective agents', 'conduits through which civilisation was passed', was well-embedded in middle- and upper-class thinking before the end of the eighteenth century.[168] Earlier, in 1739, Alexander Monro, Professor of Anatomy at the University of Edinburgh, had advised his daughter that while she might look on spinning, sewing, knitting and similar 'women's work' as 'low and mean', such skills could come in useful in harder times, while knowledge of them would prevent her 'being imposed on as the Ignorant alwaies are'.[169] A sharp class distinction however distinguished females of this rank who had some choice in the matter from those whose role was simply to labour. In 1735 when one advocate of an expanded linen industry explained how 'All our Women .... may be employed in Spinning', he was careful to add that he spoke 'only of the Poor'.[170]

Fortuitously, then, eighteenth-century Scotland was blessed with an underemployed army of females whose penurious circumstances made them hungry for work. It was this which facilitated the remarkable expansion of the Scottish linen industry, with each weaver requiring the output of yarn from four or five spinners. With the introduction of new spinning technology in the form of single- and double-handed wheels delayed until the 1750s, yarn merchants depended not only upon making more efficient use of existing spinners but also on their ability to draw in new recruits. This was done by extending the network of spinners geographically and tapping sources of female labour in Bute, Kintyre and Argyll – and as far west as Iona by mid-century – in the first phase of expansion, and in the 1740s by merchant flax spinners spreading their net into Highland Perthshire, western Aberdeenshire and even further north.

Productivity was improved and output gains were made with the use of the spinning wheel (although as this tied its users to the home, it was not always well-received), as well as by encouraging spinners to increase the number of weeks they worked, and employing yet more spinners at low rates of pay. There was a point below which spinners would not work however, while good harvests too tended to discourage females from spinning. When they were poor, or failed altogether, they were much more willing, as in 1772 when fifteen hundred women in the distressed Lochaber district were reported to be looking for lint to spin.[171] In short, other than in the Lothians, one of the few regions in Scotland not to have a significant presence in spinning, urban merchants and manufacturers were able to reap considerable benefits from the impoverished and largely unreformed system of rural employment in the rest of Lowland Scotland which freed women for work outside the harvest season. In the Highlands, small-scale subsistence farming also left women with time and the incentive to spin at rates low enough to compensate for the transport costs which Lowland flax merchants would incur, although such was the scale of army recruitment in some areas that rising wages encouraged estate factors to drive widows and single women from the land into the labour market.[172] It was the British Linen Company however which did most to extend spinning into the north, first in Orkney and then in the seaward districts of the counties of Ross, Cromarty, Sutherland and Caithness, generating many thousands of mainly part-time jobs between 1746 and 1773.[173]

One result of the extension of hand spinning appears to have been to stabilise the household incomes of the labouring classes, and in some cases to facilitate additional consumption. If, as seems to have been the case, there was an overall increase in the numbers of women and children engaged in paid work, this would have had a favourable effect on the level of demand, although even by the end of the century large sections of the working classes in Scotland struggled to make ends meet. Within Scotland the mass market for manufactured goods therefore was slow to develop.

However there is evidence which indicates that domestic demand strengthened in the central belt from the 1760s and 1770s. There were considerable intra-county variations in wage rates but the best were usually paid in and around the towns, particularly Edinburgh and Glasgow.[174] The other reasons for rises in working class living standards were complex: further employment of women and children was one factor, rises in money wages another, but important too was the increasing substitution of the cheaper potato for oatmeal (potatoes had appeared in the Hebrides in the 1690s and in Leith by 1741, although at first they are likely to have been a luxury), and more regular employment in town and country as economic conditions improved.

Although population growth was relatively slow in Scotland prior to 1800, the uniquely rapid rate of urban expansion observed earlier had a profound effect on demand. This was most evident in the western Lowlands, where, compared to the national rate of population increase of 27.1 per cent between 1755 and 1801, in-migration contributed to an increase of 82.7 per cent, although this was but part of a process where population growth in Scotland was concentrated in a 40 km-wide belt between Greenock and Arbroath.[175] In the same period, the proportion of Scots living in large towns (of over ten thousand people) almost doubled, to 17.2 per cent (the comparable figure for Ireland in 1800 was 7 per cent); that is a remarkable and rapid increase of 132 per cent, as compared to 83 per cent in England and Wales.[176] If smaller towns of 2,500–plus are included the figure rises to 36.1 per cent for 1801, 26 per cent in the 1790s.[177]

All this generated a market not only for additional foodstuffs (for animals – mainly horses – as well as humans), drink and clothing, but also for building stone and slates, and coal for domestic heat and cooking, along with pots, grates and other household items. Average annual *per capita* consumption of coal in coal-using towns such as Dundee, Edinburgh and Glasgow, is unlikely to have been much less than 0.75 tons. Without this source of heat and fuel for cooking it is difficult to see how urban expansion could have been sustained. Coal output in Scotland appears to have begun to rise from around 1740, with a sharper increase after 1760. Significantly, it was the coal port of Alloa, from where coal was shipped primarily to Leith, which experienced one of the fastest increases in coastal shipments in Scotland between 1760 and 1784.[178]

In large part, the growth of urban demand was due to the increasing prosperity of the middle and upper ranks, although landed wealth too 'enhanced some towns as centres of consumption and entertainment'. The numbers and wealth of the urban middle classes grew substantially after *c.* 1760, led by overseas merchants. Equally important numerically but less wealthy and of somewhat lower status were those in domestic commerce and distribution, while the category also includes manufacturers, lawyers, teachers and physicians. New professions were either being created or expanded, as in banking where at the Bank of Scotland, for example, the number of clerks, tellers and other servants expanded sixfold between 1770 and 1807, while over a slightly longer period tellers' salaries rose from between £70–£105 *per annum* to between £150 and as much as £450.[179] Professionalisation, with payment according to qualifications, and the introduction of age-related salaries, not only widened the salary range but also boosted middle-class earnings.

Comprising only 10–15 per cent of the population of some towns in the mid-eighteenth century (but expanding thereafter), the middle classes led building booms in both Edinburgh and Glasgow which had been presaged by earlier, smaller developments in housing – some in the fashionable classical and neo-Palladian styles designed by the best architects available, and public buildings such as hospitals, infirmaries and town houses (William Adam designed and built one in Dundee during the 1730s). They effected significant changes in the physical appearance of their respective towns by leading moves westwards in Glasgow and to the New Town in Edinburgh, the last the more dramatic both because Edinburgh had seen little construction work since the 1690s and as the planned suburb was to be built on a virgin site.[180] Less ambitious schemes in other towns with a substantial middle-class presence followed, although in some – Paisley, Falkirk and Dundee, for instance – this was relatively small, illustrated in the last case by the presence of one female servant for every thirty-six families, compared to one in eight in Edinburgh.

Improved commercial opportunities and the rising social aspirations of the landed classes too were translated into the construction of great houses designed by members of the Adam family or the less well-known Mylnes and others, and on improving the surrounding policies under the direction of influential land surveyors such as Peter May, 'the best ... in Scotland', who was active from mid-century through to the 1790s, and improvers like Alexander Fairlie in Ayrshire, who advised James Boswell at Auchinleck over a period of seventeen years.[181] All this required considerable amounts of labour, building, ditching, dyking and hedge planting as well as specialist farm workers like ploughmen and carters. Largely led by landowners and implemented by a sizeable pool of willing, well-educated and market-oriented tenant farmers, the process of agricultural improvement depended too on the abilities of zealous estate factors who instructed and where necessary coerced those less willing to engage in what has been described as a 'gigantic strategy of social and economic engineering'.[182]

Although landed house and estate improvements had been taking place prior to 1750, the more general movement of the 1750s and 1760s depended in large part on the greater opportunities there were for profit, 'the forces of commercialism' nurtured by the expanding demands of the increasing urban population and those industrial processes which were carried on in the countryside. The importance of price rises in stimulating agrarian change and improvement can be gauged using figures from Fife, which in comparison to Lanarkshire, for example, was not particularly heavily industrialised by the end of the 1770s. These reveal that oatmeal prices rose by 300 per cent between 1725–50 and 1800–10; 212 per cent if the base period used is 1751–70. The outcome was sizeable rent rises from the 1760s (followed by a second wave of increases from the 1790s), illustrated by the rental of an estate such as Douglas in Lanarkshire, which rose from £1,426 in 1737 to £3,593 in 1774, a 152 per cent increase.[183]

Middle- and upper-class expenditure made clearly identifiable contributions to Scottish economic growth in the 1750s, 1760s and 1770s, the multiplier effects of their spending reverberating through urban services, agricultural output, notably of meat, wheat and dairy produce, as well as fruit (evidently an item of conspicuous consumption) and vegetables, and interconnecting roads. The evidence is to be seen in the four-fold increase there was in paper production in the two decades from 1750–54, as well as the rise in the numbers of books published; consumer-goods industries and services as a whole appear to have done well, including coaches and coaching inns and even iron products such as drainpipes, railings and lamp-posts. In Edinburgh, the number of sedan chairs rose from six in 1687 to ninety by 1753.[184]

Notes

1 Smout, 'Scotland and England', 619–20; Devine, 'English Connection', 18–19.
2 Gibson and Smout, *Prices, Food and Wages*, 276; E. H. Hunt, 'Industrialisation and regional inequality: wages in Britain, 1760–1914', *Journal of Economic History*, XLVI (December 1986), 941.
3 Campbell, *Scotland Since 1707*, 8.
4 NAS, State Papers, Scottish, Series 2, SP54, RH2/4/384, Letter, Linen Manufacturers of Edinburgh to Lord Advocate, 1779.
5 L. Weatherill, 'Marketing English pottery in Scotland, 1750–1820: a study in the inland trade', *Scottish Economic & Social History*, II (1982), 20.
6 Turnbull, 'Scottish glass industry'.
7 See NLS, Cadell Papers, Acc. 5381, Box 28 (2), relating to Carron.
8 For an accessible introduction to the debate, see L. A. Clarkson, *Proto-Industrialisation: The First Phase of Industrialisation?* (London, 1985).
9 M. J. Daunton, *Progress and Poverty: An Economic and Social History of Britain, 1700–1850* (Oxford, 1995), 148–70.
10 Whyte, 'Proto-industrialisation', 228–51; for a modern and positive

approach to proto-industrial studies in Europe, see S. C. Ogilvie and M. Cerman (eds), *European Proto-Industrialisation* (Cambridge, 1996).

11 Whyte, 'Proto-industrialisation', 234. This judgement however seems more applicable to the seventeeth century than the eighteenth and, as will be seen, cannot be applied to Aberdeenshire.

12 S. C. Ogilvie, 'Social institutions and proto-industrialisation', in Ogilvie and Carman, *European Proto-Industrialisation*, 33–7.

13 Gerschenkron, *Economic Backwardness*, 5–30.

14 See C. J. Berry, *Social Theory of the Scottish Enlightenment* (Edinburgh, 1997), 12, 52–73; J. Dwyer and A. Murdoch, 'Paradigms and politics: manners, morals and the rise of Henry Dundas, 1770–1784', in J. Dywer, R. A. Mason and A. Murdoch (eds), *New Perspectives on the Politics and Culture of Early Modern Scotland* (Edinburgh, 1983), 222–3.

15 G. Marshall, *Presbyteries and Profits: Calvinism and the Development of Capitalism in Scotland, 1560–1707* (Edinburgh, 1980), 247, 272.

16 R. H. Campbell, 'The influence of religion on economic growth in Scotland in the eighteenth century', in Devine and Dickson, *Ireland and Scotland*, 226; R. H. Campbell *The Rise and Fall of Scottish Industry, 1707–1939* (Edinburgh, 1980), 28; van Strien, *British Travellers*, 194–5, 199, 218.

17 Durie, *Scottish Linen Industry*, 143–57.

18 R. Finlay, 'Caledonia or North Britain? Scottish identity in the eighteenth century', in Broun, Finlay and Lynch, *Image and Identity*, 145; the same case is put somewhat more judiciously in Devine, 'Union of 1707', 28; see too Saville, 'Scottish modernisation', 20.

19 Cullen, 'Scotland and Ireland', 234, 237; Shaw, *Management*, 36.

20 For an exploratory study of this topic from a Scottish perspective, see I. Donnachie, 'The enterprising Scot?',in Donnachie and Whatley, *The Manufacture of Scottish History*, 90–105; for a wider discussion, still valuable is P. L. Payne, *British Entrepreneurship in the Nineteenth Century* (London, 1974).

21 Cullen, 'Scotland and Ireland', 241.

22 ECA, CRB, Moses Collection, SL30/226, 'Memorial from the Earl of Wemyss ... directed to the Lord Provost of Edinburgh', 1709.

23 L. Davidson, 'Introduction. The reactive state: English governance and society, 1689–1750', in L. Davidson, T. Hitchcock, T. Keir and R. B. Shoemaker (eds), *Stilling the Grumbling Hive: The Response to Social and Economic Problems in England, 1689–1750* (Stroud, 1992), xli.

24 Graham, 'Impact of mercantilism', 125–37.

25 D. A. Baugh, 'Maritime strength and Atlantic commerce', in L. Stone (ed.), *An Imperial State at War: Britain from 1689 to 1815* (London, 1994), 190–203.

26 See, for example, the perceptive but undeveloped comments on this by Mitchison, *Lordship to Patronage*, 167–9.

27 Graham, 'Impact of mercantilism', 169–79.

28 ECA, CRB, Moses Collection, SL30/242, Provost Drummond to Archibald McAulay, 17 March 1726, Drummond to Annual Committee of the Royal Burghs of Scotland, 19 March 1726; M. Jubb, 'Economic policy and economic development', in Black, *Britain in the Age of Walpole*, 124; A. Murdoch, *The People Above: Politics and Administration in Mid-Eighteenth*

Century Scotland (Edinburgh, 1980), 82–3; P. Langford, *A Polite and Commercial People: England 1727–1783* (Oxford, 1989), 215.

29 P. K. O'Brien, 'The security of the realm and the growth of the economy, 1688–1914', in P. Clarke and C. Trebilcock (eds), *Understanding Decline: Perceptions and Realities of British Economic Performance* (Cambridge, 1997), 49.

30 Examples are Devine, 'English connection'; Devine, 'Union of 1707'; Smout, 'Scotland and England'.

31 E. Hughes, *Studies in Administration and Finance, 1558–1825* (Manchester, 1934), 419.

32 Murdoch, *The People Above*, 7–8, 82–3.

33 Carlisle Record Office (CRO), Lonsdale MSS, D/Lons/W2/1/11, Sir James Lowther to John Spedding, 19 April 1750; Nash, 'English and Scottish tobacco trades', 365–6.

34 Price, 'Glasgow', 27.

35 CRO, D/Lons/W2/1/112, Sir James Lowther to John Spedding, 18 September 1750.

36 Mitchison, *Lordship to Patronage*, 167–8.

37 R. F. Dell, 'The operational record of the Clyde tobacco fleet, 1747–1775', *Scottish Economic & Social History*, II (1982), 1–17.

38 Price, *France*, Volume I, 596.

39 *Ibid.*, 663.

40 *Ibid.*, 610.

41 Devine, 'Golden age of tobacco', 155–6.

42 Murdoch, *The People Above*, 62–8, 83–4, 111.

43 NAS, Henderson of Fordell MSS, GD 172/496/32, 'Observations on the Proposed Repeal of the Coal and Salt Tax', n.d.

44 P. K. O'Brien, T. Griffiths and P. Hunt, 'Political components of the industrial revolution: Parliament and the English cotton textile industry, 1660–1774', *Economic History Review*, XLIV (August 1991), 408–9.

45 R. Harris, 'Jacobitism', in Cooke, *et al.*, *Modern Scottish History*, 30–1.

46 See Bob Harris and C. A. Whatley, '"To solemnise his majesty's birthday": new perspectives on loyalism in George II's Britain', *History*, LXXXIII (July 1998), 409–11.

47 J. Lindsay, *The Interest of Scotland Considered* (London, 1736), 1–2.

48 Quoted in Withers, *Urban Highlanders*, 49.

49 For the Highlands, see Smith, *Jacobite Estates of the Forty-Five*, 110–42.

50 O'Brien, Griffiths and Hunt, 'Political components', 410.

51 ECA, CRB, Moses Collection, SL 30/244, Letter, Alex Dundas, London, anent Duty on Foreign Linen Exported, 1 December 1737.

52 Quoted in O'Brien, Griffiths and Hunt, 'Political components', 412.

53 NLS, Erskine Murray Papers, Acc. 5127, fo. 82, 'Reasons for Continuing the Bounty on low priced British Linens', 24 November 1752.

54 Murdoch, *People Above*, 68–73; Saville, *Bank of Scotland*, 127.

55 ECA, CRB, Moses Collection, SL 30/4/6, 'Memorial for Neil McVicar, Daniel Wallace and John Colville, Commissioners appointed by the last Convention of Royal Burghs to Solicit the Aid of Parliament in favour of the Linen manufacture', 1770.

56 Price, 'Imperial economy', 88.

57 Durie, *Scottish Linen Industry*, 50.

58 A. J. Durie, 'Market forces or government intervention: the spectacular growth of the linen industry in eighteenth-century Scotland', *Scotia*, XV (1991), 1–12; Signet Library, Court of Session Papers, CSP, 'Information for George Brown and ors. master-weavers in Glasgow, defenders, in process of reduction v. those brought by David Nicholson and ors', 1768.

59 Anon., *A Candid and Impartial Discussion, By A Friend of Great Britain* (1747), 40.

60 Durie, 'Market forces', 9.

61 PKCA, Perth Burgh Records, B59/24/8/17, Provost of Perth to Sir William Dalrymple, 21 April 1742.

62 Saville, *Bank of Scotland*, 126; Durie, *Scottish Linen Industry*, 117; Shaw, *Management*, 154–61.

63 Gulvin, *Tweedmakers*, 33; C. Gulvin, *The Scottish Hosiery and Knitwear Industry, 1680–1980* (Edinburgh, 1984), 12; Tyson, 'Rise and fall', 65.

64 Donnachie, *Brewing Industry*, 13; Cochran, *Scottish Trade*, 3.

65 Devine, 'Golden age of tobacco', 157, 164, 170.

66 T. M. Devine, *The Tobacco Lords: A Study of the Tobacco Merchants of Glasgow and their Trading Activities, c. 1740–90* (Edinburgh, 1976), 34–51.

67 *Ibid.*, 18–19.

68 Cullen, 'Scotland and Ireland', 238.

69 Hancock, *Citizens of the World*, 230–7; Murdoch, *People Above*, 126–7.

70 Macinnes, *Clanship*, 229–30.

71 I. Adams and M. Somerville, *Cargoes of Despair and Hope: Scottish Emigration to North America, 1603–1803* (Edinburgh, 1993), 35–50.

72 T. M. Devine, *Clanship to Crofters' War: The Social Transformation of the Scottish Highlands* (Manchester, 1994), 178–9; J. Hunter, *A Dance Called America: The Scottish Highlands, the United States and Canada* (Edinburgh, 1994), 23–48.

73 J. Horn, 'The British diaspora: emigration from Britain, 1680–1815', in Marshall, *British Empire*, Volume II, 31.

74 Campbell, *Scotland Since 1707*, 14.

75 M. McLean, *The People of Glengarry: Highlanders in Transition, 1745–1820* (Montreal, 1993 ed.), 78–97.

76 Hunter, *Dance called America*, 54–6, 73–4.

77 See A. W. Parker, *Scottish Highlanders in Colonial Georgia: The Recruitment, Emigration, and Settlement at Darien, 1735–1741* (Athens, Georgia, 1997).

78 A. McKillop, 'The social and economic dimensions of Highland military recruitment, 1746–1815', *Scottish Local History*, XLIII (Summer 1998), 7–12; A. Murdoch, 'More "reluctant heroes". New light on military recruiting in north east Scotland, 1759–1760', *Northern Scotland*, VI (1985), 157–68.

79 NAS, State Papers, Scottish Series 2, SP 54, RH2/4/384, Archibald Campbell to Lord Justice Clerk, 3 March 1774; Hunter, *Dance Called America*, 36–41; Devine, *Clanship*, 181–2.

80 NAS, State Papers, Scottish Series 2, SP 54, RH2/4/763, Lord Advocate to the Admiral Depute, 4 September 1775; A. MacKillop, 'Highland estate

change and tenant emigration', in Devine and Young, *Eighteenth Century Scotland*, 244–5, 249.

81 J. G. Parker, 'Scottish enterprise in India, 1750–1914', in R. A. Cage (ed.), *The Scots Abroad: Labour, Capital and Enterprise, 1750–1914* (London, 1985), 191–219; G. J. Bryant, 'Scots in India in the eighteenth century', *Scottish Historical Review*, LXIV (April 1985), 22–41; Fry, *The Dundas Despotism*, 112; Macinnes, *Clanship*, 230–1.

82 Cochran, *Scottish Trade*, 110; C. A. Whatley, 'Labour in the industrialising city, *c.* 1660 to 1830', in Devine and Jackson, *Glasgow*, 380–1.

83 Cochran, *Scottish Trade*, 15–16, 77, 175.

84 *Ibid.*, 46–9; Graham, 'Impact of mercantilism', 190–7.

85 G. Jackson, 'Government bounties and the establishment of the Scottish whaling trade, 1750–1800', in Butt and Ward, *Scottish Themes*, 46–66.

86 Shaw, *Water Power*, 171, 221–2; Lindsay, 'Iron industry', 55–6; Durie, *Scottish Linen Industry*, 55–9.

87 *Glasgow Courant*, 16 March 1747; CAA, Press 18, Bundle 9, 'Memorial for the Woolen Manufacturers of Aberdeen', 10 July 1762.

88 B. F. Duckham, 'English influences in the Scottish coal industry, 1700–1815', in Butt and Ward, *Scottish Themes*, 28–45.

89 Whatley, 'New light on Nef's numbers', 6–7, 18; Devine, 'The development of Glasgow to 1830: medieval burgh to industrial city', in Devine and Jackson, *Glasgow*, 7.

90 J. Butt, 'Capital and enterprise in the Scottish iron industry, 1780–1840', in Butt and Ward, *Scottish Themes*, 75.

91 Duckham, 'English influences', 40.

92 NLS, Cadell Papers, Acc. 5381, Box 28 (2), Samuel Garbett to Wm. Cadell and Son, 30 June 1759.

93 Shaw, *Water Power*, 102–13.

94 Anon., *The Present State of Scotland Considered*, 1–9.

95 C. Kidd, 'North Britishness and the nature of eighteenth-century British patriotisms', *Historical Journal*, XXXIX (1996), 366.

96 C. Kidd, 'North Britishness', 369–70; Campbell, 'Influence of religion', 221.

97 Quoted in Murdoch, *The People Above*, 124.

98 Home, *Sketches*, I, 101; see too Phillipson, 'Culture and society', 436–8.

99 Glendinning, Macinnes and Mackenzie, *History of Scottish Architecture*, 109–31.

100 Holloway, *Patrons and Painters*, 108–9; C. McKean, 'James Craig and Edinburgh's New Town', in K. Cruft and A. Walker (eds), *James Craig, 1744–1795* (Edinburgh, 1995), 48–56; F. A. Walker, 'Urban forms, 1750–1850', in D. Mays (ed.), *The Architecture of Scottish Cities* (East Linton, 1997), 66.

101 CRO, Lonsdale MSS, D/Lons/W2/1/112, Sir James Lowther to John Spedding, 20 December 1750.

102 Dwyer and Murdoch, 'Paradigms and Politics', 219.

103 ECA, CRB, Moses Collection, SL 30/4/6, 'Petition for the Manufacturers and Dealers of Linen in Scotland', 14 July 1772.

104 ECA, CRB, Moses Collection, SL 30/4/6, George Ross to Walter Hamilton, 28 January 1779.

105 ECA, CRB, Moses Collection, SL 30/4/6, 'Accounts Anent Linen Manufactures', 1755–56.

106 Smout, 'Where had the Scottish economy got to?', 69.

107 Murdoch, *The People Above*, 1–27.

108 E. Cregeen, 'The changing role of the house of Argyll in the Scottish Highlands', in Phillipson and Mitchison, *Scotland in the Age of Improvement*, 10.

109 NLS, Saltoun Papers, MS 16566, fos 197–8, James Home to Lord Justice Clerk, August 1736; N. P. Hankins and J. Strawhorn (eds), *The Correspondence of James Boswell with James Bruce and Andrew Gibb, Overseers of the Auchinleck Estate* (Edinburgh and Yale, 1998), lv.

110 Hancock, *Citizens of the World*, 279–85.

111 Shaw, *Management*, 118.

112 *Ibid.*, 173–4.

113 CEA, CRB, Moses Collection, G. Drummond to Archibald McAulay, 17 March 1726.

114 Murdoch, *The People Above*, 72–3.

115 See Fry, *The Dundas Despotism*.

116 R. H. Campbell, 'The Enlightenment and the economy', in R. H. Campbell and A. S. Skinner (eds), *The Origins and Nature of the Scottish Enlightenment* (Edinburgh, 1982), 8–25.

117 E. J. Hobsbawm, 'Scottish reformers of the eighteenth century and capitalist agriculture', in E. J. Hobsbawm (ed.), *Peasants in History* (Oxford, 1980), 3–29.

118 Dwyer and Murdoch, 'Paradigms and politics', 223–4.

119 Campbell, 'Enlightenment and the economy', 13.

120 See D. Allan, *Virtue, Learning and the Scottish Enlightenment* (Edinburgh, 1993); D. Withrington, 'What was distinctive about the Scottish Enlightenment?', in J. S. Carter and J. H. Pittock (eds), *Aberdeen and the Enlightenment* (Aberdeen, 1987), 16; Kidd, 'North Britishness', 373.

121 J. Robertson, 'The Scottish Enlightenment', *Rivista Storica Italiana*, CVIII (1996), 82–8; Devine, *Transformation*, 65.

122 Whatley, *Industrial Revolution*, 49.

123 I. S. Ross, *Lord Kames and the Scotland of his Day* (Oxford, 1972), 43, 172.

124 D. Lieberman, 'The legal needs of a commercial society: the jurisprudence of Lord Kames', in Hont and Ignatieff, *Wealth and Virtue*, 203–34.

125 Shaw, *Management*, 254–8.

126 W. C. Lehmann, *Henry Home, Lord Kames, and the Scottish Enlightenment* (The Hague, 1971), 114.

127 Quoted in Simpson, *Lord Kames*, 363.

128 Duckham, *Scottish Coal*, 243–5.

129 I. Hont, 'The "rich country–poor country" debate in Scottish classical political economy', in Hont and Ignatieff, *Wealth and Virtue*, 271–315.

130 Hobsbawm, 'Scottish reformers', 6.

131 NAS, West Register House, CS 238/S/10/9, George Glasgow to Walter Scott, 21 February, 2 March 1774.

132 Quoted in I. S. Ross, *The Life of Adam Smith* (Oxford, 1995), 323.

133 A. B. Campbell, *The Lanarkshire Miners: A Social History of their Trade*

Unions, 1775–1874 (Edinburgh, 1979), 13–17.

134 A. Hook and R. Sher (eds), *The Glasgow Enlightenment* (East Linton, 1995), 'Introduction'.

135 R. Sher, 'Commerce, religion and the enlightenment in eighteenth-century Glasgow', in Devine and Jackson, *Glasgow*, 316.

136 *Ibid.*, 341–51.

137 NAS, Carron Company, GD 58/2/1/1, General Meetings Minute Book, 1763–1774, 22 February 1763, 33; see too, for example, NLS, Saltoun Papers, MS 17594, Copy of Scroll to Mr Goodchild, 1744.

138 NLS, Minto Papers, MS 13257, Robert Beatson to Sir Gilbert Elliot, 28 September 1767.

139 Fraser, *Conflict and Class*, 23–4.

140 Durie, *Scottish Linen Industry*, 79.

141 Whatley, 'Labour in the industrialising city', 363; Saville, *Bank of Scotland*, 125.

142 NLS, Cadell Papers, Acc. 5381, Box 29/1, 'Account of Nails Made at Carron, St Ninians and Kilsyth', n.d., *c.* 1767.

143 Whatley, 'Labour in the industrialising city', 365.

144 Duckham, 'English influences', 37.

145 NAS, Carron Company, General Meetings Minute Book, August 1765, 171.

146 C. A. Whatley, 'The experience of labour', in Devine and Mitchison, *People and Society*, 238.

147 Whyte, 'Proto-industrialisation', 246.

148 Gibson and Smout, *Prices, Food and Wages*, 281.

149 For broader discussion of this and other issues relating to women's work, see B. Hill, *Women, Work, and Sexual Politics in Eighteenth-Century England* (1994 ed.).

150 *Ibid.*, 289–90.

151 NLS, Saltoun Papers, MS 17595 fo. 103, 'Memorial relating to the Bleachfield of Saltoun', 1762.

152 C. A. Whatley, 'Women and the economic transformation of Scotland, *c.* 1740–1830', *Scottish Economic & Social History*, XIV (1994), 27.

153 Signet Library, Court of Session Papers, CSP 87:8, Information for Robert White, 1762.

154 Sanderson, *Women and Work*, 74–6.

155 Whatley, 'Women and the economic transformation', 33.

156 C. A. Whatley, 'Collier serfdom in mid-eighteenth century Scotland: new light from the Rothes manuscripts', *Archives*, XXII (April 1995), 31–3.

157 R. Mitchison, 'Who were the poor in Scotland, 1690–1830?', in Mitchison and Roebuck, *Economy and Society*, 145.

158 Whatley, 'Women and the economic transformation', 20.

159 CAA, Enactment Books, 1730–41, 24 November 1740.

160 Whyte, 'Proto-industrialisation', 246–7.

161 Gibson and Smout, *Prices, Food and Wages*, 348–56; Houston, *Social Change*, 79–81.

162 Tyson, 'Rise and fall', 69–71.

163 See Houston, *Social Change*, 79, and Hill, *Women, Work and Sexual Politics*, 262.

164 Durie, *British Linen Company*, 30.

165 Whyte and Whyte, 'Geographical mobility of women', 88.

166 Withers, *Urban Highlanders*, 63–4.

167 Whyte and Whyte, 'Geographical mobility of women', 97; Gibson and Smout, *Prices, Food and Wages*, 289.

168 See Dwyer, *Virtuous Discourse*; Dwyer, *The Age of the Passions*, 180–1.

169 P. A. G. Monro, 'The professor's daughter: an essay on female conduct', *Proceedings of the Royal College of Physicians of Edinburgh*, XXVI (January 1996), 12–13.

170 Lindsay, *Reasons for Encouraging the Linen Manufacture*, 52.

171 Adams and Somerville, *Cargoes of Despair and Hope*, 82.

172 McKillop, 'Social and economic dimensions of Highland military recruitment', 9–10.

173 Durie, *Scottish Linen Industry*, 124–8.

174 Gibson and Smout, *Prices, Food and Wages*, 291–2.

175 Tyson, 'Contrasting regimes', 66; Whyte, 'Urbanisation in eighteenth-century Scotland', 184.

176 Devine, 'Urbanisation', 29–31.

177 Whyte, 'Scottish and Irish urbanisation', 16.

178 Jackson, 'Scottish shipping', 123.

179 S. Nenadic, 'The rise of the urban middle classes', in Devine and Mitchison, *People and Society*, 114–18; Nenadic, 'The middle ranks and modernisation', in Devine and Jackson, *Glasgow*, 279–85; H. M. Boot, 'Salaries and career earnings in the Bank of Scotland, 1730–1880', *Economic History Review*, XLIV (November 1991), 629, 635–6.

180 T. A. Markus, P. Robinson and F. A. Walker, 'The shape of the city in space and stone', in Devine and Jackson, *Glasgow*, 115–19.

181 I. H. Adams (ed.), *Papers on Peter May, Land Surveyor, 1749–1793* (Edinburgh, 1979), xxiii; Hankins and Strawhorn, *Correspondence of James Boswell*, xliv; Campbell, 'The Landed Classes', 102–3.

182 Devine, *Transformation*, 70.

183 *Ibid.*, 37, 46.

184 Smout, 'Where had the Scottish economy got to?', 62; Houston, *Social Change*, 226.

4

Scottish society, c. 1707–c. 1778 (I): investigating stability and protest

An uninflammable people?

Thus far, our main focus has been on economic development, the middling and upper ranks in their role as agents of change, the state and economic legislation. The labouring classes have been included only in relation to their role as consumers and as factors of production. This chapter pays greater attention to the labouring poor as actors on the historical stage. It is also concerned with social relations in a society which was experiencing dramatic fluctuations in its economic fortunes; profound political change in the shape of the Union and arrival of the Hanoverians in 1714; the encroachment into north Britain of the policies and agencies of the British state; and the early stages of concentrated and self-conscious economic and social reformation.

The traditional view of Scottish society in the eighteenth century is of quite remarkable social stability through to, and in the opinion of some historians through, the French Revolution, which broke out within the first decades of Scotland's early Industrial Revolution.[1] This is a depiction which has its roots in the eighteenth century itself, wherein the Union was credited with transforming Scottish manners and rescuing Scotland from barbarism, anarchy and unruliness, introducing in their place economic development, political order and cultural enlightenment.[2] The shorter period with which this chapter is concerned, the three-quarters of a century which preceded the Industrial and French Revolutions, has until very recently been portrayed by most historians as one of exceptional social calm, with the thick crust of paternalism and deference only being broken through on a handful of occasions like the Levellers' Revolt in Galloway (1724–5), the Shawfield Riot in Glasgow (1725) and the Porteous Riot in Edinburgh in 1736, when a mob lynched the captain of the town guard (Porteous), whose soldiers had previously shot and killed unarmed citizens. Serious disorder and threats to the tranquillity of Argathelian Scotland are generally thought to have been largely confined to the Highlands and Episcopalian strongholds in the Lowlands, where Jacobitism continued to attract militant support until 1745.[3] Otherwise, however, apart from some grumbling in the burghs, Lowland Scots were 'Quiet and law-abiding', and Glaswegians, for example, 'well-ordered folk'.[4]

Phrases such as these and such supporting evidence as there is, create the impression of a world of mutual interdependence, social homogeneity and 'rock-like' social stability.[5] As recently as 1980 popular protest in the eighteenth century was described as 'sporadic, largely spontaneous and short-lived ... just a trial run for the working-class struggles of the nine-teenth century'.[6] The challenge for Scottish historians it was declared, was to account for the 'relative lack of social discontent and either urban or peasant unrest'.[7]

The common people in Scotland have been typified as being deferen-tial, dutiful and even dull, ignorant of and unconcerned by great national events such as the Union of 1707, responding only unthinkingly, and not unusually with their passions roused by strong drink, to crude stimuli such as rises in the price of food.[8] Even Marxist historians have tended to write off the first half of the eighteenth century as far as the labouring classes are concerned. Little of significance is believed to have happened prior to the 1770s when what are assumed (wrongly) to have been the country's first meal riots and strikes took place.[9] This historiographical tradition has been enormously influential, affecting the ways historians have written about and interpreted other aspects of Scottish society, including politics and popular culture. Thus it has been suggested that other than in the Northern Isles and north-east Lowlands, the Scots were 'less musical' than their English, French and Welsh counterparts. Songs and poetry of protest other than those concerned with Whig and Jacobite politics were assumed to have been mainly nineteenth-century produc-tions. Although not entirely unreasonably, popular culture (as traditionally defined) has been represented as lacking energy, and both ritually and relatively impoverished.[10]

There is however a growing body of evidence which is beginning to provide the empirical basis for a challenge to what can be described as the 'orthodoxy of passivity'. That there was a higher incidence of riot and other symptoms of social conflict than was thought previously has been established.[11] What has been largely lacking from the published literature however are interpretive frameworks which enable us to identify and better understand the dynamics of social relations in eighteenth-century Scotland. What follows in this and the next chapter is a re-assessment of the Scottish evidence, together with some which has not been published hitherto. Where appropriate, models of social relations which historians have applied elsewhere have provided the initial framework, although as will be seen while these can be enormously useful, the uniqueness of the

Scottish experience imposes limits on their applicability.

This is not to say that the older view is altogether wrong or indeed that Scotland was unduly disorderly in the eighteenth century. It will be argued however that the social and political significance of the popularly-supported disorder in the first four decades of the century has been both underestimated and imperfectly understood. As has been seen and will be gathered in more detail as the chapter proceeds, the traditional interpretation does rest on enormously powerful and long-established intellectual foundations, particularly where it applies to rural society.[12] The current chapter however deals with the period before *c.* 1780; the absence of significant agrarian discontent is usually deemed to have been after this date, when in spite of undergoing massive transformation the rural Lowlands of Scotland experienced nothing like the major outbreaks of peasant unrest which occurred in Ireland in every decade between 1760 and 1840. This will be considered later.

Even so, the traditionalists have ventured opinions on the earlier decades, and are prepared to concede less than a handful of instances of resistance to change in the countryside, while some judge there to have been only one significant case of resistance to the 'claims of property.'[13] The virtual absence of 'major' instances of protest against enclosure is deemed to provide conclusive proof of the absence of significant rural discontent. What is argued here is that for the first six or seven decades of the eighteenth century there is another, less restrained, less deferential and more rumbustious and violent Scotland in both town and countryside, which this chapter seeks to reveal and analyse. But most rural change tended to be piecemeal, carried on estate by estate, and even at varying rates of speed within a particular estate. Therefore we should not expect to find large-scale outbreaks of disorder resulting from this. Instances of agrarian protest were unusual in England where, instead, rural crime as a form of social protest appears to have been commonplace.[14] We will discover however many more smaller contests over land and, on the land, between landowners, tenant farmers and their expanding army of proletarianised workers, than have been previously recognised by historians.

The social order may not have been actually endangered either in the countryside or the towns, but there were occasions when the ruling classes felt sufficiently threatened by incidents in which the 'mob' was involved, to take evasive action at the highest levels of both local and national government to blunt their cutting edge, particularly during the first four post-Union decades of political and economic integration. It is revealing, for instance, that early in 1725, a year of extraordinary unruliness during a decade which had begun with large-scale disorder induced by fears of dearth, a correspondent of the Lord Advocate regretted that 'in questions or matters of popular concern we must either follow the multitude or be looked upon as deserters of our Country's Interests'.[15] Patriotism – in this case represented by calls to resist the imposition by Westminster of a higher tax on malt (and therefore ale) – was not the sole property of the upper ranks. Throughout the rest of the period, it will be argued, the maintenance of order was dependent upon a continuing accommodation with the common people.

Structures and mechanisms of power

Central to the explanation for Scottish quiescence in the eighteenth century is the effectiveness of the structures and agents of social control. At the apex of Scottish rural society was the landowner. Long-established in most cases until the land market became more fluid after *c.* 1760, they were able to exploit their 'inherited authority' in order to achieve acceptance of change in the countryside.[16] Paternalism and the preparedness of many landowners to intervene in the market from *c.* 1740 and purchase and sell grain to the impoverished country dwellers at subsidised prices, and their *'willingness'* to be rated for poor relief, are judged to have been critical factors in maintaining the old rural social order.[17]

Arguably, Scotland had 'the most concentrated pattern of landowner-ship in Europe', with the position of the landed classes being consolidated at the expense of smaller lairds throughout the eighteenth century. Around 1770 the proportion of landholders in Scotland may have been a mere 2.3 per cent (or at most, 5 per cent) of the male population of twenty-one and over, a much lower rate of ownership than in England and Wales, Scandinavia or North America. At the same time there were around 7,800 landowners in Scotland, with the largest estates being in the Borders and the south-east (regions which were straddled by the separate estates of the biggest landowners in Scotland, the dukes of Buccleuch). The north-east and the Highlands too contained large estates. Lesser proprietors were more common in the south-west, Kinross, Stirling and Banff, the location of most of the country's 'bonnet lairds', or small owner occupiers.[18]

On their estates, landowners wielded immense power. Unlike much of the rest of Europe there were few peasant proprietors in Scotland, a factor which greatly eased the process of rural transformation, although in the Highlands peasants adhered 'tenaciously' to the traditionalist concept of *dutchchas*, discussed earlier. Both Jacobite- and Hanoverian-inclined clan chiefs abandoned customary obligations to their clansmen in favour of estate rationalisation. Nonetheless, in what in some respects was still a martial society in which personal loyalties were strong and where memories of hospitality and protection were enduring, landlord authority could be exercised even more readily than in the Lowlands;

vernacular poets tended to blame factors, legal agents, tacksmen and incoming tenant farmers (and sheep) for their ills, rarely their former clan chiefs and *fine*.[19]

In the Lowlands, tenants who held land on leases could be removed at the end of their term. Tenants, subtenants and cottars, along with other estate dwellers – craftsmen such as weavers, shoe-makers and millers – were bound by the feudal rights and privileges of their landed masters. Until the heritable jurisdictions were abolished in 1747, in the aftermath of Culloden, these included the holding of birlay and baron courts (which were retained but with much-reduced powers), and regality courts. The first were more concerned with ensuring good neighbourly relations, something like a community court; the second had been more powerful and authorised to deal with petty crimes including violence but not murder, rape, robbery and fire-raising. (These crimes had been tried in regality courts but by the end of the seventeenth century the national courts had largely superseded them.) In reality there was much overlap in terms of the business dealt with by the different courts. Punishment meted out by the barony courts included fines and imprisonment in the estate 'pit'.[20] When they were convened frequently, they appear to have had something of a restraining effect on the behaviour of estate workers: in 1719 at Wemyss, for example, it was reported that the colliers and salters had become 'unruly' because the court had not sat recently.[21] As landowners withdrew from daily or at least regular involvement in the affairs of their estate at this level, the problem of control became more difficult. Thirlage and some other remnants of 'feudal servitude' carried on for longer, although resented, into the early nineteenth century in some instances.[22]

This however was only part of the available legal apparatus. The law, both pre- and post-Union, reinforced proprietorial power beyond the confines of the estate, even though up to 1747 the legal system in Scotland appears at first sight to have been complex, variegated and highly decentralised.[23] Difficult or recalcitrant estate dwellers were sent to be dealt with by burgh magistrates or a sheriff court (which could hand down capital punishment), according to location and the nature and severity of the alleged crime.

The principal improving legislation favouring the landed interest passed by the Scottish Parliament in the later seventeenth century has already been noted. The process of land reform was further eased by an Act of Sederunt of the Lords of Council and Session in 1756. In effect this created a relatively quickly-implemented and straightforward legal mechanism for removing a tenant and his family along with any other subtenants, cottars and dependants. Landed hegemony was further buttressed by the political and social authority of their positions as legal and administrative agents of the state at county and local level. This was as Commissioners of Supply, who by the mid-eighteenth century were largely drawn from the ranks of the lesser landowners; and Justices of the Peace, created in Scotland by James VI in 1609 (with a previous attempt having been made in 1587), and periodically revived thereafter. However, they were never as powerful as in England. Most of their members were landholders, with a sprinkling of representatives from the royal burghs and some lawyers. They did grow in number during the course of the eighteenth century however, became increasingly loyal (considerable numbers of Jacobite sympathisers had managed to obtain commissions in the early decades of the century, and continued to infiltrate the system until the mid-1750s), and played a minor role in the maintenance of law and order. Mainly used to exert economic controls until mid-century, with their considerable powers in this sphere they set the wages of crafts-men and rural labourers and determined the length of contracts and conditions of service. Up until the 1780s, when employers became less enthusiastic about legal controls over wages, they had made frequent use of the courts' regulatory capacities and their belief in the subordination of workers to their masters.[24] They also contributed to commercial devel-opment by setting uniform weights and measures and improving roads and bridges.[25]

With the strengthening of the sheriff courts after the abolition of the heritable jurisdictions, the sheriffs-depute became the 'key' to the legal and administrative system in the Scottish counties. 'Invariably' leading members of the aristocracy, they were of major importance to central government which they represented within their spheres of influence (and provided crucial reinforcement for commercial developments in the local-ities). Proof of their loyalty to the Union and Hanover was of paramount importance, although in the period with which this chapter is concerned, they were appointed on the recommendation of county magnates and some Jacobites did secure places on the bench.[26] Above them was the High Court of Justiciary (dealing with criminal cases), and the main civil court, the Court of Session. Such was the legal system in Scotland, largely preserved by the Union, that there was a stronger presumption of guilt on the part of offenders than either in Ireland or England. Brought before courts, criminals in Scotland were more likely to be convicted.[27]

Patronage, it is argued, the 'filaments' of which 'went through all levels of society like the mycelium of dry rot through old woodwork', ensured the support and loyalty of the people below.[28] At the lowest levels social conformity was expected and, more often than not, obtained, through the activities of the Scottish kirk. Physical force it is suggested, was little needed or used in Scotland to maintain order.[29]

Kirk control overlapped with the power exercised by landowners, their baillies or factors, and constables appointed as parish representatives of the Justices. Kirk sessions, revitalised from the Reformation, were parish church courts, through which the impact of the Church of Scotland was mainly felt within the local communities. The sessions comprised the minister and session clerk, and from the main parish settlements, non-clerical elders. As they were usually men of some substance, they might include one or more landowners from within the parish, although in the towns the elders would typically be merchants, craftsmen and professionals, with considerable overlap in the personnel of civil and kirk office-holders.[30] Relatively little has been published on the operations and impact of the kirk sessions in the towns. The indications however are that the church and town councils shared similar objectives and worked closely together as adherence to Protestantism spread in the second half of the sixteenth century.[31] They were united in their detestation of 'whores' and brothels. That burgh and kirk were working hand in hand by the end of the seventeenth century in Aberdeen can be seen from the 'Instructions' issued to the town's constables in 1697. A lengthy list of their responsibilities included apprehending vagabonds, sturdy beggars and those who would not 'take themselves to some trade', and demanding testimonials from strangers, but they were also to 'delate' or inform upon fornicators, 'whoremongers', sabbath breakers as well as disobedient children, servants and those who stole from their masters. Aberdeen was unusual however in having separate courts for secular and ecclesiastical crimes; elsewhere in the eighteenth century it was usual for kirk sessions to call upon the civil authorities to buttress their authority where offenders were being recalcitrant for instance, or to deal with cases where the alleged offender was deemed 'not to be a fit object of church discipline' – a Roman Catholic for example.[32]

Church law made no distinctions of rank, but while some landowners did appear before kirk sessions, such occasions were rare, despite – for instance – evidence of the involvement of young men of that class in Edinburgh's little-known Hell-Fire Club in the early eighteenth century, notorious apparently for its orgiastic activities. Anstruther's 'Beggars Benison', was founded in 1732 and allegedly included aristocrats, customs officers and even parish ministers among its members, whose initiation rites included penis exposure.[33] If at the lower levels of society females felt the strictures of kirk discipline more acutely than males, women from the gentry and the wealthier ranks could usually find a way of evading rebuke.[34] With the Patronage Act of 1712, landowner influence over the choice of minister was regained (after this right had been removed in 1690), as it was by other powerful patrons, the Crown, town councils and the universities. For the former the advantage was that the kirk session was 'hardly likely to beard him [the appointing landowner] for minor or even major peccadilloes.'[35] Boards of heritors (owners of heritable property), separate from the kirk session, but composed of parish landowners, were responsible for the provision and upkeep of the church and the payment of the minister; in the royal burghs the heritors were the town councils.

Mainly concerned with ecclesiastical offences, and zealous above all in its dealings with perpetrators of sexual immorality, the kirk session, comparable to a 'parish state', also dealt with matters such as social welfare (poor relief), education, rites of passage (birth, marriage and death) and social order, condemning for example 'profane language', excessive drinking and failure to observe the sabbath. Even 'standing idle', travelling and carrying water on Sundays brought reprimands.[36] The parish court structure was widely spread, interlocking and tightly organised, and rigorous in its procedures – much more so than the English system, as well as being ruthless and fairly uniform in its concerns about and attitudes to sin until the 1770s and 1780s, although there were some regional variations, notably between the Lowlands and the Highlands.[37] Penalties were harsh and often humiliating, all but the most minor rebukes being carried out in full public gaze, the sinner perched upon the 'cutty stool' or 'stool of repentance' in front of the congregation, or stood at the church door clad in sackcloth.[38] The effectiveness of kirk control is best seen in the low rates of illegitimacy in those parts of Scotland where the rule of the kirk was strongest; that is, the central belt of Lowland Scotland. Where levels were higher, as in Ayrshire and Galloway and the north-east, these can reasonably be accounted for by specific cultural factors, Covenanting sentiment and resistance to Church of Scotland rule in the former, and the tradition of Episcopalianism in the latter. 'Testificats', certificates of good behaviour necessary for both men and women who wished to move from one parish to another, 'were not issued as a matter of course'. Indeed the kirk in Scotland has been described as the 'handmaiden of nascent capitalism', accustoming the poor to social discipline through preaching and the exercise of 'Godly Discipline'. Above all, this included the ubiquitous parish schools – 'bastions of social order' – thereby inculcating the values of 'restraint and hard work'.[39]

Challenging the 'orthodoxy of passivity'

This is an impressive body of evidence and some of it is beyond dispute. Yet the structures of power and the mechanisms by which it was maintained are not to be confused with their effectiveness, nor should the overwhelming grandeur of its external appearance – the theatrical props of rank and authority such as powdered wigs, fine clothing and 'hauteur of bearing and expression', even the slow and deliberate procession of the judges for each sitting of the Circuit Court, lit by torches after dark.[40] The structures of power and authority in Scotland were in some respects awesome, but there were issues of such importance and beliefs which were sufficiently strongly held, that there were those who were prepared to risk the penalties and punishments which their actions in defence of them might invoke. There are flaws in the 'orthodoxy of passivity'. Three of these will be investigated in depth here.

Considerable emphasis has been placed on the concepts of paternalism and deference in eighteenth-century Scotland. Yet the former has rarely been defined when applied to the Scottish situation, and in order to have any force as an analytical concept it has to be.[41] Usually implicit is the notion of patriarchy, a stern but warm and also one-sided relationship, its operation determined by the whims and wishes of the benevolent laird or lord, or in the towns by the urban elites. This is not to deny the existence of many genuine acts of benevolence on the part of the upper ranks, in the provision of aid in the form of money, meal or housing for aged estate employees, for example, or for the sick and the poor. But, unqualified, it is a 'model of the social order as it is seen from above', in which the price of filial deference is assumed to be low, a confusion of the actual with the ideal.[42] It pervades much of the historical literature however, even that written relatively recently, as where a historian of the Scottish coal industry celebrates the 'humane employer [the duke of Buccleuch]' for *allowing* his men to return to their homes near Dalkeith 'almost as soon' as a new colliery at Canonbie in Dumfriesshire had been won.[43] Yet a quick look, perhaps with a more cynical eye, at the Buccleuch estate's deputy chamberlain's journal for 1768 shows quite clearly that the colliers' stay at Canonbie had been fraught with frequent disputes and that in September they were dismissed and sent home in favour of local coal workers: the Lothian men had simply been too troublesome and expensive.[44]

An older but equally telling example is the late Professor Henry Hamilton's assumptions about authority on the estate of the Grants of Monymusk: 'At the centre of the social and economic life of the estate was the village or Kirkton ... with its church and its school'. Close by was the house of the heritor or landlord, 'the House of Monymusk', from whence was conducted the all-important barony court.[45] This however is an older and unsatisfactory description of a type of social relationship which is essentially reciprocal. It demands certain kinds of response on the part of the 'people above' who by defaulting in their obligations to their social inferiors could suffer individual discomfort and collective loss. There were limits to the actions those in formal positions of power and authority could take. Power and decision-making were not exercised at will, as the proprietors of barony courts who tried to manage their woodlands on commercial lines found to their cost.[46] This is not to say that the labouring poor either intended to overthrow the social order or had the means of doing so, far from it. Applicable here is what has been called the 'old dialectic of deference', a simultaneous awareness of social differentiation from the 'people above' and identification with them and, accordingly, a preparedness on the part of the common people to accept their subordination.[47] Normally this was a social system which sustained the common people, with land, employment, assistance in times of need, and supplied their spiritual needs and to varying degrees their identity and sense of belonging, to occupation or craft, community, religion, monarch and country. Yet its stability could be upset, there were those who were less dependent or not quite so subject to the apparatus of control, there were alternative definitions of the social situation, different readings of how matters should be conducted. The lower orders could be resentful when customary ways of doing things were threatened by innovations or alterations in practices which appeared to be disadvantageous, or if proper provision for their relief ceased. They could be vengeful and rebellious without being revolutionaries.

'Vertical' ties of loyalty were still strong in the early decades of the eighteenth century, and continued to provide one of the contour lines of Scottish society for much of the rest of the century, albeit much less pronounced later on. In 1708, for example, Robert Cunninghame, laird of Auchenharvie (in north Ayrshire) and a coalowner, was alleged to have raised a mob to assault a near neighbour and rival, William Blair of Blair. Sand was also poured down one of his coal pits. The 'mob' who followed Cunninghame had included not only several of his servants, colliers and coal grieves, but also sailors, skippers, merchants and craftsmen along with some of their wives and daughters who also resided in Cunninghame's burgh of barony, Saltcoats. In 1713 Major George Munro of Auchinbowie led a party of men from his barony in an attempt to break down a dam on the Bannockburn in the grounds of a neighbouring landlord as it was alleged to have been interrupting the former's flow of water.[48]

Similarly, most riots in Edinburgh in the later seventeenth and early eighteenth centuries tended to reinforce rather than weaken the social order by uniting participants from all ranks in popular opposition to 'outsiders'. The reasons why crowds formed were not always clear, and those involved might not share the same beliefs or objectives. They could be motivated by a variety of causes, depending on which issues were current at the time. However Catholics, Englishmen and the army, especially where soldiers were billeted on the inhabitants, were among the more common objects of the hostility of crowds in which apprentices especially (who were younger, needed to let off steam and had less to lose), but also journeymen featured prominently. They also had – usually – the tacit support of masters, merchants and even the magistracy, who elsewhere, as in Haddington in 1726, frequently protested against the 'great charges' and social costs – one of these was unwanted pregnancies

– of quartering soldiers. Annual pope-burning rituals continued long into the century under the watchful and nervous magistracy who were power-less to intervene.[49] Earlier, but after the Scots began to enjoy the benefits of Hanoverian imperialism, large crowds would gather in the burghs to celebrate military and naval victories, as with the 'great Rejoicings' in Glasgow in May 1747 which followed Admiral Anson's success over the French fleet, or the capture of Cape Breton in 1758. In Dundee in 1757–58 alone British victories in some seven battles or conquests were publicly celebrated.[50]

Competing loyalties, not of class but of political affiliation both united and divided urban communities in the first decades of the eighteenth century, with well-supported demonstrations involving all ranks being orchestrated on the birthdays of the reigning monarchs (not only of Britain, but also of Protestant allies) as well as those of Stuart aspirants to the throne. Supporters of the Hanoverians and Jacobite sympathisers in both Kinghorn and Stirling clashed on King George II's birthday in 1734.[51]

Contested burgh elections too could see the raising of rival mobs, as in Cupar in 1722 when an attempt was made to end the supremacy of the earls of Rothes in the town, although there was a Jacobite tinge to this disturbance which, as arms were involved, necessitated the intervention of the military.[52] In the north Ayrshire burgh of Irvine lively squabbles over the earls of Eglinton's efforts to secure the burgh for the family and their supporters were an ongoing feature in the eighteenth century.[53]

The needs and ideals of neighbourhood and community pulled people together and caused them to be hostile to perceived threats. Whether or not because of the difficult economic circumstances which marked the turn of the eighteenth century, and forced vulnerable communities to close ranks, and, on the other hand, drove some individuals to seek sexual satisfaction in non-tenable relationships, there are signs too that gender could act as a crucial link in maintaining the 'ruthless efficiency' with which the more godly rural and small burgh communities of Lowland Scotland sought to uncover sexual crimes. Older women and midwives (possibly representing a venerable moral order), aided and abetted by ministers and elders who might otherwise have missed the signs of pregnancy, were the principal agents in suspecting and identify-ing females – usually young, alone and necessarily furtive – who were accused of infanticide, a crime which prior to 1740, was likely to be punished by all-male courts by hanging.[54] Punishment by use of the branks (a metal bridle incorporating a spur which restricts speech), which continued to be applied into the early eighteenth century, was almost wholly confined to women, although other women were often the targets of the insults of the accused, who rarely came from the upper ranks.[55]

Separate and distinct trades incorporations, which had become firmly established in the Scottish burghs by the sixteenth century, continued to celebrate and defend their monopolies and privileges and blurred the differences between masters and journeymen, instead uniting in a common cause tailors, shoemakers, wrights, coopers and other tradesmen with their brethren of the same craft. The thirty or so masonic lodges which were in existence in Scotland around 1710 played a similar role in the stonemason trade, although there were lodges of journeymen only. However, the admission of non-operatives in some lodges may have served, at least for the time they remained members, to bind men of different ranks in the bonds of friendship, annual banqueting and mystic ritual.[56] Equally, trades incorporations could be, and were, fraught with internal divisions over both national and local political matters, upon which views independent of the nation's political managers and the aristocratic elite were expressed.[57] Increasingly however, masters and journeymen would turn on each other in disputes over hours and wages.

As this suggests, albeit confusedly (at least to the eye of the historian) solidarities which would later be described as those of class were emerging. By the early 1740s in Edinburgh an economically and socially distinctive and self-conscious 'middling sort' had begun to emerge, visible in changing cultural pursuits and their commercial behaviour which included the purchase of goods such as watches, coaches and tea. While in Glasgow at the same time such a mental framework was largely absent, change had become apparent throughout urban Scotland from the 1760s.[58] Indeed symbolic of the visibility of the widening divide between the labouring poor, and the middling ranks and a landed elite which in the economic sphere at least shared with merchants and others a belief in commercial values, was the nationwide campaign, begun in Aberdeen in 1759, to abolish vails, tips given to servants by departing visitors from a house. The issue was fought 'in the name of politeness' and to replace a system of crude servility and mutual dependence by one which maintained a 'measured distance between master and servant'.[59] We will return to the issue of class divisions later.

The evidence that respect for landed authority was conditional and not granted as a matter of course is difficult to ignore. Indeed it is frequently the public declarations of their property rights and authority which reveal their vulnerability, as in 1749 and 1750, when a large body of landowners from Glasgow and the west of Scotland declared their intention of coming down hard on poachers.[60] Their concern, matched within the city itself by numerous reports of thieving and beggary and other symptoms of social disorder, was part of a wider awareness – or belief – among the middling and upper classes that in the aftermath of the War of the Austrian Succession Britain was suffering from a serious and socially-destabilising crime wave.[61]

Although by no means new in the eighteenth century, there was growing resentment at the political domination of and interference in burgh affairs by landed magnates. This degenerated into violence in a number of burghs, most notably Cupar in 1722, referred to above, Duns in 1730 when the skinners led the opposition of the burgh to the intervention of the proprietors of Duns Castle who were attempting to run the town on more commercial lines. In Dumfries in 1759 craftsmen and labourers united to oppose the influence of the third duke of Queensberry. In spite of the efforts of men such as Ilay to 'deliver' tame Scottish MPs at Westminster, patronage and bribery were not always sufficient to win parliamentary elections. The three burghs referred to were by no means the only ones to experience struggles of the sort recounted here, although national-local political relationships are an aspect of political history which, like the smaller Scottish towns in general, requires further investigation before confident judgements can safely be made.[62]

The Duns example, which was only part of an ongoing dispute over custom and commercialism, demonstrates that there were challenges to landed initiatives, formal authority notwithstanding. Enclosure walls on the property of Sir James Carmichael, JP, of Bonnington, near Lanark, were torn down in 1718.[63] Something similar happened in Cromarty in 1732, when a five hundred-strong crowd pulled down a dyke and tore up trees which were designed to limit access to peat diggings.[64] In December 1724 the Commissioners of Supply for Aberdeenshire, then engaged in an ambitious programme of road and bridge improvement, found the officers they had appointed for raising funds subjected to a 'Ryot of deforcement' by the inhabitants of the town of Inverurie; two years later their new roads had been 'spoiled and abused' by people throwing stones upon them. The underlying reasons why John Cockburn should have asked in 1742 that a dozen soldiers be stationed at his new planned village of Ormiston are unclear, other than that they were to 'protect the Manufactures' from a mob which had been threatening the inhabitants. They are likely however to have been linked to his schemes for estate modernisation.[65] Lord Findlater's noble status mattered little in 1755 when he attempted to move the weekly market from Old Keith to the planned village of New Keith, which resulted in his agents being attacked, beaten and forced to flee, wigless, 'by a very great Multitude of women'.[66]

While such instances serve a purpose in showing the range and nature of conflict in the countryside, it may be objected that they are atypical, have been selected at random and reveal only sporadic tensions (although as has been suggested, this is how we might expect the evidence to emerge). Yet not only do they correspond to what is known about the changing nature of social relations in the Lowlands in the early eighteenth century but they can be placed within a broader context of emergent tensions within rural society. Not dissimilar to the cases examined above but more striking and hitherto largely unnoticed by historians were the rearguard actions being fought by a number of burghs in the early eighteenth century to resist the attempts by neighbouring landlords to recover and enclose land which the burghs had held as commons 'past memory of man'. This meant centuries in some cases, as at Dysart in Fife, where since 1543 the town's inhabitants had had the right from the St Clair estate to the gravel, clay, turf, heather, fuel and divots from the adjoining moor, along with 60 acres they had permission to labour in return for a small annual feu duty. However, from the later seventeenth century feudal superiority and common use were being subordinated to the 'explicit class interest' of landowners anxious to exploit the rights allocated to them under the Commonty Act of 1695 and to secure their properties in law and with visible boundaries.[67]

A survey of Convention of Royal Burgh papers reveals the existence of a series of what were often long-running contests of this nature in most parts of the Lowlands, spread as widely as Wick (1711), Banff (1712) and Forres (1725) in the north, Culross (1718) in the south-east, Dumbarton (1726) in the west and Lochmaben (1710) to the south-west. Local records reveal similar disputes, at Duns (1730), for example, and Cullen in the north-east, where in 1733 the earl of Findlater (who was also the burgh's hereditary Constable) announced that he was preserving for himself certain moss lands which until then had been used by the burgh's inhabitants.[68] Further searches will almost certainly uncover further instances. Some of these cases – that usually culminated in Court of Session proceedings, which most of the burghs could ill afford – involved a measure of intimidation and violence. So vexed were the baillies and councillors of the burgh of Crail in March 1719 at the 'incroachment of the town's Common muir by ... parking and inclosing' on the part of Colonel Philip Anstruther and his servants that they threatened to send out the townspeople to 'throw doune ... [the] dykes & ditches'.[69]

It was only from the 1760s and 1770s that enclosure in Lowland Scotland was carried out extensively.[70] But to dismiss such earlier attempts as there were as the misguided efforts of aristocratic amateurs interested in 'Improvement' only for its own sake is to ignore the very real conflicts there were between the parties concerned, and the resultant costs in terms of damaged social relationships. Thus in October 1707 Sir Alexander Areskine, Lord Lyon, described estate improvement as his 'great pleasure in life ... [his] only Diversion', yet he was both distressed and anxious to enhance his legal status within the Stewartry of Falkland in Fife, as then he would be better able to strike fear into those 'subtenants, servants and Cottars' who were breaking down his enclosures and destroying his young planting.[71] There is little sign here of the 'delicate ties of hierarchy and dependence' which it is claimed ensured the 'extraordinarily peaceful' transition to capitalist agriculture in eighteenth-century Scotland.[72]

Although slowly, the pace of agrarian change was accelerating, and, as has been seen, tradition and, where necessary, consensus were under attack. For those landowners concerned it was a serious business, and is almost certain to have contributed to the doubling of real rents which occurred between c. 1660 and c. 1740.[73] For the affected towns' inhabitants the effects could be grave, as at Wick where it was protested that the actions of James Dunbar of Hempriggs and others in seizing the 'hill of Wick', which allegedly involved the use of dogs, 'brings the poor Inhabitants under very Straitening Circumstances through want of grazing to their Cattle which is their main support'. They also lost their traditional right to take 'all manner of white fish from the bay', landowners poinding the nets and other equipment of those found fishing there.[74]

Notwithstanding the many competing pulls on their allegiance, the labouring poor had a strong collective sense of their perceived customary rights; equally, their rulers recognised the potential they had to cause trouble. Examples abound, but a few must suffice at this stage. In February 1698 the tenants of George Lockhart of Carnwath complained of their 'sad condition' in the aftermath of the crop failure of 1697 and previous years. They requested an abatement of their rent, although not simply by appealing to the patriarch Lockhart's generosity, but on the grounds of comparability and fairness, much as early combinations of proletarianised coal workers or tailors did in support of their demands for higher wages. Neighbouring tenants, 'who did not suffer as much', had been relieved of paying part of their rents. Lockhart conceded because, he calculated, if he did not grant an abatement his tenants would 'embezzle everything they can lay their hands on', whereby he would be 'a far greater loser'.[75] Others were slower to recognise the subtle shift which was taking place in relations between classes as landed interest in the commercial exploitation of their property grew (although theft from fields and orchards was nothing new).[76] In 1724 John Gray, baillie of the burgh and barony of Duns in Berwickshire, complained indignantly that his attempts to put a stop to the townspeople's annual game of football on 'Fasting's Even' had led to an attack on his house and threats to the lives of himself and his family. Worse apparently was the blow to his 'authoritie in the burgh'. This should have been, but was not, 'sufficient to have defended him against anie insult'.[77]

Open opposition to landowner initiatives in the countryside in Scotland however appears to have been unusual, although given the huge inequalities there were in the distribution of power and authority and the ferocity of some of the forms of punishment available, this should come as no surprise. This should not however be equated with docility or undue deference. As the late E. P. Thompson observed in relation to his concept of the 'anonymous tradition', in rural society, 'where any open, identified resistance to the ruling power may result in instant retaliation' for isolated and powerless smaller tenants, sub-tenants, cottars and their households, prudence demanded that such acts be carried on under cover of darkness.[78] This explains why most of the destruction of kelp and kelp tools in Orkney in 1741 and 1742 took place at night.[79] Even the Levellers of the south-west, who congregated in bands of one thousand people at a time, judged it wise to pull down enclosures at night, following the intervention of troops.[80] In the towns some food rioting too was carried on during the hours of darkness, which added to the authorities' fears. To compile a catalogue of nocturnal crime however would be difficult, and involve scouring estate papers and newspapers for those instances which happen to have been recorded. Because of the nature of such crimes however, they will only rarely appear in records such as those of the Sheriff Courts or the higher courts unless the culprits were identified, which was unusual. Inevitably then this source will greatly understate the existence of this and other crimes where culprits were difficult to identify, and it is hard to see how a reliable index could be created. But where estate court books survive or in sources such as diaries, memoranda, factors' correspondence and local histories, these reveal that behind the thin veil of public obedience the rural poor utilised an extensive range of 'weapons of the weak', such as tramping through enclosures, tampering with water supplies, writing threatening letters, incendiarism and even just removing gates from their hinges, to signify their resentment at unwanted innovations during the first half of the century.[81] Equally, because they either had or saw no alternative, and in spite of repeated warnings from estate courts, the lower orders continued to break into plantations in search of firewood or, in winter, shelter their animals in woodlands to which access had been forbidden.[82]

Thus the evidence of the court books of the barony of Urie, in Kincardineshire, led their editor to conclude that 'the proprietor ... was the greatest sufferer from the pecadillos of his tenantry. Against him one and all made common cause', pilfering, destroying property, stealing peats and trespassing. The published papers of the well-known family of Improvers, the Grants of Monymusk in Aberdeenshire, tell a similar but vivid story of covert confrontation and far from docile tenants who were prepared to use the law to defend themselves. This took place over several decades as the Grants and their factors embarked on a programme of estate reform, which included enclosing (the walls or hedges of which were not pulled down but rather broken through, presumably to maintain rights of way), the removal of sub-tenants and tree-planting, which was met with some open resistance but also numerous instances of sabotage, surliness and foot-dragging.[83] What is being observed here are more extreme instances of what agrarian improvers would continue to complain about even during the era of rapid change in the later eighteenth and early nineteenth centuries:

> Notwithstanding the influence of the proprietors, it must be evident to any person acquainted with human nature, that there is a reluctance among the lower ranks of men, to change old customs or to relinquish habits which have acquired the sanction of time, and are established by the authority of ages .... In vain will you threaten; in vain will you prosecute and fine; in vain will you plead the authority of statutes and the articles of leases.[84]

Indeed it is hard to find an estate of which this was not true, at least to some extent. Even a landowner like James Boswell, who revelled in his paternalist role but who was also a spirited improver of his Ayrshire lands, 'fretted at the cunning of the country people', and despaired of 'the little regard which appeared ... to be felt for my prosperity'.[85]

Very different and later in the eighteenth century, but illustrating how necessary was the judicious exercise of formal power and the conscious operation of paternalist strategy in the service of the economic development of Scotland – a central theme of this book which will be re-visited later in this chapter – is a case concerning Thomas Miller, Lord Barskimming, a Justiciary Court judge on the Western Circuit which sat at Glasgow in October 1773. Weavers in Paisley, organised in an unlawful combination to raise wages had, among other things, threatened to 'go off in a body to America' and, according to Miller, made the trial, at which seven of the twelve ringleaders were found guilty, 'very delicate'. Accordingly, Miller felt it prudent to speak to the guilty 'with warmth and tenderness for their situation' and reduced their period of imprisonment, thereby emphasising 'the lenity with which they had been treated'. Miller's fervent hope was that order would be restored and that the weavers would remain in Paisley: 'I pray God', he wrote to the Lord Justice Clerk, 'for the sake of this Country, that the Idea of Migration to America [a subject of considerable concern] may not become epidemical amongst the most useful class of our People'.[86]

Tensions in the towns

Despite the expectations and hopes of civic leaders that their status and importance would be acknowledged, respect for their authority was not forthcoming as a matter of course. Yet, as was noted earlier, in the towns as in the countryside, the lines along which the inhabitants of the towns mobilised were neither as clear nor as static as the historian in search of clear patterns of social affiliation might wish. For example, the justifiable temptation to conclude that a firm division between the burghs and the interests of the landed sector was emerging has to be tempered with the knowledge that some of the burghs too were enclosing, letting out and improving their common grounds in order to generate income, although this was done at Lochmaben in 1710 partly to stop the encroachment of neighbouring heritors.[87] Scattered in the burgh records are reports of depredations on the part of residents whose identities were largely unknown, as the towns' burgesses strove to enclose and put to commercial use land which had formerly been acquired for the 'ease' of the community, or to protect the interests of favoured landowners in the vicinity. The example of Irvine, where there was a rash of riots opposed to the enclosure of part of the town's moor in the 1740s and 1750s, pinpoints just such a divide. It lay between commercially ambitious merchants on one side, who wanted to lease land for industrial and other revenue-generating purposes, and, on the other, the more conservative trades incorporations, who were inclined to protect the interests of wage workers and the burgh's poorer inhabitants.[88]

Sometimes it can be difficult to draw a dividing line between some forms of popular protest and illegal action which might also be taken collectively, as a result of household or individual desperation – what can usefully if loosely be considered as social crime.[89] So severe had the problem of nocturnal potato stealing become in the depressed year of 1773 that Perth's dean of guild John Ramsay, who farmed land at nearby Broxden, declared his willingness, whatever the cost, to take legal action against one of those apprehended, which would be 'a terrour & example to others'.[90] As we have seen, within the larger towns such as Glasgow there was a perception among the rising property-conscious middle classes that crimes such as theft were increasing, and in 1753 fifty or so 'gentlemen of Glasgow' (one hundred a year later) formed the Glasgow Friendly Society as a vigilante body, the aim of which was to bring private prosecutions against offenders (although these were less common in Scotland than England. In Scotland the Lord Advocate and the procurators-fiscal who were responsible to him, instigated most major criminal prosecutions).[91] In the smaller towns and villages such periods of lawlessness more obviously tended to coincide with downturns in trade or poor harvests, and the consequent influx of the begging poor. The early 1770s was one such period and thus in Banff in March 1775 it was complained that the town was being 'infested' with troublesome incomers of this description from the surrounding countryside.[92] Many disputes were simply quarrels between neighbours, 'flytings' or highly expressive and energetic verbal exchanges which had escalated to the point of violence, or drunken squabbles.[93] But even here intriguing evidence from Stirling suggests that the branks, used for women who were guilty of verbal abuse, were utilised not to punish quarrelling neighbours but by the authorities who wished to silence females who were particularly argumentative – and therefore potentially troublesome.[94]

The burgh authorities felt somewhat less secure than has generally been assumed, for good reason. There were long periods of outward calm in most places, but even so town councils could not afford to drop their guard and remained concerned to ensure that levels of disorder were kept to a minimum. The Riot Act of 1715, introduced throughout Britain by a Whig government which was unsettled by Tory-led discontent, and which was read by magistrates intent on dispersing threatening crowds of more than twelve persons, appears in Scotland, as in England, to have been ignored more often than it was observed. It is ironic – given the views reported above on the place of music and popular culture in eighteenth-century Scotland – that in 1731 the town council in Aberdeen felt it necessary to ban Andrew Ferguson, a piper, from playing at night, as this had the effect of raising 'mobs & tumults in the streets'.[95] The ubiquitous fiddlers – in 1719 it was complained in Dundee that so many were coming in from the country that some of the town's 'vilers' were under-employed – could have the same effect.[96] Nor was concern with the energising effects of loud rhythmic music and dance unusual. The later seventeenth and early eighteenth centuries had witnessed growing numbers of resolutions from the General Assembly down to the parish level expressing disapproval at the number of penny weddings being celebrated. Their popularity and the drink, dancing and 'great debauching' which accompanied them were seen as offensive to God and a danger to public morals – and order.[97] Less offensive were the numerous dancing schools which were set up in the burghs, who employed a 'dancing master' as a 'dancing boom' swept the country, with fiddle music becoming so fashionable from mid-century that the town council of Dundee invited and paid Niel Gow, 'fiddler from Dunkeld', to play at the burgh's coronation ball for King George III in 1760.[98]

As has been seen, there were events and occasions which could unite much of the urban community. This was certainly the case with the earlier post-1707 attacks on customs and excise officers. This topic will be explored further later, although it should be noted that these involved both urban and rural dwellers, as did some food riots in places where the contest was over the shipment outwards of grain, suggesting that the historiographical line which distinguishes quiescent country dwellers from the inhabitants of the more turbulent towns is sharper than it appears in the historical record, which emphasises the extent to which the two were linked in the early modern period. Even the larger towns in Scotland retained a 'strong rural character'. An exaggerated but telling example of a smaller burgh in which this was also true is Dingwall in 1712, where economic distress had reduced the inhabitants to having no other work but 'labouring the Neighbouring lands'.[99]

The monarch's birthday celebrations, held with remarkable regularity throughout the towns of Lowland Scotland in the eighteenth century, seem to have been designed to serve the same unifying purpose, even though up until the 1740s Jacobites sometimes contrived to orchestrate competing festivities. The crowd on these occasions was a 'necessary actor in the enforcement and enactment of public authority', endorsing public demonstrations of both national and local state power.[100] In Scotland, with a parliamentary electorate of only some four thousand – one in a thousand males – events of this kind may have assumed an even greater significance as a channel for political communication. Even when these ended in violence, with clashes between the stone- and dead-cat-throwing lower orders on one side and the magistrates, town councillors, their guests and the town guards on the other, all the worse for drink, the effect was usually to reinforce the existing urban hierarchy. Indeed in the light of the fewer calendrical occasions of this sort there were in Reformed Scotland compared to England, the role of the monarch's birthday in acting as a 'safety valve' within the burghs' communities is considerably enhanced.[101] 'Rituals of revolt' (my emphasis), carnivalesque events such as this one, which had its counterparts both south of the border and on a grander scale in southern Europe, provided both momentary liberation from daily burdens as well as an opportunity for the lower orders to release tensions and pent up hostility towards those who ruled over them.[102] Charivari-like customs such as 'riding the stang', known throughout much of England as 'ridings', served a similar purpose in east-coast burghs, where they seem to have been more common than in the west, particularly during times of economic distress. An 'extra-legal enforcer of community norms', they were a form of ritual humiliation used against those who were judged to have offended against community values – a merchant demanding unnecessarily high prices for meal during a period of shortage, for example – which involved trying to remain upright while being carried, seated, on a long narrow pole.[103] Much rarer than in England, customs of this kind have generally been overlooked by social historians of Scotland, where in harness with the kirk, the ruling classes in the towns were more inclined to repress popular rituals which might usurp magisterial authority, but not always successfully.[104]

As has been hinted however, there were issues which could divide Scotland's urban communities along lines approximating class. Noted above, and as will be seen in greater detail below, one such fault line lay between those who were primarily wage workers and those – usually of higher rank – who derived their livelihoods by other means. Visible during periods of hardship and particularly when there were grounds for acting in defence of the 'moral economy', these could create within the affected localities crisis conditions which necessitated the use of force to reimpose the *status quo*. The town guards employed in the larger burghs – drawn in Edinburgh from the ranks of discharged soldiers – or the one or two constables in the smaller places were sufficient only to deal with minor skirmishes or to apprehend drunkards and delinquents. Nor could they always be relied upon to follow the magistrates' instructions, especially where they sympathised with the cause of those they were directed to arrest.[105]

Troops, however, were required to quell disorder in the Lowlands much more often than has been recognised, although the information we have on military deployment outwith Highland Scotland and other than during the peak periods of Jacobite activity is currently scanty, not least because of a gap in the records prior to 1756.[106] The subject badly requires further investigation. The claim that as paternalism became a less effective device later in the century, increasing social tensions led to an increased use of force, is unproven.[107] It is argued here that the implication that little or less military force was used earlier is unsoundly based, although it may be that there was a period of *relative* calm from the mid-1740s until the 1770s, following and preceding respectively periods of greater social and political tension.[108] It is known that the Lowlands of Scotland was a specific area to which men from Britain's standing army of between ten to fifteen thousand were sent, but the proportion is currently unclear.[109] What is absolutely certain however is that all of the major outbreaks of crowd violence in Scotland from the Union to the 1770s required the use of the army to restore order. It is instructive to note that an Irish historian, comparing justice and the law in eighteenth-century Ireland and Scotland, concluded that the repression and 'subjugation by naked force' which followed the malt tax and Porteous Riots in Glasgow and Edinburgh respectively, was 'far more heavy-handed' than anything which occurred in Dublin.[110] Research into the localities also makes clear that numerous minor or, more accurately, less well-known disturbances also necessitated the use of parties of foot soldiers and dragoons whose numbers may have been small but who (like the 32nd Regiment in the later 1750s, based at Fort George) spent much of their time on duty in Scotland marching or riding to trouble spots, notwithstanding the dislike there was among the military of crowd control commissions.[111] At one time or another Jacobite sympathisers, meal and food rioters, participants in crowds which interfered with customs and excise officers in their duties, striking workers and crowds intent on liberating colleagues who had been arrested and imprisoned during popularly supported disturbances – even parishioners involved in ecclesiastical disorders – felt the fatal effects of artillery-borne gunpowder and shot, or were made to acknowledge them.

Watching from an upstairs window as anti-Union demonstrations raged through Edinburgh in the autumn months of 1706, Daniel Defoe, who must have been familiar with the sight of the London mob, reported to his paymaster, Lord Harley, that the Scottish 'rabble' was the worst of its kind', and the Scots a 'hardened, refractory and terrible people'.[112]

Order of a sort was only restored in Edinburgh – as well as Glasgow –
when the military was brought in and a proclamation issued which
obliged the deacons of trades to be responsible for the actions of their
servants and journeymen and indemnified soldiers and town guardsmen
if they killed anyone in the pursuit of their duties. The vote for this
measure in the Scottish parliament was one of a few which gave the
Court an absolute majority, hinting strongly that the crowds were largely
their own masters, and not simply the puppets of parliamentarians.
Indeed there is some powerful evidence to support the proposition that
popular opinion and the fear of 'commotion' played some part in shaping
the final Articles of the Union through concessions on excise duties on
ale, malt and salt which were reluctantly granted by the Court during the
period of the so-called 'Explanations', when the Scots had their last say
on the details of the treaty.[113] Popular resentment at the passage of the
Union however continued to simmer and, significantly, in Edinburgh on
Queen Anne's birthday in February 1707, instead of the usual grand celebrations there was only a 'Small Solemnity'. Neither the queen's
commissioner, the chancellor nor the nobility would attend at the cross,
their absence being explained by their 'fear of a mob'.[114]

The atmosphere seems to have become particularly flammable in
Scotland after the Union, with daily life and commercial intercourse
interrupted by the withdrawal of the Scots coinage and the appearance of
large numbers of tax officials.[115] The Scottish Privy Council was abolished in 1708, thereby removing a body which prior to 1707 had had its
ear to the ground and been able to take steps to nip impending trouble in
the bud, by banning the export of grain during years of poor harvests, for
example, or opening the ports. Its removal was a mistake, not wished by
the ministry but instead the consequence of the efforts of dissident Whigs
to break the power of those Scots who had formerly been identified with
the Court.[116] The ultimate responsibility for domestic tranquillity now
rested with a Secretary of State, in London. The consequences were
grave.

In Scotland, as elsewhere in early modern Europe, by inviting the military to assist in maintaining order the authorities risked inflaming the
situation further and creating an even more volatile climate. Thus while
the Shawfield Riot in Glasgow in late June 1725 was precipitated by
excise officers (101 of whom had been specially appointed) beginning to
collect the new and unpopular malt tax in nearby Hamilton, and
hastened by retaliation on the part of officers who had been assaulted by
'some idle women and boys', Glasgow only became unmanageable after
troops from Lord Deloraine's Regiment had been called in and fired on a
crowd, killing eight people outright and wounding another eighteen.
Thereafter, advised that if they stayed in Glasgow they would be 'tore to
pieces', the soldiers were forced to flee to Dumbarton. The appearance of

several butchers in the crowd gave what was not far short of a national insurrection a particularly fearsome – and continental – aspect.[117] It was two weeks later that order was restored, when General Wade, who had been directing troops to other Scottish towns where disorder seemed likely, arrived in Glasgow accompanied both by foot solders and seven troops of dragoons.[118]

But where troops were absent or when for some reason the usual forms of municipal discipline and respect had broken down, life for those in positions of authority in the Scottish burghs could be uncomfortable at best and at worst terrifying. An example is provided by the case of Alexander Livingston, sometime provost of Aberdeen. A 'man of An Opulent Fortune, & of Extensive Knowledge in Trade ... a Factor in Holland for the Scotts Merchants' and a relative newcomer to Aberdeen, Livingston was proud of his record as a creator of employment and claimed to be a humanitarian magistrate who had bought meal and sold it below the market price during periods of shortage. In 1753 however he was driven to launch an action in the High Court of Justiciary against those who had accused him of recently doubling the price of meal in Aberdeen. As a result of such slanders, it was asserted on his behalf, neither Livingston nor his wife could walk the streets with safety for fear of 'that many headed monster a Mobb' which his accusers had fomented against him; in addition he had received a letter 'threatning him & family with death'. Livingston's action in a court of this status was necessary, it was argued, as there was 'nothing more destructive to society and subversive to the peace as fire brands who go about Initiating the multitude ... to Riot violence & disorder'. 'Tumultuary leaders' should be punished.[119] Further evidence of the frequency with which the authorities in Scotland had to resort to the use of military force will be seen below.

Limitations of and fissures in the 'godly commonwealth'

A second flaw in the traditional argument for Scottish social quiescence concerns the kirk. Clearly the activities of the kirk sessions in Scotland had a moderating effect on sexual behaviour, more so in some parts of the country and certain towns than others, although overall, two-thirds of males are estimated to have acknowledged their guilt when charged with having fathered a bastard.[120] Kirk session records provide compelling evidence of an intrusive system of parish government whereby in those best organised to preserve the godly commonwealth virtually every household could expect more than one visitation each year by an elder or elders determined to ascertain the level of religious knowledge and adherence of all of its members, whether family or servants. There are some indications that in the first half of the eighteenth century there was a powerful sense of religiosity in Scotland, seen, for example, in the desire among offenders against church law for absolution and in the strong but not universal belief there appears to have been in the sacredness of the sabbath. Bible-reading too may have been commonplace – at least in parts of the Lowlands, even though the ability to write seems to have been confined to one-third of Scotland's women, and twice the proportion of males at mid-century.[121] As will be seen, there were limits to godliness, but even so the church did continue thereafter to have a powerful effect on cultural life.[122]

Yet there were those who tried to evade, or even rebelled against, the authority of the church. Some of the accused fled from the parish trying them, although in the earlier eighteenth century they were frequently discovered. Evasion could also take the form of a female denying pregnancy, in spite of being subject to the painful and demeaning but by no means uniquely Scottish process of having her breasts inspected for signs of 'green milk'. The male equivalent would be to deny paternal responsibility.[123] Dissent was expressed in the increasing frequency of irregular marriages in the eighteenth century in urban areas, that is unions celebrated without the calling of banns or the parish minister. The rate of recidivism for sexual offences was high: instances of 'quadrilapse' – and worse – in cases of fornication were not uncommon. A sizeable minority of women and even more men refused to accept the Church's punishments, the former by refusing to show their faces to the congregation, while young men are reputed to have attempted to limit the effectiveness of public humiliation by crowding round the cutty stool, making it difficult for the enquiring congregation to identify the culprit.[124] Others appeared to hold the institution of the kirk in low regard, treating it to comic insults. Nowhere are the pretensions of kirk elders pricked to greater effect than in the biting assaults of the poetry of Robert Burns.[125] Earlier, in 1756, as the ethos of voluntarism began to weaken the notion of kirk-compulsion, a Marion Gow, 'late servant to Lord Ruthven', challenged the legality of the kirk session's methods in a Court of Session action. Gow complained that over-zealous elders had broken into her apartment. The case being made, it was argued on her behalf, mattered not only to the individual concerned but:

> to all those of low Rank; that they may be safe from the Oppression of Power, and men in Office may know, that even the meanest in this free Country is not below the Protection of the Law.[126]

Insolence towards ministers, parish schoolteachers and members of the kirk session was unusual but by no means unknown, and became increasingly common, as evidenced by the popularity of Burns' poems. In July 1707 it was alleged that 'in time of sermon' in Barony church in Glasgow John Dunlop did 'shew himself & pull out his privitys', which were then touched by Jean Ferguson in what was considered to be a scandalous display of 'unchast carriage'.[127] The case is an extreme one, but while the presence in church of Dunlop and Ferguson may indicate the success of the Church's ceaseless campaign for sabbath observance, it also serves to remind us that attendance at church (or as Burns' 1785 poem on the subject suggests, an annual holy fair), and the internalisation of the Calvinist doctrine and acceptance of the kirk's moral code were not necessarily the same thing. Appearance at the kirk mattered, even for the lower ranks.[128] But drunkenness, swearing and taking the Lord's name in vain were commonplace, even among believers, while the lower orders shared a coarse culture, retained a belief in witchcraft and held on to 'superstitious' notions and practices.[129]

The extent to which preaching, teaching and demeaning punishments affected other aspects of social conduct therefore invites closer inspection. For instance, there is little evidence to suggest that the labouring classes in Scotland were any more malleable than their counterparts elsewhere in Europe when confronted with the challenge of regular, custom-free and regimented waged work (see chapter 2). Indeed the Clerks of Loanhead, who for the best part of a century after c. 1680 attempted to instill habits of good behaviour in their colliers, in part by insisting that they attend church and also by offering to educate the illiterate (mainly so that they could read the scriptures), enjoyed only limited success. Yet many coal workers in the eighteenth century were baptised, married and buried by the church. However, as was hinted earlier, colliers in Scotland also managed to defend a strong leisure preference, enjoyed a robust cultural life and, when market conditions were at their most opportune, struck work and even formed combinations. In these respects the men and women of Loanhead shared a *mentalité* not only with other communities of coal workers but also with the rest of the labouring poor in Lowland Scotland – who continued to participate in penny weddings, for example, through the rest of the century.[130]

Thus the hegemony of the Scottish kirk was in certain respects more apparent than real. It certainly acted as an important bulwark for the Hanoverians at General Assembly, presbytery, and often at parish level, being particularly active on their behalf during and in the aftermath of the '45, and a powerful antidote to Roman Catholicism, or 'Superstition & Slavery'.[131] Generally (but excepting the Cameronians), the more extreme the Calvinism, the stronger the adherence to a Protestant monarch. The pulpit and the church-door proclamations of the beddal, or parish constable, were the source of news and official views on matters of national and local importance, while fasts and periodic thanksgivings ensured that few parishioners could have been unaware of events as varied as poor harvests or other disasters such as major fires, impending threats such as plague (in 1720), the condition and treatment of

Protestants abroad, national crises, coronations and royal marriages, and British military and naval successes – or the arrival and departure of Stuart aspirants to the throne.[132] The function of Protestantism as an increasingly important factor contributing to the sense of national identity and personal self-worth in eighteenth-century Scotland should be stressed, as should its role in strengthening the British union, not least because of its emphasis on the values of thrift, industry, tenaciousness and self-sacrifice.[133] But people of all ranks could, and did, choose selectively from the varied menu of doctrines and values which Protestantism offered. In Moderate hearts and minds it generated religious tolerance, but in others it could and did breed an ugly strand of anti-Catholic prejudice.[134]

The church in Lowland Scotland, 'the mouthpiece of the lairds', tended to favour the prevailing social order. By failing to provide leadership to oppose it, and preaching acceptance of the temporal suffering which rural reorganisation produced, the Church of Scotland played a significant part in maintaining it. In the towns the trades incorporations insisted that their members swore allegiance to Protestantism, Hanover and the rule of law at national and burgh level.[135] But as the enclosing landowners of south-west Scotland discovered in 1724 and 1725 when confronted by the peasant Levellers, Calvinism was an unreliable ally. Evangelical Church of Scotland ministers and elders, loyal to Hanover, supported the Levellers, who also drew strongly on the organisational, fighting and ideological traditions of the Covenanters. Religious revivalism at Cambuslang in 1742 was feared by local heritors – and persecuted – not welcomed.[136] Godliness, or more specifically the search for spiritual salvation, and the Scottish kirk were not always perceived as being compatible. Government attempts to prise out information about the Porteous rioters were partly foiled by the refusal of ministers to read out the terms of the relevant act from their pulpits, or only to do so halfheartedly. The religious revivals at Cambuslang (and Kilsyth) just referred to, caused irritation for landowners who suffered the temporary loss of farm workers. Partly for this reason, communions, during which it was rare for more than 20 per cent of parishioners to receive the sacrament but which were popular holiday occasions, were held less regularly.[137] The Church of Scotland therefore was less of a monolithic agent of the establishment than some historians have supposed. In the Highlands and Islands the influence of the kirk spread only slowly and unevenly, notwithstanding the formation of the Scottish Society for the Propagation of Christian Knowledge (SSPCK) in 1709 – which established schools as well as some spinning schools – and vigorous government efforts to establish the Protestant religion between the 1740s and 1770s. Even by the end of the century clerical authority was far from assured, and landlords who failed to consider their parishioners' views when appointing a new minister could suffer for their negligence.[138]

The kirk itself was both the locus and source of legitimacy for certain forms of disorder. Those men and women – mainly servants – who were accused of crimes of 'Ryot and violence' when they had interfered with divine service at East Kilpatrick in an attempt to stop a new minister, Andrew Gray, from preaching, were evidently devout Presbyterians. This however was insufficient to inculcate within them respect for the civil law. For failing to appear at the West Circuit Court sitting in Glasgow in October 1731 they were declared to be outlaws.[139] Another variant of the same theme is exemplified by a disputed council election in Dumfries in 1759, when a mob which had taken over the council chamber 'sustained its spirits by singing hymns' – and drinking the councillors' wine.[140] Earlier, in Fraserburgh, a 'most attrocious Ryot' of two days duration, which saw customs officers and soldiers from Hamilton's Regiment attacked and fired upon, had begun with members of the congregation leaving the church and meeting house on Sunday 16 February 'gazing' upon the soldiers. Tensions rose with name-calling, while women among the crowd protested about the fact that their houses had been searched for illegal goods on the sabbath; violence against the soldiers however appears not to have been committed until the Monday.[141] Far and away the most dramatic episode however was in 1778 and 1779 when the virulence of anti-Catholic preaching of clergymen attached to the Popular Party of the kirk – fearing for the security of government and society – awoke slumbering anti-popery in Scotland and, along with the militant Protestant Association, incited outbursts of rioting so serious in Edinburgh and Glasgow that the government was forced to withdraw its proposed measure for Roman Catholic relief from Scotland. One witness described an attack on Catholic worshippers, several of whom were Highlanders, as being 'grosser ... than I ever knew done in Britain'.[142]

The Patronage Act of 1712, referred to above, which restored the rights of hereditary patrons to appoint (or 'present') ministers, and in part designed as a measure to enhance crown and state control at the parish level in Scotland, could divide congregations and incite opposition to landed hegemony. On the other hand, where a presentation was acceptable, the effect was to reinforce the social hierarchy. The ordination of a new minister in Longforgan parish in 1737 was followed by a gathering of over 120 people who included the heritors, the members of the presbyteries of Dundee and Meigle, and several 'gentlemen' from the countryside, 'besides a great Concourse of Country people', all of whom were treated to 'plentiful Entertainment and plenty of Wine'.[143]

Although the precise number of disputed presentations is unknown and more research into the subject is required, such was their scale that they have been described as the 'most persistent and geographically widespread cause of popular unrest in Scotland between 1730 and 1843'.[144]

These frequently involved the use of physical force, as at Alloa in 1750 when a crowd 'assembled riotously' to prevent the settlement of a new minister, rang the church bell 'from morning till night and, in the afternoon, displayed a flag from the steeple in token of victory'. At Aberfoyle in 1771, such was the strength of feeling against the calling of a new minister who spoke no Gaelic that, following 'railing, Curses and Imprecations' and threats to the property of one of his supporters, the presbytery was forced to meet in a field to consider their course of action.[145] Once more, Presbyterian conscience did not preclude the use of violence in the search for spiritual sustenance. There was no single path to righteousness however. Not unusually, resort was had to the military to effect the entry of the landowners' candidates, while those found guilty of blocking their way by violent means could be fined, incarcerated in a house of correction or prison, or banished to the plantations.

Disturbances of this sort were not protests against church rule as such; rather they were inspired in part by hostility to the effects of the rise of the Moderate Party within the Church of Scotland, seen by stricter Presbyterians as morally lax and landowner-dominated.[146] Nor were those who participated in them drawn solely from the lowest ranks, although these were better represented prior to the 1790s. Artisans and tenant farmers – even some small landowners in country parishes – were to form the bedrock of Presbyterian dissent, which at its most extreme resulted in the formation of secession congregations which initially at least, joined the Secession Church. By 1766 there may have been one hundred thousand seceders in Scotland.

Nevertheless protest within the Church of Scotland can be interpreted as anti-aristocratic as well as a form of opposition to unwanted innovations and exclusion which were underpinned by a desire on the part of the parish elites to proclaim differences of social status. On the other side, seceders were the first to dispense with the habit of lifting their hats to the gentry.[147] Not only did congregations want to choose their minister but they also demanded their rights to an affordable pew or even entry to the kirk, and continued participation in worship for those without bibles or reading skills through the practice of 'reading the line' prior to the singing of psalms.[148] The extent to which patronage disputes can be linked with opposition to agrarian change is unclear, although the connection has been refuted in one study.[149] That sizeable numbers of dissenters were from the middling ranks of rural society certainly weakens the postulated connection with cottar clearance and enclosure, as does the fact that patronage disputes occurred too in towns. However, that for most of the eighteenth century religious dissent featured most strongly in the countryside or in semi-urban parishes suggests that to discount any linkage between this and rural social change may be premature, particularly in the light of the absence of detailed research into the affected localities. More subtle tensions may have been created through changes in landownership or social distancing, the increasing employment of estate factors, looked on with suspicion by the tenantry as they were generally 'strangers', and the growing divergence in attitudes to land and estate management and the concomitant if gradual and uneven crushing of custom. It was not unusual for the parish glebe to be targeted, hinting perhaps at the construction in the minds of the congregation of an association of the kirk with an increasingly exploitative agricultural system, particularly as income from such lands could make ministers in some parishes extremely wealthy men, better off than many lairds.[150]

Introducing popular protest

The third flaw in the received view is empirical, and concerns claims of the sort that popular protest was relatively unusual in Scotland. This however has to be treated with some caution, as do the inferences which have been drawn from it about the nature of Scottish society, outlined at the beginning of this chapter. Crowd activity, Professor H. T. Dickinson has observed, 'was a major form of group expression by the common people of eighteenth-century Britain'.[151] Is Scotland to be excepted from this judgement, which should more properly perhaps apply solely to England?

It must be conceded that the careful quantification which has accompanied studies of riot and disorder in England and some parts of Europe is largely lacking for Scotland in the period before 1780.[152] In the absence of a central record or readily usable source in Scotland such a task, which is fraught with methodological difficulties, would be immensely complex. The growth of newspapers in Scotland was considerably slower than in England in the eighteenth century and those which were published were mainly confined to Edinburgh and Glasgow.[153] However, the strong impression created by casting a research net widely in both national and local archives is that there was much more collective popular action than has been supposed hitherto, and fresh discoveries in the localities are to be made with remarkable frequency.[154] Nevertheless, as far as it is possible to tell at this juncture, proportionate to the two countries' populations, there were fewer riots in Scotland than in England. And regarding Edinburgh, the capital, with a population of around fifty-seven thousand in 1755, there is no suggestion that the number comes anywhere near to that of London, where crowd disturbances, some admittedly very minor, could afflict the city every other day.[155] On the other hand, in terms of their scale, social composition, the growing independence of the crowd from the 'people above' (although some crowd actions were incited by the upper ranks), and the myriad of causes, there were many similarities with those which punctuated civic life in London. But smaller numbers need not be indicative of greater social stability; on the contrary, this may well be an indicator of political and social immaturity, and signify fragility rather than robustness in the body politic.

However the extent to which popular disturbances did occur in Scotland has not been widely recognised beyond the specialist literature. Food riots, for example, broke out in various places as prices rose in Scotland in 1699, 1709–10, 1720, 1727, 1740–41, 1756–57, 1763, 1767, 1771–74, 1778 and 1783 – even 1794–96, when until recently there were thought to have been none north of the border, and 1800–1. Thus all of the major waves of food rioting in England, the most common kind in the eighteenth century, had their counterparts in Scotland.

The tendency of historians to focus on the more spectacular popular disturbances has caused them to overlook the fact that, for instance, the Shawfield Riot in Glasgow in 1725 over the imposition of the malt tax had smaller counterparts in Ayr, Dundee, Elgin, Paisley and Stirling. 'Tumults' looked likely in Edinburgh in August, but by stationing additional dragoons in the city and by taking other preventative action, the authorities managed to contain the situation. Similarly, food rioting in 1740–41 was not confined to Edinburgh and Leith, but also broke out in Aberdeen, Ayr, Banff, Cromarty, Dingwall, Hamilton, Montrose, Musselburgh, Prestonpans, Tain and other unnamed 'Towns in the North'.[156] They even spread north to Orkney where food shortages were partly blamed on the smoke from the kilns of the relatively new kelping industry, with attacks subsequently being directed towards the buildings, materials and workers employed by the islands' lairds and more substantial farmers, who were also exporters of grain.[157]

Customs and excise riots, mentioned in chapter 1, if they are noticed at all in the literature, have rarely been accorded the attention which they deserve, even though they continued to be endemic across large swathes of Lowland Scotland at least until the 1740s. These were far and away the most common type of popular disorder in Scotland in the first half of the eighteenth century. To portray smuggling and the riots against customs and excise officers and attacks on the King's warehouses, as a 'national sport' fails to convey the severity and character of these disorders (to be discussed more fully in chapter 5).[158] It is true that in the first post-Union years there was almost certainly a patriotic dimension to the attacks on customs and excise officers. But notwithstanding the proclivity of Jacobite JPs and others from the middling and upper ranks to ignore them, they would within a few years be considered by authorities loyal to the Hanoverian state as a much more serious problem, described by a despairing Stirling town council in 1728, for example, as an 'abominable practice'.[159]

Nor does the sporting metaphor convey the gravity of the matter either for the state, in the form of a shortfall in anticipated revenues, or for burgh magistrates or the officers on the ground who could be bloodied, beaten, and imprisoned by ferocious crowds rarely comprising less than thirty or forty people, often more, who used stones, clubs, staves, pitch-forks and occasionally firearms to obtain their ends. From virtually every part of the seaward parts of Lowland Scotland, but notably Ayr and Dumfries in the west, as well as Greenock and Port Glasgow, and in the east the coastline between but also including Dundee and Montrose, comes evidence of quite extraordinary disorder, much more than in the pre-Union decades.[160] Comptrollers and collectors from virtually all precincts sent frequent and desperate pleas to the Board of Customs in Edinburgh, and to the Excise Commissioners, for military assistance, without which they swore that it was impossible for them to do their duty. Typical is a report from Perth in 1722, in which the local customs officers, learning of the temporary withdrawal of forces from the town during the forthcoming parliamentary election, declared that unless half the garrison then stationed in the town remained, 'we shall certainly be mobbed, and our warehouse be broke open'; or another from Dumfriesshire in the same year, reporting that after customs officers had seized five casks of brandy an Andrew Hoatson had 'rais'd the whole Country about ... who came with Stons Clubs & firearms and Violently Deforc'd' them. They begged that a 'party of Souldiers' be sent to assist them. In Dundee in 1736 the local military commander had had to call for another company of soldiers as 'the Duty of late has been so hard' those on station were 'not able to bear it'.[161]

If in a rapidly-growing manufacturing and commercial town like Glasgow there were comparatively few violent confrontations over food, and none when the most serious disturbances of this sort were taking place elsewhere in Scotland, this had nothing to do with the imagined meekness of the inhabitants, or the hegemonic influence of kirk, burgh or state. Nor does the almost complete absence of customs and excise riots, the 1725 explosion apart. It owes a great deal however to geography. Throughout Britain, it was at ports and other places from which meal or grain were being sent off during periods of scarcity which caused the greatest popular indignation.[162] Thus most food riots in Scotland in the eighteenth century erupted on the north-east coast and in ports like Dundee which lay on the edge of grain-growing agricultural hinterlands, as well as along the southern shores of the shires of Dumfries and Galloway. Imported goods however were not landed directly at Glasgow itself until the Clyde was deepened up-river in the 1770s, and much of its trade therefore was carried on through Greenock and Port Glasgow. It was in these places that customs officials felt the brunt of popular anger. Glasgow however does satisfy the second principal precondition for food rioting, in that it contained a large non-agricultural population of wage workers. But like the industrial north-east of England, where too there were few food riots compared to East Anglia or Cornwall, Glasgow was close to the coast and was able therefore to import oats and oatmeal not only from the south-west of Scotland but also from Ireland, which not only periodically plugged gaps in the grain markets of the west of Scotland but also had a major and favourable impact on prices.[163] The very distance of Glasgow from its main grain supplies meant that it was virtually impossible for urban workers to confront the suppliers of their food by marching out into the countryside. In this sense Glasgow had much in common with Manchester where food riots also were less frequent than in food exporting counties such as Devon.[164]

Food riots in Scotland shared the rituals, symbols and forms which typified such disturbances in England or France.[165] That such a 'language' of popular protest could be mobilised with such remarkable swiftness so often in eighteenth-century Scotland provides us with another reason for casting doubt on the dominant characterisations of Scottish society. That 'execrations', swearing, chanting and singing were also part of the crowds' repertoire is significant in this regard too, and suggests a certain longevity about these practices, although the harder evidence for this type of activity is more prevalent for the later eighteenth century and beyond.

The 'community character' which has been accorded to protest over food in England is seen in the way the crowds invariably included a drummer or piper among their number, or even someone banging an iron girdle, to raise the alarm and attract maximum attention. Marching or parading through the locality concerned too was usual, as householders and onlookers were encouraged to join in. On some occasions the town's handbell might be seized or the tolbooth bells rung, a practical measure but also a symbolic indication that a temporary transfer of the panoply of local power had taken place. A similar message was conveyed by the use of formal notices which were posted up, listing grievances and the punishments which would be meted out to transgressors, thus mirroring the official 'solemn and public' proclamations made on behalf of the authorities. While the threat of physical force was both implied and intended by the carrying of sticks, poles or stones – occasionally a gun or sword – normally these also served a symbolic purpose, and violence was controlled and targeted selectively.

Offenders against the traditional rights which crowds had formed to defend were beaten, bloodied and bruised, but rarely killed and then *usually* only accidentally. Deaths were almost always due to the actions of the burgh authorities whose responsibility it was to request a military presence and who were responsible for giving the order to fire. Soldiers often felt nervous or panic-stricken when confronted by an angry, braying, intimidating mob who were not averse to taking and breaking their weapons. Unwritten codes governed the conduct of both sides: soldiers were expected to fire blanks, or to aim above the heads of the rioters, or at their legs; attempts on the part of the authorities to take prisoners were resisted, interpreted as actions which had no legitimacy, and emboldened efforts were made on the crowd's part to release anyone who was arrested or imprisoned.[166]

Those who were deemed to have been profiteering or hoarding victuals were punished by the destruction of their grain or meal, or in the case of more affluent merchants by breaking the windows of their houses and the destruction of moveable goods. Theft was unusual and quantities of seized victual were usually sold, but normally below the market price. Indeed as with food riots virtually everywhere, what is striking is the degree of orderliness with which the crowds pursued their ends. At Cockenzie in 1740 for instance a crowd from Musselburgh ordered the duchess of Gordon's factor to sell some meal they had discovered not for 8*d*. a peck but for 6*d*., 'alledging it to be North country meall ... & consequently not worth the same price as ... Lothian meall'.[167] At the same time however food rioters in Scotland as elsewhere were uncompromising in their determination to succeed, and were dispersed only with the utmost difficulty.

Notes

1 Smout, *History of the Scottish People*, 223, 227–9, 442–5; T. M. Devine, 'The failure of radical reform in Scotland in the late eighteenth century: the social and economic context', in Devine (ed.), *Conflict and Stability in Scottish Society, 1700–1850* (Edinburgh, 1990), 51–64.

2 For a brief survey of the literature, see C. A. Whatley, 'An uninflammable people?', in Donnachie and Whatley, *Manufacture*, 51–3.

3 Mitchison, *Lordship*, 163–7.

4 Graham, *The Social Life of Scotland in the Eighteenth Century*, 139.

5 Lenman, *Integration, Enlightenment, and Industrialisation*, 25.

6 K. J. Logue, 'Eighteenth-century popular protest: aspects of the people's past', in E. J. Cowan (ed.), *The People's Past* (Edinburgh, 1980), 109.

7 C. Larner, *Enemies of God: The Witch-hunt in Scotland* (London, 1981), 50.

8 Lenman, *Integration, Enlightenment, and Industrialisation*, 11; Fry, *Dundas Despotism*, 167–8; Mitchison, *Lordship*, 136; Finlay, 'Caledonia', who argues that the Union 'hardly impinged on the ordinary Scot', 145; colliers and salters are generally described in the least flattering terms, see T. S. Ashton and J. Sykes, *The Coal Industry of the Eighteenth Century* (Manchester, 1929), 70.

9 J. D. Young, *The Rousing of the Scottish Working Class* (London, 1979), 42.

10 See J. Robertson, *The Scottish Enlightenment and the Militia Issue* (Edinburgh, 1985), 179–80; T. Crawford, 'Political and protest songs in eighteenth-century Scotland II, songs of the left', *Scottish Studies*, XIV (1970), 116–17; T. Crawford, *Society and the Lyric: A Study of the Song Culture of Eighteenth-Century Scotland* (Edinburgh, 1979), 159; R. A. Houston and I. D. Whyte, 'Introduction' in Houston and Whyte, *Scottish Society*, 34; for a recent discussion of the problems of defining popular culture see T. Harris, 'Problematising popular culture', in T. Harris (ed.), *Popular Culture in England, c. 1500–1850* (London, 1995), 1–27.

11 See C. A. Whatley, 'How tame were the Scottish Lowlanders during the eighteenth century?', in Devine, *Conflict and Stability*, 1–30; I. D. Whyte, 'Scottish population and social structure in the seventeenth and eighteenth centuries: new sources and perspectives', *Archives*, XX (April 1993), 30–41.

12 This is particularly true of rural social structure and protest. See, for example, T. M. Devine, 'Unrest and stability in rural Ireland and Scotland', in Mitchison and Roebuck, *Economy and Society*, 126–39.

13 *Ibid.*, 126; Smout, *History of the Scottish People*, 324–31; Mitchison, *Lordship*, 155–6.

14 J. Rule and R. Wells, 'Crime, protest and radicalism', in Rule and Wells (eds), *Crime, Protest and Popular Politics in Southern England, 1740–1850* (London, 1997), 8.

15 National Register of Archives (Scotland) (NRA(S)), 3246, Dundas of Arniston MSS, vol. 32, Letters, II, 1724–45, 51, James Steuart to Lord Advocate, 2 January 1725.

16 Devine, 'Unrest and stability', 128.

17 Smout, 'Famine and famine-relief in Scotland', in Cullen and Smout, *Comparative Aspects*, 25–6; Devine, 'Failure of radical reform', 61.

18 L. Soltow, 'Inequality of wealth in land in Scotland in the eighteenth century', *Scottish Economic & Social History*, X (1990), 40–1; L. Timperley, 'The pattern of landholding in eighteenth-century Scotland', in M. L. Parry and T. R. Slater (eds), *The Making of the Scottish Countryside* (London, 1980), 14–54.

19 Macinnes, 'Scottish gaeldom', 72.

20 For a clear and comprehensive survey, see T. C. Smout, 'Peasant and lord in Scotland: institutions controlling Scottish society, 1500–1800', *Recueils De La Société Jean Bodin Pour L'Histoire Comparative Des Institutions*, XLIV (1987), 507–516; a useful case study is provided in L. Leneman, *Living in Atholl: A Social History of the Estates, 1685–1785* (Edinburgh, 1986), 147–71.

21 NLS, Wemyss MSS, MS 5723, Tutors Sederunt Book, 1719–33, 9 Oct. 1719; see too Watson, 'Rights and responsibilities', 102.

22 Devine, *Transformation*, 63.

23 S. J. Davies, 'The courts and the Scottish legal system, 1600–1747: the case of Stirlingshire', in V. A. C. Gatrell, B. Lenman and G. Parker (eds), *Crime and the Law: The Social History of Crime in Western Europe since 1500* (London, 1980); see too A. Whetstone, *Scottish County Government in the Eighteenth and Nineteenth Centuries* (Edinburgh, 1981).

24 Fraser, *Conflict and Class*, 64–5.

25 See E. K. Carmichael, 'Jacobitism in the Scottish commission of the peace, 1707–1760', *Scottish Historical Review*, LVIII (April 1979), 65–9; Whetstone, *Scottish County Government*, 27–51.

26 Lenman, *Integration, Enlightenment, and Industrialisation*, 25.

27 S. J. Connolly, 'Albion's fatal twigs: justice and law in the eighteenth century', in Mitchison and Roebuck, *Economy and Society*, 121.

28 Mitchison, *Lordship*, 162; for fuller discussion and a partial challenge to received wisdom on the grip which patronage had on freeholders and burgh voters, see R. M. Sunter, *Patronage and Politics in Scotland, 1707–1832* (Edinburgh, 1986).

29 Lenman, *Integration, Enlightenment and Industrialisation*, 11.

30 Smout, 'Peasant and lord', 514; see too R. Mitchison and L. Leneman, *Sin in the City: Sexuality and Social Control in Urban Scotland, 1660–1780* (Edinburgh, 1988), 20.

31 B. Lenman, 'The limits of godly discipline in the early modern period with particular reference to England and Scotland', in K. von Greyerz (ed.), *Religion and Society in Early Modern Europe, 1500–1800* (1984), 134–9; L. Leneman, 'The kirk session and social control in the early modern Scottish cities', in *Popular Religion and Society* (St Andrews, 1991), 78–89.

32 CAA, 18/65 A 15, 'Instructions to the Constables', 1697; Mitchison and Leneman, *Sin in the City*, 24.

33 R. Chambers, *Traditions of Edinburgh* (Edinburgh, 1868 ed.), 153–4; N. Smith, 'Sexual mores and attitudes in Enlightenment Scotland', in P. G. Bouce (ed.), *Sexuality in Eighteenth-Century Britain* (Manchester, 1982), 58–9; R. Mitchison and L. Leneman, *Sexuality and Social Control: Scotland, 1660–1780* (Oxford, 1989), 63–5, 70–1.

34 Mitchison and Leneman, *Sin in the City*, 88–9.

35 Lenman, 'Limits of godly discipline', 135.

36 C. Brown, 'Religion', in Cooke, *et al.*, *Modern Scottish History*, 64–5; L. Leneman, 'Prophaning the Lord's day: sabbath breach in early modern Scotland', *History*, LXIV, (1989), 220; see too Smith, 'Sexual mores', 51–8.

37 Mitchison and Leneman, *Sexuality*, 33–5.

38 Smith, 'Sexual mores', 55.

39 G. Parker, 'The "kirk by law established" and the origins of the "taming of Scotland": St Andrews, 1559–1600', in Leneman, *Perspectives*, 18–19; Mitchison, *Lordship*, 175; Lenman, *Integration, Enlightenment, and Industrialisation*, 10–11; Devine, 'Unrest and stability', 129.

40 Lord Cockburn, *Memorials of his Time* (Edinburgh, 1945 ed.), 198–9; H. Arnot, *The History of Edinburgh* (Edinburgh, 1788 ed.), 191.

41 E. P. Thompson, *Customs in Common* (London, 1993 ed.), 24.

42 *Ibid.*; J. Ferguson, *Lowland Lairds* (Glasgow, n. d.), 15, describes 'a kinship of feeling, a realisation of common interest, a sense of loyalty to the soil on which and from which both of them [laird and tenant] lived', which survived into the twentieth century. The evidence for this is at least ambiguous, as will be seen. To be fair, it should be pointed out that there are historians in Scotland who have recognised that there was a price to pay for lower class deference or acquiescence: see, for example, Fraser, 'Patterns of protest', in Devine and Mitchison, *People and Society*, 274.

43 Duckham, *Scottish Coal*, 248–9.

44 NAS, Buccleuch MSS, GD 224, 240/6, 1st Journal of Matthew Little, Deputy Chamberlain of Canonbie.

45 H. Hamilton (ed.), *Selections from the Monymusk papers, 1713–1755* (Edinburgh, 1945), x,xxxiv–xxxvi.

46 Thompson, *Customs in Common*, 57; Watson, 'Rights and responsibilities', 110–11.

47 D. Levine and K. Wrightson, *The Making of an Industrial Society: Whickham, 1560–1765* (Oxford, 1991), 375. The rest of this paragraph is heavily influenced by this study.

48 NAS, High Court of Justiciary, JC26/85, Bill Letters of Recrimination, Blair of that Ilk v. Cunninghame of Auchenharvie, 3 July 1708; JC7/6, High Court Minute Book D, 1712–1714, case between John Glass of Sauchie and ors. v. Major George Munro of Auchenbowie, 1713.

49 Houston, *Social Change*, 290–319; Chambers, *Traditions of Edinburgh*, 188; ECA, CRB, SL30/239, State of the Town of Haddington, 1726.

50 *Glasgow Courant*, 18 May 1747; see too Bob Harris, '"American idols": empire, war and the middling ranks in mid-eighteenth-century Britain', *Past & Present*, CL (February 1996), 116–7; CDA, Dundee Burgh Treasurer's Accounts, 1753–78.

51 Harris and Whatley, '"To solemnise his majesty's birthday"', 402–5, 415.

52 NAS, State Papers, Scotland, RH2/4/314, Robert Dundas to His Majesty, 17 Oct. 1722.

53 J. Strawhorn, *The History of Irvine: Royal Burgh and New Town* (Edinburgh, 1985), 64–5.

54 Symonds, *Weep Not for Me*, 71–83, 93–4.

55 J. G. Harrison, 'Women and the branks in Stirling, *c.* 1600–*c.* 1730', *Scottish Economic & Social History*, XVIII (1998), 114–31.

56 Fraser, *Conflict and Class*, 17–20; D. Stevenson, *The Origins of Freemasonry: Scotland's Century, 1590–1710* (Cambridge, 1990 ed.), 190–212.

57 Fraser, *Conflict and Class*, 44; Rab Houston, 'Popular politics in the reign of George II: the Edinburgh cordiners', *Scottish Historical Review*, LXXII (October 1993), 183–9.

58 Houston, *Social Change*, 232–3; S. Nenadic, 'The rise of the urban middle class', in Devine and Mitchison, *People and Society*, 114–18; 'The middle ranks and modernisation', in Devine and Jackson, *Glasgow*, 278–9.

59 Robertson, *Scottish Enlightenment and the Militia Issue*, 181.

60 *Glasgow Courant*, 28 August 1749, 18 June 1750.

61 Langford, *A Polite and Commercial People*, 158–62; Bob Harris, 'The *London Evening Post* and mid-eighteenth century British politics', *English Historical Review*, CX (November 1995), 11–44.

62 Historical Manuscripts Commission, *Report on MSS in Various Collections, V, MS of Col. Mordaunt-Hay of Duns Castle* (London, 1909), 49–51; A. Murdoch, 'Politics and the people in the burgh of Dumfries, 1758–1760', *Scottish Historical Review*, LXX (October 1991), 151–71;

63 C. A. Malcolm (ed.), *Minutes of the JPs for Lanarkshire, 1707–23* (Edinburgh, 1931), lxxv.

64 I am grateful to David Alston for this information.

65 NAS, State Papers, Scotland, RH 2/9/399, Letter Books 1742–6, Marquis of Tweeddale to General Clayton, 27 May 1742.

66 Grampian Regional Archives, 1/1/1, Minute Book of the Commissioners of Supply, Aberdeenshire, 1713–28, 17 December 1724, 5 May 1726; Whatley, 'How tame', 5.

67 Whyte, *Agriculture and Society*, 100–12; I. D. Whyte, *Scotland's Society and Economy in Transition, c. 1500–c. 1760* (London, 1997), 38, 44–5; Hancock, *Citizens of the World*, 297; on Dysart, NAS, Rosslyn MSS, GD 164/419, Memorial of the Burgh of Dysart, 1717; Fife Council, Kirkcaldy Town House, Dysart Council Records, 1674–1761, 5 May 1715, 8 April, 16 October 1717, 23 June 1718.

68 ECA, CRB, Moses Collection, SL30/226, Petition for the Burgh of Lochmaben, 1710; SL30/233, Representation and Petition, The Commissioner for the Burgh of Culross, 1718; SL30/239, Petition for the Magistrates of the Burgh of Forres, 1725, Petition of the Town of Dumbarton, 1726; SL30/242, Petition of the Burgh of Pittenweem, 1731; W. Cramond, *The Annals of Cullen* (Buckie, 1904), 57, 63, 69, 74; see too NAS, B 48/9/8, Linlithgow Council Minute Book, 1717–28, 30 August 1718.

69 University of St Andrews Archives and Muniments (USAAM), B10/10/1, Crail Council Minute Book, 1708–33, 11 March 1719.

70 Devine, *Transformation of Rural Scotland*, 30.

71 Blair Atholl Castle, Atholl MSS, Box 43 (7), 189, Alexander Areskine to Atholl, 20 October 1707.

72 T. M. Devine, 'The English connection and Irish and Scottish development in the eighteenth century', in Devine and Dickson, *Ireland and Scotland*, 22.

73 Whyte, *Scotland's Society*, 44–5; Timperley, 'Landholding', 141.

74 ECA, CRB, Moses Collection, SL30/228, Petition from the Town of Wick, 1712; SL30/232, Petition for John Calder, Baillie of Wick, 1717.

75 Szechi, *Letters of George Lockhart*, 1.

76 W. Hector, *Selections from the Judicial Records of Renfrewshire* (Paisley, 1876), 38–9.

77 Historical Manuscripts Commission, *MS of Col. Mordaunt-Hay of Duns Castle*, 43–4.

78 E. P. Thompson, 'Patrician society, plebeian culture', *Journal of Social History*, VII (1974), 388; see too Rule and Wells, 'Crime, protest', 8.

79 Thomson, *Kelp-Making*, 75.

80 Smout, *History of the Scottish People*, 326.

81 See Whatley, 'How tame', 22.

82 Smout, 'The improvers and the Scottish environment', 221; Watson, 'Rights and responsibilities', 111; Leneman, *Living in Atholl*, 185–91.

83 D. G. Barrow (ed.), *The Court Book of the Barony of Urie in Kincardineshire, 1604–1747* (Edinburgh, 1892), li; Hamilton, *Selections from the Monymusk Papers*, xxii, xxiv, lxix, 201; Symonds, *Weep Not for Me*, 99–104.

84 J. Robertson, *General View of the Agriculture in the County of Perth* (Perth, 1813), xv–xvi.

85 Hankins and Strawhorn, *Correspondence of James Boswell*, 24, 68, n. 5.

86 NAS, State Papers, Scotland, RH2/4/384, Thomas Miller, Lord Barskimming, to the Lord Justice Clerk, 25 October 1773.

87 See, for example, ECA, CRB, Moses Collection, SL30/239, Petition of the Burgh of Annan, 1726.

88 PKCA, Perth Burgh Records, B 59/24/1/23, Proclamation re. enclosures, 1720; CAA, Enactment Books, 1730–41, 26 February 1734, 4 March 1736, 28 July 1741; Strawhorn, *History of Irvine*, 64, 84.

89 For discussion of this problem, see J. Rule, 'Social crime in the rural south in the eighteenth and early nineteenth centuries', in Rule and Wells, *Crime, Protest and Popular Politics*, 153–68.

90 PKCA, Perth Burgh Records, PE 51/Bundle 2, John Ramsay to James Chalmers, 11 September 1773.

91 Whatley, 'Labour in the industrialising city', 383; *Scots Magazine*, November 1754, 548; *Scots Magazine,* January 1755, 47; D. Hay and F. Snyder, 'Using the criminal law, 1750–1850: policing, private prosecution and the state', in Hay and Snyder (eds), *Policing and Prosecution in Britain, 1750–1850* (Oxford, 1989), 28–9.

92 Grampian Regional Archives, 1/1/2, Banff Town Council Minute Book, 1765–76, 25 March 1775; see too Leneman, *Living in Atholl*, 161–2.

93 K. Simpson, 'The legacy of flyting', *Studies in Scottish Literature*, XXVI (1991), 503–14.

94 Harrison, 'Women and the branks', 127–8.

95 CAA, Enactment Books, 1730–41, 18 October 1731.

96 CDCA, General Petitions, Petition from Alex Neilsone and George Morrison, 1718.

97 Smith, 'Sexual mores', 58; CAA, Aberdeen Town Council Minutes, 58, 1700–21, 1 December 1708; USAAM, CH2/82/5, Cupar Presbytery Minutes, 1715–23, 20 January, 15 December 1719. It is striking that the earl of Rothes, sheriff principal of Fife, appears to have been behind this particular campaign.

98 Houston and Whyte, 'Introduction', 34; J. Purser, *Scotland's Music* (Edinburgh, 1992), 202–6; CDA, Dundee Burgh Treasurer's Accounts, 1753–78.

99 M. Lynch, 'Introduction', in Lynch (ed.), *The Early Modern Town in Scotland* (1987), 23; Whyte, *Scotland Before the Industrial Revolution*, 206; ECA, CRB, Moses Collection, SL30/228, Petition from the Burgh of Dingwall, 1712.

100 For a recent elaboration of this idea, see N. Rogers, *Crowds, Culture and Politics in Georgian Britain* (Oxford, 1998), 13.

101 B. Reay 'Introduction', in Reay (ed.), *Popular Culture in Early Modern England* (London, 1985), 8–9; for the holiday and calendrical occasions which could produce inversionary disorder in England see P. Burke, 'Popular culture in seventeenth-century London', in Reay, *Popular Culture*, 35–8.

102 C. A. Whatley, '"The privilege which the rabble have to be riotous": carnivalesque and the monarch's birthday in Scotland, *c*. 1700–1860', in I. Blanchard (ed.), *Labour and Leisure in Historical Perspective, Thirteenth to Twentieth Centuries* (Stuttgart, 1994), 89–100.

103 M. Ingram, 'Ridings, rough music and mocking rhymes in early modern England', in Reay, *Popular Culture*, 167–78; C. A. Whatley, 'Royal day, people's day: the monarch's birthday in Scotland', in R. Mason and N. MacDougall (eds), *People and Power in Scotland: Essays in Honour of T. C. Smout* (Edinburgh, 1992), 182; Cramond, *Annals of Cullen*, 79; A. Smart, *Songs of Labour and Domestic Life* (Edinburgh, 1860), 'Montrose fifty years since', 127.

104 Harrison, 'Women and the branks', 118.

105 See CAA, Aberdeen Enactment Book, 1736–41, 5 December 1735.

106 T. Hayter, *The Army and the Crowd in Mid-Georgian England* (London, 1978), 2.

107 Fraser, 'Patterns of protest', 274.

108 Such a pattern, but with a longer period of calm, has been identified by Smout, *History of the Scottish People*, 227.

109 J. Brewer, *The Sinews of Power: War, Money and the English State, 1688–1783* (New York, 1989), 51; on the same issue see too J. R. Weston, *The English Militia in the Eighteenth Century* (London, 1965), but this too has little to say on Scotland.

110 Connolly, 'Albion's fatal twigs', 122.

111 See J. A. Cheyne, 'Reluctant heroes: conscription in Aberdeenshire, 1756–1758', *Northern Studies*, IV (1981), 47.

112 G. H. Healey (ed.), *The Letters of Daniel Defoe* (Oxford, 1955), 132–66; it is interesting that a visiting Englishman commented on the greater ferocity of the Edinburgh crowd over a century later: Rogers, *Crowds*, 274.

113 Whatley, *Bought and Sold*, 44.

114 Blair Atholl Castle, Atholl MSS, Patrick Scott to the Duchess of Atholl, 8 February 1707.

115 See, for example, Dumfries Archives, Dumfries burgh records, petitions, 543, 'Petition, James Milligan, late deacon and tacksman of the common mills, Dumfries', 545, 'Petition, Robert Hewall, tacksman of the mills of Dumfries', 1709.

116 Murdoch, *The People Above*, 3.

117 For a discussion of the Malt Tax disturbances and the events leading up to them, see Lenman, *Jacobite Risings*, 206–14.

118 Whatley, 'How tame', 8–9.

119 NAS, High Court Records, JC11/18, North Circuit Minute Book, May 1753–April 1754, case of Alexander Livingston v. James Smith, 74–79; University of Nottingham, Department of Manuscripts and Special Collections, Pelham Papers, NeC 2144/1, H. Colquhoun to H. Pelham, 19 April 1752. I am indebted to Dr Bob Harris for these references.

120 Mitchison and Leneman, *Sexuality*, 201, 230.

121 R. A. Houston, 'The literacy myth?: Illiteracy in Scotland, 1630–1760', *Past & Present*, XCVI (August 1982), 81–102.

122 For an example of the strength of sabbatarianism, even in the absence of a minister, see MacArthur, *Iona*, 177.

123 Mitchison and Leneman, *Sexuality*, 201; C. Brown, *Religion and Society in Scotland since 1707* (London, 1997 ed.), 72.

124 Mitchison and Leneman, *Sin in the City*, 128–44; Mitchison and Leneman,

Sexuality, 145–6; Smith, 'Sexual mores', 56

125 Mitchison and Leneman, *Sin in the City*, 92–3; C. A. Whatley, 'Burns: work, kirk and community in later eighteenth-century Scotland', in K. Simpson (ed.) *Burns Now* (Edinburgh, 1994), 102–4.

126 Signet Library, Court of Session papers, CSP 20:9, 'Petition of Marion Gow', 1756; see too Mitchison and Leneman, *Sin in the City*, 36.

127 Mitchell Library, Glasgow City Archives, CH2/173/2, Barony Parish Kirk Session Minutes, 1699–1727, 5 July 1707.

128 For an informed discussion, see Houston, *Social Change*, 185–192, 210–11; T. C. Smout, 'Born again at Cambuslang: new evidence on popular religion and literacy in eighteenth-century Scotland', reprinted in A. Cooke, *et al.* (eds), *Modern Scottish History, 1707 to the Present* (Edinburgh, 1998), Volume III, 59.

129 Leneman, 'Kirk session and social control', 35; Larner, *Enemies of God*, 78–9; detailed on superstition in one part of Scotland is M. Martin, *A Description of the Western Islands of Scotland c. 1695* (Edinburgh, 1994 ed.); see too D. Buchan, *Folk Tradition and Folk Medicine in Scotland: The Writings of David Rorie* (Edinburgh, 1994); A. Fenton, 'The people below: Dougal Graham's chapbooks as a mirror of the lower classes in eighteenth century Scotland', in A. Gardner-Medwin and J. Hadley Williams (eds), *A Day Festival: Essays on the Music, Poetry and History of Scotland and England* (Aberdeen, 1990), 69–80.

130 Rab Houston, 'Coal, class and culture: labour relations in a Scottish mining community, 1650–1750', *Social History*, VIII (January 1983), 1–18; Whatley, 'Fettering bonds', 144–6; Whatley, 'Scottish "collier serfs"', 240–3; Smith, 'Sexual mores', 58.

131 USAAM, MS BX9075, A1, General Assembly Minutes, 1746–50, 58–61; CH2/1132/5, St Andrews Presbytery Minute Book, 1740–51, 217–18; CH2/82/9, Cupar Presbytery Minute Book, 1742–59, 115.

132 One of the fullest and most accessible is W. M. Inglis, *An Angus Parish in the Eighteenth Century* (Dundee, 1904).

133 Brown, *Religion and Society*, 78; L. Colley, *Britons: Forging the Nation, 1707–1837* (Yale, 1992), 22–3; D. Allan, 'Protestantism, presbyterianism and national identity in eighteenth-century Scottish history', in T. Claydon and I. McBride (eds), *Chosen Peoples? Protestantism and National Identity in Britain and Ireland, c. 1650–1850* (Cambridge, 1998), 197–8.

134 See R. B. Sher, *Church and University in the Scottish Enlightenment: The Moderate Literati of Edinburgh* (Edinburgh, 1985); for a recent re-interpretation of the Popular Party's (the Evangelicals) stance on theological and secular matters, see J. R. McIntosh, *Church and Theology in Enlightenment Scotland: The Popular Party, 1740–1800* (East Linton, 1998).

135 Smout, *History of the Scottish People*, 329–31; see too, for example, DCA, Weaver Trade Records, GD/TD/W/1/3, Locket Book, 1631–1762.

136 K. J. Logue, 'The Levellers revolt in Galloway in 1724', *Scottish Labour History Society Journal*, XIV (May 1980), 8–19; Smout, *History of the Scottish People*, 329; 'Born again at Cambuslang', 57–8.

137 Brown, *Religion and Society*, 73.

138 Brown, *Religion and Society*, 86; Smith, *Annexed Estates*, 34–7;

Withrington, 'Schooling, literacy and society', 164–71; Richards and Clough, *Cromartie*, 160–1; D. M. M. Paton, 'Brought to a wilderness: the Rev. David Mackenzie of Farr and the Sutherland clearances', *Northern Scotland*, XIII (1993), 80.

139 NAS, High Court Records, JC 13/6, West Circuit Minute Book, 1726–33, 5 October 1731.
140 Murdoch, 'Politics and the people', 152.
141 CAA, Press 18, Bundle 80a, Fraserburgh riot, 1735.
142 R. K. Donovan, 'Voices of distrust: the expression of anti-Catholic feeling in Scotland, 1778–1781', *Innes Review*, XXX (1979), 62–76; *Scots Magazine*, December 1778, 684–5; see too C. Haydon, *Anti-Catholicism in Eighteenth-Century England, c. 1714–80* (Manchester, 1993), 17, 212–3.
143 Glamis Castle, Glamis Papers, Box 103/Bundle 2, John Leslie to the earl of Glamis, 23 September 1738.
144 C. Brown, 'Protest in the pews. Interpreting presbyterianism and society in fracture during the Scottish economic revolution', in Devine, *Conflict and Stability*, 99. It is unlikely that this claim is correct for the period up to 1750.
145 *Scots Magazine*, January 1751, 50–1; NAS, Church of Scotland Records, CH2/723/11, Dunblane Kirk Session Minute Book, 5 February 1771.
146 C. Brown, *The People in the Pews: Religion and Society in Scotland since 1780* (Glasgow, 1993), 10.
147 Smout, *History of the Scottish People*, 281.
148 Brown, 'Protest in the pews', 91–7.
149 Devine, *Transformation*, 159–60.
150 Whyte, *Scotland's Society*, 49.
151 H. T. Dickinson, *The Politics of the People in Eighteenth-Century Britain* (London, 1994), 125.
152 But for a pioneering study of the post-1780 period, see Logue, *Popular Disturbances in Scotland*.
153 Bob Harris, *Politics and the Rise of the Press: Britain and France, 1620–1800* (London, 1996), 12; for the problems, see R. Wells, 'Counting riots in eighteenth-century England', *Bulletin of the Labour History Society*, XXXVII (1978), 68–72.
154 See Whatley, 'How tame'; Whatley, 'An uninflammable people?'.
155 R. B. Shoemaker, 'The London "mob" in the early eighteenth century', in P. Borsay (ed.), *The Eighteenth-Century Town: A Reader in English Urban History, 1688–1820* (London, 1990), 188–222; N. Rogers, 'Popular protest in early Hanoverian London', *Past & Present*, LXXIX (1978), 70–100.
156 Whatley, 'How tame', 14–15.
157 Thomson, *Kelp-Making*, 77–8.
158 Lenman, 'Client society', 87; B. Lenman, *The Jacobite Cause* (Edinburgh, 1986), 51.
159 Central Regional Archives, B 66/21, Stirling Council Minutes, 1728–32, 25 November 1728.
160 Whatley, 'How tame', 7–8.
161 PKCA, Perth Customs Letter Books, Collector to Board, 1721–38, 23 March 1722, NAS, CE 51/1/2, Dumfries Customs Letter Books, Collector to Board,

1721–35, 12 September, 1 October 1722; Whatley, 'An uninflammable people?', 61.

162 J. Stevenson, *Popular Disturbances in England 1700–1832* (1992 ed.), 117.

163 Whatley, 'Labour in the industrialising city', 381.

164 J. Bohstedt, *Riots and Community Politics in England and Wales, 1790–1810* (Harvard, 1983), 87.

165 See A. Randall, A. Charlesworth, R. Sheldon and D. Walsh, 'Markets, Market Culture and Popular Protest in Eighteenth-Century Britain and Ireland', in A. Randall and A. Charlesworth (eds), *Markets, Market Culture and Popular Protest in Eighteenth-Century Britain and Ireland* (Liverpool, 1996), 18–23; Thompson, *Customs in Common*; C. A. Bouton, *The Flour War: Gender, Class, and Community in Late Ancien Regime French Society* (Pennsylvania, 1993).

166 For a general survey which admirably describes this, see Dickinson, *Politics of the People*, 148–55; Whatley, 'How tame', 18–20.

167 NAS, Clerk of Penicuik MSS, GD 18/5423/13, Robert Pringle to Sir John Clerk, 28 October 1740.

5

Scottish society, c. 1707–c. 1778 (II): political integration and the struggle over the market economy

Integration and early improvement

The Articles of Union had passed through the Scottish Parliament during the last months of 1706 to a roaring crescendo of popular outrage in the streets of Edinburgh. Other towns and shires witnessed similar passionate outbursts of anti-Union feeling, with many ministers 'roaring' against the proposed incorporating union from their pulpits, at least until the future of the Scottish church was secured by a separate Act. Not all clergymen were placated however and for nonconformist Presbyterians, principally the Covenanters who rejected the settlement of 1690, incorporation with England along the lines being proposed in 1706 was 'anathema'. Anti-union petitioning was rife, particularly in the shires. The Articles of Union were burned at the town crosses of Dumfries, Kirkudbright and Stirling. An armed insurrection was reportedly planned and began to be marshalled in the west, as well as on the duke of Atholl's Perthshire estates.[1]

For the next four decades Scotland seethed with popular discontent. Many of the disturbances have been noted already. The existence of others which have made no impression hitherto, or whose brief bursts on to the historical stage are recorded only by short, obscure remarks in the documents of the period, or which make only fleeting appearances in the historical literature, should however be acknowledged. Restrictions of space prohibit the inclusion here of more than two of the smaller disturbances which are omitted altogether from the historiography. In August 1707 an account reached the duke of Atholl of a 'solemne battle' which had taken place in the Borders between gangs of English and Scottish fishermen. The 'quarrel', it was reported, was 'nationall'. Also, a few days earlier, it had been reported from Edinburgh where most brewers had stopped brewing 'by reason of the Severity of the [newly-appointed] Gadgers', that a 'mob' had put out the fires of those who continued to work.[2] Far and away the most important of the neglected disturbances however was a series of riots – ostensibly about food – which swept 'like a fire or contagion' through several east-coast towns and villages from near Edinburgh north to Montrose between January and March 1720.[3] In its geographical extent and severity this outbreak of food rioting was almost certainly the worst in Scotland's early modern history. It was followed by another, better-known, bout of food rioting in 1740–41.[4]

These of course were in addition to the aborted Jacobite invasion of 1708, the incursion by the Spaniards in Glenshiel in 1719 and the risings of 1715 and 1745. The '15 received considerable popular support, albeit tacitly and without widespread resort to arms. There are suggestions that in the painful aftermath of Union an 'active' Jacobite musical and poetic culture blossomed alongside the erotic, the former manifesting itself in vigorous street ballads and fiddle tunes.[5] Recent calculations of the size and geographical background of the recruits into Jacobite armies of 1715 and 1745 claim to confirm the strength of Lowland support for the former, not only among Episcopalians, and that for the '45 substantial recruiting took place in the Lowlands, south as well as north of the Tay, of nobility, officers and men.[6] But most of the Jacobite army were clansmen, and some of the Lowland contingents were extremely small. The minute numbers from Fife – a cavalry force of ninety in 1715 and a total of 120 men in 1745 – are hardly indicative of an untapped seam of militant Jacobitism. The strength of Protestantism and the degree of support there was for the Hanoverians should not be underestimated, not only but especially in the west, where a very different picture prevailed. Sizeable loyalist volunteer forces were raised in towns such as Ayr and Irvine in 1715 and 1745, for example.[7] But in the north-east too, even in counties such as Angus where Episcopalianism had rooted deeply, there was a spirited Hanoverian presence, often nurtured by the kirk, the spiritual curse of Jacobitism. Even in Cromarty, which bordered the Highlands north and west of Inverness, but a stronghold of Presbyterianism, popular tradition held that only one person dared to wear a white cockade in public in 1745, and he was immediately 'apprehended by a party of his neighbours'.[8] It was the mainly Episcopalian Highland clans, who comprised some 67 per cent of the Jacobite combatants at Culloden, which continued to provide the bulk of the fighting force of militant Jacobitism, not Presbyterian Lowlanders.[9]

When portraying and analysing the period from 1707 to 1746 historians have emphasised the pre-eminence of the fortunes of the Jacobites, which ebbed and flowed in accordance with the shifting priorities in the foreign policies of anti-Hanoverian European princes, although it has been argued that within Scotland the abolition of the Privy Council was a major enabling factor in the risings of 1715 and 1745.[10] Without Spanish or French support, Jacobitism in Britain had little hope of success. The geographical focus has been the Highlands, the more troublesome parts of which were eventually brought to heel within a united Hanoverian Britain by a combination of road and garrison construction (under the supervision of General Wade and his successors), the spinning wheel and the weavers' shuttle, with force of arms – 'systematic state terrorism' – being used with uncompromising savagery in the wake of Culloden.[11] Hostile to Whig ambitions in religion (but fellow travellers in their commitment to property and commercial progress), Jacobite strongholds in the Gaelic-speaking Highlands of either Roman Catholicism but more commonly non-juring Episcopalianism were exposed to the preaching of state-supported 'shocktroops' of Presbyterianism, the missionaries of the SSPCK, who in the early decades and until 1767 were intent on doing their work in the English tongue.[12]

Although, as has just been seen, greater emphasis is now placed upon popular Jacobitism and its identification with opposition to the Union, as was noted at the start of the previous chapter, the consensus among most historians (but not shared here, or supported by evidence already presented) is that the effects of the Union passed the common people by. The search for political ascendancy and royal favour in London at magnate level was in Scotland the driving force of British political integration, and is assumed to be the proper object of the attention of students of the period. It was here, in the competition between the parties attached to the Court on one side and on the other the opposition Squadrone, rather than from any pressure from below, that the greatest difficulties arose.[13] In the Lowlands, it is asserted, relative calm prevailed under the firm hand of Westminster rule, with urban crowds causing fewer problems than they had in the sixteenth and seventeenth centuries other than the Shawfield and Porteous riots. These have been closely studied, but in isolation not only from each other but also from the other causes of complaint in post-Union Scotland.

It would be foolish to deny the momentous importance of the Jacobite risings in either Scottish or British history. The '15 was a close-run thing, relatively strongly-supported not least because it promised to repeal the Union, but failing in Scotland almost wholly because of the inadequacies attributed to its leader, the earl of Mar, described scathingly by one historian as a 'self-centred, montrously incompetent poltroon' (although one contemporary was of the opinion that most Scottish Jacobites were 'Generally fools').[14] There are historians who are inclined to believe – not without good cause, from a short-term military perspective – that the '45 was less obviously doomed than Charles Edward Stuart's council of war concluded when they recommended in December 1745 that the Jacobite army retreat from Derby, when all that lay between it and the capital was 'a mob of nervous militia at Finchley'.[15]

There is enormous substance in the argument that as far as the authorities in London were concerned the Scottish 'problem' was the revolution of 1689 and the threat thereafter posed by a resurgent Stuart cause.[16] Yet with the benefit of hindsight it is legitimate for the historian to ask how far this perception was borne out in reality on the ground in Scotland. It will be argued here that while Jacobitism was a potent destabilising factor in post-Union Scotland, it was by no means the only one. When in 1964 P. W. J. Riley described Scotland in this period as 'an almost uncontrollable region', he was referring to the epidemic of assaults on customs and excise officers, not high politics.[17] This however was only one manifestation of what was primarily but by no means only lower-class discontent, albeit a major one.

As was outlined in chapter 2, contemporaries who commented on law and order in post-Union Scotland frequently remarked on the 'spirit of mobbing and robbery' which had 'possessed the populace of this country'. So serious had this become in Angus and the Mearns by 1721 that it was feared if nothing was done to remove this 'devil', and should the troops currently stationed there disappear, 'noe body could be one moment secure from being ruined who has anything to lose'.[18] Two decades later, in April 1742, the marquis of Tweeddale, newly-appointed Secretary for Scotland (who held office until 1746), wrote that he was 'vexed' to find 'a mobbish disposition prevail so much in our country'. It should not be allowed, he continued, 'unless we are resolved to let the mob be our Masters'. This 'licentiousness in the lower sort of the people', he thought, had been encouraged by the failure of those in authority to 'bring criminals to punishment'.[19] Such remarks referred to the Lowlands. In some districts – around Airth on the upper navigable reaches of the river Forth, for example – the forces of law and order (in the form of constables) were said to be non-existent, and a grievous loss for the customs service and its frequently maltreated officers.[20]

Some indication has already been given of the nature of the problems the authorities faced. To these can be added another variant. In the autumn of 1742 Tweeddale's fellow officer of state, Robert Craigie, Lord Advocate, gave his response to news of a 'riot' of journeymen weavers in Leith. Describing this as the first 'overt' act of a series of combinations that 'have long been carrying on among the journeymen', and as previous attempts to stop 'such Tumults' had been unsuccessful, he recommended that those guilty should be punished 'pretty smartly'.[21] Labour historians have noted too the emergence of well-organised craft unions from the 1720s, as well as an increased level of collective action among urban workers who were confronted with threats to their labour monopolies at a time when trade was generally depressed.[22]

What seems inescapable is that it was during the 1720s and 1730s (and prior to the threatened invasion of England by French forces in 1744), when the Stuart cause had been largely dormant, that civil disorder in Lowland Scotland was at its height.[23] Contrary to what has sometimes been asserted, patriotic Scots who were dissatisfied with the Union did have alternative outlets for their discontent.[24] During the aforementioned two decades at least sixty fatalities in Scotland resulted just from conflicts which were either directly or indirectly concerned with taxation, while an unknown (albeit smaller) number also lost their lives during food riots, strikes and conflicts between townspeople and soldiers. The period from 1720 to 1725, which commenced with the food riots of 1720 and thereafter saw the Levellers Revolt and the malt tax riots, was one of much greater civil disorder in the Lowlands than occurred throughout the whole of Scotland during any of the Jacobite risings.[25] Indeed it was after 1716 and during the 1720s that Jacobitism in Scotland was at a particularly low ebb, many of its leaders having been forced into exile and reluctant to risk their lives and livelihoods once again in a cause of which they heartily despaired.[26]

That Jacobite elements attached themselves to some of these disturbances is unquestionable. In pamphlets from the pens of the discontented, analogies were drawn between the Israelites and the Scots, the last subjected by the Hanoverian King George to tyrannies which in the eyes of God would justify the use of violent methods to withdraw from the clutches of England (Egypt) and break the Union.[27] Propagandists like Robert Freebairn exploited the ailing economy and the 'Ruine of Trade' for the same end, arguing for example that:

> Before the Union we had no Taxes but were laid on by our own Parliaments, and those very easie, and spent within our own Country. Now we have not only the Cess or Land Tax, and Customs conform to the English Book of Rates, near the Triple what we formerly pay'd, and Excise, both most rigorously exacted by a Parcel of Strangers sent down to us from England, but also the Malt-Tax, the Salt-Tax, the Leather-Tax, the Window-Tax, the Taxes upon Candles, Soap, Stearch ... the Tax upon stamped Paper and Parchments ... most of ... which are bound upon us for 64, and some of them for 99 years to come.[28]

As will be seen, while such sentiments struck a popular chord and helped to sustain opposition to the Union, there is rather little evidence that they served the cause of Jacobitism in Scotland particularly well. Jacobites from the upper, literate ranks had little truck with the unpredictable mob, which they despised and feared, while the Whig regime were sure that plebeian Jacobitism could do little damage without patrician leadership and endorsement.[29]

Viewed collectively rather than individually, the popular disturbances of the period can be interpreted as the consequences of the operation of a matrix of deep and powerful stress-inducing forces, although within particular localities the balance of these was different, and sometimes additional factors were also at work.[30] Primarily, the main pressures were, on the one side, increasing commercialism, especially but not exclusively in the agrarian sector, which as has been seen became more pronounced in the later seventeenth century. Allied to this were the consequences of incorporating union. On the other side, were poverty, economic uncertainties and the beliefs and perceptions of the common people. E. P. Thompson's concept of the 'moral economy' of the crowd is clearly of relevance, although recent research in both England and France has suggested that popular disorder of the sort being examined here is better understood within the regional and local contexts in which rioters calculated and acted.[31] The suggestion was made in chapter 2 that Scotland in the 1720s and 1730s was confronted by nothing less than a crisis in the twin processes of integration and early economic improvement. It has been said of food rioting which occurred in England in the seventeenth century that in a society in which 'inequalities were marked, poverty endemic and powers of repression limited', any outbreak of disorder was potentially dangerous.[32] With even greater force, the same remarks may be applied to early eighteenth-century Scotland, where the state's authority was weaker.

The food riots of 1720 provide us with a route into the evidence with which to begin to illuminate this hypothesis. At the outset it is important to underline the seriousness of these disturbances. They engulfed coastal burghs in three counties, Angus, Fife and Perthshire (see map 3). Crowds ranged in size from around fifty to two thousand, and marched and broke open the barns and storehouses of those farmers and merchants who were suspected of withholding oatmeal and grain from the market. Sailors were driven from their vessels in several harbours by men and women wielding axes, hammers, batons and stones. Vessels being laden with grain were variously disabled, by their sails being torn down, the removal of rudders or with holes being cut or smashed into hulls. In Edinburgh and Whitehall the authorities, including King George I, were both alarmed and outraged by what were described as 'Insurrections'. While prior to the Union the Privy Council would have mobilised help for the distressed communities by banning exports, subsidising imports (as happened in 1699), as well as insisting that parishes intervene to support the destitute, supported by fasts ordered by the kirk, in 1720 this was no longer an option. No easily mobilised mechanism remained to blunt the sharp edge of commercial aspiration. Accordingly, the armed forces in Scotland were ordered to act 'with all the vigour and severity that is warrantable by law', to suppress a series of disturbances which it was feared would get out of hand.[33] Trials of those accused of taking part in them, some of whom were accused of sedition, were held throughout the spring and summer, but even these were conducted against a backcloth of popular outrage. At Cupar, where the High Court sat for the trials, dragoons had to be stationed, 'for suppressing the mobs'.

In the context of early modern Europe where large-scale food riots like

Map 3   Locations of food riots in Scotland, 1720

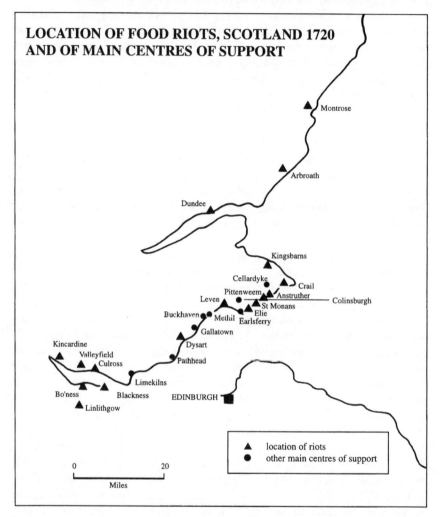

this were not uncommon, the Scottish food riots of 1720 are of no great consequence. However, as has been noted, in their scale this series of food riots was unprecedented in Scotland. In England, a tradition of food rioting stretching back to the sixteenth century has been traced.[34] In few of the towns where rioting broke out did anything on the same scale happen again. If it is the case, as has been argued recently, that the tensions which accompanied the transformation of Britain in the eighteenth century are to be seen more clearly in relation to the market for food than in industrial relations or agrarian reform (the measure which, invariably, historians in Scotland have used), this enhances their potential significance as a focus for historical analysis. There may be no more sensitive indicator of social and political relations in a period of transition than that which is revealed by the response of those who depended wholly or mainly on the wages of their labour to high prices or shortages in the food market.[35] As with most food riots in early modern England, the 1720 disturbances in Scotland were revolts of urban or semi-urban proletarians, and in several cases representatives of their masters, the deacons of the Trades, with the occupations of those involved closely correlating with the economic function and occupational composition of the affected burghs. Thus in the coal mining and salt manufacturing burgh of Methil in Fife, for example, colliers and salters were prominent members of a crowd which also comprised a wright, a shoemaker, maltmen and mariners.[36]

The outbreak of the 1720 riots owed little to rising prices, although that there was a slight upwards trend in the three years to 1720 may have caused some concern. There were modest increases only however in the price of oats and oatmeal in the affected counties between the harvests of 1718 and 1719. The 3.4 per cent increase in Fife, for example, can be contrasted with rises of 100 per cent between 1694 and 1695 and 1707 and 1708, and lower but substantial rises between 1697 and 1698 and 1713 and 1714.[37] Not surprisingly, given that nowhere else were severe famine and famine mortality conducive to riot, there were only occasional outbreaks of disorder over food in Scotland during the demographically disastrous years of the second half of the 1690s, when the Privy Council had mercilessly hounded dealers who hoarded victuals.[38] Despite the suspicion in the aftermath of the skirmish with pro-Jacobite Spanish forces in Glenshiel in 1719 that the rioting of the 'Giddy Mob' had been fomented by enemies of the government, there is not a single scrap of hard evidence to justify such a belief.

Rather, the principal precipitating cause was shortage of food in most of the respective burghs' market places.[39] This is where the protesting crowds first began to gather. That their intention was to prevent the movement of foodstuffs out of the afflicted burghs was freely admitted by those apprehended for taking part in the disturbances. Equally, and behind the rhetoric born of their paranoia about disaffection, the authorities too were clear about what was at the root of the crowds' 'seditious' behaviour: by interfering with shipments of grain, those concerned had defied laws passed by the pre-union Parliament, as well as the 6th Article of Union, which together had granted bounties to merchants and exporters of victuals in order to promote 'the tillage and Improvement of the Trade of the Kingdome to the best advantage'. Thus at least one of those found guilty had his crime – of unlawfully interfering with commerce – written on a placard on his chest, which he was forced to display in the public market place on two market days. The market cross was the focal point for the community, and therefore the stage upon which the theatre and counter-theatre of competing social values was acted out.

Without exception, assessments of the impact of the Union have been broadly focused, dealing with the *Scottish* economy. This tends not only to conceal regional variations but equally importantly the uneven effects of the Union on the social classes. The considerable benefits accruing to the landed classes from the Union of 1707 have already been described. So too have landed incursions into common land, part of a process of territorial aggrandisement which resulted in increased landholdings on the part of large landowners throughout Scotland in the opening decades of the eighteenth century. It is of no small significance that four of the burghs in which disturbances took place in 1720 – Crail, Culross, Dysart and Linlithgow – were, or had recently been, involved in disputes with neighbouring landowners over common land. The extent to which economic pressure and disappointed expectations could cause the labouring people to shed their cloak of deference is vividly recorded in a rhyming broadsheet celebration of the so-called 'Battle of Dysart', which had lasted for at least three days, with the crowd holding the upper hand for most of this time and driving off a party of soldiers. The crowd was led in this case by a bayonet-wielding female, one of the 'Valiant Wives of Dysart', who, in search of meal:

> ... skipped through the Gate,
> And pass'd throw the Kirk-yard,
> Calling where is that stinking Beast,
> The Ugly Swine the Laird?[40]

Elsewhere, threats of violence were issued, and carried out, leaving leading merchants such as George Dempster in Dundee in fear of his life.[41]

Similarly, the double-edged nature of the freedom granted by the Union to Scots to drive black cattle into England is seen in the Levellers Revolt of 1724–25, when dispossessed peasants waged a violent reactive war by tearing down the walls of cattle enclosures which had been created from land they had formerly occupied.

Some indications have been given of the adverse effects on employment of the depressed trading conditions in the immediate post-1707 decades. These were compounded by other factors which added to the vulnerability of the labouring poor in the autumn and winter months of 1719–20. Far and away the most serious of these was the threat posed to the struggling Scottish linen industry by the efforts of English weavers of silk and stuffs to obtain a ban on the wearing of printed calicoes and linens. The Scottish burghs were actively campaigning against this both in public and private in November and December 1719, the fear of the disastrous consequences on employment of both full- and part-time outworkers being felt most acutely in Perth and Dundee, Linlithgow and Montrose. Ominously, the Secretary of State, the duke of Roxburghe, was warned that if anything further was done to prejudice the linen trade in Scotland, the consequences would be 'very bad', and that it was 'very much in the Interest of the government to concern themselves in it'.[42]

What has not been mentioned thus far however is the effect of increased grain exports on the inhabitants of those east-coast coastal burghs from which grain and meal were shipped. The grain market in Scotland was becoming increasingly integrated during the eighteenth century, with the strongest flow being from east to west by the third quarter.[43] The outflow of victuals was a matter of the greatest consternation in the burghs concerned, all of which to a greater or lesser extent were experiencing severe economic difficulties and in many cases acute localised problems, as at Linlithgow where the 'great whoring' of General Carpenter's dragoons along with other misdemeanours had 'turned very uneasy with the Inhabitants', or in Dysart in March 1719 where the town council had to waive burial fees as their inhabitants were 'not in Conditione to pay'.[44] While it is impossible to be certain, it is at least conceivable that the renewed and determined campaign by the Kirk – and some burghs – to restrict the number and size of penny weddings which appears to have come to a head in or around 1719 (as, apparently, did the Kirk's attack on sinfulness generally), added to the simmering mix of lower class resentment.[45]

Most of the burghs concerned not only bordered grain-growing estates, they were themselves partly agricultural. Few if any of their inhabitants would have been unaware of the state of the crops, or that the harvest of 1719 was a good one, and as has been seen the effects of recent instances of landed aggrandisement were still being felt in some localities where connections may have been drawn between enclosure and dearth. The disastrous harvests of the 1690s could be understood as the judgement of a wrathful deity, but this was different. The sense of injustice at what was a man-made shortage then can only have been intense, as artisans and other wage workers and households scraping by on the margins of subsistence discovered only scanty supplies of victuals being offered for sale, but watched as landowners and merchant grain dealers prospered from grain exports which had grown since the Union being shipped openly before them. What the anxious wage-dependent inhabitants of the affected burghs are likely to have feared in the winter months of 1720 was a return to the nightmare conditions of the 1690s, which were still within living memory. Fear of famine continued to haunt the minds of the poor and vulnerable in urban Scotland well into the second half of the eighteenth century, when it could still act as a spur to riot.[46]

The importance of chronic economic privation as the underlying explanatory factor in popular disturbances in early eighteenth-century Scotland has been underestimated.[47] The connection has been made between popular support for (or at least acceptance of) smuggling. This was often given tacit encouragement by Justices of the Peace and burgh magistrates whose Jacobite leanings were such that they were prepared to overlook their oaths of loyalty to the house of Hanover and countenance the illegal importation of French wines and brandy, for instance, which brought both financial rewards and personal palatal satisfaction.[48] Jacobite or not, there were magistrates and town councillors who also had considerable sympathy with the suffering of the labouring poor, and were prepared to collude with them in their crimes, evasion or flight. It was 'Gentlemen' who were accused of countenancing smuggling in the Dumfries customs precinct in 1711, while in 1724 they were also strongly suspected of illegally importing Irish cattle.[49]

Such behaviour partly accounts for the innumerable difficulties which customs officers and the courts faced when attempting to implement the law. So too does the fact that in the first round of post-Union appointments so many customs and excise officers who appeared in 'Shoalls' in Scotland were Englishmen.[50] This, and the unpopularity of the Union, were the reasons why, according to Daniel Defoe, he and his companions were treated so coldly by the 'common people' in the east of Scotland in the mid-1720s, not because of the recent defeats of the Jacobites.[51] Barely visible from this distance in time, there was a xenophobic tinge to many of the popular disturbances in the period, a whipping up of anti-English feeling which had no obvious connections with Jacobitism. The Edinburgh tailors, for example, wished ardently for an end to the Union, but appear to have shown no interest in a return of the Stuarts.[52] It would have been remarkable too if in Scotland, encroaching into which were the agents of the increasingly powerful British fiscal-military state and its centrally-generated laws and regulations, there had been none of the popular hostility which greeted the hated tax gatherer throughout Europe, regardless of nationality. Indeed compelling evidence that there was is to be found in the collective hostility which had accompanied the arrival of newly-appointed excise officers in Edinburgh and Glasgow in the autumn of 1707.[53]

The violence and extent of the assaults on customs and excise officers however requires further explanation. Significantly, from those parts of the country where such disorders were more than usually common – the east coast and the south west and Borders, which by 1733 were being described as being almost 'as Rebellious again as formerly' – there were frequent complaints of economic hardship, and observations about the numbers of poor people or beggars. Thus Montrose, for example, a notoriously riotous town, was described in 1743 as being 'full of idle, Abandoned, Beggarly people' and in the 1710s, 1720s and 1730s it was people of this description who were often identified as having joined in and even on occasion sparked riots. The participants in an attack on the king's warehouse in Kirkcudbright in 1724 were described as being 'all Servants of little acc't'.[54] Indeed as conditions worsened periodically, reports of assaults increased. On its own, of course, such a crude materialist explanation for rioting of this sort ('crass economic reductionism'), as for outbreaks of food rioting, has serious limitations.[55] Nonetheless, in the Dumfries precinct the upturn in the number of customs and excise riots between 1724 and 1726 followed localised food shortages which first became apparent in 1724, while there is another close correlation between the two events in 1733.[56] There were occasions too when it is difficult to distinguish an assault against customs and excise officers from a food riot, as at Ayr in March 1742 when, in the absence of a military presence and in spite of entreaties of the magistrates and the attempts of the tidesmen to stop them, a mob 'in a tumultous manner went to the Key, and took from on board a vessel bound for Norway the whole cargo of oatmeal'.[57]

We have established that such disturbances, in which the concepts of deference and respect for the law were mocked, were endemic in Scotland. A recent reassessment of the nature and extent of smuggling in the south of England does point to a degree of convergence between English and Scottish experience – in resisting and routing excise officers, for example, or the involvement of the populace as customers. Previously, it appeared that it was only with Sussex, where in the 1740s a 'guerrilla war' was waged between smugglers and customs officers, that there were strong similarities. Even so, what seems clear is that in England this type of crime was much more localised than in Scotland, less damaging to the revenue, and that containing it was a less pressing problem for the government.[58] Generally speaking, smuggling in England was organised on business lines by men of substance, supported by paid armed gangs.[59] This was true of Scotland and Ireland too, although more is known about this in the second half of the eighteenth century than earlier.[60] The ubiquity of popularly-supported smuggling in Scotland however, certainly up to and including the 1740s, after which it declined, appears to have owed much to its connection with subsistence. There are no reasons to suspect that this owed much to violence and intimidation on the part of the smugglers. After the '45 the authorities made more determined efforts to stamp out the unruly behaviour associated with smuggling, more informers came forward and, as the economy began to show real signs of improvement, popular disturbances in support of smugglers were considerably less numerous. There are even instances of officers being assisted in carrying out their duties, as in July 1753 when, at Kinkell on the River Earn, James Dick, excise officer, and his constable, beaten by armed smugglers as they tried to intercept a cargo of illegally imported tea, were rescued 'by several Country People', who then recovered the tea.[61] Indeed as early as 1745 one contemporary thought he could detect a 'forwardness lately shown by all ranks of men, to express their detestation of it [smuggling], and to bind themselves to one another and to the publick ... to discourage that villanous [sic] traffick'.[62] Increasingly, smuggling gangs fought their own battles with the authorities.[63]

Such was the extent of smuggling in Scotland, one contemporary explained, that the nature of the offence was very different north and south of the border. In England, where run goods formed a smaller proportion of the whole, and could be sold at more or less the legal price, smugglers profited by benefiting from virtually the entire unpaid duty. In Scotland, by contrast, smugglers, most of whom operated on a much smaller scale, were 'frequently obliged to sell ... Goods *cheaper* than they cost [in the open market]'. Such was the supply of run goods in Scotland that they invited 'the very poorest of the people to become Purchasers' in the black economy, and as in Sussex this is likely to have been seen as 'a legitimate part' of the local means of making a living.[64] In addition, payments from the casual employment by smuggling gangs are likely to have provided welcome windfalls for penurious individuals and households in those districts where such opportunities arose: one of these was the south-west where much 'running' was done by 'country people' who were able to conceal single barrels of brandy or other small quantities of smuggled goods in the inhospitable moss lands. Lengthy stretches of low-lying shoreline or rocky coasts indented with quiet creeks provided the optimum environment.

The seizure of run goods and their dealers by customs officers therefore was deemed to be an offence against the moral economy of the common people. A similar sense of legitimacy justified rioting against the attempts of officers in Greenock and Port Glasgow in 1707 to enforce the pre-1707 ban on the importation of Irish victuals which had been reinforced in the VIth Article of Union, at the instigation of sections of the Scottish landed class.[65] There is here, as in the bulk of the popular disturbances concerned with food examined, evidence of the notion of 'entitlement', of the right to an adequate supply of the means of subsistence at reasonable prices; that is, without the imposition of additional costs imposed by the state, or shortages created by interventions in the market place which skewed it too far in the interests of the producers and sellers.[66] It is tempting too to see here as in the customs and excise riots an *element* of class war, and to varying degrees a hostile response to state centralisation and the monopolisation in less sympathetic hands of wealth and power. Thus were social crime and protest inextricably linked.

Gender and community

There is a third reason for linking so many of the popular disturbances which occurred in early eighteenth-century Scotland with difficult economic conditions at the levels of the community and individual household. This was the degree to which females participated in them, their presence perhaps signalling a determination and a measure of distress of the most desperate kind.[67] It was a nineteenth-century local historian of Renfrewshire who first observed something of this phenomenon in Scotland, noting that in the earlier customs and excise riots in both Greenock and Port Glasgow, 'women ... of a class above the lowest – were active participants in the riots that generally accompanied seizures of contraband articles'.[68]

They were not alone, of course, and indeed what analysis of the lists of 'panels' (those accused of crimes in Scotland) shows is that males predominated, although allowance should be made for the reluctance of the authorities to indict females, which may explain why their presence in eye-witness accounts of disturbances is not matched by their appearances in court. Females, for example, accounted for only 9 per cent of the panels listed after the food riots of 1720. In this respect, as in France – but possibly more so than in England – women's participation in riots in Scotland represented part of a prudent strategy on the part of the crowd, and is the most likely explanation why, not unusually, male rioters donned female attire. There may also have been a wish to tease and confuse the authorities who were racked with uncertainties about how they could respond legally to public disorders without escalating the dangers they represented.[69] In many disturbances of which we have descriptions, women – and often children – were the first to torment town guards, customs and excise officials, soldiers and magistrates. This was standard practice in early modern Europe, the apparent innocence of the young defying the authorities to deny their modest demands for relief.[70] The first signs of disturbances in Glasgow in 1725 were seen on 24 June with 'Several Assemblies of riotous & Disorderly people consisting mostly of Women & Boys running through the Streets & exclaiming against the Malt Tax'.[71] There are several instances of all- or predominantly-female crowds of both food and customs and excise rioters. These come from all parts of the country, but on the basis of the current state of knowledge they appear to have been more prevalent in Dumfries and Galloway, where between 1711 and 1718 there were at least four major incidents involving virtually all-female crowds of one hundred and up to two hundred people.[72]

Largely owing to the inadequacies of the historiography of riot in Scotland the matter of whether or not women in Scotland played a more significant role than their counterparts elsewhere can at this stage be judged only impressionistically, although at least one historian who has little of relevance to say on the issue in the eighteenth century is convinced that, witch-hunting notwithstanding, the Reformation in Scotland enabled women to participate more fully in the 'democratic' dissenting movements of the seventeenth century than their counterparts in England.[73] We know that females – especially younger, unmarried women – were drawn in large numbers to the conventicles which erupted during the six months of the religious revivalism which centred on Cambuslang in 1742.[74] The Covenanting tradition in the south-west, in which women were deeply embroiled, is again (as in the case of the Levellers' Revolt) likely to provide at least a partial explanation for the prominence of their involvement in the popular disturbances of the eighteenth century. Such figures as we do have suggest participation rates in food riots which are very similar to those for England (between 9 and 32 per cent), but that the extent to which they participated in other confrontations – mainly with customs and excise officers – was greater. But in contrast to England, female participation seems to have been greater early in the century than later.[75] While further investigation is required, and more systematic work could be done with the Scottish evidence, quantification of female involvement in popular disturbances is and will almost certainly remain a notoriously inexact science.[76]

What can be said with more certainty is that females who were involved in collective activity in Scotland were more inclined to use force in order to achieve their ends. Females 'were frequently the most violent in mobs', wrote our early student of the subject in Renfrewshire, while in the counties of Scotland to the south-west of and including Lanarkshire women were at least as likely as men to engage in 'aggravated assault' upon persons of authority, such as law officers, messengers, constables or sheriff-officers. It was attacks by armed females on the queen's warehouses and their fellow officers that terrified the customs service in Dumfries in the first post-Union years.[77] In others they appear not only to have been the instigators but the most threatening members of a crowd, as in Edinburgh in 1740, for example, when a magistrate who had negotiated his release from the clutches of a meal mob had to be protected 'from the Women & most dangerous part of ye Mob ... who called out to knock him down'.[78] While in the European context there is nothing unusual about this, what is notable – if again unsurprising – is the ability of women to sustain a collective action. Thus after four consecutive days of food rioting at Montrose in 1757, Anne Lamond, the ring-leader, and eleven other women were arrested and imprisoned by a party of soldiers who had purposely been marched in from Dundee. It is striking that by the early 1770s the authorities in some parts of Scotland at least had reached the end of their tether. In Perth in 1773, during a period of ferocious meal rioting along the banks of the river Tay, the magistracy and the military had had to stand aside as an 'Enraged and Desperate Multitude' released some of those who had earlier been imprisoned.[79] Consequently the lord provost was advised that as it had been 'generally observed' that women bore a 'considerable part' of the responsibility for such riots, and 'to show that Sex gives no privilege to commit Mischief', some of the women more actively involved should be taken into custody and brought to trial, even if their punishments were more lenient.[80]

That women featured so prominently is partly explained by their 'lynchpin roles in family survival' and sensitivity to prices and the availability of necessities, adopting the marketplace perhaps as principally their own space as males strove to maximise such opportunities for income-generating employment as they could find elsewhere – although this is not to accord them the anachronistic title of 'housewives'.[81] The recent finding that some two-thirds of females brought before the Justiciary Court in the south-western counties of Scotland were unmarried, mainly spinsters but with a scattering of widows, while only a tiny proportion of food rioters acted in association with relatives, further limits the effectiveness of the argument. Their motivation has to be sought elsewhere, in their status as servant members of households rather than families, or in the desperation of their personal circumstances. We should not however minimise the potential significance of their feelings of solidarity with the communities or neighbourhoods of which they were part. Certainly this, rather than concerns about poverty, would appear to have motivated those women near Loch Rannoch in 1749 who rescued a kilt-wearing neighbour from soldiers who had arrested him for wearing Highland dress, banned in the face of considerable resentment in the affected parts of Scotland after the final Jacobite defeat.[82] In 1766 it was a crowd led by women and mainly consisting of women and men in women's clothes which put up ferocious resistance to the presentation in their parish of a new minister, Patrick Grant, on the grounds that he had no right to be in 'Fraser Country'. Most of the parishioners were tenants on the annexed Lovat estate.[83] That witness after witness at the trial of seventeen females accused of deforcing customs officers near Dumfries in 1711 found it impossible to identify those responsible, even though they had witnessed the riot, underlines this sense of community-centred plebeian loyalty. The 'utter backwardness' of witnesses to reveal names, 'owing partly to fear & partly to favour', continued to be a problem for the authorities in dealing with this and similar sorts of disturbances raised in defence of the community for much of the rest of the century.[84]

Unfortunately, only the barest details have survived about such females – their ages, marital status and sometimes their occupations. There are however some sources which strongly suggest that those individuals (male or female) which contemporaries referred to as 'fire brands', 'chief actors' or simply ringleaders in crowd disturbances were, not unusually, well-known within their local communities or neighbour-hoods. They were able to articulate principles relating to the operation of the 'moral economy' and natural justice, and could evidently inspire others to march in the defence of these against those who were deemed to be causing unnecessary hardship through their exploitation of the market system. Effective speakers, probably literate and moderately subversive, they appear on the historical stage only fleetingly and are usually accorded a certain grotesqueness by those who describe them in pejora-tive terms. Thus in Perth in the 1770s there were James Wilson, a barber and a 'gaunt looking personage, with a spare, cavaderous visage', and Blair Flight, an 'odd-looking' watchmaker; prominent in Edinburgh crowds in the middle decades of the eighteenth century was a 'low and deformed' cobbler, Joseph Smith, who was credited with being able 'on a birthday', to summons 'thousands of Ragamuffins to demolish houses of fame, break windows, burn unfriendly effigies and other glorious achievements.'[85] These of course were males, but the evidence examined above strongly suggests that they had their female counterparts. Neither is there much doubt that within their respective communities they exer-cised enormous authority, as in the case of the aforementioned 'General' Joseph Smith in Edinburgh:

> The magistrates ... assembled every Wednesday forenoon to manage the affairs and deliberate upon the improvements of the city; but their power was merely that of a viceroyalty ... Smith, was the only true potentate; and their resolutions could only be carried into effect when not inconsistent with his views of policy ... the magistracy ... patronised him rather from fear than respect.

That he had died was a matter of some small relief to the authorities in Edinburgh as they anxiously anticipated the King's birthday in June 1792.[86]

Stilling Scotland

The question now arises of what the significance was of this period of political and social confrontation. The British government's response to the Jacobite uprisings has in part been dealt with. Among other measures implemented were: the appointment of Commissioners to oversee the forfeiture of 'the Estates of certain Traitors in ... Scotland in 1716'; the sacking of Sir David Dalrymple as Lord Advocate because of his lack of zeal in prosecuting Jacobites after 1715; and his replacement in 1720 with the firmer hand of Robert Dundas of Arniston. The brutal punitive action in the Highlands under the direction of the duke of Cumberland following Culloden has been mentioned, but not the trials, executions and transportation of Jacobite prisoners, as well as a second round of forfeiture of the rebels' estates.[87] The implication is that as Westminster's authority grew in the Lowlands and as Jacobite sympathisers were both torn and teased out from the Highlands, Scotland become more tranquil. With the abolition of the heritable jurisdictions, it is argued, the 'problem of law and order gradually became more tractable'.[88]

This is a line of argument which both demands and rightly commands considerable respect. But despite its force and pedigree it is incomplete. Again, its focus is Jacobitism and the Highlands. Although it does not quite exclude the Lowlands, they are clearly of only secondary and implicitly, minor importance. Yet the Lowlands were the locus of most of the disorder which has featured in the chapter. To lose the Lowlands was to lose the Union. It was not only the duke of Cumberland's victory at Culloden which would secure it. The Secretary of State, the duke of Newcastle, recognised as much in the wake of the malt tax riots which had concentrated government minds over the summer of 1725: if the 'spirit as now appears in that Kingdom [Scotland]' was 'not got the better of', he wrote to Lord Carlisle, and considering too the current 'ill humour' in Ireland, the consequences for England would be 'fatal'.[89] In order to save the Union and bolster Westminster rule, maintain order and reduce the likelihood that the discontented would look for their salvation in militant Jacobitism (even though its appeal to ordinary Lowland Scots had greatly diminished as a realistic course of action by the 1740s), the state and those in positions of authority within Scotland itself had to intervene south as well as north of the Highland line. A high proportion of Scottish riots in the first half of the eighteenth century were of the variety which demanded firm government action, as they did in London for instance. Some of them had been large. Violent attacks on individuals had been commonplace, there had been destruction of property – and, albeit indirectly in most instances, government policies had been challenged.[90]

Some of the steps taken have become part of the historiographical record. Others however have been overlooked. Combined, they suggest that the effects of Union on Lowland Scotland, both real and perceived, direct and indirect, had a profound and lasting influence on the pace and nature of economic and social change and the management of Scottish society. The raft of measures adopted by the state and quasi-state organisations to boost the Scottish economy and thereby create employment and eliminate poverty and its clamour- and sedition-inducing counterpart, 'Idleness', have already been outlined in chapter 2. Although of enormous importance, these were only part of the process of containment.

Of the rest, the short- and medium-term are easiest to deal with. The food rioters of 1720 achieved their objective almost immediately.

Nobody starved. Anstruther town council's appeal to the JPs that they should order the absent mealsellers back to the meal market for example had 'a good effect the very next day and ever since' it was noted in March. Further north, in Arbroath and Montrose, crowds successfully negotiated meal at a price which was below that prevailing in the market. It can hardly be coincidental that in spite of a good run of harvests, the quantities of oats and oatmeal shipped outwards from Scotland plummeted after 1720 and did not exceed the earlier level until 1735 (although this and the instability in the grain market in Scotland during the 1720s and 1730s may also owe something to the strengthening of demand from Glasgow and the west). Grain exports from England by contrast, continued to rise until 1750.[91] Significantly, and in spite of the pleas of some landowners and merchants that it would ruin them (grain prices in the home market remained more or less flat), the bounties on grain exported from Scotland were withdrawn – temporarily at first – from June 1725.[92] The interests of land, which in this regard had been secured in 1707, were subordinated to those of domestic consumers, with the savings on bounty payments being used to compensate the Treasury for the lower rate of malt duty which was to be applied to Scotland. The mid-1720s subjected a blow to landowners in the south-west too, where the Levellers' actions appear to have halted the process of agrarian improvement there, and it is by no means inconceivable that they slowed the process elsewhere too.[93] Even King George I took an interest in the affair (although in this period it was not unusual for government – recognising the limitations of suppression by force – to adopt a conciliatory approach, and to investigate the causes of disturbances), asking what legal right those concerned had to 'eject so many Tenants at once as to render them, and the Country desolate' and 'what provisions the law has to make for the Tenants so ejected'.[94] There was a recognition in some quarters too that further progress had to await improved market conditions and that these rather than intimidation would provide a better means of achieving productivity gains in the countryside.

Contemporaries and historians alike have credited the Scottish landed class with much of the success which was achieved in the manufacturing and trading sectors in Scotland in the 1720s, 1730s and 1740s – and beyond. A contributor to the *Scots Magazine* in 1752 noted the role played by finance and legislation in the years since 1746, but the 'great spring', he argued, 'which ... set the whole thing in motion, is, that spirit, liberality, and application with which our nobility and landed gentlemen have of late engaged'.[95] This is fully in accordance with the arguments developed in earlier chapters. Given that the next great period of improvement in Scottish agriculture awaited the later 1760s and 1770s and the appearance of a much more buoyant market for foodstuffs, it is tempting to speculate that in a very general sense, learning from the troubled experience of the earlier decades, the Scottish landed classes had turned their attention to those economic activities which would create the conditions in which agrarian capitalism could better flourish. Concern among the class-conscious upper classes in Lowland Scotland that they might provoke unrest on the part of the people below certainly governed their thinking in key areas of social policy, most significantly perhaps in causing them to doubt the wisdom of establishing a Scottish militia, although there were other reasons too why this proposal was rejected.[96]

The operation of the food market however is worth exploring further. The widespread outbreak of food rioting in 1740–41 has been described as a 'landmark' in the development of famine relief in Scotland.[97] Even though the harvests of 1739 and 1740 were poor – the worst for forty years – the mortality crisis which was feared in Scotland did not materialise.[98] Instead, as was noted in chapter 2, historians have observed that landed proprietors and burgh authorities alike organised quickly to buy and then sell meal at below the market price, the favoured strategy too in early modern France. The improvement in social provision this activity represents has in Scotland been ascribed to the higher incomes of the charity-giving classes, improved provision for the poor by the kirk sessions and landowners, and pressure from rioters in 1740. The last however cannot account for the better preparations which were made prior to 1740; these, it seems entirely reasonable to suppose, owed much to the warning that the conflagration of 1720 had provided, along with the subsequent poverty-related disorder. Crisis conditions in northern France in 1709 had led to similar lessons being learned, not least the need to placate the city populations.[99] What had not altered was the inability of those in formal positions of authority to contain the situation, despite the use of troops. Also obvious in 1740 and 1741 was that, as in 1720, there was still considerable confusion in the burghs about how to deal with the dearth, about what legal rights they had over the rioters or troops, and about whether they had the right to demand that those suspected of hoarding grain or meal bring it to market. The cause of what in some cases bordered on chaos was unambiguous: the absence of the Privy Council or a substitute body with the power to issue legal directives to which justices of the peace and burgh magistrates could have 'speedy resort' to enable them to deal with the crisis.[100] It was not just the Jacobite risings that its abolition had facilitated.

What the riots of 1740 in Edinburgh had also revealed was a profound shift in social relations. Unlike most previous riots in the city which, like some of those described earlier in this chapter, were integrative, 'reinforcing a consensus within urban society', those of 1740 exposed fractures, in sectionalism, an unwillingness to give and take, an absence of dialogue and the ready resort to violence on both sides.[101] Yet divisions along the lines of class, but more important, conflicts over the operation of the market system (but not capitalism as such, of which most rioters were part), were also evident throughout this extended period of disorder in early modern Scotland. Some pointers in this direction have been provided in this chapter. Evidence presented earlier also shows that the edges of social conflict were neither as sharp nor as clear cut as they would be later in the century, or in the early nineteenth. Thus during the food riots of 1720 we find splits within the burghs' ruling elites, whose commitment to market-led mercantilism was by no means uniform. At Pittenweem, for example, a rift between the forces of commercial self-interest and controlled, community-conscious capitalism was exposed when John Martin and two other town councillors had refused to assist in dispersing the crowd, with Martin declaring that 'he looked upon those that were carryers of such Shoalls of victuall off the Country were ruinous to the Country and the place they lived in And he looked upon some of the Magistrates as partys.'[102] There was a pronounced unwilling-ness on the part of the authorities in Dundee to pursue those suspected of being involved there, while the magistrates of Linlithgow made deter-mined but ultimately unsuccessful efforts to organise trials for their own inhabitants in the burgh courts rather than under the auspices of the High Court.[103] In rural society too similar differences in attitude are to be found. Thus in 1742 the earl of Morton was inclined to treat the Orkney kelp rioters leniently, in order to maintain good relations, whereas the local justices, who included seven merchants, imposed heavy exemplary sentences on those found guilty.[104]

Notwithstanding the complex patterning of the cross-hatched lines of social identity however, divisions between expansive, commercially-orientated landowners, the larger tenant farmers, and the overseas and coastal merchants on the one hand, and the labouring poor on the other (frequently aided and abetted in the burghs by the trades incorporations) can be discerned. We have already observed the particular vulnerability of wage workers and the prominence of urban artisans, servants, mariners and those of similar rank in the lists of the panels in the trials which followed the 1720 food riots. The gulf between the two sides was exposed in Dundee, described as a 'wicked place' by the leading and pros-perous merchant George Dempster, whose fine townhouse and its furnishings were singled out and badly damaged by the mob; that five years later the MP Daniel Campbell's newly-built Shawfield mansion was the target of rioters in Glasgow may well have owed much to the moder-nity and distinctiveness and ill-gotten wealth which it flaunted, even though the suspicions there were that Campbell's support of the malt tax was the principal cause of the crowd's ire.[105] Overwhelmingly, the crowds who battled with customs and excise officers comprised urban and rural artisans, sailors, small tenant farmers, sub-tenants, servants and cottars who in different times and places coalesced on the streets, at harbours and on the moors, to form a chain of popular subversive activity.

It is significant that the concept of class antagonism has also been applied to those peasants who fought against enclosure in the south-west during 1724 and 1725.[106] In 1722 it was apparently tenant farmers on the duke of Queensberry's estate, provided by the factor, who had protected a cargo of brandy seized from smugglers when officers had been confronted by a crowd raised from 'the whole Countrey about', and armed with 'Stons Clubs & fierarms'.[107] Similar divisions were apparent in Orkney in 1741 and 1742. The rioters tended to be small farmers and their dependents, their targets landowners and bigger farmers whose interests lay in the extension of commerce rather than survival. What most of those concerned appear to have had in common was a desperation to make a living and an awareness of their vulnerability in a society which as yet made only the barest attempts to provide for its poor. Schemes for poor relief extended only slowly during the first half of the century.[108] As has been observed of mainland Europe in the early modern era, the poor, and those whose employment and incomes were insecure and could so easily slip down into their ranks, are likely to have been 'obsessed by either the image or the memory of hunger', and to have responded accordingly.[109]

Paternalism revisited

In the previous chapter attention was drawn to the considerable emphasis historians in Scotland have placed on the part played by paternalism in the achievement of social stability in the second half of the eighteenth century. With the full extent of the problem of maintaining order in Scotland now having been described, just how crucial the adoption of such a strategy was can be better understood. It is argued here that far from being a voluntary change of direction, the governing classes in Scotland had no choice but to return to the pro-active and effective paternalist regime which in the area of food prices, for instance, had operated prior to 1707.[110] This is because rather than being dedicated primarily to the relief of the poor, the main function of paternalism was to defend authority.[111] At the same time, some licence had necessarily to be accorded to the lower ranks, or relations between the classes would stiffen and become more confrontational.

What remains to be done in this chapter is to explain with greater precision than has been the case hitherto, how the system operated. What will be shown is how between them the state in Scotland, represented by the Court of Session and, less consistently, the Convention of Royal Burghs and the burgh authorities, managed through the crucial mid-

decades of the eighteenth century to keep the lid on, although not eliminate altogether, popular protest. This was a major achievement at a time
when as we have seen, the Scottish economy was being transformed from
one which in the 1730s had altered little since the 1680s but which by the
1770s was on the threshold of industrialisation. Accommodation and
anxious ameliorisation formed but part of the equation though; where
this failed, recourse was had to the full force of the military and the law,
used – not always with the desired outcome – in ways which have been
outlined above.

Recent research into the food market in England has shown how in
Bristol, for example, serious rioting in 1753 led to 'continuous, forceful
and contested manipulation of the assize of bread', in order to keep the
price down and safeguard social welfare and public order.[112] Market
forces were held in check as a result of what had been 'an object lesson in
the vulnerability of civic order during scarcity'.[113] In the current state of
knowledge – about the role of government, for example – it is impossible
to judge with any degree of accuracy the relative importance of 'prag-
matic paternalism' in the two countries. What can be confidently claimed
however is that north of the border high prices and shortages of basic
foodstuffs – that is, primarily, oats and oatmeal – were tackled by
concerted action at national and local level.[114]

As food rioting continued through the spring of 1741, Westminster
handed to the Lords of the Court of Session the responsibility, which had
until 1708 been in the hands of the Scottish Privy Council, for opening
the ports for the importation of victuals from Ireland and elsewhere when
necessary. The point at which this was allowed had been determined by
an Act of the Scottish Parliament in 1703, the terms of which were maintained under the legislation of 1741. What this meant was that after a
fairly swift but comprehensive adjudication process (which lasted around
three weeks), the Lords of Session could order the Scottish ports open for
the importation of oats and oatmeal if the price rose above £8 Scots (13s.
4d. sterling) per boll. The regulations and pre-Union price trigger therefore remained in force – and according to the Convention of Royal
Burghs worked well – until 1773 when Parliament raised the trigger price
to 16s., causing howls of outrage from the alarmed burghs.

In Glasgow there was concern not only about the condition of their
inhabitants, but also about the danger that manufacturing costs would
rise.[115]

Accompanying the Session judges in their work were the energetic
efforts of the individual burgh authorities to ensure that shortages of victuals did not occur. Town council minute books and associated
correspondence which have been studied for burghs such as Aberdeen,
Banff, Dumfries, Montrose and Perth, provide eloquent testimony to the
commitment of their elected members to the adequate provision of food-

stuffs, as well as their fear of disorder and the financial cost of their failure to keep the peace.[116] The most common measure was, at the first sign of scarcity, for the magistrates to buy in meal and to sell it, often at below the market price, to the 'poorer Sort of the Inhabitants', thus snuffing out the potential for unruliness or keeping such disturbances as did break out to a minimum. The press played its part in encouraging public order, by printing optimistic forecasts of the forthcoming harvest.[117] Argument and persuasion were used too, as in November 1751, following a food riot in Leith, which troops had been used to quell, although in Glasgow in 1767 a similar attempt failed abysmally, as serious rioting which lasted two or three days broke out, with 'retailers' and meal-makers who bought in bulk (and raised the selling price) being blamed for the diminishing quantities of meal which were available in the public market.[118] Some days after the Leith disturbance *A Seasonable Advice to the Common People of Scotland, With Regard to Mobbing*, was published in Edinburgh, which exhorted them to recognise the 'blessing of God' in providing so many fair harvests, the good fortune in having a legal system which arbitrated between 'man and man, and one set of men and another', and the foolishness, but above all the sinfulness, of 'tumult, riot, and mobbing'. Included too was an exposition of the benefits of the market economy, while advice was offered to work hard, save more and drink less, and to love neighbour and country, which otherwise would be perceived as a 'parcel of lawless creatures'.

It is not stretching our analysis too far to apply the analogy of a volcanic region to some parts of Scottish urban society in the period under review. The supply of grain to the towns, uncertainty about crop failures and an underlying fear of shortage and the disorder which would almost certainly accompany it, were widely recognised causes of urban unease.[119] A mob 'risen from want of food is of all others likely to be the most furious', declared one anxious Glasgow resident.[120] There were frequent 'murmerings' and even occasional outbursts of disorder in years of shortage, such as 1766, but superficially at least a sense of social harmony reigned, reinforced by some shared attitudes and values and, after *c.* 1760, rising real incomes. Undoubtedly too, good weather contributed to this, with a run of good harvests during most of the 1750s and through to the wet year of 1764.[121] Yet within certain communities and in times of crisis, underlying and uncontainable tensions crashed through to the surface as the authorities were provided with forceful reminders that they had not met their obligations to the common people.

The personal anguish suffered by Aberdeen's lord provost in 1753 in such circumstances has already been described. In Perth too the authorities had clearly been alarmed during an occurrence of intimidating food rioting in 1778, after which the magistrates determined to apply to the Board of Ordinance for '200 Stand of Fire Arms for the use of the

Inhabitants to be lodged in the Artillery Barracks & to be used by the Order & at the direction of the Magistrates'.[122] The most telling example however comes from Dumfries in 1771. A coastal burgh from whence considerable quantities of grain were sent coastwise to the Clyde, it is a place where we might expect to find periodic clashes between the inhabitants and merchant exporters, especially given the demise of the tobacco trade. During the 1750s and 1760s however the town council had struggled admirably to ensure that shortages were kept to a minimum.

Yet in March and April 1771 reports reached the Lord Advocate of fearsome crowd activity, which stretched into May.[123] This often happened at night, during which the magistrates and merchants who were involved in the grain trade were attacked and warned that if they did not desist from shipping corn and meal out from the port, which their attackers declared to be a violation of the laws of God and Nature, their houses would be burned down, while in addition the magistrates would suffer mutilation and offending merchants would have their ears cut off at the town's market cross. Despite the presence of troops from the 22nd Regiment, the situation was barely containable, with crowds of a thousand or even 1,500 gathering on some nights.[124] Indeed, admitting that his men had killed or wounded seven or eight of the rioters, Captain Alexander McDonald confessed that he was unable to judge when order would be restored: 'all the Inhabitants', he wrote, 'seem enraged and swear Revenge'. Understandably, the despairing provost and magistrates were stunned and at a loss to account for the rising, 'considering how peaceable the Inhabitants of this Burgh & Neighbourhood have ordinarily been'. For 'these fifty years', they claimed, there had been 'no mobbing, except once [in 1759], to speak of'. The magistrates' authority had been 'contemned by a riotous and disorderly set of people, who in defiance of Laws Divine and human ... assembled in the night time ... and destroyed the good order which formerly prevailed'. The risk to public order, not only in Dumfries but 'in every other well Governed community', was profound and produced from the town council in Dumfries a stern reminder to the burgh's citizens of their duty in helping to preserve the peace. More significantly however, the town's small force of constables and peace officers was augmented by men drawn from a list of fifty-three of 'the most respectable & able Bodied Residenters'. The limits of burghal paternalism had been stretched beyond repair and required henceforth the presence of a larger, virtually permanent resident force for policing the burgh.[125]

Around Scotland steps were taken to introduce such forces, drawn from the solid middle-ranking citizens of the burghs. Their purpose was not to replace the existing constables but rather to augment them. Their particular responsibility was to protect private property – and in the case of Perth's blue-uniformed 'Peace Officers' who were armed with yellow batons – to 'only give assistance' when requested to do so by the provost and magistrates, 'to quell or disperse tumultuous & Riotous Assemblies, to prevent Seditious & treasonable practices & in other Necessary purposes for preserving the public peace'.[126] Policing extended more widely than this however, and included drainage, paving, street-lighting and cleansing among its responsibilities. With its commitment to the welfare of the community and the need to maintain good order, local government in Scotland developed what would become a marked authoritarian character.[127]

The economic downturn of the early 1770s had reduced wages throughout most of Scotland and 'thrown many of the Lower Sort of People into great distress'. While the prices (and wages of the producers) of linen had fallen since 1769, grain and meal prices were rising and remained high until after 1775.[128] Food riots swept Dumfries again in 1772, as well as Tayside and Fife in 1772 and 1773. Although the export of grain had been forbidden, coastal movements had not, and indeed in 1772 the grain market in Britain had been further liberalised, with the repeal of the former statute against engrossers, forestallers and regrators. In theory at least the untrammelled market system appeared to be on the march once more, singing to the tune of Adam Smith and the political economists, although in reality the situation was confused. It is highly significant that in the previous year, along with shippers of grain, engrossers and those seen to be interfering with the supply of foodstuffs into the market had been the specific targets of the Dumfries rioters, as they had frequently been elsewhere in Britain.[129] In England, forestalling, regrating and engrossing continued to be offences at common law. The Irish legislation remained unchanged. In Scotland, on the other hand, crimes of this nature were dealt with at the very highest level, by the Lord Advocate.[130]

The food riots of the early 1770s were inspired by grievances which were virtually the same as those of 1720, as traders in the producing areas sought to benefit from the higher returns obtainable by shipping grain out, in the Tayside instance to the Edinburgh region.[131] To these pressures had been added another. As was noted above, Scotland had been hard – and unfairly – hit by a 'pernicious' clause in the Corn Law of 1773 which had raised by 2s. 8d. the trigger price at which oats and oatmeal could be imported, a benefit to landowners but a burden for the less affluent inhabitants of the burghs.

To some extent the decade drew to an end as the period with which this chapter has been concerned began, with social tensions erupting on to the streets. In some parts of the southern uplands and most of the Highlands, there was 'considerable food scarcity' throughout the decade.[132] As in 1720 the food riots between 1771 and 1773 had excited interest – and worry – at the highest levels. As before, some of the trades incorporations continued to buy victuals in bulk and sell it to their members.[133] But even as the Scottish economy was being stimulated and supported by the state to create the employment opportunities that had previously been lacking, the attention of landowners, merchants and manufacturers was not diverted for long from the crucial issues of the price of labour and labour productivity.

As has been seen, in the workplace, journeymen's organisations had been evident in the early eighteenth century, but their numbers had subsequently grown. Mainly mutual aid societies initially, as the pressures of competitive capitalism grew and relations between masters and men hardened, combinations for other purposes were formed. Wages were the main subject of collective discussion and action, with a widening pool of workers in different occupations learning to take advantage of favourable market conditions to demand increases.[134] Although it was mainly urban workers who were involved – tailors were frequently in the forefront – agricultural workers too could be found adopting the same strategy. At the end of a harvest hiring fair in Tranent, East Lothian, in 1749, farmers who had employed reapers at below the rate of 9d. per day were 'pulled off their horses, beat, and the [reaping] hooks taken from them, by the riotous reapers'.[135] Monetisation, the extension of market relations at the level of the farm and the reduction in multiple tenancies which occurred in Scottish agriculture in the first half of the eighteenth century, were creating a new social order, largely through the emergence of a class of commercially-conscious sole tenant farmers in large swathes of Lowland Scotland.[136] What has usually gone unremarked however is a corollary of this: the emergence of a class of increasingly restless agricultural workers in the more advanced agricultural regions who were also prepared to play the market system.[137] Thus in Stirlingshire in 1760, during a period of wartime-induced tightness in the labour market, farm servants were reported to have been deserting their employers and demanding higher wages, while two months later, in October, similar complaints were heard in the Lothians.[138]

In some skilled occupations – coal mining, for instance, as we have seen – combinations could be highly effective. But as that example also made clear, there were powerful countervailing pressures too as employers sought, frequently in masters' associations and often with the assistance of the courts, to hold or cut wage levels and reduce labour costs. Fears that a 'concert' was being formed among the agricultural workers in Stirling, and concern at the 'extravagant' wages being demanded in the Lothians, inspired local and national action respectively on the part of the farmers concerned, and provided for many of them a reason for opposing the militia proposal referred to earlier.[139] Labour shortages and wage pressures had become so severe in East Lothian by 1762 that farmers, manufacturers and other employers were meeting together to discuss their common difficulties.[140] The greater use by employers of the courts to fix wages induced attempts on the part of workers to defend their interests, including appearances in the Justice of the Peace courts, which continued to play a central part in defining the character of industrial relations in Scotland until the early nineteenth century.[141]

Yet care should be taken not to exaggerate the extent to which this atmosphere permeated the workplace. Associations of workers were most obvious in the textile industry, expansion in which resulted in an influx of new labour, as masters by-passed restrictions on entry like apprenticeships in handloom weaving. Handloom weavers, whose wages had been under attack from mid-century, were in the vanguard of the newer, more aggressive trade societies. In 1768, for example, a weavers' combination which levied contributions from members in order to pay officials for their services, was said to have been guilty of seizing weavers who had been working at their masters' prices from their looms, dragging them through the streets as 'a spectacle of disgrace', and beating them.[142] As is to be seen in two sailors' strikes in Greenock and Port Glasgow in 1773 and 1776 respectively, which in both cases required the intervention of soldiers from Glasgow to suppress them (leading to the shooting of two women in June 1773), the streets continued to be an important arena in which, in public, the people below articulated their causes and sought support for them.[143] In March 1779 the handloom weavers of Anderston led a march through the streets of Glasgow. The symbols and signs of a highly visual popular political culture were clearly obvious in the effigy of Lord North on horseback which in one hand held a piece of French cambric and in the other a copy of the bill allowing its importation. The protest was concluded with the effigy being taken to the 'common place of execution' with a length of French rope around its neck, and set on fire.[144] The middle classes were retreating into their purpose-built, ordered and spacially segregated districts, and from the 1770s began to adopt the more orderly 'politics of the petition'. A lengthy, bitter and often violent struggle commenced for the control of public space in Scotland's towns, which between 1750 and 1800 were growing faster than virtually anywhere else in Europe.[145]

Notes

1 J. S. Gibson, *Playing the Scottish Card: The Franco-Jacobite Invasion of 1708* (Edinburgh, 1988), 74–8; Lenman, *Jacobite Risings*, 79–106; Whatley,'*Bought and Sold for English Gold'?*, 43–4; J. MacKinnon, *The Union of England and Scotland* (1896), 273–336; C. Kidd, 'Religious realignment between the Restoration and Union', in Robertson, *A Union for*

Empire, 156; Blair Atholl Castle, Atholl MSS, Box 45 (6), 129, Ann Hay to Duke of Atholl, 5 December 1706.

2 Blair Atholl Castle, Atholl MSS, Box 45 (7), 88, Lord Stormont to Duchess of Atholl, 11 August 1707; Patrick Scott to Duchess of Atholl, 5 August 1707.

3 Whatley, 'How tame', 16.

4 Flinn, *Scottish Population*, 216–23; Houston, *Social Change*, 320–31.

5 M. G. H. Pittock, *Poetry and Jacobite Politics in Eighteenth-Century Britain and Ireland* (Cambridge, 1994), 133–49; M. G. H. Pittock, *The Myth of the Jacobite Clans* (Edinburgh, 1995), 52.

6 *Ibid.*, 43–87.

7 Strawhorn, *History of Irvine*, 65, 69; J. Strawhorn, *The History of Ayr* (Edinburgh, 1989), 90; Harris and Whatley, '"To solemnise His Majesty's birthday"', 403–4.

8 Inglis, *An Angus Parish*, 61–75, 118–32; H. Miller, *Scenes and Legends of the North of Scotland: Or, The Traditional History of Cromarty* (Edinburgh, 1889 ed.), 317–8.

9 Lenman, *Jacobite Risings*, 137–8; Macinnes, *Clanship*, 163.

10 J. Black, *Culloden and the '45* (Stroud, 1990); Davies, 'Courts and the Scottish legal system', 151–4.

11 M. Lynch, *Scotland: A New History* (London, 1991), 318–23; Lenman, *Jacobite Risings*, 260–82; Macinnes, *Clanship*, 210–17; the topic is dealt with in greater detail in A. I. Macinnes, 'Scottish Gaeldom and the aftermath of the '45: the creation of silence?', in M. Lynch (ed.), *Jacobitism and the '45* (London, 1995), 71–83.

12 Macinnes, *Clanship*, 217–21.

13 D. Szechi and D. Hayton, 'John Bull's other kingdoms: the English government of Scotland and Ireland', in C. Jones (ed.), *Britain in the First Age of Party, 1680–1750* (London, 1987), 243, 253–5.

14 Lenman, *Jacobite Risings*, 154; NAS, Montrose MSS, GD 220/5/440 (7), Earl of Rothes to J. Cockburn, 25 December 1714.

15 D. Szechi, *The Jacobites: Britain and Europe, 1688–1788* (Manchester, 1994), 100; Black, *Culloden*, 115–17.

16 Smout, *History of the Scottish People*, 223; Szechi and Hayton, 'John Bull's other kingdoms', 248–9.

17 Riley, *English Ministers*, 135.

18 NAS, Dalhousie MSS, GD 45/14/386, J. Kinloch to Master H. Maule, 16 February 1721.

19 Dundas of Arniston MSS, vol. 32, Letters, II, 1725–45, 129, Tweeddale to Lord Arniston, 7 April 1742.

20 NAS, CE 67/1/21, Alloa Customs Books, Collector to Board, 1718–25, 4 December 1721.

21 Dundas of Arniston MSS, vol. 32, Letters, II, Robert Craigie to R. Dundas, 5 September 1742.

22 Fraser, *Conflict and Class*, 2–3, 39–44.

23 For discussion of the main waves of Jacobite activity, see H. T. Dickinson, 'The Jacobite challenge', in Lynch, *Jacobitism and the '45*, 20.

24 D. Szechi, 'The Hanoverians and Scotland', in M. Greengrass (ed.),

Conquest and Coalescence (London, 1991), 126.

25 Whatley, 'How tame', 20.

26 D. Szechi, '"Cam ye o'er frae France?" Exile and the mind of Scottish Jacobitism, 1716–1727', *Journal of British Studies*, XXXVII (October 1998), 358–9.

27 See, for example, NAS, State Papers, Scotland, RH 2/4/317, Letter from Magistrates of Edinburgh, 13 January 1725. Reference is made to a pamphlet entitled, *An Historical Account of the Union Betwixt the Egyptians and the Israelites*, one of a number 'the present humour in this country has produced'.

28 R. Freebairn, *The Miserable State of Scotland* (Perth, 1720), 1.

29 NAS, Dalhousie MSS, GD 45/220/90, Countess to Earl of Panmure, 27 February 1720; Lenman, *Jacobite Risings*, 224; Szechi, 'Cam ye o'er frae France?', 364.

30 See Randall, *et al.*, 'Markets', 4–5; J. W. White, 'Economic development and sociopolitical unrest in nineteenth-century Japan', *Economic Development and Cultural Change*, XXXVII (1989), 231–60; J. Bohstedt, 'The moral economy and the discipline of historical context', *Journal of Social History* (Winter 1992), 265–84.

31 *Ibid.*, 265; Bouton, *Flour War*, xxii.

32 J. Walter and K. Wrightson, 'Dearth and the social order in early modern England', *Past & Present*, LXXII (1976), 27.

33 Public Record Office (PRO), State Papers, 55/8, copy letter, Earl of Roxburghe to Brigadier Preston, 11 February 1720.

34 A. Charlesworth (ed.), *An Atlas of Rural Protest in Britain, 1548–1900* (London, 1983).

35 Randall, *et al.*, 'Markets', 4–5.

36 NAS, High Court Processes, JC 26/103, D/1117.

37 Calculated from Gibson and Smout, *Prices, Food and Wages*, 96–7.

38 Thompson, *Customs*, 264; NAS, PC 1/51, Privy Council Acta, September 1696–July 1699, 557–8; Flinn, *Scottish Population History*, 169.

39 The main sources of evidence are voluminous court records, upon which this paragraph is based, NAS, High Court Records, JC 7/10, Minute Book, 30 March – 2 September 1720; JC 3/9, Book of Adjournment, 1718–20; Processes, JC 26/103, D/1117, 1119.

40 NLS, Ry.III.c.36 (141), *An Exact List of the Battle of Dysart, which was Fought by King Georges Forces, and the Saltors and Suttors and Coliars, with a List of the Killed and Wounded* (Edinburgh, 1720).

41 NAS, Dalhousie MSS, GD 45/14/382, George Dempster to (?), 27 February 1720.

42 Blair Atholl Castle, Atholl MSS, Box 45, Bundle 14 (126), Atholl to Duke of Roxburghe, 21 December 1719.

43 A. J. S. Gibson and T. C. Smout, 'Regional prices and market regions: the evolution of the early modern Scottish grain market', *Economic History Review*, XLVIII (May 1995), 278–9.

44 NAS, B 48/9/7, Linlithgow Town Council Minute Book, 1709–26, 8 July 1719; Kirkcaldy Town House, Dysart Council Minutes, 1674–1761, 2 March 1719.

45 See, for example, USAAM, Church of Scotland Records, CH 2/82/5, Cupar Presbytery Minutes, 1715–23, 20 January, 15 December 1719; CAA, Aberdeen Town Council Minutes, vol. 58, 1700–21, 1 December 1708.

46 See ECA, CRB, Moses Collection, Miscellaneous, SL 30/8/1, Box 1, 'Memorandum respecting the Importation of Oatmeal', 1774; Bohstedt, 'Moral economy', 269.

47 For comment on England and the relationship between dearth, petty crime and disorder, see Walter and Wrightson, 'Dearth', 24.

48 Lenman, *Jacobite Risings*, 216–7.

49 NAS, CE 51/1/1, 2, Dumfries Customs Letter Books, Collector to Board, 11 January 1711, 24 (?) October 1724.

50 Whatley, 'How tame', 6.

51 D. Defoe, *Tour Through the Whole Island of Great Britain* (London, 1979 ed.), 652.

52 NAS, State Papers, Scotland, RH2/4/317, Brigadier Fairfax to Duke of Newcastle, 26 June 1725; Fraser, *Conflict and Class*, 42.

53 Whatley, 'How tame', 10; Riley, *English Ministers*, 68–9.

54 Whatley, 'How tame', 12; NAS, CE 51/1/2, Dumfries Customs Letter Books, Collector to Board, 22 April 1724.

55 Thompson, *Customs*, 187; Walter and Wrightson, 'Dearth', 25.

56 Whatley, 'How tame', 13.

57 NAS, CE 76/1/1, Ayr Customs Letter Books, Collector to Board, 30 March 1742; see too NAS, CE 67/1/1, Alloa Customs Letter Books, Collector to Board, 1736–44, 27, 31 July 1741.

58 C. Winslow, 'Sussex smugglers', in D. Hay, P. Linebaugh, J. G. Rule, E. P. Thompson and C. Winslow (eds), *Albion's Fatal Tree: Crime and Society in Eighteenth-Century England* (London, 1975), 119–66; Rule, 'Social crime', 162–5.

59 Anon., *Some Considerations on the Present State of Scotland*, 15–17; see too C. Emsley, *Crime and Society in England, 1750–1900* (London, 1987), 4.

60 L. M. Cullen, 'Smuggling in the North Channel in the Eighteenth Century', *Scottish Economic & Social History*, VII (1987), 9–26.

61 PKCA, Perth Burgh Records, B59/31/48, 'Precognition v. smugglers for a riot on the person of James Dick, officer of the Excise', 27 July 1753.

62 Quoted in E. Dunbar Dunbar, *Social Life in Former Days, Chiefly in the Province of Moray* (Edinburgh, 1865), 69.

63 Whatley, 'How tame', 12; D. Fraser, *The Smugglers* (Montrose, 1971), 178–9.

64 *Ibid.*; Wimslow, 'Sussex smugglers', 149.

65 Hector, *Selections from the Judicial Records*, 67–8; W. Fraser, *The Melvilles* (Edinburgh, 1890), Volume II, 207.

66 A. Sen, *Poverty and Famines: An Essay on Entitlement and Deprivation* (Oxford, 1981), 49.

67 Y-M. Bercé, *Revolt and Revolution in Early Modern Europe: An Essay on the History of Political Violence* (Manchester, 1987), 106–7.

68 Hector, *Selections from the Judicial Records*, 90.

69 Bouton, *Flour War*, 18; Hayter, *Army and the Crowd*, 27–35; Angus Council Archives (ACA), M/EO/1, Petitions, 1719–65, Memorial for the

Magistrates in Answer to the Provost's of the 14 March 1741, James Graham, 18 March 1741.

70 Berce, *Revolt and Revolution*, 107.
71 NLS, MS 5127, fos 25–31, 'An Account of the Riots and Tumults that happen'd at Glasgow ... Drawn out from the Examinations taken at Glasgow by his Majesty's Advocate', 1725.
72 NAS, CE 51/1/1, Dumfries Customs Letter Books, Collector to Board, 1708–26, 16 April, 2 July, 10 October 1711, n.d., 1718, Information to Commissioners of Customs.
73 J. D. Young, *Women and Popular Struggles: A History of Scottish and English Working-Class Women, 1500–1984* (Edinburgh, 1985), 24–36.
74 Smout, 'Born again at Cambuslang', 55–7.
75 On England see Rogers, *Crowds, Culture and Politics*, 230–4.
76 Thompson, *Customs*, 307–10.
77 Hector, *Selections from the Judicial Records*, 90; A-M Kilday, 'Women and crime in south-west Scotland: a study of the Justiciary Court records, 1750–1815' (unpublished Ph.D. thesis, University of Strathclyde, 1998), 45, 53.
78 NAS, Clerk of Penicuik MSS, GD 18/5423/13, Robert Pringle to Sir John Clerk, 28 October 1740.
79 S. G. E. Lythe, 'The Tayside meal mobs 1772–3', *Scottish Historical Review*, XLVI (1967), 26–36.
80 PKCA, B 59/26/1/78, William Nairne to Walter Miller, 26 January 1773.
81 See Bouton, *Flour War*, 17; Rogers, *Crowds, Culture and Politics*, 233.
82 J. Allardice, *Historical Papers Relating to the Jacobite Period, 1699–1750*, vol. II (Aberdeen, 1896), 516, 520.
83 NAS, Grant of Monymusk MSS, GD 248/538/3, Memorial of Patrick Grant of Boleskin to the Trustees of the Annexed Estates, 1766.
84 Kilday, 'Women and crime', 125; NAS, High Court, JC 12/2, South Circuit Minute Books, 1711–18, 1 October 1711; State Papers, Scotland, RH 2/384, Provost and Council, Dumfries, to Lord Advocate, 20 March 1771; see too Walter and Wrightson, 'Dearth', 36.
85 G. Penny, *Traditions of Perth* (Coupar Angus, 1986 ed.), 46–7; Chambers, *Traditions*, 184; Blair Atholl Castle, Atholl MSS, Box 65 (10), 33, George Farquhar to Duke of Atholl, 2 June 1792.
86 *Ibid*.
87 R. Mitchison, 'The government and the Highlands, 1707–1745', in Phillipson and Mitchison, *Scotland in the Age of Improvement*, 24–46; Smith, *Jacobite Estates*, 1–6; Lenman, *Jacobite Risings*, 260–82; Macinnes, *Clanship*, 210–17; G. W. T. Omond, *The Lord Advocates of Scotland* (Edinburgh, 1883), Volume I, 281–318.
88 Riley, *English Ministers*, 289.
89 Historical Manuscripts Commission, *Manuscripts of the Earl of Carlisle* (1897), Duke of Newcastle to Lord Carlisle, 6 August 1725, 30.
90 Shoemaker, 'The London "mob"', 216–17.
91 Gibson and Smout, 'Regional prices and market regions', 271; D. G. Barnes, *A History of the English Corn Laws from 1660–1846* (London, 1930), 15–16.

92 NLS, Delvine Papers, MS 1128, fo. 215, Alexander Mackenzie to John Mackenzie, 17 December 1724; CEA, CRB, Moses Collection, SL30/242/2, John Campbell to Archibald McAulay, 22 December 1724.

93 Smout, *History of the Scottish People*, 327–8; Robertson, *Scottish Enlightenment and the Militia*, 182.

94 Dickinson, *Politics of the People*, 153; Dundas of Arniston MSS, vol. 32, Letters, II, Duke of Roxburghe to Lord Advocate, 2 July, 13 August 1724.

95 *Scots Magazine*, August 1752, 374–5.

96 Robertson, *Scottish Enlightenment and the Militia*, 182.

97 Houston, *Social Change*, 322;

98 Flinn, *Scottish Population History*, 216–23.

99 J. A. Miller, *Mastering the Market: The State and the Grain Trade in Northern France, 1700–1860* (Cambridge, 1999), 8–10, 17, 25–6.

100 ACA, M/EO/1, Memorial for the Magistrates of Montrose, 18 March 1741.

101 Houston, *Social Change*, 330–1.

102 USAAM, B 60/6/1, Pittenweem Council Books, 23 February 1720.

103 NAS, GD 45/14/382, Dalhousie MSS, George Dempster to (?), 27 February 1720; B 48/9/7, Linlithgow Town Council Minute Book, 22, 24 February 1720.

104 Thomson, *Kelp-Making*, 84–5.

105 The imposing nature of Shawfield House is described in T. A. Markus, P. Robinson, and F. A. Walker,'The shape of the city in space and stone', in Devine and Jackson, *Glasgow*, 115.

106 Smout, *History of the Scottish People*, 325.

107 NAS, CE 51/1/2, Dumfries Customs Letter Book, Collector to Board, 1 October 1722.

108 R. Mitchison, 'North and south: the development of the gulf in Poor Law practice', in Houston and Whyte, *Scottish Society*, 215–8.

109 Berce, *Revolt and Revolution*, 100–1.

110 On the substantial powers the burghs had to protect and control their economies and markets in the sixteenth and seventeenth centuries, and in some spheres into the eighteenth, see Gibson and Smout, *Prices, Food and Wages*, 19–47; Saville, 'Scottish modernisation', 15.

111 Bohstedt, 'Moral economy', 273.

112 Randall, *et al.*, 'Markets', 11–12.

113 S. Poole, 'Scarcity and the civic tradition: market management in Bristol, 1709–1815', in Randall and Charlesworth, *Markets*, 98.

114 In general terms, of course, the same can be said of England, Dickinson, *Politics of the People*, 154–5.

115 *Scots Magazine*, December 1751, 596; February 1752, 91; see too ECA, CRB, Miscellaneous, SL30/8/1, Box 1, Accounts and other Papers relating to the Corn and Meal Laws, 1695–1777; Anon., *Memorial for the Merchants, Traders, and Manufacturers of Glasgow* (Glasgow, 1777).

116 This is best seen when shortages threatened. See, for example, CAA, Enactment Book, 1730–41, 14 April 1736, 11, 27, 28, 31 March, 1 May, 19 July 1740; GRA, Banff Town Council Minute Book, 1765–76, 11 January, 28 February 1766, 13 February 1767, 3 March 1775; ACA, M/EO/1, Petitions, 1719–65, 1751, 1756–7.

117 Flinn, *Scottish Population History*, 232.
118 Mitchell Library, Glasgow, G 338.17313, *The Causes of the Scarcity of Oat-Meal in the Public Market of Glasgow*, November 1763.
119 Miller, *Mastering the Market*, 1, 7–8.
120 *Causes of the Scarcity of Oat-Meal*, 3.
121 Lythe, 'Tayside meal mobs', 30.
122 PKCA, Perth Burgh Records, PE 59/24/15/39, 'Advertisement, Magistrates and Town Council of Perth & William Mercer, Sheriff Substitute of Perthshire', 1778.
123 This paragraph is largely based on NAS, State Papers, Scotland, RH 2/4/384, Provost and Council, Dumfries, to Lord Advocate, 20 March, 4 April 1771, Captain Alex McDonald to Duke of Argyll, 4 April 1771; Dumfries Archives (DA), Dumfries Council Minute Books, 1771–76, 28 March, 18 April 1771.
124 *Scots Magazine*, June 1771, 324
125 See K. Carson and H. Idzikowska, 'The social production of Scottish policing, 1795–1900', in Hay and Snyder, *Policing and Prosecution*, 270–1.
126 PKCA, Perth Burgh Records, B59/24/11/28, Regulations for the Peace Officers; Grampian Regional Archives, 1/1/3, Banff Town Council Minute Book, 1726–92, 18 December 1776.
127 I. Maver, 'Urbanisation', in Cooke, *et al.*, *Modern Scottish History*, 158–9; R. J. Morris, 'Urbanisation and Scotland', in W. H. Fraser and R. J. Morris (eds), *People and Society in Scotland Volume II, 1830–1914* (Edinburgh, 1990), 91.
128 Lythe, 'Tayside meal mobs', 26; Flinn, *Scottish Population History*, 232–3.
129 Lythe, 'Tayside meal mobs', 32–3; Barnes, *History of the English Corn Laws*, 41.
130 See D. Hay, 'The state and the market in 1800: Lord Kenyon and Mr Waddington', *Past & Present*, CLXII (February 1999), 158.
131 Lythe, 'Tayside meal mobs', 31.
132 Flinn, *Scottish Population History*, 233.
133 Fraser, *Conflict and Class*, 60–1.
134 *Ibid.*, 55.
135 Fraser, *Conflict and Class*, 55; *Scots Magazine*, September 1749, 460.
136 Devine, *Transformation*, 19–29.
137 On the emergence of class divisions in the countryside see M. Gray, 'The social impact of agrarian change in the rural Lowlands', in Devine and Mitchison, *People and Society*, 57–62.
138 *Scots Magazine*, August 1760, 445; October 1760, 551; see too T. Barry and D. Hall, *Spottiswoode: Life and Labour on a Berwickshire Estate, 1753–1793* (East Linton, 1997), 150–1.
139 *Ibid.*
140 *Scots Magazine*, March 1762, 162–3.
141 Fraser, *Conflict and Class*, 55–6.
142 Whatley, 'Labour in the industrialising city', 375–6; Signet Library, Court of Session Papers, CSP 135:9, 'Information for George Brown and ors., master manufacturers in Glasgow and neighbourhood, defenders, in process of reduction v. them brought by David Nicholson and ors.', 1768.
143 *Scots Magazine*, June 1773; *Dundee Weekly Magazine*, 5 April 1776.

144 *Glasgow Mercury*, 18 March 1779.
145 S. Nenadic, 'Political reform and the "ordering" of middle-class protest', in Devine, *Conflict and Stability*, 65–82; Devine, 'Urbanisation', 29–30; I. D. Whyte, 'Urbanisation in eighteenth-century Scotland', 179–80, 183.

6

Scotland's first industrial revolution, c. 1778–c. 1830

Outlines of industrialisation

In 1778 cotton spinning mills were opened in Penicuik in Midlothian and, by a Sheffield partnership, at what seems to have been a more favourable site in the wetter west at Rothesay, on the island of Bute in the firth of Clyde. Raw cotton from across the Atlantic (mainly of West Indian origin until after 1800) could easily be shipped off or brought from Port Glasgow and the use of technology pirated from England might better escape notice. But at Penicuik too there was an English connection, with the mill being built to the instructions of John Hackett, an acquaintance of James Hargreaves, inventor of the spinning jenny; Hackett was also a former employee of Richard Arkwright, the patentee of the water frame, referred to briefly in chapter 3.[1] (In the early mills it was not uncommon for hand-powered spinning jennies to be housed in the same buildings as horse- or water-powered frames.)[2] In total, at least thirteen of the leading individuals involved in the formative years of the Scottish cotton industry owed much to their knowledge of, or experience in, English mills.

The introduction of mill spinning in Scotland was some ten years behind England where, following the model provided by the Lombe brothers' silk mill at Derby, Richard Arkwright and his partners had commenced larger-scale spinning in Nottingham in 1769 and set up at Cromford with a purpose-built water-powered mill in 1771.[3] But in Scotland over the next half century cotton production along with other textiles, mainly linen but also wool and silk, spearheaded the Scottish economy, accounting for some 89 per cent of all recorded manufacturing employment in the 1820s.[4] It was during this period that Scotland, building on the firmer foundations which had been laid over the previous fifty years and exploiting her natural advantages to the full, made major strides forwards as an important contributor to British economic growth, but within a market environment which was increasingly freed from controls and regulations and from which bounties on exports were being withdrawn. Those on linen for example were removed in 1832. The Board of Trustees had been stripped of most of their powers in 1823.[5] The transition from old to new is symbolised by the demise of the Scottish marine salt industry after a final surge in output in the 1790s, as war-induced shortages of superior imported 'Bay' salt along with shipments of rock salt from Liverpool raised prices and encouraged Scots producers. In 1825, after the best part of two centuries of protection, and in the wake of a vigorously-fought (but unsuccessful) campaign for compensation on the part of the Scottish saltwork proprietors, the Salt Laws were repealed. Kelp burning suffered from the same legislation, with much more severe social consequences for the fifty thousand or so highlanders and islanders who derived some part of their livelihood from this form of by-employment. As was seen in chapter 3, earlier appeals in 1792 on the part of another sectional interest, the river Forth coalmasters, that to allow the importation without restraint of Newcastle coal would be a breach of the Union, no longer carried weight with a government which in Scotland was guided by the freer market and anti-monopolistic inclinations (learned in part from Adam Smith) of Henry Dundas.[6]

Wars against the American colonies and Napoleon Bonaparte both damaged and benefited the Scottish economy, and although no historian has yet attempted to generate an authoritative balance sheet for the latter, there is a great deal of evidence to suggest that, overall, the conflict favoured Scotland, despite periodic trade depression and the fall in purchasing power which resulted from wartime price inflation.[7] The dislocation caused by the almost continuous conflict with France and her allies between 1793 and 1815 was considerably greater for the continental countries than Britain, not least because the former were all but stripped of their Atlantic trade, which became increasingly important for the Scots. Whereas the French Atlantic ports suffered under the Royal Navy's blockade, Scotland's premier Atlantic port, Glasgow, was given a virtually free hand. Vital raw materials such as cotton, and sugar and rum (imports of which doubled between 1790 and 1815), are just one aspect of this. Although by adopting a protectionist policy against British goods the continental countries were able to establish a thriving modern cotton industry after 1806, high raw material prices and the industry's late start meant that the British industry (including Scotland) was still ahead in 1815.[8] Wartime demand for military and naval stores, and rising money wages, ensured that the momentum within the manufacturing districts was maintained.[9]

In this first phase of industrialisation in Scotland exports to America and the West Indies were crucial, the last-named increasing its share of direct imports of linen from Scotland – mainly for slave clothing – from

23.5 per cent in 1765 to 78.5 per cent in 1810. Scottish-made coarse linen found few buyers on the continent of Europe. In 1815 around two-thirds of the tonnage of vessels going from Glasgow was destined for ports in the West Indies and America.[10] As with the tobacco trade, geography helped (by cutting sailing times relative to those from the south of England), but so too did the skills and experience of Glasgow traders in transatlantic shipping, which were further honing the competitive edge of the Clyde shipping fleet. Rapid turnaround times were critical. By 1841 Glasgow, Greenock and Port Glasgow boasted a fleet of 662 vessels, aggregating a remarkable 187,545 tons, a figure which had risen steadily and inexorably during the 1820s and 1830s, with cotton cloth, iron goods and other manufactures featuring prominently among the exports. Scotland's economic success, then, continued to owe much to British naval power (although Scotland's part in the French Wars should not be overlooked, either in the form of Henry Dundas as Secretary for War, or its fifty thousand military recruits) and to the markets provided by the estimated 26 per cent of the world's population which was under British authority in 1820. But within the context of the security this provided, it was the Scots themselves who ultimately harnessed the resources available to them and drove this early and most northerly Industrial Revolution.[11]

As was seen in chapter 3, the increase in economic activity in the third quarter of the eighteenth century was also partly attributable to rising levels of consumption within Scotland. These continued to grow, 'nowhere in Britain' more so than in Glasgow, where manufacturing and building expansion was driving brick- and tile-makers to the extremes of their productive capacity.[12] By the 1830s the more affluent middle classes formed some 20–25 per cent of the country's urban population.[13] Consumerism, the desire to display material possessions and the emergence of the doctrine of 'separate spheres' for men and women all had their impact on urban space, housing styles and layout and spending patterns. In the countryside too new building was going on, of stone-built two-storey tenant-farmers dwellings. More regulary-shaped single-storey workers' houses either in rows or squares replaced the vernacular structures and looser layouts of the pre-improvement fermtowns.[14] But the contribution of the middling class to industrialisation was not limited to their consumption of its products, or indeed to their role as enterprising merchant-manufacturers, managers, overseers, accountants and the like; they (and especially their womenfolk) also formed the backbone of the system of deposit accounts which had been greatly expanded from 1763, and which provided the wherewithall for the emergence of branch banking.[15]

The pace of urban growth was rapid overall, as has been seen, but stupendous in some places. Five of the thirteen largest towns in early nineteenth-century Scotland at least trebled their populations between *c.* 1750 and 1821; Glasgow's rose more than four-fold, to 137,000, and by a further 38 per cent in the following decade.[16] Not surprisingly, it was the counties of Lanarkshire and Renfrewshire which grew fastest, by 80.7 per cent and 194.6 per cent respectively between 1755 and 1801. The west of Scotland grew three times as fast as the rest of the country.[17] By and large the pacemakers were manufacturing centres, thereby firmly linking urbanisation in Scotland with industrialisation, as in Dundee where steam-driven spinning mills came later, from the 1820s, following an uncertain start between *c.* 1792 and 1818. The burgh's population, which had hardly risen at all between 1811 and 1821, increased by a massive 45 per cent over the next ten years, to reach *c.* 45,000, and, like the woollen manufacturing town of Bradford, Dundee was transformed into an industrial centre within two or three decades. Similar patterns can be discerned in many of the smaller towns too, although increasingly, the big four Scottish towns, Glasgow, Edinburgh, Dundee and Aberdeen, came to dominate urban Scotland.[18]

The number of planned villages, many of which were associated with the emergent cotton industry, also rose, with 164 being laid out between 1770 and 1799, and a further 119 in the following two decades, although both of these figures include fishing and coastal villages in the north-east and Highlands and Islands.[19] Scotland had a greater proportion of its population in small and medium-sized towns (below ten thousand) than either England or most parts of Europe for which data are available. Excluded from these calculations are the villages and smaller towns (of below two thousand inhabitants), some old, some new, which have recently been identified as forming an important and integral part of the process of rural reorganisation in Lowland Scotland, absorbing dispossessed cottars and small tenants, attracting some industry and providing accommodation for part of the rural proletariat and the growing numbers of tradesmen required to service the new market-led agricultural society.[20]

Commercialisation in the countryside increased the numbers of the poor who necessarily sought refuge in the towns, a process which was hastened in the first two or three decades of the nineteenth century. Market relations meant that the greater numbers of urban wage workers were vulnerable to sharp or substantial food price rises, or to periods of trade slackness or unemployment. But as elsewhere in Britain's industrialising regions, the trend in real wages in Scotland was upwards, at least until *c.* 1793. This positive picture reflects the position of agricultural workers as well as urban artisans, and while Scottish wage levels as a whole remained below their English comparators (but less so than in the 1750s), the effect overall was to create virtually a new class of domestic consumers, something which was largely absent in Ireland.[21]

Although at a level which reflected regional variations in income, with those in and around the central Lowland towns doing best, expenditure on food rose, and began to include items which had previously been considered luxuries – such as meat, whisky and confectionaries. On the other hand, there is some impressionistic evidence that expenditure on frivolous items like toys, trinkets and ribbons was lower in Scotland, the working classes in Glasgow preferring instead (perhaps because they had less choice) the escape provided by drink and energetic dancing.[22] Whisky consumption soared from the 1790s. Domestic consumption of Scottish-produced beer almost quadrupled between 1770 and 1800, when there were 180 public breweries. By 1825 there were 233, the heaviest concentrations of which were in and around Edinburgh and Glasgow. Clothing too was purchased in greater quantities and with an eye to changing fashions, with muslin, fine linen, cotton and silk-gauzes replacing heavy brocades and satins from the 1780s.[23] The paradox this created of more onerous work for those females involved in the monotonous trade of spinning was clearly recognised in an 1801 chapbook version of a popular traditional spinning song, 'The Rock and the Wee Pickle Tow':

> An' we maun hae pearlins, an' mabbies, an' cocks'
> An' some other things that ladies ca' smocks:
> An' how we get that, gin we tak na' our rocks,
> An' pow what we can at the spinning o't.[24]

Consumer durables – watches and clocks were particularly popular – and kettles and other household items were in heavy demand. All of this had a knock-on effect on the Scottish agricultural, extractive, manufacturing and construction industries.

The outlines of the rapid expansion of cotton spinning and weaving in Scotland are well known, and need only be briefly described here. Remarkably quickly, indeed within two decades, cotton had overtaken linen as Scotland's premier textile product, as measured by employment, volume of output and capital formation.[25] By 1788, within ten years of the first being erected, Scotland had nineteen of Britain's 143 water-powered mills. By 1800 there were around sixty in Scotland, by 1810, 110, and by 1839, 192, by which time the capital value of the industry was somewhere in the region of £4.5 million.[26] Raw cotton imports, which must serve as a proximate measure of output, rose spectacularly, increasing almost seventeen-fold to an annual average of 7.19 million pounds between 1781–86 and 1799–1804. Although most mills were small, there were also some massive undertakings, with the trend towards the large-scale mills firmly set by 1815, following a series of credit crises during the French wars which eliminated the weaker firms.[27] Almost from the outset however, large mills of four storeys and more were built, powered by massive water wheels, as at Catrine (Ayrshire), Deanston

(Perthshire) and New Lanark, which Robert Owen purchased (along with the village) in 1799 for £60,000 from the early doyen of mill spinning in Scotland, David Dale.[28] Dale was a partner or had interests in at least six large spinning concerns, a position which was enhanced by his appointment to the post of cashier of the Glasgow agency of the Royal Bank of Scotland in 1783.

But for all the new mill building, conversion of older structures for cotton spinning and the spread of hand-powered spinning jennies into sheds and small factories, which seem to have been more profuse in Ayrshire than anywhere else, Scotland's emergence as a significant producer of cotton cloth was not altogether a surprise. Fustians, fabrics comprising linen warp and cotton weft, were being made in Scotland in the 1730s, and 'mixed goods' such as Bengals saw substantial increases in output thereafter. Manchester however was the main centre of fustian manufacture in Britain, and the demands from England – and Ireland – for linen yarn had been one of the factors behind the extension of flax spinning in the 1730s and 1740s. Scotland continued to be a net exporter of yarn, although evidently owing to the inability of yarn merchants to obtain sufficient fine yarn from within Scotland, imports rose from an annual average of around 6,000 pounds in the second half of the 1750s to over a quarter of a million pounds in the early 1780s.[29] Bleachfields and printfields too, over a hundred of which were laid out between 1765 and 1790, had experience in dealing with cotton goods.

It is notable that, contrary to the long-held view that the Scottish cotton industry emerged as a result of capital being transferred from the tobacco trade following the blows to its prosperity caused by the American War, its entrepreneurial roots lay primarily in the flax, linen and silk trades. It was from the ranks of dealers in these as well as textile finishers that the largest group of the industry's entrepreneurs came, with foreign and colonial traders playing a particularly prominent part.[30] Such transitions, a form of backward integration, took place in a sector of the textile industry in which partnerships were the norm, spinning; single-owners and family concerns were more usual in weaving. The indications are that bank lending, both for capital needs and shorter-term credit requirements through bill-discounting, played an important – but still unmeasured – part in facilitating expansion in both sectors in cotton and linen, although less obviously in the case of woollens.[31] By 1802 Scottish bank assets were £12 million. *Per capita* this was a higher level than England. Banking density was greater too, and the system was more stable. The provincial banks, the number of which had risen to twenty-one by 1793, with a further twelve formations between 1802 and 1810, were often conscious of their capacity to stimulate local economic development, although the Edinburgh banks and their agencies have been credited with providing the greater part of the banking facilities required by industrial concerns in Glasgow before 1830.[32] The Scottish banks' liberal note issuing policy was undoubtedly helpful too, but even so, current indications are that personal finance, often obtained within kinship networks, and the policy of ploughing back profits, were the major sources of long-term capital.

Powerloom weaving made comparatively rapid progress in Scotland very early in the nineteenth century, but thereafter its adoption was 'fitful and slow' (partly because of its unsuitability for weaving finer fabrics) until the high wage year of 1824 when the cost benefits became overwhelmingly obvious. Even then – as before – interest in powerlooms tended to wax and wane in accordance with prevailing handloom rates.[33] It was rare for more than a hundred powerloom weavers to be employed by a single firm before 1830, and indeed the small firm remained the norm in the British weaving trade, which in cost terms was subject to the prices set by the spinners and more than ordinarily susceptible to overproduction and depression.[34] As in England, early industrialisation saw an increase in the numbers of handloom weavers, not only in cotton but also linen, concentrated in the east of Scotland, where numbers rose until 1840 (to reach around 85,000). Indeed if we include other non-mechanised processes such as the muslin embroiderers (tambourers) who were engaged in growing numbers in the Glasgow and Paisley areas from the 1780s it is easy to understand why in 1812, for example, the majority of the estimated 150,000 workers employed in cotton worked from their own homes. Handloom factories were not unknown, but as late as 1840 the typical Scottish weaver was still a domestic out-worker.[35]

There are a number of inter-related reasons for this remarkable progress in cotton, notwithstanding its dual technology. As we have seen, in the early 1770s the prospects for linen manufacture in Scotland were uncertain, and while output recovered, a number of factors had combined by the end of the decade to encourage fine linen yarn and cloth merchants and manufacturers to make the momentous move into cotton. Labour during the American War of Independence was scarce and the underlying trend in wages was upwards, thus encouraging producers to seek higher productivity levels, and indeed it was precisely this which had been behind the initial proposal for a water-driven mill in Penicuik in 1774.[36] The market for the higher-priced, finer-quality linens such as cambrics and lawns was rising, but fashion-led demand for cotton cloth was even stronger, and the yarns for this could be machine-spun from the end of the 1760s, with the inventions of Arkwright's spinning frame and James Hargreaves' spinning jenny. Crucial in explaining the timing of the beginning of the transfer from linen to cotton in Scotland towards the end of the 1770s were flax price increases which occurred alongside a halving of the price of raw cotton in the Clyde between 1776 and 1780.[37] The uncertainty there was about the government's attitude to assisting the linen industry in Scotland is likely to have been another.

When Richard Arkwright rode north to Glasgow in 1784, allegedly in search of a means to 'find a *razor* in Scotland to *shave* Manchester', whose manufacturers had resisted his attempts to uphold and extend his patent rights, he was carrying on a decades-old tradition whereby Scotland had been looked to for lower building, labour and raw material costs. The patriotic card too was played again, not only but most notably by George Dempster of Dunnichen, MP, 'the patron of manufactures in Scotland', who evidently persuaded Arkwright of the potential advantages of locating north of the border. Glasgow's Chamber of Commerce, the first in Britain, founded in 1783 to press the commercial interests of the Glasgow district, was also involved in the visit during which Arkwright was met with popular acclaim in the weaving centres of Anderston and Paisley.[38] Merchants and other ambitious men in the textile trade were anxious to impress upon him their business abilities, while owners of estates with manageable rivers had little difficulty in persuading Arkwright of their adaptability by the use of lades for spinning machinery, and there followed a flurry of large mills built either with Arkwright's direct involvement – as at New Lanark, Woodside (near Aberdeen), Stanley and Deanston (Perthshire) – or on Arkwright principles.[39] At the heart of these lay the centralisation, regulation and control of labour, which explains why three hundred shoemakers were employed under one roof by the Glasgow Tanwork Co. *c.* 1773, but the new technologies driven by a single power source provided the imperative for most of the mill and factory building of the period.[40] Previously Scotland had had some large workforces – of over fifty – at a handful of coal mines, some larger bleachfields and printworks, and at Carron, but what was spectacular from the 1780s was not only the size of the biggest mills (New Lanark was employing as many as 1,700 workers in 1816), but also the dispersal of all sorts of mills throughout much of Scotland.

Although Arkwright's interest in Scotland was short-lived – once his patent was overturned Scotland seemed a less desirable ally – it had been long enough to lay the new technological basis of cotton spinning in Scotland, and widespread enthusiasm was maintained. Mills were opened far from what was to become the industry's core location, the Glasgow and Paisley regions. A 'fever' for mill building seems to have gripped the south-west, where from 1785 and into the first half of the 1790s there was a rash of construction of both small and large units.[41] Stirlingshire, Perthshire, Dumfries and Galloway, Fife and even Angus were all penetrated by cotton mills. The most northerly large-scale cotton spinning enterprise was set in train in 1792, at Spinningdale in Sutherland. The site's coastal location and proximity to what was assumed to be a pool of suitable underemployed Highland labour persuaded Dempster and Dale, in alliance with some Glasgow merchants and local landed interests, that a works there would be to their own and the public advantage.[42] Like most pre-*c*. 1800 cotton mills in Scotland, Spinningdale was water-powered, and indeed water continued to provide a greater proportion of kinetic energy in Scotland than the north of England, the respective percentage shares in 1835 being 43.6 horse-power and 18.6 horse-power.[43]

By the end of the eighteenth century however a clear pattern of regional concentration and specialisation was emerging. Several of the more peripheral mills disappointed the expectations of their over-optimistic projectors, who experienced difficulties during times of commercial distress, as between 1792 and 1794, and in 1810 and 1811. Sixty of Perth's seventy cotton merchants and over fifty (out of sixty) manufacturing firms were reputed to have failed when continental markets were cut off in 1810.[44] Others, Spinningdale for example, which was one of the first to be abandoned, suffered from their 'remote' locations and the discovery that displaced Highlanders were not easily converted into disciplined mill and factory workers, and failed to respond to the prospect of regular wages.

Labour turnover could reach 'staggering' proportions, even where efforts had been made to soften the shock of entry to the world of industrial capitalism with the provision of housing, small gardens and other social facilities in factory villages.[45] Problems associated with the shortage of suitably experienced mill managers continued to trouble some early entrants to the industry, although in this regard Arkwright's assistance in taking and training parties of Scots in his works at Cromford helped overcome this at some favoured mills.[46]

The larger country mills survived, often through changes in ownership, and thrived, with the employment of lower-paid women and girls on a larger scale than in Lancashire (where in 1833 50 per cent of workers were in these categories), providing the Scottish mills with a price advantage over their rivals.[47] Intriguing evidence is beginning to emerge that female workers in Scotland (and perhaps males too), may have been physically stronger than their English counterparts. In spite of the restricted nature of and the prominence within the Scottish diet of oatmeal and potatoes, it produced the tallest males in the UK up to 1850 and, it would appear, fit women.[48] If the Scots manufacturer was able to work such females as well as the males, it was observed, 'he must derive a great benefit from their labour being much cheaper'; in the west of Scotland bleachfields women were to outnumber males by three to one by the start of the Victorian era.[49] Although mule spinning in the urban mills necessitated the use of scarce skilled male labour prior to the invention of the self-actor (an early variant of which was patented by William Kelly of New Lanark in 1792, but not perfected until the mid-1830s), even in these, females dominated owing to their employment as carders, reelers and piecers. Kelly's intention, as with those who strove in the same direction over the following decades, had been to replace expensive and troublesome male mule spinners (see chapter 7) with children.[50] The benefits of child labour, both for industry and society, were passionately argued.[51] Children under the ages of thirteen or fourteen were the most contented workers in the mill, it was claimed of Stanley Mills in 1833. Only when they were older did they become discontented. Raging against the parliamentary threat to the use of child labour, James Craig (of Stanley) was convinced that his rivals would 'chuckle' at the removal of 'the Pillars of the Cotton manufacture' which, by forcing employers to hire old men and women (at double the wages) who could not do as well as children, would 'destroy the exertions of the most enterprising men in the British Empire'.[52]

Two technological developments were to confirm Glasgow and its region as the centre of the cotton industry in Scotland. If Arkwright and his methods had provided the model for the initial take-off for cotton in Scotland, it was Richard Crompton, who in 1779 invented but failed to patent his mule-spinning method, who determined its later direction. Unlike the Arkwright machines, which turned out coarse yarns, mule spinning enabled yarns of the finest counts to be spun mechanically, and thus to provide the needs of the fine weavers who had earlier concentrated in Glasgow and Paisley, making cambrics and, in Paisley's case, silk. Although hand- and water-powered mules were used in the country mills it was in the urban mills, particularly in Glasgow, that the mule dominated. By 1831 there were well over half a million mule spindles in and around Glasgow, compared to some 22,000 throstles (i.e. modified water frames).[53]

The application of steam power to mill spinning machinery, in the form of James Watt's invention of rotative motion, was crucial to the emergence of Glasgow as Scotland's leading industrial city in the early nineteenth century. The limitations of the city's water power resources, which had forced merchant-millowners out into the surrounding countryside – and even further afield – were overcome as the new technology was adapted and improved to meet the needs of spinners. By 1839 Glasgow and its immediate suburbs housed some 98 mills, the counties of Lanark and Renfrew 175 of a Scottish total of 192; only a fraction of those built between 1800 and 1830 were water-powered.[54] Although human, animal and wind power were used to drive the wheels of early industrialisation, their scale was small. What mattered was coal, even before c. 1830 and the era of heavy industry in Scottish economic history. Contrary to older indictments of the Scottish coal industry, some of which have been noted already, its performance during the later eighteenth and early nineteenth centuries was impressive, registering a thirteen-fold increase in output between 1700 and 1830, and accounting for a growing share (13.3 per cent in 1800) of British coal production.[55] To combat the problem shared by mining enterprises everywhere, underground water, steam-pumping engines were applied in impressive numbers: between 1734 and 1775 only in the north-east of England were more constructed than in Scotland (and the west Midlands, which shared second place). For the century as a whole Scottish collieries accounted for 17 per cent of all steam-pumping engines erected in Britain, including the improved and more efficient Boulton and Watt engines.[56]

As before, the greater availability of coal both facilitated and encouraged growth elsewhere by satisfying the needs of the burgeoning towns, but also made it possible for cotton firms in and around Glasgow to exploit the advantages of steam power. One reason for the failure of the Irish cotton industry to grow from the 1820s was the absence of this natural advantage.[57] Dundee's lead in steam-driven spinning was made possible by the ease with which coal could be shipped into the Tay from the pits along the Forth and on Tyneside, which between them sent almost five times as much coal in 1840 as in 1820.[58] Coal was transported to Glasgow by cart, the Monkland Canal (which opened in 1793) and in growing quantities by rail and canal after 1826, when the first of a series of coal railways was laid to connect the Monklands coalfield with the city.[59] In 1831 the Garnkirk & Glasgow line was opened, backed by Glasgow coal and chemical interests, the first to directly challenge the canals.

Industrial concentration was further encouraged by the deepening and improved navigability of the Clyde, which went some way towards reducing the costs of imports into Glasgow's city centre, as well as by the intensification of the flow of labour from the Highlands but more importantly before 1851, Ireland.[60] A specific benefit of this for Glasgow and the west of Scotland was the increased numbers available for handloom weaving, wage levels and working conditions in which were rapidly deteriorating. But strengthening rural-urban migration streams (both temporary and permanent) and, on a stronger but more geographically selective basis, Irish immigration – allied to a rising rate of natural population increase from 1801 – combined to provide the altering demographic variable which was an essential component of an economy one of whose nineteenth-century strengths lay in its continuing capacity to hold down labour costs.[61]

But as has been hinted, Scotland's first Industrial Revolution was neither 'confined to cotton', nor to west-central Scotland. Linen output continued to rise, tripling in volume between 1773–77 and 1813–17 to an annual average of 26.6 million yards, some of this woven from yarn spun in mills which from the mid-1790s had retreated from cotton back into flax.[62] By 1831 Dundee alone was exporting 44 million yards. With long-established links with the Baltic and Russia, where most of the flax was derived, existing labour and entrepreneurial skills, a favourable credit structure, familiarity with markets and contacts with customers, it made sense that the industry should become increasingly concentrated in Dundee and its smaller satellite towns like Forfar, and the sub-regional centres of Dunfermline, Kirkcaldy and Montrose, each with their own specialist cloths.[63] In following this pattern of regional specialisation, one of the defining features of the British Industrial Revolution, east-central Scotland had much in common with a rapidly industrialising region such as Yorkshire.

Where Dundee and its region stands out it is in respect of its growing prominence within the British and indeed the European linen industries.[64] By 1826 Dundee had overtaken Hull as Britain's premier flax port and in the following decade was rivalling Leeds as the country's principal producer of linen. Striking too was the speed at which mechanisation was adopted, first in the spread throughout the coarse textile area of water-powered flax-spinning mills from 1787 (following the development of the new technology in Darlington), and then the application of steam-power in Dundee, where the number of mills rose from seven in 1820 to forty in 1832, a faster rate than anywhere else in either Scotland or England. Again the Napoleonic Wars had played their part, causing severe fluctuations in output in Scotland, but devastating the formerly productive linen regions of Westphalia, Saxony and Silesia – and putting almost an entire stop to French exports to the West Indies and Spanish America. By contrast, during the conflict, Scottish linen output rose. Mechanisation advanced faster than in Ireland or on mainland Europe.[65]

It is at this juncture that favourable economic and social structural factors come into play: in Lowland Scotland, the nature of agrarian advance with the move to larger farms was to prise apart farming and part-time manufacturing activity, thereby releasing labour for the urban mills. In Ireland, on the other hand, domestic flax cultivation, and the ease with which land could be sub-divided encouraged the continuation of small-scale, low-cost hand spinning and weaving.[66] Whether this advantage was as great in practice as in theory will be seen in the following chapter.

Success in linen was due too to several other factors – including, as in the Glasgow case, the dynamism of Dundee's merchants in seeking out markets abroad, notably in North America, and campaigning for vital harbour improvements and extensions from 1815. But what was crucial here as elsewhere in Scotland – as it had been since the seventeenth century – was the commitment on the part of the industry's leaders to cost competitiveness, the studious copying of manufacturing techniques utilised elsewhere, and in the later eighteenth century, their subsequent modification and improvement by mechanics who were bred in the distinctly practical environment of the Scottish Enlightenment.[67] The employment of females (a feature of the modernising economy we have already noted), the ratio of whom to males was even greater in linen than cotton, along with lower rates of pay, completed the equation in spinning.[68] In weaving (in cotton as well as linen) work was more tightly controlled, but it continued to be done by hand rather than on the power-loom, the greater abundance of cheap labour in Scotland from the 1810s enabling Scottish manufactures to delay the widespread adoption of mechanised production longer than in England.[69]

Similar patterns, of regional specialisation and the catching up of the Scottish economy with England, with some industries taking a growing share of British output, are to be seen in other sectors. Although considerably smaller than cotton and linen (which between them employed nine out of ten textile workers in Scotland in 1826), the woollen industry in Scotland not only concentrated in the Borders, the Hillfoots in central Scotland and to a lesser extent in the south west and east Aberdeenshire, but also grew. This was in sharp contrast to East Anglia and the west of England, which had declined in the face of Yorkshire competition. Spread widely in the mid-eighteenth century, the introduction in the 1810s of water- and steam-powered spinning concentrated production geographically, and in mills in which, again, there was a higher proportion of females than in England. Although there were apparently no wool spinning mills in Scotland in 1790 (when there were around seventy-seven in the rest of Britain), by 1830 7.4 per cent of them were north of the border, with fixed capital investment having risen from £3,000 to £170,000. The Hillfoots alone reckoned that they were processing the fleeces of 550,000 sheep by 1833.[70] Somewhat later, by mid-century, Scotland had supplanted the west of England in the fine woollen trade.[71]

Framework knitting in the Borders – and its smaller component in and around Dumfries – followed a virtually identical trajectory, starting relatively late, but being fairly well-established by 1815. By 1830 it was well on the way to becoming a significant contributor to the British hosiery and knitted woollens industry.[72] The route to centralised production however could be circuitous or even reach a localised dead end. In rural Aberdeenshire, for example, the domestic knitted stocking trade, organised by Aberdeen-based merchant-hosiers who gave out the wool and collected the work done by as many as thirty thousand part-time, mainly female knitters, more than quadrupled its output in the fifty years to 1793. Thereafter however the industry contracted, the French Wars causing the immediate collapse of vital foreign markets, while in the longer-run the Borders frame-knitters undercut Aberdeenshire prices. Although textile mills were opened in the Aberdeen area, their scale was never sufficient to compensate for the demise of cottage industry.[73]

In textile finishing too the outlying fields which had been laid out in the 1740s and 1750s began to be abandoned from the 1790s. But the best could stand comparison with any in Europe, and by the early 1800s the biggest, such as those in the vicinity of Perth, which could cost between £4,000 and £5,000 to set up, attracted cloth from England and, in even greater quantities, Ireland.[74] As we have seen, vitriol production, at Prestonpans, had initially (in 1749) been begun by an English partnership led by Dr John Roebuck, an outstanding Edinburgh University-educated applied scientist but less able entrepreneur, who was also one of the original partners at Carron. However, with the establishment by Charles Tennant in 1799 of the St Rollox chlorine bleaching powder works, Glasgow became a world leader in chemicals. Chlorine not only removed the need for bleachers to import ashes, but also reduced dramatically the time required to bleach cloth. By the 1830s St Rollox was the largest heavy chemicals plant in Europe. In dyeing, where too French experimentation was turned to practical use in Britain, the Scots also achieved world success, to the extent that by the early nineteenth century Turkey-red handkerchiefs dyed at Henry Monteith, Bogle & Co.'s Barrowfield Dyeworks were known throughout Europe as 'Monteith's'.[75]

Also growing in comparative terms was the Scottish paper industry which, like coal, lime and slates, was geared to the burgeoning home market. The growth in production which occurred between 1779 and 1790 has been called 'phenomenal', although this may partly reflect the effects of new administrative procedures in the collection of the excise returns from which output data have been calculated. What is beyond doubt however is that from 1824, before the end of our period, and up to 1852, the Scottish growth rate not only surpassed that of England, but Scotland also increased its share of United Kingdom paper output from 10.7 per cent to 22.2 per cent.[76] Consumer demand both north and south of the border lay behind the establishment of several new, legal whisky distilleries in Lowland Scotland in and after 1779, while further expansion followed the Wash Act of 1784. Whisky distilleries were among Scotland's largest manufacturing enterprises. One of them, belonging to James Stein in Kilbagie, housed the country's first Boulton and Watt steam engine.[77] The demands of fashion, for whalebone stays, allied to that from industry for oil, stimulated new-found interest in whaling in ports such as Aberdeen, Dundee, Montrose and Peterhead. The government bounty on whalers provided an additional inducement. First offered in 1732 but to little effect in Scotland, this almost doubled in 1749, and was further enhanced in 1781. Even before this last increase the bounty was providing the main return to Aberdeen whaling firms. Notwithstanding the favourable consequences for British whalers of the conclusion of the American War, progress was slow at first, but in the first and second decades of the nineteenth century the main Scottish whaling ports grew as rapidly as Hull in England and, between 1814 and 1817, matched the best English catches.[78]

Although iron made its greatest contribution to Scotland's economic history after 1830, its share of UK pig-iron output rising from 5 per cent in the 1820s to 25 per cent in less than ten years, the factors which were to generate this expansion were all in place earlier. The industry's locational pattern had been established too, even though it would take the spread of the rail network to the extremities of the coalfields of central Scotland to bring this to fruition. But while before 1830 it was overshadowed by textiles in terms of capital, output and numbers employed, iron manufacturing, in which some £1.5 million had been invested by blast-furnace firms by 1830 (compared to over £4 million in cotton), had already become an integral feature of the industrialising and urbanising economy. Rural society was affected too, not only by the construction of ironworks in countryside locations, but also through the works' demands for coal, ironstone and lime – and foodstuffs – which benefited estates within their vicinity. After a twenty-year gap following the establishment of Carron, a second coke-fired ironworks – again applying the smelting techniques developed by the Darbys at Coalbrookdale – was built at Wilsontown in 1779. This presaged a period of dramatic expansion, with works in Lanarkshire (five), Ayrshire (two) and Clackmannanshire and Fife (one each) raising Scottish iron-making capacity from 4,000 tons in 1780 to 32,000 by the early 1800s. Investment in new works, which were usually started during peaks in the trade cycle and then ran short of capital before they were completed, was attracted by the prospect of Scotland's lower costs, of land, minerals and labour, which goes some way to accounting for the substantial interest of English firms until the early 1800s. Unlikely locations such as Muirkirk (begun in 1787) – 'a Desart and Inland place' over twenty miles from the Ayrshire coast – were chosen largely because speculators were convinced that virtually virgin minerals could be mined, apparently with careless abandon at first, even more cheaply than elsewhere in Scotland.[79]

Landowners anxious to exploit estate minerals welcomed the coal and iron companies with open arms and modest demands for royalties, while the heavy capital costs of setting up an ironworks were met by partnerships – mainly Scottish from 1825 – which limited individual financial risks, supplemented by the ploughing back of profits and increasingly, bank credits.[80] (Although more will be said about landowners below, in their capacity as agricultural capitalists, their generally positive contribution to the early industrialisation process up to c. 1820, largely as part of their efforts to maximise estate income, should be recognised.)

Sales were anticipated from armaments and war-related demand in some cases, most notably Carron, although most were founded in hopes of finding markets in England as well as Ireland, the West Indies and North America. Within Scotland, demand was strengthening, from agriculture, for ploughs and other metal implements; from urbanisation, which required water-carrying pipes; and from industry, notably the growing business of engineering, supplying and repairing steam engines and water wheels at mines and mills. Most of the country's fifty foundries and forges in 1813 were to be found in and around Glasgow and the south west, which, with the interest in the region in practical questions relating to steam technology which had provided the enquiring environment in which James Watt could flourish, gave rise to the steamship building industry of the Clyde. Between 1812, when Henry Bell's steam-driven *Comet*, first sailed across it, and 1820, forty-two steam vessels were constructed on the Clyde.[81] Although other rivers successfully competed in the short-term, in the longer-run, the Clyde was to be ascendant.

Nevertheless there was considerable instability within the iron industry. Overseas demand was liable to fluctuations, while that from within Scotland was unable to sustain all of the works. No new ironworks were constructed in Scotland between 1801 and 1825, when iron prices rose to encourage the formation of the Monklands Iron and Steel Co. the following year. Company failures were frequent – seven English partnerships tried and failed at the Balgonie works in Fife between 1801 and 1814. The costs of transporting – by road – the finished product from inland works which were usually some distance from their markets cancelled out the initial locational benefits. But in 1802 David Mushet, of Calder ironworks, discovered iron-rich 'blackband' ironstone (in which iron nodules lay in black clay between the seams of coal). In 1828 J. B. Neilson, a Glasgow chemist and engineer, discovered a means of blowing hot rather than cold air into the blast furnaces, which improved the quality of the pig iron but much more importantly reduced the quantity of coal required for each ton of pig iron by some two-thirds. The cost savings, buttressed by the lower costs of Irish and Highland labour and aggressive labour relations policies (see chapter 7), along with the other Scottish price advantages already noted, were to give the west of Scotland an unbeatable competitive edge over English producers in UK and export markets at a time of soaring demand.[82]

In 1832, it has been argued, 'the forces of industrial change extended and accelerated in dramatic fashion.'[83] The concept of a second Industrial Revolution in Scotland is not without its attractions. Certainly there was recovery from this date, following a period of general slackness in the British economy from 1825–26. There were some severe blows to parts of the Scottish economy, apart from those mentioned earlier in this chapter. We will come across others below. To these should be added local downturns such as the fall in the number of whaling ships at Aberdeen and Peterhead between 1821 and 1825, while the lead industry saw falls in production after 1815 and 1827, the last following the removal by William Huskisson of yet another set of tariffs which had provided a useful level of protection for a weak Scottish industry.[84] There was a major cut in the output of the emergent Scottish shipbuilding industry. The Clyde had seized 60 per cent of the British output of steam shipping in the eight years between 1812 and 1820, but ten years later this had fallen to 14 per cent. After tackling allegations that it was unable to keep up with demand the west of Scotland coal industry periodically found itself burdened with surplus coal, which was dumped on the Irish market in a bid to drive up Glasgow prices. Before the end of and in the years following the wars with France, competition in and around Edinburgh was such that collieries at any distance from the capital had difficulty finding a renumerative sale.[85] After 1825 cotton never again experienced its previous levels of buoyancy; following a lengthy period of stagnation it slowly followed its Irish counterpart downwards as it ran up against competition from those continental producers which had become established during the Napoleonic Wars, and slipped further behind Lancashire which was consolidating its technological and organisational superiority over the Scots. The woollens industry was confronted with serious difficulties too, over the quality of its raw materials and products, and the apparent unwillingness of the industry's leaders to take on the fine woollen producers of Yorkshire.[86]

But the case for a break in what has been perceived as a 'two-stage' industrialisation process can be over-stated. Scotland by c. 1830 had not yet felt the impact of a full-blown Industrial Revolution, but nor had anywhere else. Although the era of heavy industry lay in the future, the foundations had been laid, in coal, iron, shipbuilding and heavy engineering. This was true not only of west-central Scotland. Albeit in a restricted form, in Aberdeen (where textiles were the single most significant single employer of labour) a small but flourishing engineering industry pre-1830, allied to an established shipbuilding sector, gave rise in the following decade to a vigorous steamship-building industry. Granite quarries too had been opened up, with the stone being used for local building puroposes as well as being shipped to London. The advent of steamers in the 1820s also enabled Aberdonians to send live cattle south.[87] Temporary if deep recessions apart, the textile industry of east-central Scotland continued to expand during the first half of the nineteenth century. New production methods were widely employed, but steam power had been used in Dundee from the 1790s. 'Massive' port development along Scotland's east coast up until the mid-Victorian era accompanied and facilitated the expansion of shipping which this entailed. Improved dock facilities were in line with developments elsewhere in Britain, where port capacity tripled between 1791 and 1841. The challenges which confronted the Borders woollen industry were fundamental and demanded radical solutions, but according to the industry's historian the remarkable expansion in the productive capacity of the industry in the succeeding decades 'was rooted in the products of the pre-tweed era'.[88]

The fact is that even by 1830 few parts of Scotland had not been touched by the tentacles of early industrialisation. Its impact in the Lowland countryside and the Highlands and Islands will be discussed below. The populations of the rural counties peaked in 1831. By the 1840s no Lowland county had a majority of its householders engaged in farming. Three regions out of eight in Scotland – Strathclyde (the largest, with Glasgow at its core, with a population of some nine-hundred thou-sand, 34.5 per cent of the total), Central and Fife, and Tayside – would have markedly higher proportions of their populations in 'revolutionised' industry than the British average.[89] Although English regions such as Lancashire contained more revolutionised industry, in England and Wales as a whole only six out of forty-three regions were above average in this respect. Figures for mid-century show that a higher proportion of Scots were employed in manufacturing (43.2 per cent) than in Britain as a whole (40.9 per cent), and a smaller percentage in the service sector.[90]

But well before 1850 contemporaries were in no doubt that they had lived and were living through a period of extraordinary change in the economic and social life of the nation. The extent of this – including the benefits – according to Charles Anderson, in his 1825 *Statement of the Experience of Scotland with Regard to the Education of the People*, had 'never [been] exhibited in the same time [thirty to forty years] in any country on the face of the earth.'[91] Commentators, tourists, novelists and poets, and in the 1790s the parish clergy who throughout Scotland contributed to the first *Statistical Account,* often reported and wrote in a similar vein, although usually with less sanguinity than Anderson.[92] Even in a middle-ranking, semi-industrialised port town like Montrose, where steam engines had swept in during the 1820s, a minor poet, Alexander Smart, could wax eloquently against the 'theorists' who argued for the advantages of steam and new labour-saving inventions and in favour of the unchecked operation of the market in which an 'invisible hand' would somehow provide alternative work for the displaced artisan:

> But had our theorist to sweat and moil
> For daily bread, he would, without a doubt,
> See the affair in quite another light,
> And bawl against machines with all his might.[93]

As will be seen in the following chapter, the social costs of industrialisa-tion were high.

Care must be taken however not to exaggerate the spread of large-scale manufacturing in Lowland Scotland, and attention should be paid to the ubiquity of small-scale enterprises with low levels of capitalisation: the independent tradesmen of Lowland Perthshire, for example, with business assets of a couple of hundred pounds who made and serviced agricultural machinery and provided for the needs of farm servants, village dwellers and country mill and factory workers.[94]

Lowland agriculture

In accounting for the emergence in Scotland of a mechanised linen industry, attention was drawn to favourable features of Scotland's changing Lowland rural society. The marked expansion in the number of planned villages and other forms of rural settlement resulting from estate rationalisation was also noted. But the ramifications of the advance of capitalist relations in the countryside were wider than this. From the 1760s, as was observed in chapters 2 and 3, the agrarian revolution in Scotland was gathering momentum, led by landowners and lairds and supported and implemented by a cadre of full-time agents, factors or 'men of business', along with some favourably-inclined tenants of larger farms. But while Scotland's Lowland rural transformation contributed to the process of industrialisation, it was urban growth, much of which was the consequence of the expansion of textile manufacturing, which provided the spur of market expansion and persuaded the landed classes to embark on a more vigorous campaign of estate reform. This was time-consuming and expensive, requiring not only substantial capital sums for direct expenditure on their own estates, but also for bridges and road improvements, essential for easing and hastening the transportation of agricultural produce to markets. Mainly undertaken in the form of turnpike trusts, some £2–3 million may have been expended on internal communication in Scotland between 1790 and 1815.[95] The prospects for rent increases, then, had to be extremely good.

Grain prices rose in the second half of the eighteenth century, as did real wages. Edinburgh and Glasgow, which by 1800 housed some 60 per cent of Scotland's urban population, created even more powerful market pulls on the agricultural sector, as to a lesser degree did the myriad of smaller centres which lay within the land corridor which lay across south-central Scotland.[96] That urban growth rates were at their fastest in this period is of immense significance, and helped reinvigorate landowner enthusiasm for costly modernisation programmes. Urban demand not only played its part in accounting for the speed of agrarian change, but also for the intensification of the process of regional specialisation the beginnings of which we noted in chapter 2. Landowners themselves contributed to urban growth and expanded their own markets by setting out more planned villages: 82 per cent of the planned villages laid out between 1700 and 1840 in the Lowlands were founded between 1760 and 1815.

Although only part of rural Lowland Scotland during the 'long' eighteenth century has been subject to recent rigorous study (the counties of Angus, Ayr, Fife and Lanark), and while there were regional and local variations and exceptions, the broad outlines of change are now reasonably clear. Research on a wider scale would be welcome but it is unlikely to radically alter any of the conclusions regarding the chronology and causes of Scotland's Agricultural Revolution reached by Professor T. M. Devine. This is not to overlook the fact of regional diversity in Scottish agricultural history, even in the Lowlands.[97] In a distinctive region such as the south-west, where family farming was more common, there was a great variety of farming types, with dairying predominating around Glasgow and the industrialised districts, and cattle farming, sheep rearing and mixed corn and cattle cultivation being the norm towards the Solway in the south. But while there was no single pattern of improvement, by 1830 almost every part of the Lowlands was farmed according to the precepts of improvement and was marked by common features which included separate holdings, rectangular fields and crop rotations. If a single region stands out it is the north east, where improvement generally began later (in the 1790s) and most farms were only moderately enlarged. Instead of shrinking, after 1800 the populations of most of the region's rural parishes grew as the number of smallholdings was *increased*, landowners retaining an enlarged labour force both to cultivate large swathes of unused land and to provide a source of local seasonal and temporary workers for the larger farmers.[98]

Market and commercial considerations penetrated all aspects of social and economic life in the countryside in the second half of the eighteenth century. Customary rights, to free grazing or to enter plantations or walk through enclosures to follow the course of an established way, for instance, were withdrawn, and the rights of property conspicuously asserted by an increasingly authoritarian landed class. Enclosure, widespread between 1763 and 1780, surged further forward in the 1790s as weather conditions and prices improved. By this decade the 'improving' lease, referred to in chapter 2, had become the norm.[99] These documents made it clear to tenants what their responsibilities in terms of land management were. Landowners and their agents determined to enforce them, backed by legal action and removal in cases of non-compliance. Their provisions, wrote Boswell to the overseer of his Auchinleck estate in 1793, 'must be followed without relaxation', and, in terms which reflected sentiments which thus far we have tended to associate with the employers of the labouring classes, he went on to remark that 'no Estate can flourish where the tenants are not kept to steady order and regularity.'[100] Tenants who were deemed to be insufficiently good farmers or committed to improvement were identified and given notice of removal, or moved to another part of the estate on a smaller holding, perhaps to be utilised as a labourer or carter. For industrialisation the most signifi-cant consequences of these radical changes, which included more scientific farming methods such as regular liming – aided by the greater availability of lime from huge commercial works such as that erected by the earl of Elgin at Charlestown (Fife) in 1777 and 1778 – and the use of new crops and rotations, were dramatic increases in yields. These aver-aged between 200 and 300 per cent in some areas between 1750 and 1800. Not only, it appears, had Scotland caught up with England in this regard (in a remarkably short period of time), but also the bulk of the country's growing manufacturing and urban population could be adequately fed.[101] Glasgow's and the west of Scotland's particularly voracious grain requirements were such that quantities had to be brought overland from the east and, after 1775, on the first stretch of the Forth and Clyde canal. Imports of oats and oatmeal from Ireland did grow over the course of the eighteenth century, and while these may have fed only some 2.5 per cent of the Scottish population in later years, there are strong suggestions that in times of crisis – 1787 and 1792, for example – imports from Ireland (as well as England and North America) played a crucial part in checking price rises and feeding the urban population of the west of Scotland.[102]

The first stages of agricultural improvement, which involved major physical alterations in the landscape along with extensive rural rebuild-ing, were highly labour-intensive. Tree and hedge planting, ditching, walling and the reconstruction of farm buildings and dwellings, as well as ploughing, sowing, tending and harvesting bigger crops, required more and not less labour, both of tradesmen such as masons and dykers as well as day labourers. Many of these – certainly the unskilled – were former cottars, removed from their holdings in the countryside but relocated, often with a smallholding, in the rural villages and small towns referred to above, some of which grew at a quite dramatic rate – six-fold in the case of Airdrie in Lanarkshire during the second half of the eighteenth century.[103] Others became part- and full-time artisan producers. Work too became available for longer periods. The end result, at least until the demographic variable shifted irrevocably in favour of capitalist interests in the early 1800s, were higher earnings at enhanced rates in those parts of Lowland Scotland where the rise of industrialisation created greatest competition for labour. Rural reorganisation, then, not only helped to create both urban and agrarian proletariats, but also played its part in generating the 'new class' of consumers identified earlier. It should be noted however that in parts of the rural Lowlands some 20 per cent or more of this comprised the emergent *petit bourgeois* class of independent tradesmen – the masons, tailors, smiths, butchers and others – small-busi-nessmen who provided for the needs of country dwellers but whose commercial dealings in the Fife burgh of Newburgh in 1800 were not sufficient to allow them to adopt the title 'merchant'.[104]

The process of improvement was not complete in 1830. The rate of enclosure, which had peaked again in 1810, remained fairly high until mid-century. Effective drainage, great strides forward in which were made by James Smith at Deanston in Perthshire after 1823, only became widespread in the 1840s, encouraged by government grants for tile-draining operations.[105] In spite of the revolutionary impact of agrarian change, aspects of rural society were marked by considerable continuity. Unlike in southern England, in Lowland Scotland farm service was much more common, largely because of the labour supply problems of the period c. 1780–1830 but also because such an arrangement was well-suited to the needs of Scottish agriculture. Mixed husbandry required labour all year round, while such was the centrality of ploughing in the new system that a regular force of skilled horsemen had to be retained. Payment in kind, which was also carried on until mid-century and beyond, reflected in part the nature of agricultural communities, which were often some distance from a market.[106]

Nevertheless a revolution had been effected in Scottish agriculture, led by a landed class which compared to its counterpart in parts of Scandinavia had considerable powers which had been used to reshape the countryside and rural social relations.[107] Scottish farming methods, once the object of ridicule, now attracted praise from admiring visitors from England and abroad. Labour productivity was particularly high. The Lothians were in the vanguard, farms there being described by William Cobbett in 1830 as 'factories for making corn and meat', but other innovations attracted attention too. Not the least of these was the threshing machine (referred to in chapter 3 and introduced by George Paterson of Castle Huntly in the Carse of Gowrie in 1787), a horse- or steam-driven device which made major labour savings. Wartime labour shortages had played their part too. By the greater use of machinery which resulted, the use of improved implements, and 'the regular subdivision of labour', agricultural operations were carried on 'with a degree of accuracy and despatch unknown in former times, and unequalled in any country.'[108]

Scottish ploughs provided the model for those made in Sweden from the early nineteenth century.[109] By 1830 the new type of farm, sole-tenanted, compact, enclosed, and using appropriate crop rotations, had swept 'into every corner of the arable Lowlands', even though it appears that the process of tenant reduction was longer drawn-out than was once thought and much less draconian than in the Highlands. In upland districts on the other hand, where pastoral farming was being encouraged, there was less of a difference, and where multiple tenancies survived, there was large-scale dispossession.[110] Large farms were much more common, stretching to between 200 and 600 acres, in the Lothians. Elsewhere – Fife, Perth and Angus – there were also large holdings, but smaller tenancies were more often found in the vicinity of industrial or semi-industrial towns. For farms in locations of this sort, high rents could be charged by offering smallholdings to villagers.[111] The average farm size in Stirling was around 50 acres. In this sense there was further continuity and less of a break with the old system. Indeed a significant proportion of farms in the western Lowlands were smaller than the 100 acres recommended by the improvers; in Ayrshire 43 per cent of farms were beneath this level, in Lanarkshire 52 per cent. In Angus – in the east – the figure was between these two.[112]

But virtually everywhere sub-tenants had gone and instead, other than in the north-east and within the vicinity of Lowland towns, a more sharply-polarised social structure had been created of tenant farmers, imbued with the values of capitalist farming, and their workers, few of whom could aspire to the rank of tenant (although this was still possible on the smaller farms).[113] Although in formations which varied around the country, this social distancing was reflected too in farm layouts and accommodation arrangements, with male farm workers in Angus, the Mearns and parts of Fife being housed in separate bothies. Relations were closer in the south-west where, typically, medium-sized farms predominated, and such extra-family labour as was employed lived in and ate with the farmer. But almost everywhere commentators were agreed that the standards of agricultural workers' living quarters were deplorable.[114]

There were of course gradations between the tenants of larger farms which might employ twenty or more workers and those on smaller properties, such as the family-run dairy farms in Ayrshire.[115] Among farm workers too there were distinctions, linked in large part to occupational specialisation. Thus on one of the earl of Mansfield's farms in Stirlingshire c. 1830 fourteen or more people were employed, ranging from permanent employees such as John Roger, the foreman, with an annual income (in cash and kind, including a 'free' house) of £32 11s., through relatively highly-paid dairymen and maids, ploughmen (now virtually full-time workers) who were paid between £20 and £22, down to day labourers, a smaller category than it had been in the previous century, which included an unspecified number of females who received 8d. for ten hours work.[116] Part-time and seasonal workers were still necessary – and available, from the Highlands and, in growing numbers, Ireland. In the south-east, harvest needs were met by the labour of the wives, daughters or womenfolk of the 'hinds', a condition of whose engagement was to provide their farmer-employer with additional labour during busy periods. 'Bondagers', who might be employed for 180 days *per annum*, were a more extreme variant of this form of employment. As in the manufacturing economy of Scotland, female labour was proportionately more important than in most parts of England, notably the south-east with its extensive pastoral farms.[117]

Commercialisation and the impact of industrialisation in the Highlands and Islands

As we have seen, the lengthy process of economic, social and cultural change whereby Highland chiefs adopted the values and roles of reforming landlords had begun by the early seventeenth century and continued into the eighteenth. Something of a crisis in the march of commercialism had occurred in the later 1760s and early 1770s when unprecedented numbers of tacksmen and subtenants fled across the Atlantic, retreating from raised rents and the failure of the new system to accommodate their rising social aspirations.[118] Direct expulsion may have been unusual but it was by no means unknown. Indirect pressures could produce the same result. But although most landowners (in the north and west) were steadfastly opposed to emigration until the 1820s, and continued to equate numbers of tenants and subtenants with wealth and prestige, the process of weeding out undesirables which was noted in chapter 3 intensified. On Breadalbane estate in the southern Highlands in Perthshire a detailed survey of tenants and cottars, which included assessments of the characters and abilities of those involved, concluded that Katherine Clark, a crofter and 'a young single woman', 'would be much better at service'. Although the fate of Donald McGrigor of Douallain is not recorded, this may be guessed from the description of him as a 'turbulent fellow' and 'a disagreeable neighbour' who was suspected of marking sheep which were not his own and refusing to meet to discuss and settle the matter. This was the hey-day of the systematic and closely-monitored process of social selection, not simply a Highland phenomenon, which ensured that only those judged to be the best would remain in the possession of farm tenancies. By 1810 the Breadalbane tenants in the districts of Ardeonaig and Clouhrain who had leases of farms were ranked according to five classes which indicated their current state of improvement; only a small proportion (13.5 per cent) remained in Class 4, 'those in a backward state in industry & improvement'. There were none in Class 5, nor – other than the estate officer – in Class 1.[119]

Highland Scotland however was not homogenous. An important distinction can be drawn between the north and west Highlands and the islands of the inner and outer Hebrides, and the mainly Gaelic-speaking areas of the southern and eastern frontiers of the Highlands which included southern Argyll, eastern Inverness, Easter Ross, and Cromarty. The former – which were to become the main crofting districts (see map 4) tended to be mountainous, less fertile, with sub-Arctic climatic conditions in some regions, wetter and subject to high winds; conditions in the latter were considerably more favourable, with the added advantage that the straths and valleys which cut through the mountains eased communications and trade with the Lowlands. With a larger proportion of arable

Map 4 The main crofting areas in the Western Highlands and Islands of Scotland

Crofting Areas

Source: derived from T. M. Devine, *The Great Highlands Famine* (Edinburgh, 1988), xvii.

ground, the south and east saw the emergence of an agricultural regime which had much in common with that of the Lowlands. Generalisations are difficult and have the potential to mislead, but what can be clearly detected is a pattern of consolidated tenancies, most of which were in the hands of capitalist-inclined members of the indigenous peasant class. Similar to the Lowlands, a class of full- and part-time agricultural workers was created, although in Inverness-shire and parts of Ross these were semi-landless cottars and crofters. Fishing provided the principal means of subsistence in some coastal districts, the Cromarty Firth, for example, being studded with small fishing hamlets. Although new farms in areas such as southern Argyll and Highland Perthshire were smaller than those of the Lothians, and while there were some large pastoral farms rearing black cattle and sheep, that most tenants concentrated on arable and mixed farming meant that there was a heavy demand for labour.[120]

The greater benevolence of the region was reinforced by the accessibility of non-agricultural employment for those made redundant in the new economic order. Outright evictions did occur.[121] Out-migration was such that between 1755 and the 1790s 60 per cent of parishes saw no increases in population; between 1801 and 1841 the net increase was 7 per cent, very small compared to the crofting region. A pattern of permanent migration from mainland Argyll and southern Inverness-shire into Lowland towns like Glasgow and especially Greenock had been established early in the eighteenth century; Argyll landowners formed a sizeable proportion of the founders of the Glasgow Highland Society (1727), which acted as a charity, by promoting apprenticeships for young highlanders, for example. Such was the close proximity of the island of Gigha to Kintyre, and thence to Glasgow, that net out-migration between in the 1790s represented 85 per cent of births, and in every decade throughout the following century at least two-thirds of those born on the island left. Cod fishing – for sale in Glasgow and Ireland – supported a sizeable proportion of the remaining male population.[122] In Lorne, slate quarrying provided several hundred jobs, the opening of the Crinan Canal in 1801 ensuring that the district maintained its dominant place as the principal provider for Lowland builders.[123]

Migrants to the towns of eastern Lowland Scotland were more likely to have been drawn from Ross and Cromarty and Sutherland.[124] Expulsion certainly played its part in this exodus but opportunity was more important at this stage. For the landless who remained there were alternative means of making a living which the region's larger acreage per head made more comfortable anyway. The average acreage was four times greater in mainland Argyll than Wester Ross and Skye.[125] Demand from Glasgow, and the lochs of Argyll, swarming with herring and white fish, coincided to create communities of full-time fishermen in the coastal districts of the west Highlands.

Illicit whisky distilling, conducted on a part-time seasonal basis, and a much smaller number of legal stills concentrated in Ferintosh in Easter Ross, provided additional income for literally thousands of tenants and peasants in the north-eastern and southern Highlands in the later eighteenth and early nineteenth centuries (and spread further north too, into Sutherland, for example). The juxtaposition of high and rising government taxes on malt and stills, and steeply rising demand from the Lowlands – and, in the early nineteenth century, from the west and northern Highlands – provided conditions for the expansion on commercial lines of what had previously been a small, private operation. The interruption of imports of French brandy and claret during the Napoleonic Wars provided an additional impetus to what could be an elaborately-organised trade which probably benefited professional smugglers, landlords and grain farmers more than it did the peasant producers. They lacked the marketing and financial muscle of the former, and were hardly in a position to resist demands for higher rents from landlords who turned only half a blind eye to their tenants' autumnal and wintertime illegal pursuits.[126]

Towns on the fringes could provide work both within their boundaries, and to those residing within the economic travelling distances of putting-out merchants, outwith them. David Dale and others established 'small branches' of the cotton manufacture in and around Oban. When the first *Statistical Account* for Inverness was compiled, 'above 1,000 men, women and children' were employed in the town's hemp factory, its bags, sacking and tarpaulin being sold in the south and the East and West Indies. Remarkably, another ten thousand were used in the various processes of flax spinning, work being organised in the surrounding counties by nineteen putting-out agents.[127] Similarly, it was in Highland Perthshire and the Angus glens, accessible to merchant-manufactures in and around Perth and Dundee, that part-time spinning was commonly carried on by females. Attempts to take spinning into the north or to the Western Islands – observed in chapter 2 – were frequently short-lived. Cromarty's hemp works, then owned by a London firm, employed fewer people than its Inverness counterpart, but the buildings were considered 'extensive beyond any for the same purpose in Britain'; another six hundred women in the nearby parishes of Nigg, Fearn and Tarbat span yarn for the factory.[128] The impact of industrialisation in places such as these was direct, and created considerable prosperity: by contrast in those Highland parishes further north and west where such works were desperately sought but rarely established, underemployment and poverty were rife. Throughout most of the region living standards were higher than in the western Highlands and Islands.

In at least one respect they appear to have been higher too in Shetland, often overlooked in discussions of Scottish agrarian history. There, animal food appears to have been eaten, as well as fish, more regularly than elsewhere in the north. Diet too was more varied.[129] Furthermore, relatively little change in either agricultural methods or land-holding occurred in the eighteenth century, although, as in the western Highlands, as population increased and sub-division of holdings intensified, spade husbandry replaced the now-uneconomic plough, and the area of land under this form of subsistence cultivation spread. Relatively little of Shetland's rocky land mass however was suitable for viable agriculture. With fishing necessarily providing the basis of economic activity, merchant-lairds encouraged population growth and residence – with the aim of increasing the numbers of fishermen, and rentals.[130] As elsewhere in much of the north of Scotland, the French Wars were enormously beneficial, bringing sharply increased demand and higher prices for exports such as butter, salt beef and kelp, as well as the relatively large sums remitted to the islands from Shetlanders serving in the Navy.[131] The first Court of Session division of common land ('scattald') case in Shetland was not begun until 1815, more than sixty years later than the Lowlands and using legislation first passed in 1695. Largely owing to the continued success of fishing until the 1830s and 1840s when first cod and then herring and whale catches declined, fundamental change was not undertaken until the mid-nineteenth century.[132] In Orkney too, apart from exceptional improving proprietors, such as Thomas Balfour on Shapinsay (aided in part by family funds accumulated in India through a post obtained by Balfour's patron, Sir Lawrence Dundas), arable land was still unenclosed and lying in runrig. Grain provided the focus of agrarian production until the steamship service inaugurated in 1833 brought the islands within the orbit of Aberdeenshire cattle dealers and a new market. Until the end of the 1820s crofters' incomes were supplemented by kelp-burning, fishing and casual labour, although, during part of the wars with France, Kirkwall and Lerwick benefited from the spending power (£675 per month at the end of 1797) of the locally-recruited Orkney and Shetland Fencibles. Sharply rising cattle prices relative to those of oats and central government loans for drains precipitated sudden changes in the later 1840s, with enclosure, eviction and, ultimately, confrontation.[133]

It was the western and northern mainland and the Hebrides which were to feel most acutely the full spectrum of the effects of the market system. To portray Highland society as one riven by a simple landowner-tenant divide is to ignore more complex inter-tenant rivalries and differences in landlord attitudes. Nevertheless it was in the west and north that growing divisions between the interests of tenants in the broadest sense and landowners more obviously came to a head before the end of the eighteenth century.[134] It is the region where after *c.* 1815 the former were more obviously exposed to the workings of the laws of comparative advantage and the negative consequences of industrial concentration. Population rose after mid-century, by just under 20 per cent between 1755 and 1801 – a lower rate than Scotland as a whole – a pattern which was maintained from 1801 until 1831. Overall however there was a rise of 54 per cent between 1755 and 1831.[135] A low age of first marriage, increased dependence upon the potato from the 1770s (although the rate of uptake varied by locality) and intensive inoculation against smallpox (the Highlands and Islands seem to be one of the few regions in Scotland where this happened), appear to explain an increase which, while modest, pressed ever-strongly against available resources.[136] There were physical limits and those determined by the rights of their tenure to how much additional land (usually marginal) tenants could bring into cultivation. There were limits too to the productivity of land which was subject to heavy leaching, notwithstanding the use of locally-available fertilisers, such as manure, seaweed, peat soil and turf, and lazy-bed cultivation. Although labour-intensive, the *caschrom* (foot-plough) could provide a yield bonus over the plough of some 33 per cent; yield bonus with the spade was a lower 25 per cent. Much-scorned by outsiders for their 'backwardness', that such methods were less labour-efficient was of little consequence for tenants whose concern was to maximise output, regardless of the cost.[137]

There were great differences in conditions throughout the region, even though the *bailtean* or township, which was neither 'uniform nor ... static' over our period and is not to be confused with an archaic survival, was the basic social and economic unit, small farming communities comprising tenants, cottars, cottagers and farm servants. Although the degree to which runrig and communal working were the same thing has been questioned, the townships, which supported anything from twenty to fifty people on acreages of arable which varied enormously, usually required some element of co-operation.[138] The smallest – of less than 100 acres – lay alongside the western seaboard and the inner Hebrides, including Skye, although as larger acreages could include ground which was exceptionally hard to cultivate, size does not necessarily indicate agricultural worth. Over time, and as population stretched the townships close to the limits of their viability as self-supporting economic units, holdings were further reduced.

Conflict occurred between, on the one hand, landowners and large tenants, whose interests lay in maximising estate income through sales of black cattle and increasingly, sheep, and, on the other, the inhabitants of the townships who, in order to survive, were required to increase crops of oats, bere and potatoes. Livestock – sales of and the manure from which had previously sustained a balanced system of support – were, necessarily, of secondary importance, despite their rising cash value.[139] For landlords, higher rentals could be obtained by converting the townships into single-tenant farms. It was this – large-scale pastoral husbandry, led by cattle but exacerbated by sheep, rental returns from which were higher – 'which led to the greatest social dislocation'.[140] Some townships had attempted to adapt to the changing market conditions and begun to breed sheep, but it was a capital-intensive business, best conducted (if returns were to be quick and hefty) on large farms managed by substantial grazier-farmers recruited from the older sheep farming districts of the Borders, where larger units had been created and tenant numbers thinned from c. 1720.[141]

Early industrialisation provided a double-opportunity for Highland landlords (and, as we have seen, for enterprise at lower social levels). Demand for wool and for mutton from the towns – along with rising prices – provided them with the impetus to convert their estates to sheep farming. The former inhabitants of the townships however would not be lost, but retained, shifted on a massive scale from the inland straths and glens and relocated to arable smallholdings in coastal crofting communities, which were surrounded by common land, usually hill pasture, for grazing. Individual crofts were small, with few paying more than £10 per annum in rent. In addition, there was a numerous cottar class, not recognised as tenants of land, living on the barest margins of subsistence, but which on some estates were almost as numerous as the crofters, and more so on Mull.[142] But while the croft lands were rarely sufficient to maintain a household, even though potatoes – a much more efficient use of land and earlier to crop than oats – were widely cultivated by the end of the century, the continued residence of the crofters in what were, in effect, quasi-industrial communities, was to be ensured by the provision of part-time work in fishing or, more often, kelping. In this way the population would not only be retained, but encouraged by earlier marriage to procreate in greater numbers.[143] In some locations, such as Sutherland, for example, there were even hopes – as there had been further south in the earlier part of the century – that work in industry could be full-time, with George Dempster proposing plans for the conversion of 'Sutherlandshire into a Lancashire'. Almost half a million pounds was ploughed into the Sutherland estate between 1811 and 1833. At Brora, coal mining, salt manufacturing and brick- and tile-making were established. Work in these occupations, declared the Sutherland estate factor David Loch, would forward 'the civilisation of the country'.[144] More generally it was anticipated that smallholders would be enticed by the prospect of gain to bring under the spade uncultivated ground, 5 acres of which settlers in Ullapool were granted, in addition to their half acre of arable.[145] This was the standard area of arable ground available per head in Wester Ross and Skye. According to the Caithness improver Sir John Sinclair, it required those on such holdings to perform an additional two hundred days a year of alternative work in order to avoid destitution. On the Sutherland estate coastal holdings were so small that they were incapable of supporting a family through the sale of a cow, for example. In this way cleared tenants from the inland straths and hills of Kildonan and Strathnaver would be forced to fish for a living and – in theory at least – cease to be a burden on the estate.[146]

From the 1760s the commercial attractions of kelp had become increasingly obvious to landowners. Used as a source of industrial alkali necessary in glass- and soap-making, its price tripled to £10 per ton in the 1790s as France cut off supplies of Spanish barilla, the preferred source. The price was to double again before the end of the war, encouraging landowners throughout the west and in the Northern Isles to expand production. Meagre wages enabled crofter households to pay their rents, while the profits made by their landed proprietors soared, in some cases providing greater income than was derived from land rentals, and this in return for a minimal capital outlay, for rakes, shovels and simple kilns. On North Uist, Lord MacDonald was reputed to have had an income of £20,000 *per annum* from kelp in the early 1800s. In this manner did the crofters on South Uist, the source of the best and most valuable kelp, and others who were within reach of the rocky shores and islands of the tidal sounds where bladder wrack grew most profusely, feel the impact of industrialisation, carrying out in miserable, wet conditions an arduous physical task which even though it was at its height from June and over the summer months, compared with the most onerous jobs which were being created in the mills and factories of the south.[147]

Fishing had long been regarded as a potential source of employment, and of sailors for the Royal Navy. The economies of favoured sea-side locations would be boosted, thereby contributing to a rise in national prosperity. Although schemes for promoting Scottish fishing pre-dated the Union, another initiative in 1720 inspired the patriotic poet Allan Ramsay to compose 'The Prospect of Plenty: A Poem on the North Sea Fishery'. This anticipated that 'Plenty shall cultivate ilk Scawp and Moor / Now Lee and bare, because the Landlord's poor', while along 'wild Shores' 'Braw Towns' would rise:

> And Houses bigget a' with Estler Stane:
> Where Schools polite shall liberal Arts display,
> And make auld barb'rous Darkness fly away.

In 1749 a number of concerns, including the wish to integrate the Highlands, through commerce, into an already deeply-divided British society, had persuaded the British parliament to support the establishment of the Free British Fishery Society. Although supported by the duke of Argyll and other Scottish Whigs, scant regard was had to the realities of Scottish conditions and it came to little in the north.[148] In 1756 the Scottish Fisheries Act was passed, partly as result of campaigning by the

Convention of Royal Burghs, but with minor results, although bounty payments were evidently sufficiently large to increase and maintain more herring busses fishing from the Clyde.[149] The Commissioners for the Annexed Estates had high hopes of establishing commercial fishing communities – partly, ironically, in order to employ sailors demobilised in 1763 – but again with no lasting success.[150] The state however was determined to improve conditions in the Highlands and to put a stop to emigration and, under Dundas, earlier repressive policies were replaced with those designed to increase employment in a region now valued for its loyalty and contribution (largely through the provision of soldiers) to the British empire, and as a repository of culture and values untainted by civilisation.[151]

In 1784 the Highland Society of Scotland was founded, with Henry Mackenzie, author of *The Man of Feeling* (1771) as its secretary. More practically-inclined however than its London counterpart formed six years earlier (and which, paradoxically, comprised 'chiefs, clan gentry and other interested parties resident in London'), it gave rise in 1786 to the British Fisheries Society.[152] Unlike previous schemes, that developed by the Fisheries Society was intended to provide capital for buildings rather than large boats, and to offer bounties on catches. It was moderately successful in establishing fishing stations at Tobermory, Ullapool and Pultneytown, but not at Lochbay (Stein) on Skye.[153] Landowners too attempted to encourage crofters now settled in the maritime districts to turn to fishing. Some did, as on Lewis and in Wester Ross, where the returns from fishing enabled those on even the smallest crofts to survive.[154] The wholesale plans for reorganisation of the Sutherland estate between 1806 and 1820 involved the creation of a number of fishing stations which processed herring, salmon, cod, haddock and, on a small-scale, lobsters. One of the stations, Helmsdale, was a considerable success, employing over two thousand people in 1841, many of whom had been evicted.[155] But even Helmsdale struggled at times. Fishing was beset with all sorts of difficulties: shortage of capital for boats and tackle, the erratic and unpredictable movements of the herring shoals from sea lochs in which they had once been abundant, the complexities of the salt laws – and in sharp contrast to the 'haaf' fisherfolk of the Shetland archipelago where fishing took precedence over farming, the considerable resistance of crofters, bred in inland, upland districts, to engage in anything other than subsistence fishing close to the coast.[156]

Although temporary and seasonal migration in search of work in the Lowlands was nothing new, its importance – and almost certainly the numbers involved – increased in the later 1700s and particularly the early 1800s, as the props which had supported the new economic and social system were knocked away after 1815. The annual movement was mainly of females searching for harvest work, with some domestic servants too managing to obtain employment before returning north in the winter, journeys in both directions being made easier in the western coasts and islands with the introduction of the steam-packet boat in the 1820s.[157] As the temporary exodus expanded it not only provided a reserve army of labour at low cost during key periods of the year for the industrialising and agrarian economies of the Lowlands but also, in encompassing increasing numbers of migrants from the far north and west, played a crucial role in sustaining the crofting communities. This was mainly through remittances and the temporary absence from hard-pressed house-holds of one or more mouths to feed, but it also supported a deeply-ingrained annual life cycle which was governed by the need to be at home during planting and harvest times.[158] But arguably the most significant shorter-term period of temporary out-movement of the Highland population was during the Napoleonic Wars when perhaps as many as 74,000 men from a regional population of three hundred thou-sand (that is one quarter of the total) served in the armed forces, the volunteers and the militia, and so relieved at an important moment pres-sures on the transforming Highland economy.[159] In ways such as this, as one writer has put it, 'the deluge was averted'.[160]

A brief survey cannot hope to convey the great variety in crofting conditions.[161] That which was universal however was uncertainty. And what became apparent after the end of the Napoleonic Wars in 1815 was how vulnerable the new agrarian-industrial order was. Demand for wool continued to rise, to the extent that the proportion of wool in the United Kingdom originating from Scotland rose from 10 per cent in 1828 to 25 per cent in the early 1840s. Its price however halved between the 1810s and the 1820s.[162] Demand for Highland soldiers and sailors however collapsed in the aftermath of Waterloo. Demand for kelp had peaked around 1810, by which time it had become the main source of income in Barra, the Uists, Lewis and Harris and parts of Skye – and an important one on Orkney, Mull and Tiree, as well as along the Ardnamurchan and Morven coasts. While the connection was not uniform, generally, the boom in kelp had been accompanied by an above average rise in the rate of population increase, from 58 per cent in Lewis between 1755 and 1811 to 118 per cent in South Uist. Kelp prices fell slowly at first, but by 1828 were just over £4 per ton, that is at or below the level at which its manufacture was profitable, although in several places (mainly Tiree, Lewis and Harris) it continued to be burned, the kelpers' wages being the only means by which rents (increasingly in arrears throughout the region) could be paid.[163] The fall in cattle prices, by half between 1810 and 1830, was a severe blow to tenants whose means of raising cash from non-agricultural sources were further reduced by government efforts to wipe out illicit whisky distilling. A dramatic rise in distillation in the years after 1815 was met by a series of measures in 1822 and 1823 which punished illicit producers more harshly and encouraged legal production. By the early 1830s peasant production for the market had all but been eliminated in districts which had previously been major producers.[164]

Fishing, expanding and concentrating along the north-east coast in the 1790s and first half of the nineteenth century, was considerably less buoyant in the north-west where, by and large, it remained a peasant by-employment, with smaller boats and nets and a less well-developed infrastructure. Although erratic in their movements, the herring shoals appeared to be migrating north and eastwards, but, in addition, bounties on herring catches were withdrawn in the 1820s and former markets for cured herring began to disappear.[165] The emancipation of the slaves in the West Indies in 1833 removed the main market for Scotland's pickled herring, the poor quality of which made it difficult to sell elsewhere. There were some successes but overall the picture is one of decline, with failure being reported on Loch Carron, Loch Sunart and on the inner and outer Hebrides. Even Ullapool, upon which some £20,000 had been spent by 1813, was unable to sustain anything other than subsistence fishing for its impoverished population.[166] State expenditure, to improve Highland communications not for military but for economic and social reasons, had little immediate effect although the short-term employment benefits generated by the £450,000 which was spent on 885 miles of 'Parliamentary roads' by 1821 should certainly not be overlooked. Indeed the provision of work for underemployed Highlanders was one of the factors which had persuaded the government not only to embark on a road-building programme but also the construction of the Caledonian Canal, work on which was begun under the direction of Thomas Telford in 1804. It was completed in 1822, not long after the road programme was finished.[167] State aid for fishing continued, with the establishment of the Fishery Board – an offshoot of the Board of Trustees – in 1809. Although the Board provided some assistance in the Western Islands, most support was provided, for harbour construction, in the east, beginning in 1829 with an improved harbour at Cellardyke in Fife.[168]

Their existence precarious enough in the post-war years, the inhabitants of the teeming crofting communities – still being created during 'silent' clearances on estates whose actions failed to attract the notoriety of the Sutherland evictions – were expelled further from the older more cohesive society in the later 1810s, 1820s and beyond.[169] Many landowners had extracted what have been described as 'extortionate' profits during the extravaganza of high wartime prices. At the height of the kelping boom, landowners were typically netting five times per ton more than the kelpers. Yet these windfalls, much of which had been dissipated on conspicuous or non-productive consumption, evaporated in the deflationary conditions of the 1820s.[170] No longer able to service their debts or to support the lifestyles enjoyed by their more southerly counterparts, an unprecedented number of landowners were forced to sell their estates between *c.* 1810 and 1850. At the very least something like fifty-five estates were exposed to sale during these years, some more than once. An example is Morven, part of the dukes of Argyll's domains in the early 1800s. The estate had not been out of Highland ownership for several centuries. Between 1813 and 1838 every property within it had changed hands.[171] Most (in Morven as elsewhere in the west and north) were purchased by Lowlanders or English interests who, with improved transport links by road and sea, now had easier access to the Highlands. What has been termed 'the final phase of clearance', then, was often in the hands of outsiders rather than the hereditary proprietors who, for all their reforming zeal, had in most (but by no means all) cases a strong sense of paternalistic responsibility for and duty to their tenants. Not uniformly, but predominantly, the new owners were less attached to older traditions and were responsible for some of the 'most brutal, notorious and extensive clearances'.[172] Some cleared without ever residing on the estate. With rational management and their populations cleared rather than relocated the estates would provide regular rentals from sheep and later deer (Glenfeshie was one of the first estates advertised for leisure shooting, in 1812). In some instances massive speculative gains were made as land values rose.[173] Neither for these proprietors, nor those attracted to the Highlands and Hebrides for their 'Romantic' or sublime appeal, was there a place in their barren panoramas for destitute crofters, cottars or squatters, other than as mute decorations.

In short, by *c.* 1830 and some sixteen years from the tragedy of the potato blight of the mid- and later-1840s the tide of early, and in some respects, artificially-stimulated industrialisation had ebbed from the north and west of Scotland, although not the hard-headed commercialism of which it was part. In the context of the flows and counter-flows of British industrialisation, the Highlands were not unique, although the effects of the peripheral position of the region were more cruel and dramatic.[174] In having to confront the relentless march of capitalist agriculture, the Highlands represented a regional variant of a Europe-wide phenomenon. Solutions however varied from country to country.[175]

In Highland Scotland agrarian change and the disappearance of alternative sources of income had left an increasingly wretched and poverty-stricken population, which out-migration and emigration could only partly alleviate. The rate of population increase was slowing, having fallen from 0.51 per cent *per annum* between 1821 and 1830 compared to 1.46 per cent *per annum* in the previous decade, but this was not enough to halt the decline in living standards among a populace which had been drawn into a market economy the benefits of which were now being withdrawn. If the Lowlands of Scotland were becoming one of the most heavily industrialised and urbanised regions in Britain the north and west had the fewest opportunities for non-agrarian employment, and the lowest incomes.[176] Emigration – now favoured by landowners old and new – was an option only for the better-off and, as far as can be judged, was still resisted by the people below them. Although the numbers of those leaving rose after 1815, there were marked fluctuations over time. Within the region the pattern was confused and, dependent upon a complex of factors including landlord policies, the rate of clearance and the availability of (a few) schemes for assisted emigration.[177] Mass emigration awaited the crisis of the 1840s. It is cruelly ironic that as in reality the peoples of the Highlands and Islands sank to the country's lowest material levels and suffered the deepest sense of loss of place, culture and identity, the cult of Highlandism and nostalgia for an older and noble way of Gaelic life were in the ascendant.[178] In 1829–30, as Felix Mendelssohn conceived and composed his 'Hebrides' Overture, the writing of which he began during a visit to Fingal's Cave on Staffa, some miles inland at North Ballachulish and Achintore, the laird of Lochiel was completing the process of 'wholesale evictions' which he had begun in 1824. The clash of cultures could scarcely have been more jarring.

Notes

1 R. S. Fitton, *The Arkwrights: Spinners of Fortune* (Manchester, 1989), 69–71.

2 See, for example, *Glasgow Mercury*, 13 August 1793.

3 S. D. Chapman, *The Cotton Industry in the Industrial Revolution* (London, 1987 ed.), 14–15; R. S. Fitton and A. P. Wadsworth, *The Strutts and the Arkwrights, 1758–1830: A Study of the Early Factory System* (Manchester, 1958), 64–8; Hamilton, *An Economic History of Scotland in the Eighteenth Century*, 170.

4 Whatley, *Industrial Revolution*, 26.

5 A. Durie and P. Solar, 'The Scottish and Irish linen industries compared, 1780–1860', in Mitchison and Roebuck, *Economy and Society*, 214.

6 Whatley, *Scottish Salt Industry*, 54; NAS, Henderson of Fordell MSS, GD 172/503/2, James Pinkerton to Sir John Henderson, 28 March 1788; J. Chalmer to Sir John Henderson, 12 June 1793; Fry, *Dundas Despotism*, 141.

7 On the economic consequences of the American War of Independence, about which there is measured optimism, see J. Butt, 'The American war of independence and Scottish economic history', in O. Dudley Edwards and G. Shepperson (eds), *Scotland, Europe and the American Revolution* (Edinburgh, 1976), 57–60; T. M. Devine, 'The American war of independence and Scottish economic history', in *ibid.*, 61–5.

8 F. Crouzet, *Britain Ascendant: Comparative Studies in Franco-British History* (Cambridge, 1880), 302–11.

9 R. Hamilton, *Observations upon the Causes of the Distress in the Country* (Glasgow, 1822), 11–12.

10 R. H. Campbell, 'The making of the industrial city', in Devine and Jackson, *Glasgow*, 202–3; Jackson, 'New horizons in trade', in *ibid.*, 227.

11 C. A. Bayly, *Imperial Meridian: The British Empire and the World, 1780–1830* (London, 1989), 3; see too P. K. O'Brien, 'Inseparable connections: trade, economy, fiscal state and the expansion of empire, 1688–1815', in Marshall, *The Eighteenth Century*, 53–77.

12 *Glasgow Mercury*, 15 March 1791; Strathclyde Regional Archives (SRA), T – MJ 332.3, John Henderson to J. Freeland, 31 January 1791.

13 Nenadic, 'Rise of the urban middle class', 110.

14 R. Naismyth, *Buildings of the Scottish Countryside* (London, 1989), 18–49.

15 Saville, *Bank of Scotland*, 267–8.

16 Devine, 'Urbanisation', 29–36.

17 R. E. Tyson, 'Demographic change', in Devine and Young, *Eighteenth Century Scotland*, 196.

18 R. J. Morris, 'Urbanisation and Scotland', in W. H. Fraser and R. J. Morris (eds), *People and Society in Scotland, Volume II: 1830–1914* (Edinburgh, 1990), 73–4.

19 Lockhart, 'Planned village development', 133–6.

20 Whyte, 'Urbanisation', 178–81; J. S. Smith, 'The background to planned village foundation in north east Scotland', in Smith and Stevenson, *Fermfolk & Fisherfolk*, 1–10; D. G. Lockhart, 'Migration to planned villages in north east Scotland', in *ibid.*, 11–25; Devine, *Transformation*, 152–3; M. Gray, The social impact of agrarian change in the rural lowlands', in Devine and Mitchison, *People and Society*, 66; C. Young, 'Rural independent artisan production in the east-central lowlands of Scotland, *c.* 1600–1850', *Scottish Economic & Social History*, XVI (1996), 17–27.

21 J. Treble, 'The standard of living of the working class', in Devine and Mitchison, *People and Society*, 194–200; Hunt, 'Industrialisation and regional inequality', 937–41; Devine, 'The English connection, 19–20.

22 E. I. Spence, *Sketches of the Present Manners, Customs and Scenery of Scotland* (London, 1811), Volume I, 97; I. Donnachie, 'Drink and society 1750–1850': some aspects of the Scottish experience', *Journal of the Scottish Labour History Society*, XIII (1979); Whatley, *Industrial Revolution*, 90.

23 W. M. Matthew, *Keillor's of Dundee: The Rise of The Marmalade Dynasty, 1800–1879* (Dundee, 1999); Donnachie, *History of the Brewing Industry*, 118–19; M. Lochrie, 'The Paisley shawl industry', in Butt and Ponting, *Scottish Textile History*, 97.

24 *The Unfortunate Fair or, the Sad Disaster* (Glasgow, 1801).

25 Durie, *Scottish Linen Industry*, 95.

26 Butt, 'Scottish cotton industry', 122.

27 *Ibid.*, 123–4.

28 J. Butt, 'Robert Owen as a businessman', in J. Butt (ed.), *Robert Owen: Prince of Cotton Spinners* (Newton Abbot, 1971), 171; see too D. J. McLaren, *David Dale of New Lanark* (Milngavie, 1983).

29 Hamilton, *Economic History of Scotland*, 161–2; Durie, *Scottish Linen Industry*, 39–40, 74–7.

30 Butt, 'Scottish cotton industry', 118–19; S. G. E. Lythe and J. Butt, *An Economic History of Scotland, 1100–1939* (London, 1975), 166–7.

31 Munn, *Scottish Provincial Banking Companies*, 211–14; Saville, *Bank of Scotland*, 272; A. J. Durie, 'Lairds, improvement and industry in eighteenth century Scotland: capital and development in a backward economy – a case study', in T. M. Devine (ed.), *Lairds and Improvement* (Dundee, 1979), 21–8.

32 Saville, *Bank of Scotland*, 277; R. Cameron, 'Banking and industrialisation in Britain in the nineteenth century', in A. Slaven and D. H. Aldcroft (eds), *Business, Banking and Urban History* (Edinburgh, 1982), 106.

33 SRA, Stirling Maxwell of Pollock Papers, T – MP, 117/1/45, James Crum to J. Maxwell, 21 June 1820.

34 Whatley, *Industrial Revolution*, 26; N. Murray, 'The regional structure of textile employment in Scotland in the nineteenth century: east of Scotland hand loom weavers in the 1830s', in Cummings and Devine, *Industry, Business and Society*, 219; N. Murray, *The Scottish Hand Loom Weavers, 1790–1850: A Social History* (Edinburgh, 1978), 65; Farnie, *The English Cotton Industry and the World Market*, 284–7.

35 J. Butt, 'Labour and industrial relations in the Scottish cotton industry during the industrial revolution', in J. Butt and K. Ponting (eds), *Scottish Textile History* (Aberdeen, 1987), 139; Murray, *Scottish Hand Loom Weavers*, 13.

36 Shaw, *Water Power*, 318.

37 This paragraph is largely based on J. Butt, 'The Scottish cotton industry during the industrial revolution 1780–1840', in Cullen and Smout, *Comparative Aspects*, 116–28.

38 Fitton, *The Arkwrights*, 71–3; A. J. Cooke, 'Richard Arkwright and the Scottish cotton industry', *Textile History*, X (1979), 196–202.

39 See, for example, A. Cooke (ed.), *Stanley: Its History and Development* (Dundee, 1977).

40 H. Lumsden, *History of the Skinners, Furriers and Glovers of Glasgow* (Glasgow, 1937), 119; see too M. Berg, *The Age of Manufactures, 1700–1820: Industry, Innovation and Work in Britain* (London, 1994 ed.), 189–90.

41 I. Donnachie, 'The textile industry in the south west of Scotland 1750–1914', in Butt and Ponting, *Scottish Textile History*, 19–28.

42 A. Cooke, 'Cotton and the Scottish highland clearances – the development of Spinningdale 1791–1806', *Textile History*, XXVI (1995), 89–94.

43 Chapman, *Cotton Industry*, 19; Shaw, *Water Power*, 331–8.

44 A. W. Harding, *Pullars of Perth* (Perth, 1991), 17.

45 Lythe and Butt, *Economic History*, 186.

46 Fitton, *The Arkwrights*, 74, 77; Cooke, 'Cotton', 92.

47 P. Bolin-Hort, *Work, Family and the State: Child Labour and the Organisation of Production in the British Cotton Industry, 1780–1920* (Lund, 1989), 54.

48 Gibson and Smout, *Prices, Food and Wages*, 243; W. Knox, *Hanging By a Thread: The Scottish Cotton Industry, c. 1850–1914* (Preston, 1995), 3; Whatley, 'Women and the economic transformation', 30.

49 British Parliamentary Papers, 1834, XIX, *Factory Inspectors (Supplementary) Reports*, 245; Whatley, 'Women and the economic trans-

formation', 28–9.

50 J. Cleland, *The Rise and Progress of the City of Glasgow* (Glasgow, 1829), 233–4; A. Ure, *The Cotton Manufacture of Great Britain* (1836), Volume II, 195–7.

51 Sir J. Sinclair, *Analysis of the Statistical Account of Scotland* (Edinburgh, 1825), Volume I, 323.

52 NAS, Breadalbane MSS, GD 112/16/1/2/10, James Craig to Lord Ormerlie, 12 August 1833.

53 Butt, 'Labour and industrial relations', 141.

54 Shaw, *Water Power*, 328–9.

55 Whatley, 'New light on Nef's numbers', 7.

56 *Ibid.*, 15.

57 D. Dickson, 'Aspects of the rise and decline of the irish cotton industry', in Cullen and Smout, *Comparative Aspects*, 111.

58 G. Jackson and K. Kinnear, *The Trade and Shipping of Dundee, 1780–1850* (Dundee, 1991), 26–7.

59 C. J. A. Robertson, *The Origins of the Scottish Railway System, 1722–1844* (Edinburgh, 1983) 44–63.

60 Campbell, 'Making of the industrial city', 197.

61 Houston, 'The demographic regime', 12–13; Withers, *Urban Highlanders*, 62–8, 84–105; R. H. Campbell, *The Rise and Fall of Scottish Industry* (Edinburgh, 1980), 15–19.

62 Shaw, *Water Power*, 327.

63 Whatley, *Industrial Revolution*, 27; C. A. Whatley, *Onwards from Osnaburgs: The Rise and Progress of a Scottish Textile Company* (Edinburgh, 1992), 19–62.

64 Crouzet, *Britain Ascendant*, 299–300.

65 L. Miskell and C. A. Whatley, '"Juteopolis" in the making: linen and the industrial transformation of Dundee, *c.* 1820–1850', *Textile History*, XXX (1999).

66 Smout, 'Scotland and England', 619–20; L. M. Cullen and T. C. Smout, 'Economic growth in Scotland and Ireland', in Cullen and Smout, *Comparative Aspects*, 10.

67 This point has been made earlier, but see too R. Sher, 'Commerce, religion and the Enlightenment in eighteenth-century Glasgow', in Devine and Jackson, *Glasgow*, 312–59; R. W. G. Anderson, 'Joseph Black', in D. Daiches, P. Jones and J. Jones (eds), *A Hotbed of Genius: The Scottish Enlightenment* (Edinburgh, 1986), 98–9; Whatley, *Industrial Revolution*, 61.

68 Whatley, 'Women and the economic transformation', 29–30.

69 W. W. Knox, *Industrial Nation: Work, Culture and Society in Scotland, 1800–Present* (Edinburgh, 1999), 35.

70 D. T. Jenkins, 'The wool textile industry 1780–1850', in C. H. Feinstein and S. Pollard (eds), *Studies in Capital Formation in the United Kingdom, 1750–1910* (Oxford, 1988); NAS, Breadalbane MSS, GD 112/16/1/2/11x, 'Resolutions of the Woollen Manufacturers of Stirling and vicinity', 12 April 1833.

71 D. T. Jenkins and K. G. Ponting, *The British Wool Textile Industry,*

1770–1914 (London, 1982), 80–2.

72 Gulvin, *Scottish Hosiery and Knitwear Industry*, 16–21.

73 Tyson, 'Manufacturing in rural Aberdeenshire', 64–82.

74 A. J. Durie, 'Textile finishing in the north east of Scotland 1727–1860', in Butt and Ponting, *Scottish Textile History*, 2.

75 N. A. Tarrant, 'The Turkey red dyeing industry in the vale of Leven', in Butt and Ponting, *Scottish Textile History*, 38–42.

76 A. G. Thomson, *The Paper Industry in Scotland, 1590–1861* (Edinburgh, 1974), 77, 192.

77 Moss and Hume, *History of the Scottish Whisky Industry*, 48–72; Lythe and Butt, *Economic History*, 172–3.

78 W. R. H. Duncan, 'Aberdeen and the early development of the whaling industry, 1750–1800', *Northern Scotland*, III (1977–8), 51–2; R. C. Michie, 'North-east Scotland and the northern whale fishing, 1752–1893', in *ibid.*, 62, 64; G. Jackson, *The British Whaling Trade* (1978), 70–90.

79 Whatley, 'Process of industrialisation', 225–6; see too J. Butt and J. R. Hume, 'Muirkirk 1786–1802: the creation of a Scottish industrial community', *Scotttish Historical Review*, XLV (October 1966), 160–83.

80 J. Butt, 'Capital and enterprise in Scottish iron, 1780–1840', in Butt and Ward, *Scottish Themes*, 67–79; Lythe and Butt, *Economic History*, 190–1.

81 A. Slaven , *The Development of the West of Scotland, 1750–1960* (London, 1975), 125–32.

82 *Ibid.*, 116–17; Butt, 'Capital and enterprise', 73–4, 79.

83 S. and O. Checkland, *Industry and Ethos: Scotland, 1832–1914* (London, 1984), 21.

84 Smout, 'Lead-mining', 106.

85 NRA(S), Dundas of Arniston Papers, vol. 149, Stobhill Colliery, Robert Bald to Lord Justice Clerk, 7 June 1809, Hugh Nibble to Messrs Cranstoun and Anderson WS, 22 December 1824.

86 Most of this paragraph is based upon Whatley, *Industrial Revolution*, 32–3.

87 T. Donnelly, 'Shipbuilding in Aberdeen, 1750–1914', *Northern Scotland*, IV (1981), 27–8; R. E. Tyson, 'The economy of Aberdeen', in J. S. Smith and D. Stevenson (eds), *Aberdeen in the Nineteenth Century: The Making of the Modern City* (Aberdeen, 1988), 25–6.

88 Gulvin, *The Tweedmakers*, 70, 85.

89 N. F. R. Crafts, *British Economic Growth during the Industrial Revolution* (Oxford, 1985), 4–5. 'Revolutionised' industry includes those in employment in general categories such as chemicals and metal manufactures and as Crafts acknowledges, the proportions genuinely engaged in what we might assume to be 'revolutionised' activities are overestimated.

90 Whatley, *Industrial Revolution*, 36; for greater detail see C. H. Lee, *British Regional Employment Statistics, 1841–1971* (Cambridge, 1979); Lee, 'Modern economic growth and structural change in Scotland: the service sector reconsidered', *Scottish Economic & Social History*, III (1983).

91 Quoted in Smout, 'Scotland and England', 612.

92 I. Donnachie, 'A tour of the works: early Scottish industry observed, 1790–1825', in Cummings and Devine, *Industry, Business and Society*, 43–57.

93 A. Smart, *Rambling Rhymes* (Edinburgh, 1834), 31–5; C. A. Whatley, 'From handcraft to factory: the growth and development of industry in Montrose, *c.* 1707–1837', in Jackson and Lythe, *Montrose*, 267–76.
94 C. Young, 'Financing the micro-scale enterprise: rural craft producers in Scotland, 1840–1914, *Business History Review*, LXIX (Fall 1995), 399–401.
95 Devine, *Transformation of Rural Scotland*, 41, 45–6; Gordon, *To Move With The Times*, 36–55.
96 Devine, *Transformation of Rural Scotland*, 39–40.
97 See invaluable studies such as R. A. Dodgshon, 'Agricultural change and its social consequences in the southern uplands of Scotland, 1600–1780', in Devine and Dickson, *Ireland and Scotland*, 46–59; I. D. Whyte, 'Agriculture in Aberdeenshire in the seventeenth and early eighteenth centuries: continuity and change', in Stevenson, *From Lairds to Louns*, 10–31.
98 M. Gray, 'Scottish emigration: the social impact of agrarian change in the rural Lowlands, 1775–1875', *Perspectives in American History*, VII (1973), 124–6, 166–7.
99 *Ibid.*, 43–4, 70–8.
100 Hankins and Strawhorn, *Correspondence of James Boswell*, 194.
101 Most of the material or this section was drawn from Devine, *Transformation of Rural Scotland*, 35–59.
102 Cochran, *Scottish Trade*, 97.
103 Devine, *Transformation of Rural Scotland*, 146–57.
104 Young, 'Rural independent artisan production', 27; *Dundee Magazine*, June 1800, 287–92.
105 G. Whittington, 'Agriculture and society in Lowland Scotland', in G. Whittington and I. D. Whyte (eds), *An Historical Geography of Scotland* (London, 1983), 145; Campbell, *Scotland Since 1707*, 159–60.
106 T. M. Devine, 'Scottish farm service in the agricultural revolution', in T. M. Devine (ed.), *Farm Servants and Labour in Lowland Scotland, 1770–1914* (Edinburgh, 1984), 2–5; A. Orr, 'Farm servants and farm labour in the Forth valley and south-east Lowlands', in *ibid.*, 44–5.
107 T. C. Smout, 'Landowners in Scotland, Ireland and Denmark in the age of improvement', *Scandinavian Journal of History*, XII (1987), 89–92.
108 Hamilton, *Observations*, 13.
109 *Ibid.*, 88–9; J. Donaldson, *General View of the Agriculture of the Carse of Gowrie, in the County of Perth* (Edinburgh, 1794), 19–20; Smout, *History of the Scottish People*, 324.
110 M. Gray, 'The social impact of agrarian change in the rural Lowlands', in Devine and Mitchison, *People and Society*, 59; Devine, *Transformation of Rural Scotland*, 111–27.
111 *Ibid.*, 132–3; NLS, Minto Papers, MS 13258, fo. 113, 'Estimate of Farms at Melgund by Mr Beatson', 21 October 1786.
112 *Ibid.*
113 Gray, 'Social impact of agrarian change', 62–9; Whittington, 'Agriculture and society', 148–52.
114 *Ibid.*, 155–61.
115 Smout, *History of the Scottish People*, 308–14.

116 Scone Palace, Mansfield Papers, second series, Bundle 156, 'List of Persons permanently employed on Balboughty Farm shewing their occupation and yearly income', n.d. (*c.* 1830); on dairy workers see R. H. Campbell, 'Agricultural labour in the south-west', in Devine, *Farm Servants*, 55–70.

117 Orr, 'Farm labour', 32–3; Whatley, 'Women and the economic transformation', 30–1.

118 A. Mackillip, 'Highland estate change and tenant emigration', in Devine and Young, *Eighteenth Century Scotland*, 247–8.

119 NAS, Breadalbane MSS, GD 112/16/13/8/7, 'Tenants proposed to be removed for exchanges and otherwise'; GD112/16/13/8/1, 'List of Lots in the Officiary of Ardeonaig & Clouhrain in Classes agreeable to Lord Breadalbane's instructions', 9 April 1810.

120 T. M. Devine, *The Great Highland Famine: Hunger, Emigration and the Scottish Highlands in the Nineteenth Century* (Edinburgh, 1988), 1–3; Devine, 'A conservative people? Scottish gaeldom in the age of improvement', in Devine and Young, *Eighteenth century Scotland*, 229–31; the need to recognise the diversity in Highland society is emphasised by MacKillop, 'Highland estate change', 241.

121 *Ibid.*, 245.

122 M. Storrie, '"They go much from home": nineteenth-century islanders of Gigha, Scotland', *Scottish Economic & Social History*, XVI (1996), 110–13.

123 J. Robson, *General View of the Agriculture of the County of Argyll* (Edinburgh, 1794), 17; Whatley, *Industrial Revolution*, 81.

124 Macinnes, *Clanship*, 225; Withers, *Urban Highlanders*, 84–6.

125 Devine, *Great Highland Famine*, 3.

126 I. R. M. Mowat, *Easter Ross, 1750–1850: The Double Frontier* (Edinburgh, 1981), 58–63; Devine, *Clanship*, 119–34.

127 Robson, *General View*, 23; Sir J. Sinclair, *The Statistical Account of Scotland, 1791–1799, Volume XVII, Inverness-shire, Ross and Cromarty* (Wakefield, 1981 ed.), 97.

128 Mowat, *Easter Ross*, 56–7.

129 S. A. Knox, *The Making of the Shetland Landscape* (Edinburgh, 1985), 9.

130 *Ibid.*, 11–16.

131 Smith, *Shetland Life and Trade*, 144.

132 *Ibid.*, 104–19.

133 R. P. Fereday, 'Thomas Balfour of Elwick (1752–99), an Orcadian improvers: a sketch of his origins and career', *Northern Studies*, XXIV (1987), 1–26; W. P. L. Thomson, *The Little General and the Rousay Crofters: Crisis and Conflict on an Orkney Estate* (Edinburgh, 1981).

134 This section has been greatly influenced by the recent writing of MacKillop, 'Highland estate change', 248–50.

135 Tyson, 'Contrasting regimes', 66; Devine, *Great Highland Famine*, 21

136 Tyson, 'Demographic change', 203, 205–6.

137 Macinnes, 'Scottish gaeldom', 75, 80; Dodgshon, *Chiefs to Landlords*, 203–4, 212–18.

138 *Ibid.*, 124–43.

139 *Ibid.*, 225–7, 243–5.

140 Devine, *Clanship*, 35.

141 M. Gray, *The Highland Economy, 1750–1850* (Edinburgh, 1957), 89–94; J. Hunter, *The Making of the Crofting Community* (Edinburgh, 1976), 15–16; Dodgshon, 'Agricultural change and its social consequences', 53–6.

142 Devine, *Great Highland Famine*, 4–9.

143 *Ibid.*, 12–18.

144 E. Richards, *The Leviathan of Wealth: The Sutherland Fortune in the Industrial Revolution* (London, 1973), 167, 226–8, 231–4; R. J. Adam (ed.), *Papers on Sutherland Estate Management, 1802–1816* (Edinburgh, 1972), 254–5.

145 J. Munro, 'The planned villages of the British Fishery Society', in Smith and Stevenson, *Fermfolk & Fisherfolk*, 55.

146 Richards, *The Leviathan of Wealth*, 203–8.

147 Hunter, *Making of the Crofting Community*, 16–17; MacArthur, *Iona*, 50–1; Macinnes, 'Scottish gaeldom', 85.

148 Mowat, *Easter Ross*, 49; Bob Harris, 'Patriotic commerce and national revival: the Free British Fishery Society and British politics, c. 1749–58', *English Historical Review*, CXIV (April 1999), 295–313.

149 Hamilton, *Economic History of Scotland*, 117.

150 Smith, *Jacobite Estates*, 156–62; E. Richards and M. Clough, *Cromartie: Highland Life, 1650–1914* (Aberdeen, 1989), 92–5.

151 Fry, *Dundas Despotism*, 137–40; Ferguson, *The Jacobite Song* 70–1.

152 R. Clyde, *From Rebel to Hero: The Image of the Highlander, 1745–1830* (East Linton, 1995), 132–4.

153 Munro, 'Planned villages of the British Fisheries Society', 50–62; Clyde, *From Rebel to Hero*, 36–8.

154 Devine, *Great Highland Famine*, 7.

155 Richards, *Leviathan of Wealth*, 222–3; Gray, *Highland Economy*, 161–3.

156 *Ibid.*; Smith, *Jacobite Estates*, 158, 162; Smith, *Shetland Life*, 88; MacArthur, *Iona*, 31–2; M. Gray, *The Fishing Industries of Scotland, 1790–1914: A Study in Regional Adaptation* (Oxford, 1978), 6–9; J. J. A. Irvine and I. A. Morrison, 'Shetlanders and fishing: historical and geographical aspects of an evolving relationship', *Northern Studies*, XXIV (1987), 43–56.

157 Withers, *Urban Highlanders*, 62–7; MacArthur, *Iona*, 51–2.

158 A. R. B. Haldane, *New Ways Through the Glens: Highland Road, Bridge and Canal Makers of the early 19th Century* (Newton Abbot, 1973 ed.), 82–3.

159 Devine, *Clanship*, 135–40.

160 P. Gaskell, *Morvern Transformed: A Highland Parish in the Nineteenth Century* (Cambridge, 1968), 8.

161 For a significant variant, see J. B. Caird, 'The making of the Gairloch crofting landscape', in Baldwin, *Peoples & Settlement*, 137–58.

162 Richards, *The Leviathan of Wealth*, 229–31; Devine, *Clanship*, 42.

163 Gray, *Highland Economy*, 156; Adams and Somerville, *Cargoes of Despair and Hope*, 203.

164 Devine, *Clanship*, 130–3.

165 J. R. Coull, 'Fisherfolk and fishing settlements of the Grampian region', in Smith and Stevenson, *Fermfolk & Fisherfolk*, 26–49; Gray, *Highland Economy*, 166–8

166 M. Gray, 'National rivalries in the North Sea herring fishery, 1790–1914', *Northern Studies*, XXVII (1990), 25; Richards and Clough, *Cromartie*, 194–7.

167 Gray, *Highland Economy*, 170; Haldane, *New Ways Through the Glens*, 191.

168 J. Coull, 'The role of the Fishery Board in the development of Scottish fishing harbours *c.* 1809–1939', *Scottish Economic & Social History*, XV (1995), 27–30.

169 E. Richards, *A History of the Highland Clearances: Agrarian Transformation and the Evictions, 1746–1886* (London, 1982), 212–14, 221–3.

170 Macinnes, 'Scottish gaeldom', 85; Gray, *Highland Economy*, 135.

171 Gaskell, *Morven Transformed*, 23.

172 Richards, *Highland Clearances*, 219; Devine, *Clanship*, 82; *Great Highland Famine*, 24.

173 *Ibid.*, 75–81; T. C. Smout, 'Tours in the Scottish highlands from the eighteenth to the twentieth centuries', *Northern Studies*, V (1983), 101–11.

174 E. Richards, 'Margins of the industrial revolution', in P. O'Brien and R. Quinault (eds), *The Industrial Revolution and British Society* (Cambridge, 1993), 203–28; Whatley, *Industrial Revolution*, 82.

175 Richards, *Highland Clearances*, 8–22.

176 I. Levitt and T. C. Smout, *The State of the Scottish Working Class in 1843* (Edinburgh, 1979), 22–35.

177 Devine, *Great Highland Famine*, 23.

178 Richards, *Highland Clearances*, 223–4; Clyde, *From Rebel to Hero*, 116–49.

Scottish society in
the age of revolutions

Workplace change, combination and unionisation

For Adam Smith, how labour was utilised was central to his prognostications on the wealth-creating potential of commercial societies. In the organisation and management of labour however there was no single through-route to industrialisation.[1] In Scotland, no less than elsewhere in the industrialising world, 'the age of manufactures' can best be portrayed as a 'complex web of improvement and decline, large- and small-scale production, machine and hand processes'. Yet if we allow for the hand-working 'jenny houses' and the considerable variety of technology and working practices in the first mills and factories, it was these institutions which presented workers with the most radical break with their previous experience of the workplace and work routines. But even here we must be careful: the number of paper mills more than trebled between 1740 and 1800, but they were not powered by a single source, nor did they house the 150–plus workers the typical cotton mill employed in the early nineteenth century. In paper the average was ten, and hand methods of production prevailed until the early 1800s.[2] The increase in the number of handloom weavers in the early nineteenth century has been noted, but what should be emphasised are the regional and local differences in their circumstances, with most in Dunfermline and Montrose being employed in factories but relatively few in Paisley.[3]

As was noted in chapter 6, as far as textiles were concerned it has been proposed that the separation of manufacturing activity in the Scottish countryside from agricultural employment formed a village-based 'quasi-proletariat' which found the transition to the new regime of specialised production relatively comfortable after *c.* 1780, allegedly another aspect of the ease with which capitalist enterprise was accommodated in Scotland.[4]

Looked at more closely however, the evidence suggests that this only partly describes what happened. As in England and elsewhere, there was considerable reluctance to enter the early mills which, in appearance and in the imaginations of those urged to work in them, were not unlike workhouses or prisons. Real wages were buoyant in most occupations until the mid-1790s and more desirable employment was not hard to find. Robert Owen of New Lanark despaired of 'the Scotch peasantry' who 'disdained the idea of working early and late, day after day'. Even the provision of village-type accommodation to entice families was unsuccessful at first, and tended to attract 'persons destitute of friends, employment, and character'.[5] Labour turnover in the mills was high, which suggests that workers in early industrial Scotland could not be persuaded to stay for long.[6] Unusual in the extremity of their response but arguably less so in their sentiments were the female domestic hand spinners of Forfarshire who were reported to have been 'all up in arms' against the new flax-spinning mills, which they threatened to burn down. They may have feared the loss of the congenial female-run working environment they had established, which incorporated a culture in which song and courtship were prominent. They also valued their independence. The fear of losing this continued to act as a disincentive to better-paid factory work or domestic service in some places until the 1830s.[7] The initial tightness of the labour market was such that women could exercise at least some degree of choice, so much so that in coal mining female bearers were evidently harder to find in the 1790s than male hewers, and could not readily be persuaded to engage in underground work.[8] Consequently, but also due to the technical requirements of much mill and factory employment, a high percentage of the labour force comprised pauper children, as well as females between their early teens and mid-twenties. In the early nineteenth century almost two-thirds of manufacturing workers in Scotland were women, youths and children.

It is difficult to determine by quantitative means whether the proportion of women and children in employment in 1830 was greater than a century earlier.[9] Observers relatively early in the eighteenth century did note concentrations of female and child workers in the west of Scotland. In the east, at the spinning and weaving town of Ormiston in 1737, all children were said to have been occupied, and were restricted to one hour of play daily.[10] But the indications drawn from impressionistic sources are that by the turn of the nineteenth century not only were women and children more likely to be part of the formal economy, but they were also exposed more often to the revolutionary aspects of mechanised production; that is, through their employment in the water- and steam-powered mills which by the early 1830s were typically working for twelve hours six days a week (Saturdays excepted) for some 306 days *per annum* in a hot and humid energy-sapping environment.[11] What can be said with even greater certainty is that the range of opportunities open to them was fairly sharply circumscribed and, in common with women elsewhere in

Britain, a clear sexual division of labour confined most females to lower-paid tasks.[12] Where they did jobs which had formerly been the preserve of males – handloom weaving, for example – this was when craft control had been weakened, wages were falling and, it was reported of Glasgow in 1820, 'every weaver makes his family weavers ... because poverty leaves him with little choice'. By the 1830s at least a quarter of looms in the south of Scotland were worked by females, more (perhaps one-third) if children are included, although where fancy fabrics were produced, as in Paisley and Dunfermline, far fewer were employed.[13] From the outset powerlooms were operated by females, usually those who were young and single.

Children, who comprised a remarkable 84 per cent of the employees in Renfrewshire's forty-one cotton mills in 1809, and 36 per cent of the workforce of Glasgow's cotton mills in 1833, as opposed to 23 per cent in Manchester, were often the conscripted shock troops of a somewhat tardy Scottish industrial army, taken at the age of six or seven from charity houses on long indentures, and virtually imprisoned in some country and semi-urban mills in barrack-like accommodation. They were paid not much more than subsistence wages and in most cases trained in regular habits rather than useful skills which, traditionally, apprentices could exploit during adulthood.[14] To escape was to risk imprisonment, fines or beatings, as well as an extension of the indenture by twice the number of days the culprit was absent. Yet absconding was common-place, not only among young millworkers, but also from the ranks of apprentices in occupations such as nail-making and calico-printing. It is clear that they were being ruthlessly exploited in their employers' attempts to force down labour costs and, by way of retaliation, were insubordinate, took collective action or sought instead a life in the army or abroad.[15] At home the alternatives were often dismal: chimney sweep-ing, tobacco spinning and pin heading (the last two in return for 1s. a week in the early 1800s compared to over 4s. a day for a coal miner), or calico-printing, where the young were 'the hardest-worked employees ... and the worst paid'. If necessity drove them further down the occupa-tional ladder they could join the 'hundreds' who included the elderly and 'worn out prostitutes' who in 1834 were reported in Glasgow to have been eking out a living on the fringes of the labour market, 'gathering manure, old iron, rags and similar articles from dunghills', commodities which they sold, subsidised by meagre poor relief and their own wretchedness, to be reinvested in the production process.[16]

Highlanders too could be tempted by mill and factory work, although how many had experience of part-time domestic production is not clear (but this is hardly likely other than in spinning and perhaps not at all when recruits were drawn from the inland parts of distant counties such as Caithness).[17] They were favoured by employers as they would work for lower wages than Lowland adults, and because it was believed (mistakenly) that they would be relatively easy to train. There were exceptions, but they had few advocates among mill and factory proprietors and, while there was a sizeable group of merchants of Highland origin in Glasgow, Port Glasgow and Greenock, it seems that most Highlanders were engaged in labouring of various sorts. Nowhere was this more so than in Greenock, where in 1801 29 per cent of the population was Highland-born.[18] Where skilled adult male labour was needed, often when greater physical strength was involved as well, as in mule spinning, the shortfall in the supply of indigenous adult males was made good by recruiting from the ranks of the immigrant Irish, the previous trickle of which into the west was becoming a stream, exacerbated by the Irish rebellion of 1798, which produced a flood of refugees. The migrants included women and children, to the extent that in the early nineteenth century at least half of the workforce in the cotton mills and textile factories of Glasgow and Paisley were first-generation Irish migrants and their descendants who, in the early years, partly owing to their need for paid work, were willing and comparatively trouble-free employees.[19]

Fortuitously, large-scale Irish immigration had begun just as the first urban spinning mills were being built in the west of Scotland and unlike the Scots they were not averse to mill and factory work.[20] Significantly, this critical bottleneck in the supply of labour for Scottish industry was broken through not with former inhabitants of the Scottish countryside but instead with workers from Ireland, mainly in the west of Ulster, precisely where domestic textile production and agriculture had developed hand in hand. The same was partly true of the Dundee textile industry, with a rising proportion of the labour force for the spinning mills which were erected from the 1820s being former hand spinners, mainly female adolescents and young adults along with adult weavers from the Irish counties of Cavan, Monaghan and Fermanagh. Most migrants however were drawn from the town's rural hinterland.[21]

The greater rationality in the use of labour was not confined to large-scale, centralised workplaces. We have seen that similar principles, rooted in the notion of the division of labour, were applied in the countryside. Customary work practices were no more welcome there than in the factory.[22] Fines, payment by the piece, detailed contracts of employment, the threat of dismissal and even corporal punishment were used to alter working habits. Urban craftsmen found that they were subject to the same forces as their counterparts in the mills.[23] 'De-skilling' was one aspect of the process of worker subordination, although this was not an even development over time nor is it necessarily one which is uni-directional.[24] The trends during our period however are sufficiently clear not only in the leading sectors but in others too. In 1812 the journeymen bookbinders in Edinburgh complained that the lighter parts of their work were being done by boys and girls, so that even an outsider could observe that the journeymen were doing heavier work, which brought the trade 'very nearly within the circle of laborious occupations.' Formerly, they argued, their work was 'inconstant' whereas they now had to work solidly for eleven hours for their wages under a 'new division of labour', in 'severer' conditions which, because of the growing taste for hammered gilt ornamental binding, were harmful to their health.[25] While wages and living standards were arguably the workers' prime concern, working conditions and the degree to which they controlled the production process were also fought over. Hours too were contested, with employers in several trades attempting to recover some of their heavier outlays on wages by increasing hours. Workers, on the other hand, taking advantage of the wartime labour shortage, combined to reduce them, as in the case of the journeymen smiths at one firm in Perth, who refused to work an additional hour in 1803 on the grounds that 'the General rule of the Town was only Ten hours'.[26] Hours as well as wages were the issues which instigated a formal combination of farm servants in the Carse of Gowrie in Perthshire in 1805. Disputes over working practices had first come to light in the district two decades earlier as the process of rural proletarianisation had intensified, and would periodically break out into open conflict thereafter in this and other parts of rural Scotland where farm servants who had common interests to protect – as ploughmen, for example – were sufficiently numerous.[27]

While for many thousands of the labouring poor the new urban industrial system marked a sudden and even shocking break with their past experience, for most the transition was slower and more manageable, a mingling of old and new, represented most obviously in the way that handloom weavers in some parts of the country left their looms during spring and autumn, to sow, cut peat and gather crops, and 'gamboled' at new year, the so-called 'daft days' of pre-industrialised Scotland. The season's excesses in Dundee in January 1830 were recorded in a diary entry by a local businessman:

> An innumerable number of Men & Women Crowding the Streets particularly in the afternoon, and mostly less or more inebriated – some say eight people are missing ... thought to have wandered in drink down about the Harbour & fallen in.[28]

At least until the 1780s some handloom weavers in Glasgow were able to grow and sell potatoes within the burgh's boundaries.[29] Seasonal and 'step' migration meant that for many their induction into the industrial system was gradual, and even assisted in breaking down language barriers (invariably at the expense of Gaelic).[30] There is some evidence too that where the physical boundaries between town and countryside were blurred – as cartographic evidence shows they were even in industrial

Glasgow and Dundee – members of the same semi-urban household could be employed as farm workers, as well as in manufacturing. In the early 1790s when seven-year-old Alexander Moncur's family moved into Dundee from the neighbouring countryside, his father continued to work as a ploughman, his mother spun yarn, while Alexander himself operated a pirn wheel (for winding yarn on to bobbins), except during the harvest, when he acted as a cowherd.[31] In some artisanal trades, as well as coal-mining, workers managed to maintain earlier work rhythms and practices, and recognised the Scottish equivalent of 'St Monday'. Parliamentary elections in contested seats provided excuses to leave the loom or bench for some fun, free drink and a noisy spectacle, as well as an opportunity to influence the electors to vote for a favoured candidate.[32]

Ways too were found to counter the psychological deadening of mill monotony and the physical fatigue of the factory, by bantering and singing during worktime, for example. Song, wrote the weaver poet William Thom, as he recalled his seventeen years as a factory weaver in Aberdeen, 'was the dew drops that gathered during the long night of despondency', a substitute for the sermon. Song too was a means by which workers – females especially – signified their 'command of space' within the workplace and expressed collective feelings about their status, conditions or employers.[33] For handloom weavers who may have enjoyed the headier years of greater independence and higher wages, song- and poetry-writing provided a connection with their former culturally-enriched way of life.[34] So too did religion. Dissenting churches provided a source of comfort for some of the uprooted: the planned villages in which weavers were commonly congregated, as well as the larger factory villages and concentrations of industrial workers such as miners and calico printers, often bred 'feverish religious enthusiasm'.[35]

Intoxicating drink had long played a practical part and symbolic role for Scottish workers in the countryside, as well as the town, being given out by employers, for example, on a man's agreement to engage as a servant or at the completion of a particularly arduous task. Short drinking sessions broke up the working day and could act as a temporary spur to greater endeavour. Whisky was increasingly resorted to as a means of release from the 1790s, with consumption soaring between c. 1800 and c. 1830. Both legal and illicitly-distilled spirits were sold from dram shops or 'tippling houses' of which there was at least one for every twenty families in most parts of the west of Scotland, in addition to public houses and inns.[36] Dressing up in their purchases of cheap fashionable clothing helped raise the spirits of the young. Among the unskilled in the towns and in parts of the rural Lowlands there was considerable labour mobility and variety of work, albeit that the search for gainful employment was usually determined by the conclusion of a fixed term contract or necessitated by the temporary nature of many tasks.[37]

As has been noted, the greater use which employers and employees in Scotland made of the courts, both local and national, was a distinctive feature of industrial relations north of the border. It can be argued that the practice engendered a certain orderliness in the conduct of labour disputes, as magistrates and judges sought to conciliate between the two sides. Claims and counter-claims – in some instances at a fairly sophisticated level – had to be articulated, made in writing, and represented by agents and advocates, thereby further encouraging calm and respectability. On the other hand, the same process was an inducement to workers to organise collectively and effectively, to raise money for cases and to brief legal representatives.[38] That appeals to magistrates and the JPs came increasingly from the workers' side from the 1780s is indicative of a growing distrust and further social distancing between masters and men that we have observed in previous chapters. That trades incorporations were less likely than they had in the past to act in the interests of the craft as a whole, through the purchase of meal for their members, for example, is another sign of a growing gulf, which also encouraged workers to form their own organisations, if only in the first instance to provide for relief in times of distress or old age.[39] Friendly societies, established on the basis of both trade and neighbourhood, were ubiquitous by the end of the century, and continued to be formed into the nineteenth. Urbanisation and the lack of alternative means of support of those who had severed their links with the countryside and their former parishes added a further incentive.[40] There was a greater awareness and resentment of the increasing prosperity of employers – the case of the Edinburgh journeymen bookbinders, for example, was based partly on their observation that their masters' profits had risen at times without any benefit to them. The coal miners saw things in much the same way. Outside the workplace the towns in Scotland – as in much of the rest of Britain – were becoming more tense and disorderly, and relations between the classes were hardening.[41] Such developments had repercussions for employers, to the extent that in 1815 it was complained that even among servant girls cases of insolence to their employers had 'of late ... become frequent'.[42]

Employer alarm and pressure to reduce costs and raise labour productivity intensified during the 1790s and early 1800s, when workers had managed to obtain significant wage increases, and in some trades to impose their will on workplace practices. There are signs too of cross-border labour organisation by the early nineteenth century, on the part of calico printers, paper-makers and handloom weavers, for example.[43] Parity of wages in Britain however was anathema to most Scottish employers. In some sectors they acted collectively, forming associations either to secure parliamentary support for their industry or to exercise more effective control over workers in their respective trades.

Coalmasters working collieries along the Forth were among the first to do so, in the 1770s, in an attempt to raise the price of coal by restricting output, and to reduce colliers' wages.[44] Although the coalmasters in Scotland were divided on east–west coast lines, proprietors at those collieries where competition was most intense – mainly in the west – obtained legislation in 1799 which was designed primarily to outlaw combinations which the muddled law of 1775 had failed to check. In the pits, the colliers had become even more powerful, setting restrictions on output and the number of days worked, and organised on a local and regional basis. Demand for coal, intensified due to the rush of ironworks which were established in the 1780s and 1790s, had assisted in driving up wages beyond the levels of most of the rest of the working classes.[45] In 1808, following what was virtually a nationwide strike of paper workers in Scotland in May 1807, it was alleged that a collective body of the master paper-makers had 'subsisted for many years'. In 1799 they had attempted to reduce their workers' wages by 2s. a week.[46] Others followed. In the cotton industry, where the spinners may have been organised from c. 1800, it quickly became clear that the malleability of the Irish mule spinners was more apparent than real and that they too had begun to act collectively, securing what was a skilled occupation to themselves and their families, sometimes with the use of violent tactics. Colliers, not without justification, faced the same charges.[47] The spinners' aims, it was alleged, were 'to cramp and fetter the Masters in the employment of their time, talents & capital', to determine who they would employ and to 'raise the prices of labour; and in other respects, to bring the Masters under the control of the Leaders of the Combination, in the prosecution of their business'.[48]

In Glasgow the employers responded in 1810 by forming the Association of Master Cotton Spinners, the primary aim of which was to break the spinners' combination. In the courts however there was a reassertion of paternalism. The judiciary, drawn largely from the ranks of the landed classes, tried to seek conciliation through an even-handed approach in which the welfare of the worker was a prime consideration. For those workers who managed to obtain legal redress for their grievances – and those located in Edinburgh appeared to have achieved most in this respect – market forces were kept in check.[49]

However not all employers adopted the overtly aggressive approach to labour management seen above, although most were single-minded in their determination to secure the same end. Paternalism and the laying out and creation of self-contained factory villages offering housing, leisure facilities, such as plots for growing vegetables, and education, were employed by men such as David Dale at Catrine and New Lanark. In several works throughout Scotland the king's birthday was adopted by employers as an occasion for a holiday, the provision of food, drink and entertainment, which included the singing of 'national loyal airs'.[50] Religious instruction was used as a means of inculcating in child workers moral values, cleanliness, stoic endurance in the face of adversity (which was essential, given the long hours they worked, often in appalling conditions) and respect for authority, temporal as well as spiritual.[51] Few were as liberal as at Carron however, of which it was boasted (in somewhat exaggerated terms) in 1820 that the works had 'never been troubled with Combinations or Mutineers', owing to the policy the company had of allowing workers to leave if they wished to try for better conditions elsewhere: 'under this freedom', the manager declared, 'the men are as much afraid of Losing good Bread as we are afraid of losing their Service'.

A turning point was reached in 1812 however, as tension grew in the preceding years between employers and workers who were both organising their respective interests collectively. Master–worker solidarities transcended the usual sectoral boundaries. At the forefront of the workers' movement were the weavers, periodically organised in the eighteenth century, but who from at least as early as 1808, in response to falling wages and the dilution of workforce through mass entry into the trade, as well as other complaints, formed, from Glasgow, a national organisation, the General Association of Operative Weavers in Scotland. The Association however did admit females, provided they had entered the trade prior to 1808, or if they were working for a male member. The principle over which they clashed with the employers was political economy, the handloom weavers arguing in defence of the traditional interventionist strategy and fair wages – a moral economy of pay. Open in its dealings, respectable and largely law-abiding, in 1812 the Association sought and obtained the support of the JPs of Lanarkshire for a table of wages they presented. Strike action followed the refusal of most masters to accept the weavers' prices, but although there was little violence and Luddite overtures and methods were rejected, the government – with Lord Sidmouth as Home Secretary and in Scotland represented by the Lord Advocate and other leading legal officers – determined to suppress what they feared might become an armed political rising. The weavers' leaders were arrested, combination was declared illegal in Scotland, and throughout Britain statutes concerning wage regulation dating back to the sixteenth century were repealed.[52] Formally, from 1813, the market was in the driving seat as long-standing assumptions about the social economy were hastily scuttled by legal theorists and in practice in the courts in favour of employers and *laissez-faire*.[53] Although the odds against their success had suddenly lengthened, the weavers continued to campaign for a cause which was not simply about wages. The defence of the table of prices was of such importance that John Stewart, a Wishaw weaver, warned his fellow workers that if they failed to stand out until it was accepted, 'their Children would cause it to be wrote on their Coffins to their dishonour'.[54]

The gloves were cast off as, in and around the workplace, 'labour consciousness', merging on occasion with a consciousness of class in the community, embroiled much of Lowland Scotland, the west in particular, in what threatened to become an open class war (see chapter 8). In September 1824 the *Glasgow Courier* reported uneasily that 'a spirit of opposition to the authority of their masters has sprung up amongst our manufacturing population'. Glasgow, described as the 'Scottish focus of organised systems of combination', was the crucible in which the harder-edge of industrial relations in Scotland was formed. Even the 'redeemingly deferential' coal miners of the Lothians, who normally demonstrated little of the spirit of the 'independent collier' fraternity of the west of Scotland, struck work and managed to weaken their landed masters' grip on the industry until 1842.[55]

The employers were led by uncompromising advocates of the market system such as the textile magnates Kirkman Finlay, Henry Houldsworth and James Dunlop, while in coal and iron, landed interests combined with those of the newer companies to cut labour costs by simplifying underground operations and, where possible, removing existing colliers and replacing them with unemployed weavers and labourers.[56] They were supported by lawyers such as George Salmond, Glasgow's procurator-fiscal, who left no stone unturned as he grimly went about his business of rooting out combinations.[57] The mix was made more potent with peri-odic injections, on the workers' side, of the rhetoric and ideas of political radicalism and by the involvement of weavers, spinners, colliers and others who evidently had a foothold in both camps.[58]

The pattern of industrial relations was partly determined by the prevailing economic conditions. As these worsened and wages were cut in the immediate aftermath of the Napoleonic Wars, workers who had previously been organised, as well as others who had not, agitated both over wages and the deeper-seated issue of apprentices. In a number of trades, including the strategically-placed industries of cotton spinning, coal-mining and, to an increasing degree, iron-making and founding, as well as older trades like shoe-making, employers were attempting to increase production and to weaken worker influence over output and wages by expanding the number of entrants. Although successful resis-tance was mounted at first, the demographic variable was shifting in the interests of capital. For reasons which are not entirely clear to demo-graphic historians, mortality levels had been falling in the later eighteenth century and, as a result, the rate of population growth rose, virtually matching that of England and Wales in the first decades of the nineteenth century (where the rise was largely due to birth-rate improvement) and rising as high as 1.6 per cent *per annum* between 1821 and 1831.[59] Pressures in the labour market in the Lowlands were further eased for employers by increased immigration from Ireland and a stronger flow of Highland migrants after 1815, as well as by many thousands of disbanded soldiers and sailors. But further advantages were sought. Given their attachment to child labour, it should come as no surprise to find that Scottish factory masters were the most ardent opponents of shorter working hours in the United Kingdom.[60]

The struggle over workplace control – intimately linked with the market in and the price of labour – reached its climax during the mid-1820s. The immediate background was the economic boom of 1824–5 (which led to demands for higher wages), and the sharp downturn thereafter. At issue too however were the work practices which specific groups of workers had managed to introduce during the short period of their ascendancy, as in printworks in the Maryhill suburb of Glasgow, where a culture of whisky drinking determined the pattern of the working day and the arrival of a new apprentice was the occasion of a drunken bout lasting a day or longer.[61] Combinations too were under attack – competition and combination being 'as opposed as light and darkness' – especially after the repeal of the Combination Acts in 1824.[62] As noted earlier in relation to cotton spinning, masters were anxious to gain control of the management of their works, and to determine who worked for them, and at what price. By the early 1820s the Association of Operative Cotton Spinners had managed to raise the spinners' wages in Glasgow to over two guineas a week. In some older established industries, coal mining, for example, worker habits, attitudes and practices such as 'brothering' were deeply-ingrained, dating back perhaps to the 1720s, and a century later had been reinforced by the taking of secret oaths and use of passwords and 'grips'. These were also part of the cotton spinners' armoury.[63] The conflicts which resulted were of immense economic and social significance and form a vital component of the history of labour and social relations in Scotland during the 1820s and 1830s. The involvement of thousands of coal miners across the main Scottish coalfields between 1824 and 1826 was of such a length, ferocity and nature – one commentator compared the activities of the Colliers' Association with 'the worst days of the French Revolution' – that it contributed to the 1825 revision by parliament of the Repeal of the Combination Acts (1824).[64]

In the short-term the employers gained the upper hand, although not irrevocably.[65] Contests over workplace domination did not end in the 1820s; there was a resurgence of collier organisation in 1830 through to 1834, engineers and calico printers came head to head with their masters in the early 1830s, as did the flax hecklers of Dundee who until 1830 had been one of the most effectively organised groups of workers in the country.[66] Firmness on the part of the employers concerned, court rulings, exemplary punishments, wage cuts and the use of 'blacklegs' hastened the demise of workers' organisations however and signalled the limits of their power to resist. The tailors, another group of workers who were no strangers to collective action, struck in 1823 but, after the break-ing of their society in the same year, remained unorganised for four decades. The builders too achieved wage gains initially, but were subse-quently forced back.[67] The handloom weavers, organised again from 1824, but now in the General Association of Weavers in Scotland, were broken by the arrest and trial of their leaders, a drain on their funds by members holding out against employers who offered below table prices, and the adverse movement of the trade cycle in 1826. They re-organised again after 1832, but apart from some factory weavers and those in fancy work, their increasing poverty left them without the means or spirit for further contest.[68] Indeed, although real wages for skilled workers such as Glasgow machine makers rose as prices tumbled after 1815, for coal miners, the semi-skilled and the unskilled, material conditions improved little if at all between 1815 and 1830. Handloom weavers experienced further falls in their living standards in real terms – one-third between 1810 and 1830 in Dundee – and for other groups such as building labourers, real wages in 1830 were lower than they had been in 1792. At the end of the first phase of industrialisation in Scotland, poverty was still endemic.[69]

The saga of the cotton mule spinners is best-known, partly because of the longevity of their drawn-out struggle, which culminated in the strike of 1837, the crushing of which in the courts did much to set back the cause of trade unionism in Scotland for several decades.[70] Like the coal miners however the mule spinners' had effectively begun to lose their battle over the management of the workplace in 1825.[71] It was this issue which incited most of the violence with which the industry is associated (until another wave broke out in the months prior to the 1837 conflict). Fatalities and serious woundings occurred during strikes and lockouts and masters were in receipt of a stream of anonymous intimidating letters threatening death and injury. Spirit drinking has been used as a means of explaining away the number and brutality of assaults, but the language of confrontation as revealed in 'Nob Songs' – sung by females and children inside and outside the mills – indicates that hostility towards masters and blacklegs ran deep. One asked rhetorically whether a blackleg, 'auld Graham' (John Graham, who was shot in the back), 'wasn't ... a fool to come out and be Shot'.[72]

But the cotton spinners were not alone in having recourse to physical force in support of their cause. Some of the poetry written by the Paisley weaver Alexander Wilson in the 1790s was distinctly inflammatory and interpreted as such by the authorities, causing Wilson to flee to America in 1794. After the blow of 1812 there are reports of handloom weavers engaging in episodes of vitriol-burning. Tenters at Charles Todd's powerloom weaving factory used it to drive off unwanted replacements.[73] In coal mining, some unwelcome entrants had their ears cut off. In 1817 stocking weavers in Jedburgh who were accused of working below the agreed prices were threatened by men claiming to have orders from 'General Ludd' that their frames would be broken (although this was a comparatively minor occurrence of a phenomenon which appeared in Scotland only sporadically). Violence or the threat of it were common-place in calico-printing and the heckling trade.[74] But neither the spinners nor the others were simply the mindlessly violent, greedy 'brutes' depicted pejoratively by some historians.[75] They were proud of their skill and position within the mill hierarchy, committed to the British commer-cial empire and probably, in the main (but see chapter 8), attached to the monarchy. When stated by the mule spinners their demands appear more reasonable than the versions which were reported by their masters. They included an end to cruelty to piecers, the employment of overseers who were 'just', and a supply of 'wholesome water to drink, and a refreshment in the afternoon if need require'. Nor were their interests simply sectional. The spinners' campaign for shorter hours embraced all factory workers.[76]

It would be misleading however if the impression was given of a phalanx of workers in Scotland solidly united in its opposition to an employing class which was engaged in a particularly vigorous bout of cost cutting. Others adopted alternative, less confrontational and non-violent means of maintaining a semblance of control over the market system. Co-operative schemes were one, designed at the short-lived Owenite community at Orbiston in 1825 to eliminate the harmful effects of competitive capitalism. Co-operative retailing societies were set up, encouraged by one of the Orbiston partners, the influential joiner Alexander Campbell, who established an Owenite labour exchange in the east end of Glasgow in the later 1820s, in which time-labour notes rather than money changed hands for jobs done.[77] Socialist ideas too began to gather some momentum as organised labour began to recover from the economic depression of the mid- and later-1820s. These were articulated from 1830 by the *Herald to the Trades Advocate*, which urged that workers should become their own 'capitalists and employers', although this early attempt by workers to establish their own press collapsed in 1831. There were divisions however, between those who advocated trade union activity and the supporters of co-operative schemes, who were themselves split, Owenites being perceived as being antipathetic to reli-gion. By the end of the decade the same tension had separated Chartism in Scotland from Owenism.[78] The political route to the resolution of the sufferings of the labouring classes however had been adopted earlier, as will be seen more clearly in chapter 8.

While the compartmentalism which some historians have argued weakened working-class resistance is belied by the evidence there is of mutual interest and support among workers in different trades, there were weak spots and fissures in labour's embryonic army.[79] Attention has already been drawn to the differential pace of economic change, the effect of which was to disperse potential solidarities. There were groups of skilled workers whose material circumstances greatly improved in the fifteen years after 1815. Even though those of the handloom weavers fell, their education, a high moral tone and religiosity acquired during the so-called 'golden age' of the 1780s and 1790s may have caused some of those working in the higher classes of work to stand apart from other proletarians. (Although whether this distinction was as great as has been suggested is open to question: some highly paid mule spinners were reputed to have placed considerable emphasis on the home, organised by their wives, as well as their own and their children's education, even though out of necessity they had to employ them as piecers. They also expressed concerns about overseers taking sexual advantage of their authority over young females in the mills.)[80] Class relations between mill and factory workers and their masters were more sharply differentiated than between the small manufacturers and fancy weavers of Paisley, although genuine sympathy for the weavers' plight was mingled with concern that their worsening conditions were likely to dilute their 'loyalty' and lead to intemperate habits.[81] Even within the same workplace there was rivalry between different grades of employee and exploitation of worker by worker, as of piecers by spinners. In June 1820 the piecers in Milngavie mills struck work in protest at the spinners' decision to cut their rates by more than the drop the spinners were to endure.[82]

Among immigrant Irish males, solidarities of gender, nationality and religion were torn apart by, on the one hand, mule spinners who were defending their privileged position in the occupational hierarchy, and, on the other, those who before 1830 were used as blackleg labour in coal and ironstone mines. While most Irish migrants were Roman Catholics, a sizeable minority – perhaps as much as a third of the total – were Protestants, more in some localities. At least half the Irish households in Irvine in 1820 were Protestant. Religious differences could also inflame inter-Irish violence, and indigenous Scottish anti-Catholicism was never far from the surface. Not without precedent, Orangeism arrived in the weaving and shoe-making villages of south-west Scotland in 1799 and had become established in and around Glasgow and Paisley by 1820.[83]

Arguably in Scotland, however, where textiles played a more important role in early industrialisation than south of the border, gender divisions were less marked than in London for example, where artisan labour was more prominent. In most artisanal trades female workers were unwelcome.[84] Nor indeed were children, unless they were legitimately indentured apprentices. This is not to say that patriarchy was not a strong ideological force in Scotland or that fraternity and assumptions about masculinity and female inferiority did not contribute to the formation of strong and exclusive bonds between men. (Women too had some separate organisations of their own, notably friendly societies.) In handloom weaving, up to the end of the eighteenth century, patriarchical values predominated in a culture of female subordination. While the situation in handloom weaving was to change, in coal mining there is no suggestion that other than in exceptional cases, hewing was a male preserve. Coal bearing was the province of poorly-paid women and children (and pit ponies), the former to be substituted by male colliers when demand for coal was slack. So exploited were the 'fremit' bearers (unrelated to the colliers) at Pencaitland colliery in 1803 that the proprietors decided that the bearers would belong to the master and that before a bearer was allocated to a hewer he would have to undertake to give her 'proper work & wages'.[85]

In cotton, manufacturers in Glasgow and Paisley replaced male mule spinners, as well as carders, with females, who were subject to periodic attacks from male-led groups. Male replacements were also brought in however and in such cases women and children crossed the gender divide to defend the jobs of male mule spinners with whom they worked and whose neighbourhoods they shared; united against particularly harsh masters or overseers, their commitment to spinning and pride in were occupation were celebrated in the strike songs of their own creation, sung to the tunes of traditional spinning songs from the countryside. In 'The Rock and the Wee Pickle Tow' they boasted that they were the 'braw chiels that belongs to the wheel / That earns their bread by the spinning o't'. Female power-loom weavers hissed, abused and pelted with dirt new male tenters, who were brought in by their masters to replace those they had worked under previously. In handloom weaving, which many thousands of females had taken up by the 1820s, opposition to weavers who worked below table prices emanated from both sexes.[86] In one especially revealing case in 1824 a crowd estimated at between seven to eight hundred people, in which women were 'particularly active', whipped an effigy and attacked the loomshop of a handloom weaver in Camlachie (Glasgow) who was not only working at low prices but who had also allegedly failed to support the Radical rising of 1820. The crowd thereafter marched in search of other offenders in the neighbouring villages of Parkhead, Dunsmore and Westmuir, cohesive communities in which handloom weavers were particularly thick on the ground.[87] That women and children joined in the periodic drinking sessions indulged in by calico printers may explain the 'intense' labour solidarity found in calico-printing villages.[88]

Towns and urban social conditions

Work in the urban areas was not without its compensations. Indeed it was the prospect of these which eased the exodus of people from rural Scotland – as well as from Ireland – into the towns and cities. Drinking and dancing to the music of fiddle and bagpipe were the main components of a vigorous and rough popular culture (although in consuming large quantities of alcohol the lower orders were ably matched by their social superiors). Young men in particular participated in street games like football and shinty, although more restrained sports like bowling and curling were popular among weavers. Stone throwing was commonplace in Glasgow, and involved pitched battles between gangs allied in their opposition to each other by street and neighbourhood.[89]

If holidays were fewer in Scotland owing to the rejection by the kirk of pre-Reformation festivals, those work-free days that were taken as holidays – Handsel Monday, the monarch's birthday, new year, market days and fairs – were the scene of boisterous and energetic enjoyment. (Working-class adherents of the secession churches also found fulfilment in the six or so fast days which they held by the end of the eighteenth century.) Bonfires were frequently lit during the first two. Markets and fairs were often accompanied by travelling circuses, shows and similar entertainments – such as W. H. Moss and Thomas Bell, Perth comedians, who in 1800 requested permission to perform 'Tragedies, Comedies etc' in Dundee – although there are hints that at Scottish fairs there may have been less of the gayness, frivolity and spectacle of their English equivalents.[90] Baser pleasures may have been deemed more important – and obtainable – by the poorer part of the population, temporarily freed from their masters' supervision. The annual Glasgow fair, for example, held in July (right in the middle of the 'season for outdoor sex'), was judged to be an important forum both for plebeian match-making and marriage, while hiring fairs provided both temptation and opportunity for the young of both sexes.[91] Despite the efforts of the urban authorities to remove the more convivial (and potentially disruptive) elements of the monarch's birthday celebrations from the streets and to dampen down the popular rumbustiousness of a day in which town dwellers but also expectant visitors from the countryside mingled together, it remained the occasion which was most likely to lead to plebeian disorder until the middle of the nineteenth century.[92]

At the same time however there was a fairly robust reading culture, if not of books (other than the bible, and Blind Harry's *Wallace*), which were expensive, but of cheap chapbooks, sold by hawkers and packed with ballads and popular histories. Heavily-taxed newspapers were purchased by men clubbing together and often read in groups. Chapbooks, it was claimed of Glasgow in the early nineteenth century, were 'found in almost every house', and read avidly. They supplemented the transmission of stories by oral means, often at the mother's knee, or by other informal methods used to educate the young in the eighteenth century.[93] School attendance however had a favourable impact upon literacy levels, and even though schooling was not free, among the working classes in Scotland there was marked enthusiasm to learn how to read, but less for writing. Although, in general, family traditions and attitudes to learning probably had a greater bearing on literacy levels than parental occupation, there is evidence which suggests that the children of labourers were less likely to be able to read and much less likely to be able to write and do arithmetical calculations than the sons and daughters of craftsmen, farmers and those of higher rank.[94] Among the working classes however few matched the handloom weavers, who prior to the demise in their status and living standards demonstrated a deep commitment to learning, literacy and cultural expression.[95] Overall however, attendance levels in the schools of the industrialising towns were probably declining in the 1820s, not, it is argued, because of a shortfall in provision or indeed a lack of enthusiasm for reading and writing among the parent population. Instead the explanation seems to lie between the need of households for their offspring to earn money and a perception that schooling would produce little advantage for the lower orders in the machine age. The influx of the Irish too may have added to the pool of those whose skills were deficient in reading, writing and arithmetic. On the other hand, in the smaller towns – the thriving port of Portpatrick for example – eighteenth-century literacy levels (as measured by ability to read) were maintained among the native-born population into the nineteenth century.[96]

For most however, material conditions were worsening. The more fortunate members of the middle and upper ranks were able to escape to the new streets and squares of four- and five-roomed terraced houses, and to semi-rural detached houses and gardens. Edinburgh and Glasgow led the way in attempting to impose some order on urban growth, and were followed in the early nineteenth century by Aberdeen, Greenock and, to a lesser extent, Paisley. They also were followed but in a less co-ordinated fashion in Dundee.[97] Similarly ambitious if less spectacular developments, which also included raising prominent public buildings such as churches, academies, theatres and libraries, were also begun in smaller places such as the county town of Ayr, the population of which had almost doubled to fifteen thousand between 1801 and 1831.[98] The specification of rooms by their function, as, for instance, dining-room and bedroom, reveals a new internal order, as well as increased purchasing power, spent on large dining tables, matching sets of chairs and glassware, which became essential accompaniments of middle-class lifestyles from the 1760s. Soo too did muslins, silks, lace and, later,

French perfumes. By 1830 the distinguishing feature of a middle-class public gathering in inclement weather had become the sea of opened umbrellas.[99] It was the men and women of this class who could make most use of the sixty-one stage coaches which were said to have been available in Glasgow, the second city of the British empire, in the early 1830s.

Yet it was in Glasgow that the paradox of economic achievement which at the same time produced acute social suffering, was most apparent. Death rates, for example, which by 1811 had improved considerably since the last decade of the previous century, began to rise again and by 1841 the city had the worst record in Scotland. Although Edinburgh came close, Aberdeen's death rate, sixteen per thousand of the population, was almost twice as good as Glasgow's rate of thirty-one per thousand. Life expectancy fell too, reduced by five years to an average of forty years for women between 1821 and 1841.[100] Although mortality levels rose after 1818–19 in rural as well as urban areas, they were higher in the Lowlands. The major killers were infectious diseases, which accounted for some 60 per cent of all deaths (in Glasgow) in the first half of the nineteenth century.[101] Fatalities from smallpox had almost disappeared from some places by the 1810s, although measles partly replaced this among the infant population, the hardest hit in any mortality crisis. Tuberculosis was the single-largest killer, but cases of 'fever' or typhus increased in a series of surges after 1818. In 1831 cholera made its first appearance in Scotland. 'Almost as terrifying as the plague in the seventeenth century', the disease swept west, north and south from its landfall in Haddington.[102] Overcrowding – early identified as a major cause of infection – was rife, in Glasgow and the other towns into which manufacturing industry was penetrating rapidly. The incoming population, comprised largely of the poorer elements of rural society, poured into the older medieval central districts to sub-let property and added to the growing number of lodgers and those whose conditions were so wretched that they had no formal abode – casual workers, beggars, vagabonds and the unemployed. They were the stragglers in Scotland's reserve army of labour, whose numbers appear to have risen dramatically during the 1810s and 1820s. Strongly influenced by Malthusian principles, the Scottish Poor Laws were re-interpreted after 1820 as having no responsibility for those whose poverty resulted from unemployment. Poor rate income failed to rise with need. Landed resistance to compulsory payments grew, sustained by a belief that over-generous provision for the poor was morally unsustainable. In 1817 the Rev. Thomas Chalmers, ministering to a Glasgow parish, argued that charitable relief, voluntarily given and allied to Christian teaching, served God's purpose better. Chalmers' attempt to run St John's parish in Glasgow on these lines however was a failure. Along with the requirement that applicants should have been resident within a parish for at least three years before receiving relief, many of the urban poor in Scotland were unable to halt their descent into penury.[103]

But while it has been conditions in the larger conglomerations, Glasgow in particular, which have attracted most attention of historians, other towns in Scotland were experiencing similar difficulties. By 1841, for example, the Rev. George Lewis of Dundee, after a visit to Bolton, Manchester and other manufacturing towns in the north of England, declared that he was 'struck with the superiority in cleanliness and comfort of their most neglected districts', compared to those of Dundee (and Glasgow).[104] Although precise occupational data is not available pre-1841, it appears that the economies of Glasgow, Dundee and Paisley were more dependent on textiles than those of the other large towns, thus making them highly susceptible to fluctuations in the trade cycle.[105] With relatively small proportions of their populations in the middle-class occupations of commerce or the professions, they employed correspondingly fewer domestic servants who, like their employers, tended to have more secure – if greatly inferior – incomes. There were however massive variations within the towns: both Dundee and Glasgow were overwhelmingly working-class in their social composition, yet in Glasgow's fashionable Ramshorn the ratio of domestic servants to inhabitants was 1:6, whereas in the textile working district of Calton, it was 1:92.[106] The point however is that it was Edinburgh and, to a lesser extent, Aberdeen, with their better-balanced economies, which enjoyed the cushion of middle-class purchasing power that shielded these cities from the worst effects of an economic downturn.

Although on a smaller scale, to varying degrees and with different chronologies, it appears that the depth of social suffering was greater in some smaller burghs or industrial villages in which there were few or none of the middle-class subscribers to voluntary hospitals and like institutions which ameliorated some of the social problems of the larger towns. Worst-off were those mushrooming towns and villages and their surrounding districts in which burgh control was weak or altogether absent and where handloom weaving and coal mining were carried on. Into the last category comes Clackmannan, which, the earl of Mansfield was informed in 1824, was:

> without exception the most wretched parish in this ... part of the Country [Stirlingshire]. The rickle of ruined houses which is dignified with the appellation of the County Town is a receptacle of poverty, filth and vice; a great proportion of the inhabitants are actual paupers, and with them the numerous poor belonging to the Collieries in the parish, occasion demands on the parish funds far beyond what occurs in any of the neighbouring parishes.[107]

Clackmannan was not without its rivals, and before long would be joined by the colliery and ironworking villages of Lanarkshire and Ayrshire which would spring up with astounding speed during the 1830s and 1840s. These were one of the social consequences of rapid expansion. By contrast, some of the areas (outside the Highlands) where rural manufacturing had previously prospered had to deal with the consequences of decline, as in Kilconquhar in Fife, where in 1831 it was reported that owing to the erection of mills 'the only persons' who felt the 'pressure of the times' were the single women who had previously spun flax. In Aberdeenshire hand-knitters faced a bleak future too from the 1790s, with war cutting off former markets, and competition from the Borders' frame-knitters. In 1811 the county had some 41,000 people – mainly females – employed full- and part-time in textiles. A slow and painful shrinkage of hand manufacturing was begun, which reduced the labour force to less than a quarter within four decades.[108]

Order, protest and crime

For the urban middle-classes, the more pressing concern was social order. The relative calm of the period c. 1750–80 was elevated in the minds of the authorities, social commentators and some members of the 'respectable' working class into a sylvan age of social harmony. However in both town and countryside paternalist tactics were less effectively deployed under the pressure of social dislocation and the fears, uncertainties and material pain this produced for the labouring classes. Under the Scottish Poor Laws, which provided less relief than their English equivalents, the responsibility for providing for the poor during periods of hardship fell on the shoulders of the town authorities (and in the countryside the heritors), who, as the problem became worse, had to appeal for financial aid to Westminster, which was reluctant to help.[109] The kirk's hold over moral behaviour which, as we have seen, was never comprehensive, was loosened further as the urban population swelled. Detection of sexual misbehaviour became more difficult. To a lesser extent, kirk control was weakening in the rural districts too, and although we do not know precisely when, illegitimacy ratios began to rise some time after 1780 and before the middle of the nineteenth century, other than in the south-west and Ayrshire, where there had been an increase from the 1750s and 1760 respectively.[110] But there were changes within the church as well, as moderate influence grew, and fines replaced public appearances on the cutty stool in some towns, although the concession was less likely to be granted to the lower orders prior to the 1820s.[111]

Robert Heron noticed on a visit to Glasgow in 1792 that the city had lost 'much of its ancient piety', although his comments could have been applied equally well to Aberdeen, Dundee or Stirling. Research results for smaller growing towns are likely to be similar. The 'degree of superstition and reverence' which there had been for the sabbath had largely disappeared from the ranks of the working classes. The 'more worthless and licentious part of the labouring citizens' simply drank and caroused from Saturday until Monday afternoon; others, whose 'manners were less profligate' visited the country or ate a bigger meal. The 'third division' did attend church and possibly even read the bible, but spent most of the day at amusements, albeit of the 'harmless variety'. Even manufacturers and merchants appropriated the afternoon and evening for 'convivial enjoyment'.[112]

With so many 'strangers' in the towns, burgh officials were no longer as able as they had been formerly to nip trouble in the bud by interceding early on during a tumult, often by means of personal appeal to the leaders of a mob, or by ordering alternative supplies of victuals for distribution at a fair price. Both measures continued to be implemented, with some success. In Dundee, for example, the concept of 'community politics' was still applicable in the early nineteenth century. Provost Alexander Riddoch was certain that meal mobs and other disorderly incidents posed no threat to the *status quo*, and that participants would return home after their passion had been spent, or following gentle persuasion on his part that they should retire.[113] Dundee's population growth had slackened however, and rose by only 3,777 between 1801 and 1821, to 30,575. In Aberdeen, where numbers doubled between 1755 and the early 1790s, there was rather more concern, and in 1785 the lord provost initiated a campaign on the part of larger burghs to stop the fencible regiments from being disbanded, on the grounds that to keep the peace during periods when food was scarce, a military presence might be needed.[114] As was seen earlier, where disturbances were of a serious nature, the town guards were unable to cope. Throughout Britain the problem became more acute in the larger towns.

The authorities in Glasgow, who had relatively little experience of handling food riots, were little short of panic-stricken in February 1800, with one proclamation from the provost and magistrates advising the city's inhabitants that such was the severity of the grain shortage that 'dearth ... to a certain degree must be submitted to, with resignation to the Will of Heaven'. Grain prices had rocketed over the course of the preceding year, peaking at 3s. 7d. a peck in April, compared to 1s. the previous January and double the unprecedentedly high price of 1s. 8d. in 1795. Rioting also broke out in the surrounding counties, as well as in Edinburgh, with military intervention being required on several occasions. The pleas of the burgh authorities for relief measures from the Treasury however had fallen on deaf ears. With the Union now much more secure than it had been sixty years earlier and the authorities in

Whitehall anxious about security south of the border too, Scottish demands that a ban should be imposed on distilling in England in order to preserve grain were rejected. 'To lay the Barley under any restraint would be the cause of as great an evil as it attempts to cure', the Lord Chancellor wrote, 'and an Insurrection in London is a bad Remedy for one in Glasgow'.[115] With the blockading by mobs of grain-shipping ports in the south-west and the north-east of Scotland (where without military assistance there was not 'the most distant chance' of quelling the disorder), the situation for those charged with the maintenance of law and order was, for a short time, perilous. That radicals, Scots as well as some Irishmen (who are suspected of being behind particularly ferocious riots in Kilmarnock, where they were employed in the Home Secretary, the duke of Portland's, coal pits), appear to have made attempts to harness and steer discontent down the channel of sedition, may well have made matters worse.[116] This is a theme to which we will return in chapter 8.

The changing nature of the monarch's birthday celebrations provides us with further insight into the character and growing scale of the law and order problem with which urban magistrates had to grapple. That what was the most important calendrical occasion in urban Scotland acted as a means of reinforcing the existing social order was established in chapter 4. In many respects it continued to serve this function. Thus after a particularly rowdy king's birthday in Dundee in 1817, Robert Rintoul, the radical editor of the *Dundee, Perth and Cupar Advertiser*, defended the 'priviledge of the rabble to be riotous' and their right to insult 'respectable inhabitants with impunity'. Not only were the day's activities firmly established, he argued, but without this means of release, 'anarchy and confusion' would result, and the 'venerable fabric' of the established political order would 'tumble down'. Certainly attempts on the part of the authorities to interfere with the activities of boys and youths who seemed to be the main actors on such occasions turned boisterous crowds into dangerous ones.[117] It was this sense of the day as a ritualised outpouring of tension followed by the healing brought about by the return of normality which was captured by Robert Fergusson in his 1772 poem, 'The King's Birthday in Edinburgh'. From the vantage point of Montrose *c*. 1830, Thomas Allan looked back on the fourth of June (George III's birthday) as 'the merriest day of all the year', a holiday, with bell-ringing, bonfires, fireworks, gun-fire, drunkenness and effigy-burning, but above all it was a popular declaration of loyalty to king and country.[118] Monarch's birthday crowds in Scotland, even the most fearsome, were normally immensely loyal.

If there was a particularly pressing concern within a community, the king's birthday was often the channel through which feelings on particular issues were made publicly-known. The crowd assured the legitimacy of their action by their very public pledge of allegiance to the monarch and their conviction, genuine or otherwise, that he would listen to his people's complaints and act to resolve them. Their purpose was not solely to seek solace in a drunken spree. Thus in 1784 a king's birthday crowd in Edinburgh, dismissed by one sneering historian as 'all dead drunk', attacked Haig's recently-constructed distillery at Leith, in accordance with a pre-arranged plan – in protest against the use of scarce grain for whisky production.[119] In June 1792 there were riots in many towns in Lowland Scotland. It has long been recognised in the literature that while these may have owed something to the adoption of Thomas Paine's principles among the lower orders, the immediate causes of the rioting were a series of grievances, mainly of a local nature, as in Lanark where the magistrates had recently feued out some burgh land. Even in Edinburgh, where the crowd targeted Henry Dundas, Edinburgh's Member of Parliament and William Pitt's Scottish political overlord, and James Stirling, provost of the city, one investigator into the causes of the riot was convinced that they were unconnected with French 'levelling ideas', and instead that they had been precipitated by the appearance of troops on the streets.[120] Burning effigies of Henry Dundas might signify dissatisfaction with government and its policies, and in particular with the steep increase in the excise on beer imposed in 1789 (which would explain why the supervisor of the excise was another object of the crowd's fury). It does not necessarily signify a demand for universal suffrage, support for which seems to have been variable. There were reports from Glasgow that effigies of both Thomas Wilkes and Thomas Paine were burned during this period.[121]

However, periodically beforehand, but much more so from around 1780, the king's birthday became a scene of major and sometimes uncontrollable disorder. Fatalities too began to be reported. On the rare occasions when the day did not end in riot and disorder, it was considered by the authorities to be a matter of self-congratulation. Equally, outbreaks of crowd violence which were more serious than king's birthday riots were judged to be extraordinarily dangerous. Ironically, the most terrifying monarch's birthday disturbances happened in the years after *c*. 1810, when burgh provosts and councils attempted stealthily to withdraw their support for the event. As early as 1784, during the Haig's distillery riot, soldiers had turned on the crowd and killed somebody. At least one person died during the June 1792 disturbance in Edinburgh. In 1802 in Aberdeen, four people lost their lives while many more were injured during a confrontation with the Ross and Cromarty Rangers. Worse was to come and in Glasgow in 1819, a massive bonfire was set alight near the city's medieval heart, the Saltmarket, fuelled by timber taken from roofs and old houses as well as carts, police boxes, lamp posts, sign posts, full tar barrels and anything else which was combustible. The episode was brought to a halt by the use of water hoses but not before some looting of shops had taken place. In 1821 'the proceedings of the *mob*', it was reported, were 'as violent and as uncontrollable ... as have been experienced here'. Not only was the authority of the lord provost and magistrates 'derided and defied', roared the *Glasgow Courier*, 'but their persons as well as the persons of the military, were most grossly insulted, severely beaten and bruised'. An unknown number of fatalities and numerous injuries resulted when a bridge at Glasgow Green collapsed under the weight of citizens fleeing from a cavalry charge.[122]

It can be deduced from what has just been said that the issues which lit the short fuse which led to explosive crowd activity in Scotland after *c*. 1780 were similar to those which were examined earlier. A strong sense of a 'moral economy' clearly survived early industrialisation and rapid urbanisation. This was a code of behaviour which the authorities understood, even if their inclination was to scuttle it in favour of the market economy. What they had greater difficulty dealing with was what seemed to be an increase in wanton, aimless violence, and what was believed to be a growing volume of crime against property. Historians however have greater difficulty in arriving at firm conclusions on crime levels. The methodological difficulties in creating time series for crime, and then interpreting them, are considerable.[123] More committals can simply mean that more police were employed, and in Scotland each of the main urban centres established formal police forces by private act of parliament between 1795 (Aberdeen) and 1824 (Dundee).[124] Highly relevant to the period in question is the suggestion that in some counties procurators fiscal had insufficient funds to prosecute suspected criminals. Those involved in riots, thefts and assaults were said to have been escaping with 'impunity' in Peebleshire in 1821, for example.[125] With different legal systems and criminal codes in England and Scotland, it is difficult to make satisfactory cross-border comparisons. However, although there was a disproportionately low number of hangings in Scotland, a recent study has concluded that in the first decades of the nineteenth century Scots were less likely to have their sentences commuted. The figures tend to confirm the hard-headedness of the Scottish bench observed earlier and 'do not indicate any squeamishness on the part of the Scottish judiciary', who were determined to hand down exemplary punishments.[126]

For single years or short periods it is relatively easy to establish the scale and significance of riot and disorder which appears to have had little or no connection with either the moral economy or political radicalism (to be discussed in the next chapter). Burgh and police court records from the early nineteenth century reveal an extraordinarily rich menu of minor criminal activity, which could range from leaving a shop door open at night, through the case of William McDowell and his wife who were charged in Glasgow in 1813 with 'Singing and causing a crowd in the street', to gang fighting.[127] Squabbles between neighbours, arguments and fights between couples – Matthew Watson was accused of throwing herring brine over his wife – and dogs which had been allowed to run wild were also matters for the burgh constables. So too was wife-beating, a practice from which no social class was immune, but which according to the evidence of cases brought to court in Glasgow, became increasingly common among textile workers and the unskilled.[128] Not surprisingly given the responsibility the first police forces had for ensuring that the inhabitants of towns obeyed local bye-laws concerned with lighting, paving and sanitation, offences over these loom large in the figures. In Dundee in the two years from 1828 until 1830, for example, breaches of the burgh's statutes accounted for 31.7 per cent of all offences dealt with by the police court. The largest single category of offence however was described as 'riotous and disorderly conduct and assault', which accounted for 51.3 per cent of all cases dealt with.[129] Evidence from Glasgow suggests that the work of the burgh court increased, from 464 cases in 1812 to 1,028 in 1820.

Even allowing for the pitfalls in compiling and interpreting crime statistics, such few figures as are available do support contemporary impressions. Indictment rates for serious crimes, non-violent rather than violent, and tried in the High Court of Justiciary, do appear to have risen faster in the west of Scotland than the national rate of population increase between the mid-eighteenth century and 1815.[130] What can also be discerned is a steeply rising rate from the mid-1780s, peaking sharply in 1792. Figures for the whole of Scotland record an annual average of 187 precognitions between 1815–19 (precognitions measure the investigation rate rather than the crime rate), which almost doubled to 349 *per annum* between 1825–29. High Court trials rose from thirty or forty each year in the 1810s to 302 in 1830. The growth rate in precognitions was fastest in the period 1812–20, and was almost certainly linked to the dislocation of the post-Napoleonic Wars period. To some extent this is supported by the increase in the proportion of crimes against property that were investigated, which rose from around half of the total in 1810 to three-quarters by 1830.[131] Most were cases of theft, mainly of money, food and clothing. Generally too they involved relatively small values, and one-third of those suspected were females, a higher proportion than were involved in all serious crimes. Not surprisingly, the highest rates tended to be in counties in which there were large manufacturing towns.[132]

Of growing concern however was crime in the countryside. By the 1820s some of this was spilling over from the manufacturing centres. Thus in June 1821 'idle persons from Glasgow' were thought to have been responsible for setting fire to a large plantation at Cadder estate.[133] In the following decade highway robberies were complained of on 'all roads leading into Glasgow', while orchards and plantations 'for several miles around' were:

> continually plundered, broken down, and destroyed, by crowds of persons who come out of the City, particularly on Sundays, often armed with guns, or in a state of intoxification, and in such numbers, as completely to overawe all attempts at individual resistance.

Similar complaints were to be heard elsewhere, with organised gangs operating in some places.[134] The problems faced by Game Associations, established from 1805 in some counties, were not dissimilar, with textile workers and coal miners being among those found guilty of poaching in Fife.[135] Indeed it was the counties in Scotland which took the lead in establishing regular police forces in the early nineteenth century, principally to combat the twin evils of vagrancy and crime.[136] But the inhabitants of the countryside too were contributing to the discomfort which was felt by some of those who were in the driving seat of change in the Lowland agrarian economy.

The dominant view of the Scottish countryside during the period 1780–1830 is one of relative social stability. In one important respect this is a perfectly valid judgement. In Lowland Scotland there was none of the mass peasant action which was so much a feature of Irish rural society after 1760.[137] Cottars cleared from Lowland farms were usually able to find some alternative means of subsistence in the rural villages and the manufacturing towns. That living standards of agricultural workers were rising prior to the mid-1790s further helped to soften the blow of compulsory expulsion and 'eased the transition to a new economic and social order.' There was 'pain, anxiety, insecurity' and misery, detectable to the modern ear in those Burns poems which rage against the sufferings of the small tenant farmer, but, it is argued, what is most remarkable is the virtual absence of overt opposition to the spectacular transformation of rural Lowland Scotland, and the existence of only 'scattered acts of [covert] activity'.[138]

But given the favourable conditions just outlined, and the powers of the Scottish landed class and their domination of a legal system which showed little mercy to those the judiciary found guilty, it seems reasonable to ask if a different response should have been expected. As in parts of Ireland levels of 'intense and current violence' were extraordinary, this particular comparator is bound to exaggerate the degree of Scottish quiescence.[139] In addition, the piecemeal nature of change noted earlier militated against large-scale opposition on the part of cottars and sub-tenants bereft of rights, especially as they could maintain something of a foothold in the countryside if they found accommodation and employment in the rural villages. But what of those who remained in the countryside itself, or indeed the proletarianised agricultural workers just referred to, who had access only to small plots of land for their own use, or none at all, the wage-labourers, handloom weavers and rural artisans of the settlements, villages and towns which lay within or skirted the agricultural districts? They too were subject to the workings of the market economy and the demands of the new system, and, in times of distress, could be moved to take direct action.

This was clearly evident in the grain-exporting counties such as Dumfries, Angus and Perthshire. In 1795 a crowd of several hundred, led by a piper, marched from Longtown in Cumberland to the port of Annan in Dumfriesshire in an effort to stop the shipment of grain. Steps had been taken however to distribute grain in the parishes in the region, and the leaders of the meal mob were arrested by soldiers, imprisoned and subject to lengthy interrogation. As a result, it was reported, 'They were so effectually frightened' that it was highly unlikely that 'they will ever adventure upon a similar exploit'.[140] Pro-active paternalism allied to the use of state-backed terror were powerful weapons where the crushing of open confrontation was concerned. Thus resort was necessarily had to nocturnal raids on the yards and even the houses of landowners and substantial tenant farmers. A case of this kind occurred in the Carse of Gowrie in 1800, when 'Dundee people', acting in concert with workmen from Rossie estate, had burned an effigy of a grain exporter and attempted to set fires alight in certain farm yards. In order to prevent further disturbance however, discipline was to be exercised less openly but equally effectively: those estate employees suspected of being guilty would simply be removed at the end of their terms, 'the quietest way of getting rid of them'.[141]

What is at issue then is the extent of covert acts of resentment of this sort. As we might expect, few cases appear in sheriff court records for the period in question.[142] Notwithstanding the counties' early start in policing, few had a police force in 1830; it was during that decade that most acted, and none was established in Lanarkshire until 1857. Thus, as in the first half of the eighteenth century, most incidents were undetected, and there was no systematic way of reporting them. Impressionistic evidence then has to bear the burden of proof, as in December 1819 when the duke of Hamilton was informed that 'an immense number of depredations' had been committed in Hamilton and its neighbourhood but 'without the slightest trace of the offenders being discerned'.[143] Judging from reports in newspapers and other incidental references that can be found, there *appears* to have been an increase in covert rural crime, some of which comes into the category of protest. In order to make this distinction the evidence which survives requires to be interrogated sensitively, distinguishing, for example, between acts of need like the still widespread practice of stealing wood from enclosures, and what were more likely to have been communal acts of revenge, as happened in Perthshire in 1801 and 1802, when John Hagart lost at least two avenues of established trees which were 'most maliciously cut down and destroyed' by disgruntled parishioners.[144]

However it is categorised, two tentative conclusions can be drawn from what is admittedly scanty hard evidence of rural misdemeanours. The first is that they tended to be concentrated within periods of general distress or political excitement. Thus early in 1801 the *Dundee Magazine* claimed that it had had reports from various parts of the country of raids on farms, the stealing of fowls and grain, and arson attacks.[145] Another flurry of reports of disorder and incendiarism can be identified around Glasgow in 1819 and 1820.[146] The second is that at least in parts of rural Scotland there was considerable animosity between landowners, tenant farmers and agricultural servants.

The social fissures in the rural Lowlands were nowhere more clearly exposed than during the anti-militia disturbances of the autumn months of 1797. However, that these were less deep, of a different character and not tainted with Defenderism or combined with other underlying issues as they were in Ireland, is partly demonstrated by the fact that during the Irish anti-militia disturbances of 1793 something in the region of 230 lives were lost, some as a result of shootings by the resisters, as opposed to eleven in Scotland, all of whom were shot by troops.[147] The Scottish Militia Act had been passed in July, with the compulsory levy, by ballot, of men aged between nineteen and twenty-three, being designed to strengthen Britain's defences against French invasion. Attempts to implement the Act however were met with widespread opposition throughout most of Lowland Scotland, in large and small towns and villages, and in Highland Perthshire. Much of this was violent, so much so that lists compiled by schoolmasters with the names of those to be balloted were destroyed and the recruiting process was interrupted and delayed.[148]

The precise causes of the strength of popular feeling against the militia are difficult to unravel. Various explanations were given by those involved: opposition to compulsory military service and to the ballot which would determine who served, the harm which would be done to household economies by the absence of a key contributor, and objections in some quarters to defending the privileges and property of the rich. There are suggestions too that the radical United Scotsmen, formed in 1796 or early in 1797 and modelled along the lines of the United Irishmen, may have played a part by inflating popular fears about the effect of the measure, although it would seem more likely that what the United Scotsmen did was push the resistance movement eastwards, into Cupar in Fife, for example, and into the rural areas.[149] Whatever the motives of those who congregated outside church doors to oppose the Militia Act, those charged with implementing it, the lords and deputy lieutenants of the counties, were quickly made aware of how dangerous was the undercurrent of latent hostility. At Ingleston, Captain Maitland was advised not to call out the yeomanry to put a stop to rioting there as most of those concerned were 'our own servants', who would know personally who was involved in suppressing them. Our lives and property, wrote one concerned tenant farmer, 'are continually in their mercy' and, should the servants act against them, they would easily evade detection by that 'most diabolical' act, 'wilful Fire Raising'. Elsewhere such threats were carried out. On the outskirts of Glasgow, Garscube House was attacked.[150] It was not that the 'country people' who played such a large part in the disturbances were uninflammable but rather that their protests were limited to a demand for the *status quo*. To defuse the situation the authorities had to adopt the usual mix of force and compromise. English troops were called in, although in insufficient numbers at first and in Lanark the duke of Hamilton had to suspend the execution of the Act. In some Glasgow parishes arrangements were made to raise money to offer bounties to those who agreed to be balloted.[151] Trials of the ring-leaders were held from August into the following spring, but after the first exemplary punishments were handed down by Lord Braxfield, most juries were inclined to be lenient, although on Iona the duke of Argyll removed tenants who had refused – with violent means – to release their sons for militia duty.[152]

Where there is greater unanimity among historians is that in the Highlands there was considerable open opposition to the changes brought about by the greater commercialisation of Highland estates. Again, this was less marked or severe than in Ireland, but much more common than was once believed.[153] But the scale, speed and nature of the transformation in the Highlands and Western Islands resulted too in cultural disorientation. In part and in ways which are difficult to link directly with the material changes in the region, one reaction in large parts of gaeldom was to seek solace in evangelical religion and spiritual poetry. Resented and resisted at first, SSPCK-sponsored Presbyterianism made greater progress after it had begun to countenance the use of Gaelic in its schools, and in 1767 published a Gaelic version of the new testament. *Na Daoine* (the 'Men'), elders and lay preachers whose impact was first felt in Easter Ross in the 1740s, formed a charismatic elite who succeeded the tacksmen in providing communal leadership, and provided a strict puritanical code which gave hope, comfort and the promise of salvation in a world wracked by insecurity, anxiety and fear of starvation. Unlike the emigrants of the eighteenth century, after 1815 the displaced could not easily find refuge overseas, unless they had financial assistance. What Professor Devine has termed a 'religious revolution' swept the Highlands, manifested in a series of revivals which between the 1790s and the early 1830s erupted in parts of Highland Perthshire, Arran, Skye and Lewis.[154] The intensity of religious experience in the last-named is conveyed in reports of believers being 'seized with spasms, convulsions, fits, and screaming aloud'. Southern missionaries, 'preaching an open evangelical gospel tinged with Painite ideas about the dignity of man', further excited religious enthusiasm as they swept north – as far as Orkney and Shetland – and west into the Hebrides between the 1790s and 1830s.[155]

While the resort to religion almost certainly numbed the pain of dispossession and in some communities channelled anger away from thoughts of temporal revenge, mostly this happened later, after 1792, the 'Year of the Sheep'. This was a watershed event in Highland history, the culmination of years of small-scale and largely unreported resistance to the introduction of sheep. One of the first incidents had taken place in 1782, when a party of women had beaten up a sheep farmer at Letterfinlay in Inverness-shire.[156] The clash of 1792 was a remarkable confrontation between, on the one side, hundreds of the small tenantry from numerous parishes in the counties of Ross and Inverness threatened by removal to make way for sheep, and, on the other, a large body of landowners intent on opening their estates to sheep farming. The intention of the 'Insurgents' was no less than to drive out all of the sheep from the counties of Ross and Sutherland, in the cause of land rights at a time of intense social dislocation, rising rents and subsistence difficulties. Government in London and the Lord Advocate in Edinburgh, fearful that something more sinister may have inspired the insurrection, were outraged at what has been described as 'the greatest threat to order in the Highlands since the Jacobite Rebellion'.[157] Troops were rushed into the region and by early in August (the first disturbances had taken place in June) the rising – notable for the relative absence of violence – had been crushed. But despite public antipathy in the south to the policies and actions of the landowners, the way was opened for more sheep farms; thereafter opposition to sheep farming was partly driven underground and often manifested itself in theft or maiming. Illicit whisky distillation was another means of maintaining a livelihood on an inland holding and, where landowners were not themselves benefiting indirectly from the trade, of defying authority. In turn however, after the Excise Act of 1823 had reduced the cost advantages of illicit distilling, peasant distillers too were turned off, replaced in some cases by licensed producers.[158]

Overt confrontations continued to occur, but unlike the Ross-shire rising, they tended to be localised. Tenants had little or no bargaining power, and not having access to arms or, as loyal subjects, much inclination to take them up, they usually dispersed when faced by troops. Fort George, constructed at massive expense in the aftermath of the '45, but too late to be of much use for combating Jacobites, found a purpose as a base for the defence of agrarian capitalism in the north. Even so, on some estates, notably that managed by the marchioness of Stafford, large-scale clashes between factors, sheep farmers and shepherds, sometimes accompanied by sheriff's officers, and the tenants who were to be cleared, could be ugly, bloody and violent. As in the case of some forms of Lowland protest, ritual humiliation played its part, as where officers were stripped naked and threatened with fire or drowning by crowds in which women often took the lead.[159] In 1820 and 1821 clearances in Culrain, Ross-shire, and Sutherland respectively, were only effected with the use of guns and swords.[160]

Notes

1 Berg, *Age of Manufactures*, 57–76.
2 C. A. Whatley, 'The experience of work', in Devine and Mitchison, *People and Society*, 232.
3 T. Clarke and T. Dickson, 'Class and class consciousness in early industrial capitalism: Paisley, 1770–1850', in T. Dickson (ed.), *Capital and Class in Scotland* (Edinburgh, 1982), 17.
4 Devine, 'The English connection and Irish-Scottish development', 20.
5 R. Owen, *A New View of Society and Other Writings* (London, 1966 ed.), 26–7.
6 J. Butt, 'Labour and industrial relations', 142–5.
7 University of Dundee Archives (DUA), MS 11/5/14, C. Mackie, 'History of flax spinning from 1806 to 1866'; Whatley, 'Experience of work', 242; 'Women and the economic transformation of Scotland', 34; Aitken MacKinnon Papers, recollections of John MacKinnon, Carnbroe Ironworks, December 1858. Transcript kindly lent to me by T. C. Smout.
8 Whatley, 'Collier serfdom', 32.
9 For a discussion of this and related problems, see P. Sharpe (ed.) *Women's Work: The English Experience, 1650–1914* (London, 1998), 1–17, 26–8.
10 Whatley, 'Labour in the industrialising city', 368; *Historical Manuscripts Commission 67: MS of Lord Polwarth, Vol V, 1725–1780* (1961), Letter, Sir James Hall to the Earl of Marchmont, n.d., 1737, 3.
11 Whatley, 'Labour in the industrialising city, 367; see too M. Berg, 'What difference did women's work make to the industrial revolution?', *History Workshop Journal*, XXXV (1993), 26–31; Sinclair, *Analysis*, I, 323–34.
12 D. Valenze, *The First Industrial Woman* (Oxford, 1995), 90–1.
13 Murray, *The Scottish Hand Loom Weavers*, 28–31.
14 *Ibid.*, 244–6; Bolin-Hort, *Work, Family and the State*, 54; A. Clark, *The Struggle for the Breeches: Gender and the Making of the British Working Class* (Berkeley and Los Angeles, California, 1997 ed.), 21.
15 PKCA, PE 51/60, 'Petition to the Sheriff, of Messrs Young, Ross, Richardson & Co.', 1808, PE 51/17, 'Petition of Messrs Young, Ross, Richardson & Co., calico printers at Ruthven', 1810, PE 51/228, 'Petition to Sheriff of Perthshire, Messrs Carruthers, Wylie & Co., cotton and linen printers at Cromwell Park', 1804; see too Highland Regional Archives, Inverness Burgh Records, CTI/IB/9/113, Bundle, 'Indentures and related documents, 1787–1799'.

16 Whatley, 'Labour in the industrialising city', 371.

17 I. Donnachie and G. Hewitt, *Historic New Lanark: The Dale and Owen Industrial Community since 1785* (Edinburgh, 1993), 37–9.

18 Withers, *Urban Highlanders*, 134–7; Tyson, 'Demographic change', 196.

19 Whatley, 'Labour in the industrialising city', 366–7.

20 M. Mitchell, *The Irish in the West of Scotland, 1797–1848: Trade Unions, Strikes and Political Movements* (Edinburgh, 1998), 20–1.

21 See B. E. Collins, 'Aspects of Irish immigration into two Scottish towns (Dundee and Paisley) by the mid-nineteenth century' (unpublished M.Phil. thesis, University of Edinburgh, 1979); Collins, 'The origins of Irish immigration to Scotland in the nineteenth and twentieth centuries', in T. M. Devine (ed.), *Irish Immigration and Scottish Society* (Edinburgh, 1991), 5–6.

22 Young, 'Rural independent artisan production', 30–1; see, for example, PKCA, Judicial Papers, PE 51/17, 'Petition of Stewart Scales, tenant at Nether Durdy, to the sheriff', March 1811.

23 W. Sloan, 'The supply of labour for cotton spinning in Glasgow, c. 1780–1836' (unpublished B.A. Honours dissertation, University of Strathclyde, 1980), 48; Whatley, 'The experience of work', 235–9; Fraser, *Conflict and Class*, 131.

24 For fuller discussion, see Knox, *Industrial Nation*, 6–10.

25 NAS, Court of Session cases, I. Inglis B6/7, 'Journeymen bookbinders v. masters', 1812.

26 PKCA, PE 59/29/149, 'Declaration of Alexander Cuthbert and other journeymen smiths, servants to W. Gray', 1803.

27 Whatley, 'An uninflammable people?', 58; G. Houston, 'Labour relations in Scottish agriculture before 1870', *Agricultural History Review*, VI (1958), 34–41.

28 DUA, MS 15/114/2, Diary of Thomas Handyside Baxter, 1829–30, 1 January 1830.

29 SRA, Pamphlets series, 'State of the conjoined processes, Alexander Ferguson and ors. v. the magistrates and town council of Glasgow', 1783.

30 Withers, *Urban Highlanders*, 61–83.

31 See DCA, GD/X99/10, 'Memoir of Alexander Moncur', September 1869; Aitken MacKinnon Papers.

32 DUA, MS 15/114/2, Diary of Thomas Handyside Baxter, 1829–30, 21 June 1830.

33 C. Behagg, 'Narratives of control: informalism and the workplace in Britain, 1800–1900', in O. Ashton, R. Fyson and S. Roberts (eds), *The Duty of Discontent: Essays for Dorothy Thompson* (London, 1995), 132.

34 Campbell, *The Lanarkshire Miners*, 36–8; W. Thom, *Rhymes and Recollections of a Handloom Weaver* (London, 1845), 14–15; see too Murray, *The Scottish Hand Loom Weavers*, 168–72.

35 Brown, *Religion and Society*, 83.

36 Donnachie, 'Drink and society', 10–14.

37 See, for example, A. Somerville, *Autobiography of a Working Man* (London, 1951 ed.), chapters III–XI.

38 Fraser, *Conflict and Class*, 55–6, 64–5, 78; 'Patterns of protest', in Devine and Mitchison, *People and Society*, 279–81.

39 See A. M. Smith, *The Nine Trades of Dundee* (Dundee, 1995), 35–8, 52–3.

40 R. Mitchison, 'The poor law', in Devine and Mitchison, *People and Society*, 254–6.

41 Campbell, *The Lanarkshire Miners*, 76; C. Emsley, *British Society and the French Wars, 1793–1815* (London, 1979), 6; see too the changing tone of some weavers' poetry in T. Leonard (ed.), *Radical Renfrew: Poetry from the French Revolution to the First World War* (Edinburgh, 1990); and W. Finlayson, *Simple Scottish Rhymes* (Paisley, 1815), 'Saunders and John', 119–26 .

42 *Dundee Magazine*, May 1815, 445–6.

43 Fraser, *Conflict and Class*, 79.

44 NLS, Cadell Papers, Acc. 5381, Box 12/1, Minutes of the River Forth Coal Proprietors, 10 January 1776.

45 Duckham, *History of the Scottish Coal Industry*, 271–3; A. Campbell, *The Lanarkshire Miners: A Social History of their Trade Unions, 1775–1974* (Edinburgh, 1979), 13–17.

46 *Dundee, Perth and Cupar Advertiser*, 29 May 1807; NAS, JC8/5, High Court Minute Books, 1806–8, 'Information for James Taylor, James Thomson, William Dawson and James Mackle, journeymen paper makers v. Archibald Colquhoun, HM Advocate', 1808.

47 Campbell, *The Lanarkshire Miners*, 77.

48 SRA, T – MJ, Minute Book, Association of Master Cotton Spinners, Glasgow, 1810–11.

49 Fraser, 'Patterns of protest', 281; *Conflict and Class*, 79.

50 Dundee, *Perth and Cupar Advertiser*, 10 June 1814.

51 Z. G. Brassay, 'The cotton spinners in Glasgow and the west of Scotland, *c.* 1790–1840' (unpublished M.Litt. thesis, University of Strathclyde, 1974), 7–8; Donnachie and Hewitt, *Historic New Lanark*, 35–58; *Glasgow Courier*, 8 July 1819.

52 Fraser, *Conflict and Class*, 85–96.

53 *Ibid.*, 98–9.

54 NAS, Lord Advocates Papers, AD 14/13/14, 'Precognition as to Wishaw town disturbances', 1813.

55 J. A. Hassan, 'The landed estate, paternalism and the coal industry in Midlothian, 1800–1880', *Scottish Historical Review*, LIX (April 1980), 79–80.

56 See Anon., *Observations on the Laws Relating to the Colliers in Scotland* (Glasgow, 1825); and SRA, T – MJ 100, 'Sederunt book of the cotton spinners and other manufacturers', 1816; Campbell, *The Lanarkshire Miners*, 72–3; Whatley, 'Labour in the industrialising city', 377.

57 NAS, Lord Advocate's Papers, AD14/23/241, George Salmond to Crown Agent, 23 April 1823, George Salmond to Crown Agent, 6 August 1823.

58 Murray, *The Scottish Hand Loom Weavers*, 191; Campbell, *The Lanarkshire Miners*, 74–6; Mitchell, *The Irish in the West of Scotland*, 33.

59 Houston, 'The demographic regime, 12–14; Tyson, 'Demographic change', 199.

60 Ward, 'Textile trade unionism', 138.

61 A. Thomson, *Maryhill 1750–1894* (Glasgow, 1895), 16–17.

62 Anon., *Observations on the Laws Relating to the Colliers*, 63.
63 Brassay, 'The cotton spinners in Glasgow', 41.
64 Campbell, *The Lanarkshire Miners*, 62, 74.
65 See Knox, *Industrial Nation*, chapters 13–18.
66 J. T. Ward, 'Textile trade unionism in nineteenth-century Scotland', in Butt and Ponting, *Scottish Textile History*, 134–6.
67 Whatley, 'Labour in the industrialising city', 377.
68 Smout, *History of the Scottish People*, 420–30; Murray, *The Scottish Hand Loom Weavers*, 194–7; Ward, 'Textile trade unionism', 130–1, 137.
69 Treble, 'The standard of living', 203–6.
70 W. H. Fraser, 'The Glasgow cotton spinners, 1837', in Butt and Ward, *Scottish Themes*, 80.
71 Brassay, 'The cotton spinners in Glasgow', 117.
72 NAS, Lord Advocates Papers, AD 14/25/192, 'Case against John Kean and others', 1825.
73 Leonard, *Radical Renfrew*, 8–9; see too C. A. Whatley, 'Sound and song in the ritual of popular protest: continuity and the Glasgow "nob songs" of 1825', in E. J. Cowan (ed.), *The Ballad in Scotland* (provisional title, East Linton, forthcoming); NAS, Lord Advocate's Papers, AD 14/23/241, Petition of Procurator-Fiscal to Sheriff-Depute of Lanark, 31 July 1823.
74 NAS, Lord Advocates Papers, AD 14/17/163, 'Declaration of Benjamin McKall', 'Information for Thomas Veitch', 7 November 1817; Murray, *The Scottish Hand Loom Weavers*, 190; Ward, 'Textile trade unionism', 135–7.
75 See *ibid.*, 132, 136; for the rejection of this approach in the case of salters and colliers, see Whatley, *Scottish Salt Industry*, chapter 5; and Whatley, 'Scottish "collier serfs" in the 17th and 18th centuries', 248–51.
76 Anon., *Statement by the Proprietors of Cotton Works in Glasgow and Vicinity* (Glasgow, 1825), with which is bound Anon., *Case of the Operative Cotton Spinners in Glasgow*, 8, 13–27; Mitchell, *The Irish in the West of Scotland*, 33.
77 Fraser, *Conflict and Class*, 131–8.
78 W. H. Fraser, 'Owenite socialism in Scotland', *Scottish Economic & Social History*, XVI (1996), 60–80.
79 For the 'compartmentalist' case, see Smout, *History of the Scottish People*, 440–8; and a measured rebuttal, T. Clarke and T. Dickson, 'The birth of class?', in Devine and Mitchison, *People and Society*, 294–5.
80 Anon., *Case of the Operative Cotton Spinners of Glasgow*, 23–4; Clark, *The Struggle for the Breeches*, 20.
81 Clarke and Dickson, 'Class and class consciousness', 21–33.
82 SRA, Papers concerning Lochwinnoch Mill, T – MJ, 320/1, 'Old Mill, 12 March 1822: Regulations of spinners regarding piecers'; NAS, Lord Advocates Papers, AD 14/20/60, 'Precognitions in the case of the Milngavie riots', 1820.
83 *Glasgow Courier*, 13 July 1822, 4 May 1824; E. McFarland, *Protestants First: Orangeism in 19th Century Scotland* (Edinburgh, 1990), 47–55; Mitchell, *The Irish in the West of Scotland*, 4–5; Strawhorn, *History of Irvine*, 116.
84 Clark, *The Struggle for the Breeches*, 5.

85 NAS, Hamilton of Pencaitland MSS, RH 15/119/16/11, 'Memorandum concerning Pencaitland colliery', September 1803.

86 For the distinctiveness of this in Scotland see Young, *Women and Popular Struggles*, 60–70.

87 *Glasgow Courier*, 11 September 1824; see too Clark, *The Struggle for the Breeches*, 26–7, 203–19.

88 *Ibid.*, 33.

89 Murray, *The Scottish Hand Loom Weavers*, 172–3; *Regulations for the Master of Police of the Barony of Gorbals* (Glasgow, 1809); SRA, B3/1/1/1, Glasgow Police Court Records, 28 January–3 July 1813, 14 February 1813; Senex, *Glasgow, Past and Present* (Glasgow, 1849), Volume I, 261; J. J. Dunstone, *Reminiscences of Glasgow* (Glasgow, 1874), 15.

90 Brown, *Religion and Society*, 80; DCA, Acc 12/2/1, Forfarshire JP Minute Book, 1791–1828, 10 June 1800; Penny, *Traditions of Perth*, 38–41; E. I. Spence, *Sketches of the Present Manners, Customs and Scenery of Scotland* (1811), Volume I, 97; *Glasgow Mercury*, 19 July 1791, *Glasgow Courier*, 28 November 1824.

91 *Glasgow Courier*, 17 July 1824; L. Leneman and R. Mitchison, *Girls in Trouble: Sexuality and Social Control in Rural Scotland, 1660–1780* (Edinburgh, 1998), 96.

92 Whatley, 'Royal day, people's day', 184–5.

93 Aitken MacKinnon Papers; W. J. Milne, *Reminiscences of an Old Boy: Being Autobiographical Sketches of Scottish Rural Life from 1832 to 1856* (Forfar, 1901), 23; Somerville, *The Autobiography of a Working Man*, 42–3.

94 N. Tranter, 'Schooling and literacy in early nineteenth century Scotland: some additional evidence and its implications', *Scottish Economic & Social History*, XVII (1997), 34–40.

95 Murray, *The Scottish Hand Loom Weavers*, 173.

96 R. D. Anderson, *Scottish Education Since the Reformation* (Glasgow, 1997), 9, 27; Withrington, 'Schooling, literacy and society', 183–5; Tranter, 'Schooling and literacy', 31.

97 Walker, 'Urban form', 60–7; Maver, 'Urbanisation', 161–3.

98 Strawhorn, *The History of Ayr*, 132–40; see too *History of Irvine*, 116–17.

99 Nenadic, 'The middle ranks', 285–91; DUA, MS 15/114/2, 1829–30, 30 June 1830.

100 W. H. Fraser and I. Maver, 'The social problems of the city', in Fraser and Maver (eds), *Glasgow, Volume II; 1830–1912* (Manchester, 1996), 352.

101 Flinn, *Scottish Population History*, 389.

102 *Ibid.*, 369–70.

103 T. M. Devine, 'The urban crisis', in Devine and Jackson, *Glasgow*, 408–9; R. Mitchison, 'The poor law', in Devine and Mitchison, *People and Society*, 257–66; 'Who were the poor in Scotland?', in Mitchison and Roebuck, *Economy and Society*, 145.

104 Rev. G. Lewis, *The Filth and Fever Bills of Dundee, and What Might be Made of Them* (Dundee, 1841), 3.

105 R. Rodger, 'Employment, wages and poverty in the Scottish cities, 1841–1914', in G. Gordon (ed.), *Perspectives of the Scottish City* (Aberdeen, 1985), 28–41.

106 J. Cleland, *Enumeration of the Inhabitants of the City of Glasgow* (Glasgow, 1820), 1–4; Devine, 'Urban crisis', 410–12.

107 Scone Palace, Perth, Mansfield Papers, Box 106/2, Robert Jamieson to the Earl of Mansfield, 15 October 1824.

108 Whatley, 'Women and the economic transformation of Scotland', 34–5.

109 NRA(S), Hamilton of Lennoxlove Papers, TD 94/57/797, Lord Liverpool to Duke of Hamilton, 18 November 1819.

110 Leneman and Mitchison, *Sin in the City*, 35–6; *Sexuality and Social Control*, 144–5.

111 Brown, *Religion and Society*, 72.

112 R. Heron, *Observations Made in a Journey through the Western Counties of Scotland in the Autumn of 1792* (Perth, 1793), Volume II, 381; Leneman and Mitchison, *Sin in the City*, 48–9; Brown, *Religion and Society*, 95–6.

113 See Bohstedt, *Riots and Community Politics*; C. A. Whatley, 'The making of "Juteopolis" – and how it was', in C. A. Whatley (ed.), *The Remaking of Juteopolis, Dundee, c. 1891–1991* (Dundee, 1992), 11.

114 PKCA, Perth Burgh Records, B59/32/63, Provost of Aberdeen to magistrates of Perth, 2 March 1783.

115 NLS, Stuart Stevenson Papers, MS 5391, fo. 150, Lord Chancellor to A. Stuart, 2 March 1800.

116 NAS, Grant of Monymusk MSS, GD 248/699/4, George Robertson, provost of Banff, to James Grant, 16 February 1800; Logue, *Popular Disturbances*, 30–1, 36–7; E. McFarland, *Ireland and Scotland in the Age of Revolution: Planting the Green Bough* (Edinburgh, 1994), 216–9.

117 *Dundee, Perth and Cupar Advertiser*, 6 June 1817; NAS, Lord Advocates Papers, AD 14/20/147, 'Papers regarding king's birthday riot in Aberdeen', 24 April 1820.

118 Allan, *Rambling Rhymes*, 97–100.

119 Fry, *The Dundas Despotism*, 167.

120 W. H. Meikle, *Scotland and the French Revolution* (New York, 1969 ed.), 81–3; Smout, *History of the Scottish People*, 444.

121 Anon., *An Impartial Account of the Conduct of the Excise Towards the Breweries in Scotland Particularly Edinburgh; Pointing out the Beneficial Effects of the New Mode of Survey* (Edinburgh, 1791); NAS, RH2/4.209, fos 3–8, 'Riot in Edinburgh, anonymous memorandum', n.d; Penny, *Traditions of Perth*, 39; Smout, *History of the Scottish People*, 444; Whatley, 'Royal day, people's day', 183.

122 Whatley, 'The privilege which the rabble have', 94; *Glasgow Courier*, 5 June 1819, 24, 26 April 1821.

123 See V. A. C. Gatrell and T. B. Hadden, 'Criminal statistics and their interpretation', in E. A. Wrigley (ed.), *Nineteenth-Century Society* (Cambridge, 1972), 372–8.

124 Carson and Idzikowska, 'The social production of Scottish policing', 271.

125 M. A. Crowther, Crime, prosecution and mercy: English influence and Scottish practice in the early nineteenth century', in S. J. Connolly (ed.), *Kingdoms United? Great Britain and Ireland Since 1500: Integration and Diversity* (Dublin, 1998), 234.

126 *Ibid.*, 233.

127 SRA, B3/1/1/1, Police Court Records, 28 January to 3 July 1813, 30 June 1813.

128 Derived from Clark, *The Struggle for the Breeches*, 76.

129 Calculated from DCA, Dundee Police Board Minutes, 1824–32, 'Comparative view of the numbers and description of cases from this and the previous year', 12 July 1830.

130 A. M. Kilday, 'Women and crime', chapter 7.

131 I. Donnachie, '"The darker side": a speculative survey of Scottish crime during the first half of the nineteenth century', *Scottish Economic & Social History*, XV (1995), 5–19.

132 NRA(S), Hamilton of Lennoxlove MSS, TD 94/57/1483, 'Memorial of the noblemen, sheriffs, justices of the peace, magistrates, merchants, bankers, manufacturers and others in Lanarkshire and the adjacent counties of Renfrew, Dumbarton and Stirling', 1838.

133 *Glasgow Courier*, 29 June 1821.

134 For example, PKCA, Petitions, PE 51/281, 'Petition to sheriff of Perthshire from William Cunningham, tacksman of the farms of Goodlyburn and Claypotts', 24 November 1810; PE 51/17, 'Petition to the sheriff of Perthshire from John Rutherford, writer in Perth', 25 November 1811.

135 Donnachie, '"The darker side"', 19.

136 PKCA, Perth Burgh Records, B59/24/1/108 (1) – (7), Letters concerning Game Associations in the counties of Dumfries and Perth, 1807–9; Carson and Idzikowska, 'The social production of Scottish policing', 272–3.

137 Devine, 'Unrest and stability', 127–8.

138 On Burns and agrarian change see J. C. Weston, 'Robert Burns's satire', in R. D. S. Jack and A. Noble (eds), *The Art of Robert Burns* (London, 1982), 36–58; Devine, *The Transformation of Rural Scotland*, 159–60.

139 Devine, *Clanship to Crofters' War*, 210.

140 Scone Palace, Mansfield MSS, Box 111(1), J. Murray to Earl of Mansfield, 11 December 1795.

141 PKCA, Rossie Priory Papers, MS 100 (36), Robert Cranston to Lord Kinnaird, 8 February 1800.

142 Devine, *The Transformation of Rural Scotland*, 158.

143 NRA(S), Hamilton of Lennoxlove MSS, TD 94/57/1477, W. Home to Duke of Hamilton, 28 December 1819.

144 PKCA, Petitions, PE 51/152, 'Petition to the sheriff of Perth from John Hagart of Cairnmuir', 7 February 1801.

145 *Dundee Magazine*, III (1801), 164, 216.

146 *Glasgow Courier*, 16 March, 16 December 1820.

147 McFarland, *Ireland and Scotland*, 164; T. Bartlett, 'The end to moral economy: the Irish militia disturbances of 1793', *Past and Present*, XCIX (May 1983), 41–64.

148 Logue, *Popular Disturbances*, 78–102.

149 McFarland, *Ireland and Scotland*, 166; *Glasgow Courier*, 7 December 1797.

150 NRA(S), 1889, Maitland Family Papers, Bundle 12, J. G. to Captain Maitland, 26 August 1797, Thomas Allan to Captain Maitland, 1 September 1797; Logue, *Popular Disturbances*, 81.

151 *Glasgow Courier*, 29, 31 August, 2, 12 September 1797.

152 Logue, *Popular Disturbances*, 101; MacArthur, *Iona*, 35.
153 See E. Richards, 'How tame were the highlanders during the clearances?', *Scottish Studies*, XVII (1973).
154 Devine, *Clanship to Crofters' War*, 100–9.
155 Brown, *Religion and Society*, 84–92.
156 Richards, *A History of the Highland Clearances*, 249–83; Logue, *Popular Disturbances*, 55–6.
157 Richards, *A History of the Highland Clearances*, 261.
158 T. M. Devine, 'The rise and fall of illicit whisky-making in northern Scotland, *c.* 1780–1840', *Scottish Historical Review*, LIV (1975), 173–5.
159 Richards, *The Leviathan of Wealth*, 213–14.
160 Richards, *A History of the Highland Clearances*, 339, 345–8.

Making and breaking of the Scottish working class

The French Revolution and the 1790s

News of the Revolution in France was at first welcomed, although not acclaimed, in Scotland.[1] Enthusiasm for political reform grew from 1791 after the publication of part one of Thomas Paine's *Rights of Man* in March of that year, and from the summer of 1792 and 1793 Friends of the People societies were founded. Their 'immediate stimulus' however was the House of Commons' refusal to countenance reform of the oligarchical Scottish burghs, which, along with the corrupting effects of political and kirk patronage, had been the main concerns of Scottish reformers in the 1780s. The leadership was drawn from the ranks of Edinburgh lawyers such as Thomas Muir of Huntershill, gentlemen Whigs like John Francis Erskine of Mar, and merchants, small manufacturers and professionals. With enthusiasm for the Friends of the People movement soaring, by the end of 1792 'virtually every town south of Aberdeen had its own parliamentary reform society as did many of the villages of central Scotland'.[2] Popular support for the French revolutionists also appeared to manifest itself in crowd disturbances and the planting in several places of trees of liberty. Alarm grew however as the authorities began to discern a 'levelling spirit' among the lower orders. With the 'September Massacres' in the autumn of 1792 the revolution in France had become more bloody, and therefore more fearsome for the ruling class in Scotland.[3] From Henry Dundas (who was convinced that he had been singled out as a target by radicals) and down through the ranks of the landed, the lawyers and the manufacturing middle classes, some of whom had earlier advocated reform, pressure was exerted on the leaders of the Friends of the People movement to rein in their supporters and to emphasise their loyalty to the constitution and their opposition to riot and disorder. Most were willing to comply. Although a first national convention of the Friends of the People was held in December 1792 in Edinburgh (where the Friends drew most support), increased unease among middle-class reformers caused most of them – but not all, there were exceptions such as the liberal advocate Henry Erskine – to withdraw from the movement altogether.

Intensive intelligence gathering activity conjoined with fierce repressive tactics on the part of the government – from February 1793 at war with France, and legitimately concerned with treasonable speeches and acts – and the arrival in Scotland of English delegates and representatives of the United Irishmen, led to the breaking up of the increasingly radical third convention in December 1793. With Muir having been sentenced to fourteen years' transportation in August, followed in September by Thomas Fyshe Palmer, a Unitarian minister in Dundee, and further sentences of similar duration for leading delegates at the convention, what remained of the support for political radicalism in Scotland, now firmly in working-class hands, was either driven underground or left unorganised and, mostly, demoralised.[4]

Most historians have been inclined to play down the significance of working-class involvement in the Friends of the People movement in Scotland during 1792 and 1793. Where this was in evidence it appears to have mainly come from the ranks of the handloom weavers, shoemakers and small independent tradesmen, who had at least some acquaintance with the discourse of political reform, which was rare elsewhere in Scotland at the lower social levels.[5] Many popular disturbances during these years were caused by specific local grievances and do not indicate widespread enthusiasm for political radicalism. Indeed in Dundee at the end of November 1792 there was no response from the inhabitants, even though radical symbolism seems to have been used to mobilise wider support for attacks on local excise officers and an unloaded grain-carrying ship which was lying at the harbour. The price and availability of meal, and the greater difficulties the Corn Laws created in Scotland, were issues which were generating unrest at the time. Nonetheless, the 'Disposition of the Inhabitants' of Dundee, the Lord Advocate Robert Dundas (and Henry Dundas's nephew) wrote, was 'for Quiet & peace'.[6]

Sanguine opinions of this sort however could be contradicted by another correspondent or informer only days later. Evidence that James Matthew, a Dundee weaver who was arrested for having been involved in publishing, printing and distributing a seditious paper in July 1793 suggests too that such confidence may not have been entirely soundly-based.[7] It is also clear that there was considerable variation in the strength of radical activity across the country, with very little happening in Berwickshire and the Lothians, for example.[8] But what the evidence presently indicates is that working-class radicalism was mainly confined to a small – if zealous – minority, even in Glasgow and Paisley and their satellite villages, where most supporters were found by the end of 1793.

From 1794 until the anti-militia riots of 1797 there were reports of

strikes and worker combinations, some food rioting and cases of mutiny-
ing or deserting soldiers. In the east, Perth was simmering and would
reward in-depth research, as would some of the smaller but largely unin-
vestigated weaving towns such as Forfar and Kirriemuir, which were
also reported to be troublesome. So too were some Borders' villages. In
February 1794 the Relief church minister in Perth was reported to have
been preaching along seditious lines by denouncing the war with France.
In April firearms from England had been delivered to 'Evil disposed
persons' in the burgh, and the parapet walls of the bridge over the Tay
had been daubed with republican slogans which included, 'Damn all
Kings' and 'Who would want a King to eat the Bread of twenty five
thousand men?'. Such republican sentiments stemmed directly from
Scottish radical connections in England. Troops were stationed in the
town but the activities of recruiting parties and the spoiling by the
cavalry of the burgh's inches (greens) had generated fierce resentment.
Soldiers were frequently assaulted. On top of this a poor harvest in 1795
and speculative purchases of grain by merchants had caused prices to
rise and produced what the provost and magistrates declared to the privy
council was a 'truly alarming' situation. Reinforcements were called for
and an additional six troops of dragoons were quartered in Perth in
August. This however only inflamed the situation, which may have been
made worse because the new regiment was Irish. In order to defend
themselves horse patrols had begun to go through the town with drawn
sabres. In the magistrates' opinion this put 'an End to Civil Authority',
and in order to retain some semblance of normalcy in the governance
of the burgh – not least their own standing in it – they had no choice
but to request, on the last day of October, the 'immediate Removal' of
the 31st Regiment.[9] Perth seems to have remained unsteady in terms of
its loyalty and the ease with which it could be governed throughout
much of the duration of the French Wars, and in 1811, for instance,
provost Robert Ross had to ask for additional troops to be sent to what
was a garrison town on the eve of a public execution, in order to secure
the 'peace & safety' of the burgh.[10]

Local studies may reveal more cases of this sort, and there were reports
of disturbances in Aberdeen, Dingwall, Inverness, Peterhead and Ross-
shire, some of which had to be put down by Volunteers.[11] Otherwise,
however, the over-riding impression (which the authorities were certainly
anxious to create) is of remarkable social stability and national unity of
purpose, of Volunteers being raised, and conflict-free and well-supported
king's birthdays. Entirely without precedent, at the September sitting of the
western circuit of the High Court in 1796, there was only a single indictment for trial.[12] This was without doubt a triumphant year for Henry
Dundas, 'Harry the Ninth', who in the general election managed to organise the return from Scotland of MPs sympathetic to the government in all

but a handful of seats.[13] It follows then that what requires to be explained is the apparent 'failure' of Scottish radicalism in the 1790s.

Rightly, in one multi-faceted explanation for this, the long-held view that 'the uninflammable character' of the Scottish people was a prime cause of the weakness of popular radicalism has been rejected.[14] It should be clear by now that neither the labouring poor nor the artisans and small shopkeepers and others of that rank were in any sense unusually docile in Scotland. The suggestion however that government repression from 1793 did not play a major part in suppressing dissent seems somewhat eccentric in the light of the evidence of harsh sentences meted out to printers, booksellers and other radical supporters, mass arrests of radicals in 1794, the suspension in Scotland of *habeas corpus*, acts of parliament restricting free speech and public assembly, the plethora of spies appointed by Dundas and the all-pervasive, oppressive anti-liberal mood which enveloped the country. George Mealmaker, the renowned Dundee radical, fled to Arbroath in 1794, only to be attacked by a loyalist mob.[15]

Unconvincing too is the argument that the rise in the standard of living of the working classes in Scotland provided a 'cushion' which helped to alleviate the worst effects of social change and neutralised potential unrest. It is not clear that the rising trend in real wages was sufficient to compensate workers during periods of depression, low prices and unemployment. Even the handloom weavers, beneficiaries, as we have seen, of what has somewhat generously been called a 'golden age' of living standards in the 1780s and 1790s up to 1797, were involved in disputes over prices and wages in 1767–68, 1779, 1784, 1786 and 1787. So confrontational was the last of these that several rioting weavers were shot by troops in Glasgow.[16] That weavers' wages were at least static and might even have risen between 1789 and 1792 may partly account for their quiescence in the first part of this period, but there were price rises in 1793 and severe food shortages in 1795–96.[17] The fact is that it was the handloom weavers who formed the largest segment of working-class support for political radicalism in the 1790s. What is more, although the numbers were small, it was handloom weavers who appear to have been among its more militant supporters, committed to adult male suffrage, the secret ballot and annual parliaments.

A more convincing part of any explanation for plebeian political quiescence is that which emphasises the security in Scotland of the landed classes. The formal power of the landlord class in Scotland has been acknowledged earlier in this volume, and its relevance in this period is partly confirmed by the considerable success Scottish landowners had in raising volunteer corps from among their tenants, although poorer economic conditions are also likely to have been one of a complex set of factors which determined whether or not men otherwise denied the right to 'active citizenship' would take up arms.[18] Some employers managed to achieve a similar end.

It has been observed however that notwithstanding the hegemonic position enjoyed by the landed classes, the social and political order was 'a peculiar mixture of latent strength and precariousness'.[19] Indeed it can be argued that it was the real fear and panic which resulted from watching affairs in France (and spreading unrest in Scotland) which not only gave new life to prudent paternalism among a ruling class which was still uncertain about how best to maintain order, but also produced such a vigorous defence of the political *status quo* on the part of the state, loyalist activists, north and south of the border, and the kirk.

Yet even without prodding or other forms of encouragement, it would appear that there was a strong genuine sense of popular loyalism in Britain. The significance of this, as well as the importance of the usual rise in wartime patriotism which occurred as French invasion worries grew, has almost certainly been underestimated by historians in Scotland.[20] Something of this sort was noted earlier in this volume, when discussing Jacobitism. The popularity of the Hanoverians continued to grow during the eighteenth century, especially under George III. Public celebrations at the news of British achievements abroad continued in Scotland into the 1770s, 1780s and beyond. Thus in June 1780, reports of the British victory at Charleston, caused bells to be rung, windows to be illuminated and a great 'concourse' of people to turn out in Glasgow, with similar happenings in Port Glasgow, Greenock and Paisley.[21] We have seen already that Paine's work was burned in Glasgow during one king's birthday holiday during the 1790s by a mob which the city's lord provost assured Dundas in 1794 was '*Loyal* by a good majority'.[22] It is unlikely that this had happened entirely by chance however. King's birthdays enjoyed a renaissance as loyal and patriotic spectacles, with Volunteers in Edinburgh and Glasgow going through complex manoeuvres before huge audiences.[23] That the convention of royal burghs felt strongly enough to thank the Edinburgh Constitutional Association for its 'many excellent and useful publications' which had helped to 'strengthen and to guard the loyalty of Scotsmen at this alarming juncture', suggests that in some towns such propaganda efforts had served their purpose.[24]

From 1792 loyalism among church-goers was bolstered and re-invigorated by the established church which launched a veritable barrage of sermons, spoken and printed (ten thousand of just one were printed in 1792), in defence of the God-given constitution and against liberty and equality, a campaign which it maintained through to the end of the 1790s. Wholehearted support was given by ministers to the war against France, while violent mob activity at home was denounced as wicked, and likely to plunge the country into anarchy and chaos.[25] Large numbers of handloom weavers would have been exposed to such views, and sympathised with them.[26] Those belonging to Secessionist congregations would have heard less strident opposition as opinion among seceders was rather more mixed. There were radical ministers among their number, however, in Dundee, Kilmarnock, Montrose, Perth and Paisley, and perhaps elsewhere.[27] Nevertheless, on the whole, seceding and dissenting ministers tended to be moderate reformers who denied that their sermons were seditious, disassociated themselves from violence and preached submission and humility.[28] Those who overstepped the mark – like David Sangster, the Relief church minister in Perth referred to earlier – had to be prepared to deal with the accusations of informers, who were even drawn from their own brethren. The strength of working-class loyalism is demonstrated by the fact that the witnesses who reported Sangster's disloyal sermon in some detail were a carter, a glover, a bleacher and a weaver.[29]

The period 1792–97 however was of considerable longer-term significance for class relations in Scotland. The seeds of political radicalism had been sown among the working classes. Emissaries from the avowedly-insurrectionist United Irishmen, sent across from Belfast late in 1795 or early in 1796, found Scots who were willing to act in some sort of alliance with them. It is enormously revealing that in February 1820, as fears of a radical rising in Scotland mounted, Alexander Boswell (of Auchinleck), vice lord-lieutenant of Ayrshire and commander of the county's yeomanry cavalry, reported to Sidmouth that the two north-Ayrshire weaving villages of Newmills and Galston, had been 'poisoned since the year 1794' and that 'the evil' had 'fester'd ever since'.[30] It is not known whether this was due to United Irish influence. Certainly by 1796 the United Scotsmen had been formed, with members being sworn in by secret oath in Dundee, Ayrshire and Renfrewshire.[31] An elaborate system of oaths, signs and passwords, and caution in the use and sending of written communications, meant that the society's activities were hard to discern, despite the introduction by the Home Secretary and, in Scotland, the Lord Advocate of an ambitious but flawed scheme for gathering information. Long suspected, there is now very strong evidence that much of the work in disseminating seditious ideas in Scotland was done by United Irishmen who were among those who sought refuge in Scotland from the savagely coercive policies of Dublin Castle and the army in Ireland in 1796 and 1797.[32]

Although there were no indications of open radical political activity, by the end of the decade and into the first years of the new century, firmly ensconced in some of the textile towns of Ayrshire and the neighbourhoods of Glasgow and Paisley where cotton manufacturing was carried on, were thousands of Irish workers, many of whom turned to handloom weaving. Others, as we saw in chapter 7, entered the new spinning mills. The migrants included a cadre of working-class radicals who were not only ideologically more advanced than most of their Scottish counterparts, but were drawn from a revolutionary political culture which, since at least 1795 or possibly earlier, had been prepared to countenance physical force. Hitherto, where force had been used in popular movements in Scotland it was mainly to threaten and intimidate and to strike fear in rulers' hearts, to bruise and bloody perhaps, but only inadvertently to kill or maim, even where weapons were present. The former spy Robert Watt's 'Pike Plot' in 1794, in which an armed uprising had been planned but was pre-empted by the discovery by the authorities in Edinburgh of the revolutionaries' small cache of weaponry (about a dozen pike heads), had mustered little popular support, if indeed any at all outside Watt's head.[33] At most it was the work of a well-intentioned, angry, but atypical fringe.

Class and Scotland's 'Radical War'

There has been considerable debate about the issues of class and class consciousness in early nineteenth-century Scotland. Essentially, historians have been trying to grapple with the applicability to the Scottish situation of the claim made by E. P. Thompson in 1963 that in England between the 1790s and 1831–32 a class-conscious working class was 'made', that working people came to feel and articulate an identity of interests which crossed barriers of trade, occupation and neighbourhood, in opposition to the employers and the ruling class.[34] The debate has come a long way since, with a plethora of books and articles amplifying, modifying and contesting Thompson's hypothesis.[35]

The first issue, concerning the creation of an objective working class, that is one of wage labourers as distinct from the owners of capital – landowners, larger tenant farmers and manufacturers – is more easily resolved. That a working class was being created in Scotland by the economic changes which were examined in chapters 3 and 6 is clear, albeit with complications like the fancy weavers of Paisley who had much in common, including physical proximity, with the burgh's relatively humble merchants and manufacturers. There was considerable fluidity between the two groups and, accordingly, class distinctions were blurred.[36]

On the second, more difficult, issue, something of a consensus is emerging that in Scotland in the second and third decades of the nineteenth century, an awareness among workers of a class interest can be identified. It should be emphasised however that the evidence for this is strongest in and around Glasgow (stretching north through manufacturing villages such as Campsie and Kilsyth to Stirling) and Paisley, including Ayrshire to the south. Far too little is known about Edinburgh in this period, which had a sizeable manufacturing sector but where handicraft trades continued to flourish during the construction and fitting out of the New Town. The smaller towns in the east and north of Scotland, like Cupar and Inverness, both of which were important regional centres, are virtually uncharted territory for the historian. On the other hand, as Glasgow was Scotland's leading and fastest-growing industrial town, containing within its boundaries Barony parish, the second most populous in Britain (and housing 34 per cent of Glasgow's population), what happened there is of considerable importance to our understanding of class relations in early nineteenth-century Scotland. Furthermore, as was noted earlier in relation to combinations, Glasgow's influence spread far beyond its burghal limits. Revealing in this respect were the remarks of the earl of Cassillis when reporting from Culzean castle on the political state of Ayrshire in December 1819:

> the Trade of Glasgow governs entirely the whole of this county ... Keep Glasgow [and Paisley] quiet and all Ayrshire will be quiet. Keep the Body in a due state of Health and the Legs and Arms will do their duty.[37]

Inextricably linked to the question of class in early nineteenth-century Scotland is what has been called the Radical War, or Scottish Insurrection, of 1820. Strictly speaking, the term applies to an announcement by radicals in the counties of Ayr, Dumbarton, Glasgow and Renfrew on 1 April 1820 that a provisional government of Scotland was to be established. In support a national strike was called and responded to by an estimated fifty to sixty thousand workers, principally weavers ('all' of them in Glasgow and Paisley, according to one contemporary account) and cotton spinners, but also coal miners and some machine-makers and foundry workers, who struck work for several days.[38] An armed rising was also called for. This was to be part of a general insurrection in the north of England and Lowland Scotland. In some quarters there were fears that Ireland too was to be involved.[39] The signal to commence in Paisley and Glasgow was the non-appearance of the mail coaches from England on 4 April. They arrived, and the rising, during which it was reported that several hundred men had taken up arms, with muskets, pistols and pikes, collapsed.[40]

Some of the radicals however were determined to proceed, and on 5 April a party of around thirty-five or forty weavers embarked on a march to Carron Iron Works to secure armaments. After a skirmish they were scattered by troops at Bonnymuir, and eighteen of the radicals were arrested.[41] Later, others marched from Bridgeton, and from Strathaven in Lanarkshire in search of a scattered radical army and a putative rising. On 8 April some five radicals who had been arrested and imprisoned in Greenock were released following a fierce battle during which some of the rescuers were killed, but by the following day according to one source, 'Lowland Scotland was pacified'. By the 11th, in the more expressive words of Colonel Alexander Boswell, the 'Vipers' had 'returned to their retreats disappointed and deceived by the delegates', hastily abandoning their weapons, caches of which had been discovered 'hourly' in the preceding days.[42] Thereafter, throughout the region, those suspected radicals who had not fled were harried and caught, in some cases turned out of their beds during night-time raids, and arrested.[43]

Some historians have been inclined to take these events extremely seriously. In one account the Radical War amounted to nothing less than a challenge 'to the very foundations on which Scottish society rested'.[44] Hitherto however there has been little support for this interpretation. Others have been less impressed, and portray the rising as a 'pathetic' failure.[45] The belief that it was simply the work of *agents provocateurs* however, has been soundly refuted and finds no substantial evidence in its support.[46]

To focus solely on the first days of April 1820 may provide amusement for historians intent on deflating left-wing pretensions (as well as those of writers who are convinced that the rising was nationalist), but it is a mistake. Taking a wider approach it can be concluded that the events of 1819 and 1820 together 'were more serious than anything in England, not excluding Peterloo'.[47] Although the immediate effects were largely confined to west and central Scotland, their reverberations were felt much further afield, with the Berwickshire schoolboy Alexander Somerville alarmed to hear that 'a terrible set of men' were at large, who were 'threatening to take lives and destroy the property of all good people', and who without the soldiers would have come to his own village, burned it 'and killed everybody'.[48] Contemporary reports from the east that Coupar Angus in Forfar-shire, Dundee and Kirkcaldy were places where 'turbulent measures' had been adopted in 1819 demand closer investigation. Perth's struggling weavers were rumoured to be looking to the 'Radicals coming' to resolve their difficulties.[49] The narrower focus also excludes from view the sheer scale and strength of working class anger and challenge in the period *c.* 1816 until the mid-1820s. Radicalism was but one front of a wider defensive war which was being waged by working people. The conflict of which it was part was no less important in determining the character of the Scottish economy and society than the upheavals of the 1720s, almost a century earlier. Indeed, given the numbers involved, not to mention the anxiety of the state and its determination to retain the upper hand, it can be argued that it was as important a defining moment in Scottish history as the final defeat of Jacobitism of 1746.

In chapter 7 a start was made in describing the threats to organised labour in the early 1800s. It was established too that workers had begun

to think beyond the confines of their own occupational and trade interest. Indeed one of the earliest pieces of evidence we have that workers in
different trades were aware that they faced common challenges comes
from 1799, when Glasgow weavers, understandably fearful about the
future of their bargaining position, questioned the colliers about the anti-
combination legislation which was being proposed in the mining
industry.[50] We have observed too the rise in crime, along with the
growing disorderliness on the monarch's birthday.

A further indicator of the emergence of something more than labour
consciousness is the evidence there is of overlap between occupation,
trade and neighbourhood. Thus a meal riot in Dundee in 1816 had much
of the character of the community-based food riots of the eighteenth
century. The immediate cause of the disturbance was a rise in the price of
a peck of meal, which was first charged to a flax heckler. The broader
context however was concern about wage levels. The riot was organised
in the first instance by factory weavers, who made an effigy of the
mealseller concerned, and male youths from a neighbouring ropework.
The torch- and effigy-lit march to attack the mealseller's premises began
as dark fell, with a dozen or so workers raising support, mainly it seems
from women and boys, by parading through 'different streets in the
suburbs'. In the hours that followed the shops and houses of several
merchants were attacked and looted.[51]

However, as many workers engaged in a variety of occupations during
their lifetimes, it is somewhat unrealistic to assume that those concerned
would have a particular affinity with any one of them. Street and neighbourhood were arguably more powerful sources of identity, as with
Glasgow's Calton Green Street Friendly Society, formed around 1806.
The idea of neighbourhood or community as a platform for popular
collective action finds support too in the evidence of shared leisure experience. Participation in cock shootings or the stone battles mentioned in
chapter 7 took place on the basis of street or locality, while the range of
the occupations of the parties involved in drinking sessions which ended
in street brawls serious enough to command the attention of the police
reveals that friendships, allegiances and networks were forged outside the
workplace.[52]

Glasgow's south-side comprised not a single homogenous mass of the
labouring poor, but rather a series of expanding but still discrete villages
– Anderston, Bridgeton, Calton and Camlachie, for example – communities in which weavers predominated, but which were inhabited too by
cotton spinners, other textile operatives and less numerous representatives of other trades. It is significant that so many mass meetings were
held only after the growing crowd had marched through villages such as
these, gathering adherents who, on occasion, had held discussions to
determine a community response to a particular issue. In May 1824, for

example, a good cross-section of the community of Tollcross leapt to the defence of two colliers and a weaver when sheriff's officers attempted to poind their household effects as they had failed to pay their dog taxes. As the officers began their searches, 'a numbers of evil-disposed and riotous persons', including a colliery engineman, a weaver, a collier and a 'crowd of women and children', appeared at the doors of their houses and stoned them before driving the intruders into a series of public houses as they tried to make their escape.[53] Even more instructive is the 'Harvie's dyke' riot of June 1823, when a crowd estimated to have been three thousand strong demolished two great stone walls which had been erected by Thomas Harvie, the new proprietor of Westhorn estate. The walls ran down into the River Clyde, thereby making 'an encroachment on the rights of the public' by blocking a much-used riverside path. The action however had been planned some weeks in advance by a committee chaired by a Parkhead grocer and which included small businessmen, artisans and a doctor, while the crowd was collected on a march which wound its way through Dalmarnock and Bridgeton before arriving at Westhorn. Hardly surprisingly, weaving was the best-represented occupation, accounting for 60 per cent of those thought to be most directly involved, but there was a substantial number of cotton spinners and colliers (whose skills with picks and gunpowder were utilised to hole the walls), as well as a sprinkling of other trades, including, as many such affairs did, a schoolteacher.[54] Although the crowd was driven off by a party from the Iniskillen Dragoons, the row carried on. The wall was quickly re-built, but the estate was placed under a cavalry guard to protect it from further damage and its proprietor from threatened attacks on his life.[55]

What is striking about the ten or so years after 1815 is the sheer variety of issues which could ignite popular unrest. Eye-witness reports of public meetings capture the blunderbuss nature of the working-class response in a political and economic climate in which those at all levels of authority could seem oblivious to their plight, or to the lower orders' reservations and fears about the consequences of rapid change. At the end of August 1819 the readers of one newspaper were provided with a full account of a meeting called principally by handloom weavers to demand that the Poor Laws in Scotland be put into effect. Orators, who took a 'roving view' of current grievances, spoke in favour of annual parliaments and universal suffrage, and against the corn laws, high taxation, the combination acts, the Peterloo massacre and savings or 'shavings' banks. Significantly too, and revealing the extent to which those present looked back to a time when the moral economy could be activated, one speaker argued that, 'in times of distress, it was lawful for every one to seize on what his more wealthy neighbour *ought* to have offered him'.[56] This was simply a veiled version of the sort of argument which was now being developed by supporters of physical force through-out the region. At a small meeting held in Neil McVicar's beaming shop in Glasgow's Calton in June it had been agreed that as no relief had been provided by the government for the 'suffering Weavers ... they would have recourse to the law by nature, and take it where they could at the point of a Bayonet'.[57]

Glasgow and Paisley were racked as they had never been before by social tensions and violent disturbances. This was in addition to those noted already, and involved attacks on persons and property with stones, flame and firearms, which intensified during periods of economic distress. Street and house lamps were commonly smashed, easily-broken symbols of the propertied classes' anxiety to make the streets safer, and which were installed in many towns from the 1800s. Radicalism by 1815 was no longer the small-scale phenomenon it had been in working-class circles in the early 1790s. Instead there is a sense in which it had become the thread of hope that, with varying degrees of strength, held together the disparate sections of a working class in west-central Scotland which was becoming distinctly less respectful of rank. Rather, it was observed, 'a line of demarcation was drawn between the different ranks of society' and a 'ferocious spirit of retaliation was engendered in the minds of the labouring classes.'[58]

This included women, whose earlier experience in food riots, and more recent involvement in friendly societies, evangelical religion, the formal world of work, industrial agitation and strikes provided pathways into radical activism. For the first time, radical definitions of 'the people' began to include females, although there is little to suggest that they provided much of a leadership role, but instead played a part as emblems of working-class suffering.[59] Nevertheless, the highly theatrical and well-marshalled radical gatherings incorporated women, although they formed their own societies too. In Ayrshire, for example, the Galston Female Reformers' Society was believed to have been particularly active, as was one in Johnstone.[60] Communities were mobilised, not only in ways we have observed already, but by thousands of 'men and women four in four arm in arm' striding to reform meetings, accompanied by music bands and carrying flags, caps of liberty and 'bundles of reeds surmounted with green olive branches, emblematical of union'.[61] At one meeting in the east end of Glasgow in November 1819, the caps of liberty were mainly carried by women, forty of whom appeared on the hustings. Powerful symbolism was employed, with embroidered caps of liberty representing purity and virtue. Well-dressed female radicals in Ayr wore black silk gowns, white scarfs and elaborately-decorated white head-dresses, studded with black dots, 'to represent the mourning of the people for the persons killed at Manchester'.[62]

There are considerable gaps and inadequacies in the evidence relating to radicalism in Scotland in the period *c.* 1815–20. Nevertheless, it is reasonably clear that radical ideas like universal suffrage and annual parliaments, as advocated by men such as William Cobbett and Henry Hunt, became increasingly attractive to working people in the west of Scotland as economic conditions failed to improve in the post-war years and indeed dipped sharply in the downturns of 1816–17 and 1819–20. 1819 was appallingly bad, with unemployment levels of as much as 50 per cent in some places. The Corn Laws of 1815 raised food prices, and the abolition of income tax had resulted in higher taxes on essential commodities such as salt, tea, tobacco, sugar, candles and soap, putting further pressure on the household budgets of the working classes. The real wage gains made by skilled workers and coal miners between 1814–15 and 1831 tended to come after 1820, not before, and there were savage wage cuts in 1819.[63] In Glasgow, in the crucial period 1815 to 1819, real wages fell by around 10 per cent.[64]

The relative calm the authorities had enjoyed since the last signs of United Scotsmen activity in 1803 was replaced by increasingly serious worries about their own safety and the security of civil institutions. In a confidential letter to the duke of Buccleuch in January 1817 the Lord Advocate confessed that both he and Lord Sidmouth were 'apprehensive' about the capacity of the yeomanry in Scotland. Large meetings demanding parliamentary reform had been held in 1815 and in 1816 at Thrushgrove.[65] Of greater concern however – even more so than in 1793 – was the way that 'the Revolutionists', bound by secret oaths, were organising and collecting arms.[66] *Habeas corpus* was again suspended and in February there were mass arrests of those suspected of taking unlawful oaths, as the Tory government's infamous six 'Gagging Acts' were implemented in Scotland.[67] This however failed to quash either radical activists or the spirit of unrest. Those radicals who favoured insurrection, went underground, organised in secret societies along the lines of the United Scotsmen in the 1790s. It was in these subterranean councils that the rising of 1820 was planned. Further fuelling popular excitement, in 1819, were Union Societies which were founded quite openly under the guidance of the Englishman Joseph Brayshaw, who advocated political education and tax boycotts as means of furthering the cause of parliamentary reform.[68] Several meetings and demonstrations were organised between June and December.

But in spite of the apparent divisions between the two strategies, what is noticeable is the extent to which radical idealism bridged the gaps which might have existed with such a diversity of issues and between men and women of different occupations. Analysis of the occupations of those suspected of having taken some part in the 1820 rising reveals the extent of co-operation between workers. Weavers predominate, cotton spinners feature significantly, but also involved were bakers, bleachers, booksellers and schoolteachers. In Paisley, James Parker, a 'flower-lasher', was exceptional not only in his occupation but also because he was the only one of twenty-eight suspects in Paisley who was over the age of forty. Most were in their early- and mid-twenties.[69]

There were those who saw no conflict between industrial action and radical political activity, and indeed supported both.[70] This was certainly true of handloom weavers, cotton spinners – whose leaders 'were in jail as Radicals' in May 1820 – and coal miners, whose radical leanings have somewhat surprisingly been denied by some historians.[71] The long-held view that coal miners were a 'caste apart' in Scottish society is largely the result of historians assuming that the isolated and inland coal-mining communities of the mid-nineteenth century were typical of the eighteenth. Although some coalmasters would have preferred it to be otherwise, until the era of the railway, most colliers tended to live in and among the labouring classes in the village and town communities, sharing many of their interests, attitudes and concerns.[72]

Appeals for help for the poor or those on low wages provided a similar opportunity to combine causes. Thus in June 1819 the Glasgow weavers met on Glasgow Green to petition the Prince Regent for funds to help them emigrate: the *Glasgow Courier* however was disappointed that 'they dabble[d] too much in politics'. Of what use was it, the paper asked, for the children of a poor man 'to hear their father lecturing on universal suffrage, annual parliaments etc, when he ought to be attending to his work'.[73]

Some radical activists also managed to retain credibility while being engaged in both subversive activity and public meetings. One man who straddled a number of interests was John Fauldhouse Wilson. Wilson was a well-read weaver, secretary to the Glasgow and Clydesdale Association of Operative Colliers, and played a prominent role in the west of Scotland coal strike in 1817 and 1818. By 1820 he had become the proprietor of a 'Porter House' in Glasgow, which provided radical litera-ture for his customers to read. (Radical newspapers such as *Wooler's Gazette*, the *Manchester Observer*, the *Belfast Irishman*, *The Spirit of the Union* and the *Black Dwarf* were circulating in the west by 1819, along with works by Cobbet and Paine.) In 1823 he was again working as a weaver and was present at, and suspected of having played some part in, the attack on the Westhorn estate walls.[74]

By playing the Scottish card too, and raising national consciousness, even among the many Irish adherents to the radical cause in Scotland, support for what was essentially a British political movement was main-tained and potential rifts were camouflaged.[75] (Sectarian tensions continued to exist at the height of the radical agitation, for example, but only rarely exploded into open conflict.)[76] Thus during the intervals between the speeches at a great combined meeting of the Union Societies of Glasgow in October 1819 an orchestra played 'national airs', which included 'Scots Wha Hae' (the most popular), as well as the 'Sprig of Shillelah [sic]' and 'Rule Britannia'.[77] The first-named became something of a radical anthem after the magistrates in Paisley arrested a band of reformers who had played 'Scots Wha Hae' at a meeting on Meikleriggs Moor. According to one witness, on the band's release, 'it was played at all public meetings ... sung by the ballad singers in the streets ... [and] whistled by workmen passing to & from their work'.[78] Speakers too drew on well-known figures and events in Scottish history to inspire their listeners, one for example, declaring that the Peterloo massacre had 'no parallel except the massacre at Glencoe'.[79] More sought succour from the example of William Wallace.

As the economy slowed – indeed collapsed – in 1819 and wages and employment opportunities slumped (the real wages of Glasgow weavers had already fallen by half between 1815 and 1818), thousands of hand-loom weavers were thrown out of work. Soup kitchens were set up in the towns, in Ayrshire potatoes were distributed among the families of the needy, and work-creation schemes for the unemployed were devised. Any diversion of this sort, it was argued, tended to have a 'most desirable effect' on those who might otherwise fall under the spell of 'the mischievous and disaffected'. (The benefits for the landed were two-fold in that uncultivated land brought under the spade at rock-bottom wages could produce significant rent increases.)[80] Some however – the duke of Hamilton was one – despaired of the effectiveness of such measures. The parish system of poor relief was unable to cope with the burden thrust upon it: 'there is an enormous population' in Lanarkshire, he informed the earl of Liverpool in a plea for state aid, that was 'not their [the parishes] own':

> a population of strangers, chiefly Irish, brought in for manufacturing purposes, whom it is impossible to maintain, now exceeding ten times the natural number of paupers in the county.[81]

There was a constant flow of letters between those concerned with the maintenance of law and order in Scotland. Their tone, with few exceptions, swung backwards and forwards between sheer terror and somewhat unconvincing assurances that all was secure. Many such letters were from county and civic sources who sometimes seemed more anxious to secure ministerial approval than to report their misgivings. It is hard to convey the gravity of the political situation in the west of Scotland during 1819 and 1820. Numerous public meetings were held in addition to those reported already, some peaceable, others less so. In several what began as orderly gatherings later disintegrated into lawlessness. Thus in September 1819, following three days of rioting in Paisley, said to have been fomented by radicals, some three thousand sympathisers gathered menacingly in Glasgow. Fearing the consequences, troops were brought in from Hamilton and eventually the crowd was broken up by the cavalry. Around a hundred people were arrested and some forty charged. This was not before all 220 street and house lamps had been broken in the Gallowgate, Saltmarket, and the surrounding streets, while shops – those dealing in spirits fared worst – had been attacked in Calton, Greenhead and Tradeston, and numerous house windows broken, including those of a Methodist chapel. There was a ferocious ugliness into which frustrated radicalism could readily descend, with riots like this one – led by a torch-carrying smith or founder – striking terror into the hearts of the better-off residents of now-darkened streets.[82]

By the end of 1819 what was virtually a state of open war existed between working-class communities and the authorities. Troops or the yeomanry had simply to appear and they were assailed by braying, dirt- and stone-throwing mobs. In September recently-enrolled special constables drawn from the 'respectable householders' in Bridgeton were 'severely hurt' by stones thrown at them during their first night of duty, and faced a more severe challenge from a meeting which called for the inhabitants to arm themselves by way of response.[83] In November arrangements were made to strengthen the garrison at Carlisle, so that cavalry reinforcements could be sent north into Scotland.[84] Towards the end of December, as the Old Monklands Yeomanry Cavalry returned from a muster through the colliery village of Greenend, they were 'assaulted by a mob of young men and boys, with stones, mud etc, who followed a considerable distance, abusing and throwing at them'.[85] In January of the following year attempts were made to set fire to Shotts Iron Works and Broomward Cotton Mill (both of which were owned by fervent anti-radical proprietors), while in March buildings and a wall at Wellshot estate, Cambuslang, were attacked. Mill buildings too appear to have been set on fire in Ballantrae, Minigaff and Portpatrick.[86] By the 20th January, after communications on the respective political situations in Glasgow and Manchester had been read, Thomas Sharp informed Henry Monteith, Glasgow's provost, that the situation in Glasgow and neighbourhood was 'more serious than in this District [Lancashire]'.[87] Reports of arming and drilling – often under the command of retired soldiers from the British Army – were heard with increasing frequency; as far as can be judged, most seem to have been accurate.

The working classes in the west of Scotland, men, women and juveniles (of which there was a reform society in Paisley), were united as never before, and brashly confident in their cause. In Airdrie the previous December, radicals who had been released from jail were met two miles from the town by 'an immense crowd of people who took the horses from the carriage and drew them in triumph up and down the streets'.[88] The people, one worried contemporary observed, have shown 'that they will not act agt those of the same class'. The danger was that if a rising was to happen, it would be 'considered as a war between the lower classes & the higher so that the result cannot be anticipated'.[89] The 'times are perilous in the extreme', announced the *Glasgow Courier* on 4 April 1820, no longer able to comprehend or make sense of the disquiet as the strike spread and thousands of people milled around the streets, awaiting the signal to rise. Some days earlier the newspaper had carried a report of a raid by the magistrates and military on a machine shop in which pikes were being manufactured. But:

> On entering the building ... [they] were received with cheers, three times three, and were told by the workmen that if they were in search of Radicals they might take the whole of them, and some of them pretended to be better than the others in that respect.[90]

Why well-paid men, who had been in constant employment, immune from 'the pressure of the times', were adopting the politics of radicalism was beyond understanding.

But as we have seen, the events of the first week of April were something of a damp squib. This should not detract however from the significance of the dissatisfaction of which the rising was part, or of what for the authorities was a partial but important victory in their crusade for the hegemony of political economy. This rarely provided the language of radicalism however, or indeed, its focus. Working class anger was directed towards the symptoms of a system which in the words of Alexander Richmond, advocate for the weavers' in 1812 and 1813 who later turned informer for Kirkman Finlay, had effected:

> almost a total revolution ... in the whole frame of society; capital and the means of producing all the luxuries of life have been augmented ... yet it is questionable if, in the midst of all this apparent improvement, the substantial comfort and happiness of the great body of the people have in any degree been promoted, and whether the enlightened philanthropist will not consider they have rather retrograded.[91]

Although those who suspected there were direct – and radical – connections between the upheavals in Lowland Scotland and the disturbances directed against clearance in Sutherland and Ross at the end of 1819 were probably wrong, there was a link in that James Loch, Sutherland estate commissioner from 1812, was well versed in and broadly sympathetic to the ideology of the market economists. Non-doctrinaire in practice, he was as committed to the rational use of the resources available to him, land, labour and capital, as any southern agriculturalist or industrialist.[92] Throughout great swathes of Scotland, all concerned in implementing the new economic and social order were responsible for causing varying degrees of dislocation, pain and despair, and had to confront their victims' responses.

The manner in which the authorities coped with these is to be seen in how they snuffed out the revolutionary threat which Lowland radicalism posed in 1820. Spies and informers appointed on the instruction of the Lord Advocate, Sir William Rae, and Lord Sidmouth ensured that the authorities were invariably one step ahead of those radicals who were plotting insurrection. Indeed Rae was so confident about the arrangements he had made that in October 1819 he could declare that 'nothing material on the part of the Radicals can be attempted without my previous knowledge'.[93] Not every scrap of evidence was of use, and some information was plainly misleading, but there was enough to enable precautionary steps to be taken and to justify Richmond's fee of £50 *per annum*.[94] Rumours of insurrectionary activity were treated seriously, and met with imposing shows of military force. Thus one threat in Glasgow in December 1819 led to the assembly of most of the 7th and 10th Hussars, detachments of the 6th and 13th foot regiments, a battalion of the Rifle Brigade, ten field pieces, and in the region of five hundred men from the Midlothian and West Lothian Yeomanry Cavalry. The city remained quiet.[95] Contrary to what has been asserted in some quarters, in Glasgow and the west of Scotland, the authorities were well aware that something serious was in the wind late in March and early in April 1820.[96] By the time of the abortive rising, Glasgow was garrisoned with a 'formidable' array of troops and armaments which were stationed in key streets and squares. That Kilmarnock and some other outlying centres of support had relatively little defence to offer did not matter: the core was secure.[97] But even so, in Ayr, the town's barracks, which had been built in 1794, were re-opened as fears about an uprising mounted and housed the 10th Hussars and the 4th Royal Veteran Battalion. In the north of the county, the Yeomanry first raised in 1798 was also strengthened in 1817 and supplemented by an Armed Association of the inhabitants of Irvine in 1820.[98]

Within hours searches for weapons and suspected radicals were instigated in and around Glasgow and began to produce results. Countless arrests were made as troops scoured the surrounding counties during the subsequent days and weeks and a series of treason trials was held in Ayr, Dumbarton, Glasgow, Paisley and Stirling. Although most of those found guilty were transported to Australia, exemplary punishments, by hanging and beheading, were handed down to John Baird, Andrew Hardie and Alexander Wilson. In addition there were nine major cases in 1820 alone involving seditious publications or clergymen who had been heard uttering pro-radical sentiments.[99]

Arguably as important in defusing the militant radical threat was the pre-emptive action the authorities took in February 1820 in arresting, in a vintner's shop in Glasgow, some twenty-eight of the leading radicals in the west of Scotland. Their papers too were seized. Despite a popular outcry and calls for a rising in their support, they remained in prison for the next nine months. It is not unlikely that they represented the cream of that element in the radical movement which was committed to physical force, and thus weakened the leadership, the quality of which according to some sources, was diminishing and becoming increasingly reckless in character.[100] From Ayrshire, Alexander Boswell was able to tell the Home Secretary that while radical committees continued to meet and 'utmost vigilance' was required so that 'the loyal are not lulled into supine security', the committees had 'thin'd in numbers' and 'lost much of their poisonous influence'.[101]

Certainly there is evidence that the bulk of those who sympathised with the radical cause were unwilling to become revolutionaries. It is impossible to provide more than the crudest estimates of the number of radicals who might have answered the call for a rising (as opposed simply to the strike) early in April 1820. Reports of drilling parties around Glasgow and near Paisley give numbers of one to two hundred in most cases, as many as four to five hundred in Milngavie, and we must assume there were many others in the manufacturing villages in the landward parts of Lanarkshire which have left no trace.[102] The textile villages of north Ayrshire were each thought to contain between fifty and a hundred of the kind of radicals who concerned Alexander Boswell ('those ... desperate enough to have joined' if violence was to be employed), although there were more in Stewarton and Kilmarnock. Boswell also estimated a figure of five hundred for Galston and Newmilns. By amassing data in this uneven fashion a total figure of at least a couple of thousand seems not unreasonable.

But even if this was anything like the size of the standing radical army, the signs are that it would have had few volunteer recruits. Even those prepared to don the mantle of leader may have been harder to find than we may suppose. John Neil, a twenty-six-year-old weaver from Paisley was arrested some time after the failed rising. But, it was noted by the sheriff who was looking over the case, it was 'believed he had become alarmed and timid for some time previous to the 1st of April'. Even though he had been a delegate to the central committee he was 'not of such repute for nerve or sagacity as to entitle him to be really a leader'.[103] His 'talents' were for speaking and expressive writing. This finds an echo in Boswell's observation that beneath the ranks of the genuinely enthusiastic there were 'many who huzza a speech' but who were 'not prepared to take to the field'.[104] They might even damage property, but nothing more sinister would happen. One of the factors that had given comfort to the well-informed Lord Advocate in October 1819 was that 'the leading Reformers' were 'averse to any disturbance' and wanted only to 'ascertain their own Strength & to blow the flame until they are more fully prepared'. Notwithstanding the concern expressed by one writer at the prospect of class confrontation in 1820, he was also sure that the people were 'not disloyal'.[105] Something of the distaste which was felt about the prospect of revolutionary action is seen in a reported falling off in the attendance of some of the private radical meetings and a decline in the number of 'respectable' adherents. There was also some resentment that members of the general committee of radicals were paid for attending, and there was a view that if left alone for long enough squabbles among the leadership would cause the 'foolish spirit' to subside.[106]

Within two months of the abortive rising Sidmouth had heard enough from Ayrshire to conclude that the radicals 'were generally quiet, more submissive and less boasting'.[107] It was reported from the Kilmarnock area that the radicals were 'as quiet and humble as possible', and now recognised the futility of the violent route to reform. In Newmilns it was said that 'many of the fellows who were most violent in favour of Radicalism actually felt ashamed of their conduct and never now spoke of the subject'. Similarly, by November, Boswell was able to report that even though 'some radically bad men' were still around, 'they do not see the practicability of any success.'[108] That guns, which had been taken by radicals from farmers near Craigend in Lanarkshire, were returned (after being hidden since the rising) to their owners early in September provides some corroboration that this is likely to have been true.[109] Much to the authorities' chagrin, many had fled. Some had joined the Volunteers, to throw their pursuers off their scent. Even from what one sheriff called the 'bad [weaving] village of Kilbarchan' in Renfrewshire, only one rather weak suspect had been apprehended by July.

Violent insurrectionary action of the kind required by the physical force radicals was largely alien to Scotland's working classes, although as has been observed, older attitudes were changing.[110] But on the question of life-threatening violence, this appears not to have been by much.

The clergy were blamed for failing to provide sufficient relief for the poor. In the autumn of 1819 some radicals even began – unprecedentedly – to attack religion.[111] It was in part to counter this that in January 1820 Glasgow's lord provost ordered that a Mr Ferrie's sermon be printed and distributed: its usefulness was that it offered 'reasons for reconciling the poor to their circumstances'.[112] Loyal newspapers printed reports of pleasing spectacles such as the three hundred sabbath school children at Blantyre Cotton Mill who paraded in an orderly fashion to Blantyre parish church to hear a sermon on the theme that 'the fear of the Lord is the beginning of wisdom'.[113] It is true that even the dissenting churches were losing touch with the working classes below the status of skilled artisan. Church provision fell behind the growth of population over the period 1750–1830, and only began to catch up from the 1840s.[114] But local studies reveal a remarkable level of new congregations and new church building taking place in the 1810s and 1820s. Thus in Ayr, for example, which had a population of around six thousand in 1800, additional provision was made for worshippers from at least seven denominations between 1813 and 1832, ranging from the Moravians through Congregationalists to Roman Catholics.[115] While attendance among handloom weavers fell off 'markedly' after 1815, the church continued to exert a considerable hold in many of the handloom-weaving communities, even in radical Airdrie.[116] It is revealing that so much of the poetry written by handloom weavers and other working-class writers in the first half of the nineteenth century recognises the ills of trade, social inequalities and the depth of social suffering, but urges forbearance and hope of a better life in the hereafter rather than worldly rebellion. Thus in William Thom's 'Whisperings of the Unwashed', a hard-driving rhythmic poem which paints starkly the tribulations of the weavers, 'Wi' hungry wame and hopeless breast / Their food no feeding, their sleep no rest', the solution is to be found 'neither with bludgeon nor blow' nor in the 'ramping of demagogue rage'. Instead, salvation will come when 'Truth walks abroad all unfetter'd again':

> When the breast glows to Love and the brow
>   beams in Light –
> Oh! hasten it Heaven! MAN LONGS FOR HIS
>   RIGHT.[117]

This represented a deep-rooted tradition, from which it was hard to shake free.

Many contemporaries were convinced that the radical threat came not from native Scots, but from the Irish. The *Perth Courier* for example, remarked that the workmen in Glasgow who manifested 'symptoms of an unruly spirit' were 'not Scotchmen but Irishmen'.[118] There is certainly a coincidence between the known destinations of Irish immigrants and those towns and villages in the south and west of Scotland which were particularly unruly in the years before 1820. In Glasgow, the two most turbulent districts within Barony parish and the Royalty of Glasgow were Calton and St John's respectively, which had the highest proportions of Irish-born residents in 1819 – 20.5 and 14.5 per cent.[119] Other districts too where radical support was particularly strong held high concentrations of Irish immigrants and their descendants. In both weaving and cotton spinning, from where the bulk of active radicals were drawn, Irish workers formed one-third and at least 50 per cent of the respective workforces.[120] Recently-published research has provided fairly convincing proof that there was a substantial Irish input into the radical societies. Irish-Scottish links had also been forged through trade unionism among both handloom weavers and calico printers.[121]

The leading members of the radicals arrested in February 1817

included at least five Irishmen.[122] Whether or not these men had links
with the United Irishmen is not clear, although this was suggested, as too
was a connection with the United Scotsmen. Less is known about the
leaders arrested in February 1820, but again contemporaries alleged Irish
involvement, including that of survivors of the 1798 rebellion.[123] These
men may have been among those who managed to escape capture.
Judging on the basis of surnames in lists of those who were arrested
however, there is no suggestion of a disproportionately strong Irish representation (although this is by no means a watertight method for
identifying ethnic background). Yet the impact of even a small number of
individuals drawn from a revolutionary group which had experience of
armed struggle could have made a major difference in Lowland Scotland.
Unlike Scotland, in Ireland the older 'moral economy' had died (in 1793),
and with it certain unspoken rules about confrontations between crowds
and the magistrates and military. 'Savage ferocity' and 'organised
outrage' become the terms with which popular politics in Ireland can be
fairly characterised.[124] Soldiers were shot. Pikes began to be manufactured and used in large numbers. In the 1790s Defenders and the United
Irishmen learned how to popularise revolutionary doctrines and extend
an effective underground organisation.[125] All that can be said with
certainty however is that Irishmen and women contributed to the cause of
Scottish radicalism; their precise role may be speculated upon, but at
present cannot be proven.

One other important factor has to be taken into account in understanding why the wave of working-class radicalism failed to wreak the
havoc which some had predicted. We have already alluded to the efforts
of the civic authorities during the wars with revolutionary France to
marshall a loyalist and patriotic spirit, and to the animation of the Kirk
in its attempts to quash revolutionary idealism. With the wars lasting
virtually twenty-two years (there was a short interlude during the peace
of Amiens, 1802–3), these initiatives were clearly of major importance.
They were however but part of a campaign waged by the ruling classes in
the towns to counter the challenges to urban order presented by their
burgeoning populations, some of the consequences of which were
outlined in chapter 7.

One of the first moves in this respect – and an important one – was the
formation in Glasgow of the Sunday School movement (although the first
sabbath school was set up in Aberdeen), launched after the trauma of the
Calton weavers' disturbances of 1787. Mission schools expanded particularly rapidly between 1814 and 1818, and by 1819 the schools could
boast a roll of nine thousand, equivalent to 7 per cent of the city's population. In Scotland as a whole, 567 schools were affiliated to the Sabbath
School Union for Scotland.[126] Although by no means without precedent –
the degree of regulation in Scottish towns in the eighteenth century was

greater than in England – attempts too were made to improve civic amenities by paying greater attention to the disposal of human waste, repairing streets and walkways and feuing out ground for new housing. Another aspect of this in Glasgow was the cleaning up and laying out of the burgh's green, and the exercise of some control over the entertainment offered there during the annual fair.[127] There was often an overlap between civic involvement and the voluntary subscription societies which appeared in growing numbers from the 1780s. Infirmaries and asylums, schools and libraries were all founded or, as in the case of Aberdeen's infirmary, established in 1742, extended to meet rising demand.[128] The first two were innovative in that they were designed to remove individuals perceived to be problems from the community. This was a shift in social ordering which Stana Nenadic has called 'a chilling demonstration of the scientifically rational and ordered mind at work', a phrase which is certainly applicable where asylums were concerned, but less so for those infirmaries which confined themselves to the treatment of sick and injured bodies.[129] Formed principally in the interests of their middle-class subscribers, the societies – mainly male-run – were a means of promoting order through charitable improvement. They also aided middle-class cohesion, enhanced their status and, it was hoped, earned the gratitude and respect of the lower orders.[130] Reading accounts of the opening of a new grammar school in Irvine in 1816, when during a large procession of dignitaries and pupils it was announced that a holiday 'in all time coming' would be held on 10 December to commemorate the birthday of the twelfth earl of Eglinton, one can see the process at work.[131]

Wartime displays and patriotic entertainments put on in the theatres which most of the main towns had by 1815 were to serve the same purposes. Less obviously, but of considerable importance, is the part the propertied classes played in promoting 'civilised' models of organisation, rituals, ceremonies, processions and etiquette for the lower orders to adopt. Protest was to be peaceful, ordered and registered in writing, not by force. Preferably, women should be absent, their sensitivities and emotions directed towards the home and education of the young.[132] Paternalist strategies, adopted by some urban employers as a means of maintaining workplace harmony, could also assist in steering workers away from the politics of the crowd and community. Their reward appeared in incidents such as that reported some two weeks after the rising in 1820, when 'the whole workmen' belonging to Shotts Iron Works assembled in front of their manager's house, fired a royal salute from a field-gun, 'and drank the King's health with the greatest enthusiasm'. In other cases employers gave effusive thanks to workers who had remained in employment during the first week in April.[133]

Determination at the state level to crush radicalism, and of employers and certain law officers to neuter trade unionism, was matched at the local level in Glasgow by the work in the burgh court of the Town Clerk, James Reddie, appointed in 1804.[134] Combinations of masters of the sort referred to in chapter 7 and other private bodies added to the weight of establishment power. Thus in Glasgow at the end of the eighteenth century a Detecting Society was formed by the city's textile manufacturers and merchants to deal with the worsening problem of weavers taking webs from agents but failing to deliver them. Glasgow's Police Act was passed in 1800. In 1783 the Glasgow Chamber of Commerce had been established, the first in Britain, in order to represent the city's business interests. The point is that the emergent but not yet fully-formed class-conscious working class in west and central Scotland was faced by a much more solidly-united ruling class. Although middle-class demands for parliamentary representation grew after 1815, and a rift began to appear between the middling ranks and the landed interest and their Tory apologists, such was their alarm by 1820, bound by their mutual concern for the integrity of private property, that they were willing to close ranks against the common enemy. Indeed so disconcerting were the events leading up to and during April 1820 that large numbers of the less-prosperous middle classes flocked to join their local Volunteers, to defend their lives and property with arms if need be. Thus in Ayr, for example, lawyers and shopkeepers joined the recently re-formed Armed Association, under the command of landed commanding officers.[135]

The urban bourgeoisie and the dominant landed classes in Scotland shared other things in common, including an interest in wealth creation in a market system. They were linked too by the landholdings of many merchants and manufacturers, and the close connections there were between land, the legal profession and the state.[136] By the later 1820s, on the streets, in the fields, in and around the workplace and through the courts, a unified ruling class had faced up to and largely successfully resisted and defeated a series of challenges to their ascendancy from below. The brief period during which a class-conscious working class was being made in Scotland, was also that in which it was confronted by forces upon which it began to break up.

That some historians and several contemporaries believed that tranquillity had been restored in Lowland Scotland by the summer of 1820 was noted earlier. In one sense this is correct. The radical 'dream' (the prospect of a violent overthrow of the state and the equalisation of property and other transforming measures) was certainly over, or at least placed quietly in abeyance until the first rumblings of the Chartist agitation.[137] To date the rising as 'over' by 8 April however is probably premature. There were reports of nightly drilling still taking place in the Glasgow vicinity some days later than this and early in May it was remarked that the 'seed sown by the Radicals' was 'now beginning to ripen', as news broke that a range of buildings and the entire livestock of a prominent Renfrewshire landowner had been destroyed by fire.[138]

Nevertheless, militant radicalism had suffered a devastating blow. It would be altogether wrong however to assume that from April 1820 the working classes were silenced or ceased to represent their views forcibly. Indeed there is a sense in which working-class rage was heightened by the outcome of the Radical War. There was a two-fold reaction to the defeat of April 1820. The first was to return to traditional forms of urban protest, over issues which had long roused the lower orders into action. Revolution was a non-starter, but riot had the power to annoy, to create fear and slow the pace of or modify the progress of change where this was deemed to offend popular values. Plebeian moral codes too had to be defended. Thus in mid-February 1822 the house of a Mr Provand in Glasgow was attacked and plundered by a crowd who suspected him of 'seducing boys from the path of moral rectitude' by inviting them to 'belabour his posterior'.[139] Grave robbers too felt the crowd's wrath, as they had in the previous century.[140] In chapter 7, the animated reaction of large numbers of the inhabitants of some of Glasgow's working-class suburbs to the blocking of a right of way in 1823 and their assertion of their rights 'to take back what belonged to them before' was examined. There was no sense that this was anything other than a serious public incident. George Salmond (see chapter 7), anxious that those involved should be tried in the High Court rather than the Sheriff Court, argued that actions of this sort 'in a Community so populous ... where the mixture of Irish is so very great' should be firmly repressed. Otherwise, he feared, 'the people would soon get ahead of the Authorities'.[141] What Salmond had recognised was that the outcomes of such disorders were unpredictable where the bonds of paternalism and deference, which gave crowd action much of its theatrical quality, were weak.

There was a difference after April 1820 though, in that on some occasions crowd behaviour clearly had an added edge which was almost certainly born of resentment at the radical defeat. The first major post-rising disorder in Glasgow occurred on 28 June 1820, when soldiers from the 13th Regiment of Foot were attacked by a crowd (and some of the police) in the city's Saltmarket. The riot, which for a time 'had the most dreadful appearance, more so, perhaps, than was ever witnessed on the streets of this city', was evidently provoked by the sight of armed, whisky-drinking, Irish soldiers in the company of a local girl, but the context in which it happened is likely to have been the hatred there was for the military in the west of Scotland as radicals were rounded up. Whatever the precise cause, the solution recommended by the still-nervous authorities was the removal of the troops concerned from the city.[142]

Much more obviously connected with radicalism were the demonstrations which took place in Glasgow and elsewhere in the Lowland towns in support of the George IV's estranged wife, Queen Caroline, who had returned to Britain to reclaim her legal rights. Similar gatherings occurred in London and other parts of England, including, significantly, Lancashire. A multipotent symbol and immensely popular with the crowd, radicals flocked to her cause in part to mobilise the masses, conflating the Queen's oppression with that of their own in the wake of 1819 and 1820.[143] Interpretations vary about the meaning which should be placed on what has been described as 'the greatest [popular mobilisation] of the whole Georgian era'.[144] In Scotland however, rather than revealing the non-class character of radicalism and an issue which was 'essentially populist ... [and] restorationist', by and large, the evidence which has been examined on a topic that has attracted remarkably little notice among Scottish historians seems to point to something more complicated.[145] One observer did find that 'amongst the middling and lower orders of people' there was a 'general Sentiment, in favour of the Queen'. This was discerned even in rural Perthshire, although it was in the towns that people met and conversed on the subject, working themselves up into a 'State for desperate adventures'. Enthusiasm for such activities however seems to have been considerably stronger at the lower social levels. In Perth itself those 'respectable inhabitants' who illuminated their windows often did so 'through fear of having their windows broke' otherwise. Similar accounts came from Glasgow and Paisley.[146] The Queen's middle-class sympathisers preferred to demonstrate their support in a more genteel fashion however, and in Glasgow generated the largest petition ever raised in Scotland.[147]

There was no suggestion of any managerial encouragement or presence however as a procession of the workers from Ruthven printfield marched through the streets 'with torches and music'. Violence broke out when some sailors were prohibited from doing likewise and the military had to intervene (as they did in Edinburgh). Later however they rowed up-river to Scone, residence of the earls of Mansfield, but greatly to the surprise and relief of the estate factor, 'arranged their Boats ten in number, gave three cheers and dropped down the river', a reminder that republicanism represented only a minority aspiration among the Scottish working classes.[148] Loyalty to king and country was arguably more palpable if articulated with less subtlety at the lowest social levels. After the extraordinary carnage of the king's birthday in Glasgow in 1819 it was the 'canaille' which, after carrying off casks of whisky and rum looted from a spirit dealer's, proceeded to drink the king's health' with loud cheering'.[149] It was in Glasgow too that in November 1820 scenes of disorder, 'highly disgraceful to this city', were to be seen as fiery rituals of joy – firing guns and pistols and setting tar barrels alight, along with fencing torn up from 'a gentleman's policy' – 'broke loose into acts of outrage'. Carried on in the name of Queen Caroline, stones and bricks were thrown at the windows of 'principal houses' in both Glasgow and Paisley (where the police too were stoned), while at Ayr a boat was seized and burnt. Almost inevitably, dragoons and cavalry were called in to bring things to a halt.[150] The middle and working classes shared an enthusiasm for the Queen and her plight, but, as on royal birthdays, this particular loyal demonstration was also used as an opportunity to settle a more recent score.

It was clear that old radical scores were being settled in Greenock in December 1820, when a mob made a snowball of 'colossal' dimensions and rolled it into the doorway of a particularly unpopular former member of the Port Glasgow Armed Association.[151] That radical fires were still glowing two years later is evident from the reports there were at the end of November 1822 of bonfires and other demonstrations of 'mobical joy', in Johnstone and parts of Glasgow and Paisley, to celebrate the radical 'Orator' Hunt's release from prison.[152] The case of the Glasgow weaver George Smith, whose premises were attacked by a large crowd in 1824 which still held a grudge against him for his failure to join in the 1820 rising, was reported in the previous chapter. While the bulk of the crowd mainly comprised females of a 'savage disposition', the faintest suggestion that there remained among the population activists who may have had radical leanings is found in the presence among the leaders of Smith's attackers of Alex McPhee, a weaver and coal sinker, who had been convicted of being part of the riot against Westhorn wall the previous year.[153] But little more was seen or heard of working-class radicalism in the 1820s.

The other direction in which the working classes turned in the aftermath of April 1820 was to industrial struggle. This was intensified, first by the cotton spinners, who resumed their attacks on blackleg workers and made several attempts to set mills on fire. Although the suggestion has been made that there were no links between trade union affairs and radicalism, it does appear, initially at least, that the targets of industrial violence were spinners and mill workers who had filled the jobs of those dismissed for having been 'out' for the week of the rising.[154] But this was unusual and by 1823 serious disputes, the outcomes of which would have consequences for the manufacturing class as a whole, were taking place in cotton spinnning and calico-printing, as well as tailoring. In September 1824 concern was expressed at the 'spirit of opposition to the authority of their masters' which had arisen among the manufacturing population of the west of Scotland.[155] As was seen in chapter 7, this culminated in the industrial confrontations of 1824–6. It was with no little satisfaction that in January 1825 the newspapers were able to announce that some cotton spinners had returned to work 'upon the terms prescribed by their masters', unable to hold out any longer as they had sold their furniture and all their spare clothing for their scanty subsistence.[156]

An end of *Auld Lang Syne*

The industrial relations war was not over, but crucial battles were being won in the interests of a rampant market system. Wage cuts – savage in the case of handloom weaving – and the employment in coal mining, for example, of unemployed handloom weavers both hastened and signalled the limits of worker resistance. With militant working-class radicalism crushed, the movement for political reform was now safely back in middle-class hands.[157] Little was left of the coalition of overlapping interests which had momentarily united large sections of the labouring class in Lowland Scotland between 1819 and 1824–25. Key conditions were being put in place which would ensure the future of the low-wage Scottish economy within a remarkably stable political environment.

During the 1820s the middle-classes, the churches and the urban authorities carried on with their collaborative, evangelically-inspired work of physical and moral improvement with increased vigour. Although the degree of social homogeneity among the urban bourgeoisie in Aberdeen may have been unusual, the example is instructive. By and large, those families who provided most of the city's 120 or so kirk elders were also the source of the leading personnel in the main business and political institutions.[158] Evangelicalism, yet another source of middle-class identity, was 'not so much a theological system' as a 'framework of response to the emergence of modern urban society', which incorporated 'hundreds' of activities in addition to the more obvious ones such as church building, Sunday school provision and the distribution of religious tracts.[159] Better habits and more appropriate attitudes were inculcated not only by the sabbath school and church but by the provision of works libraries.[160] To these were added in 1828 a powerful temperance movement in Scotland, aimed at cutting out spirit drinking, which was rightly seen as a danger to morals, public order and labour productivity, although less so among the 'better class' of workmen, who tended to be 'more intellectual' and materialistic, and for whom being 'tipsy' was considered to be offensive and degrading.[161]

At the ideological level the writings of the staunch Tory and radical-hater Sir Walter Scott 'defused' the nation's history by playing their part in retrieving from Scottish radicals icons they had imbued with partisan significance. Pressing contemporary issues such as clearance and emigration were ignored as Scotland's past was conflated with that of the greatly-romanticised Highlander.[162] It was a sentimentalised, unproblematic self-image with which many (but by no means all) Scots – especially those of a Tory persuasion – evidently felt comfortable. The martial tradition in Scotland, once an object of ruling class trepidation, was tapped for the same ends, that is to protect Britain's world position and to counter revolution.[163] In August 1822, on George IV's visit to

Scotland (with Colonel David Stewart of Garth as master of ceremonies, aided by Scott), the first by a British monarch since Charles II in 1650, not only did an estimated twenty thousand of Glasgow's citizens leave for the capital by coach and canal-boat to see the tartan bedecked king and Scotland's 'Highland' peers, but so too, on foot, did some seven hundred 'artisans'.[164] Highland games were organised in the same decade, in towns such as Crieff, Dunkeld and Stirling, where Highlander and Lowlander could meet and mingle and adopt as national virtues those associated with the Highlands – strength, endurance and tartan dress. In a sleight-of-hand process which had preceded 1820 and which would carry on well into the nineteenth century, the Scottish past was turned into an 'ideologically neutral pageant', a transition which had its visual counterparts in the erection of towers and monuments that celebrated and turned into common property figures like William Wallace and Robert Burns, ploughman poet, self-made man and 'paradigm of Scottish bourgeois virtue'. Burns' dabblings with radicalism, as well as poems written in 1793 and 1794 which might have been judged treasonable, were quietly expunged from the public memory.[165]

Existing distinctions between different sections of the working classes, many of which have been mentioned already, became sharper as the looser labour market turned man against man and boy and, increasingly, men against women, as domestic rhetoric replaced the more egalitarian, community-based struggles described earlier, and in chapter 7 in the industrial context. Ironically, arguments in favour of patriarchy and the primacy of the male breadwinner came not from above, from middle-class exponents of *laissez-faire*, but instead from male trade unionists, who used the image of the passive female worker-victim to strengthen their own positions with the workplace.[166] The thin skin which had temporarily all but closed the sectarian divide was also broken, although not uniformly. In Dundee the proposals for Catholic emancipation in 1829 met with a hostile reception. A William Kirkcaldy organised a petition which, it was noted, was 'Signing in all corners of the Town by immense numbers but mostly of the Lower Class of People & Boys who understand nothing of the bearings of the question'. Although 'foolish dread of Popery' was advanced as the cause, by the following year anti-Irish disturbances were thought to have resulted from fears that Irish workers were driving down wages.[167] In Glasgow, an Orange march had gone ahead in July 1822 in spite of a ban on it imposed by the magistrates, with peace being maintained only by the temporary arrest of all the Catholics who had collected and been 'most ready to give battle'.[168]

Their attention necessarily focused more intently on the workplace, and, more interested in self-improvement of the sort mentioned above, artisans were withdrawing from the 'rough culture' of the streets and appeared much less frequently in riots associated with 'community politics' in towns such as Glasgow and Dundee in the second half of the 1820s.[169] The process whereby the 'respectable' members of the working class differentiated themselves from the rougher elements was eased by the real wage gains which began to be enjoyed by the beneficiaries of industrialisation, the machine-makers, millwrights and others who were prepared to eschew confrontation and needed little persuasion of the benefits of class collaboration. The necessity of reforming the existing political system without resorting to violence or creating a new one was the strategy espoused by working-class newspapers like the *Herald to the Trades Advocate*. It was largely funded by subscriptions from the unen-franchised, artisans who would now read more about the ideas of Jeremy Bentham than Thomas Paine.[170] How far the atmosphere had changed can be demonstrated by looking at reports of the king's birthday celebra-tions in June 1831. Nowhere was trouble reported. Instead, there were spectacular decorations which, in Paisley, were more excessive 'in the streets which are principally occupied by the working classes'. In Glasgow's Gallowgate they were said to have marched 'four and six deep', singing as workers did elsewhere, 'Up and whaur them a' Willie', a hymn of praise for the 'reforming King', William IV.[171]

The working classes in Scotland would be disappointed by the Reform Bill of 1832, although with a proportionately greater extension of the fran-chise in Scotland than England, and with the main enemy having been identified as the landed class, this was less marked than in England.[172] Chartism would provide a rallying point for working-class radicals, but Scottish Chartism was distinctly moderate, and strongly committed to the moral force approach. Among the unrulier elements there would be a return to the street disorders of earlier times, and physical-force Chartism did have its Scottish adherents. There was a series of food riots in the north-east in 1847. Nevertheless, by the mid-1820s a course of untrammelled agrarian and industrial capitalism in Scottish society was set for the next half century and beyond. It would not be until the crofters' wars of the early 1880s, the emergence of ideologically-explicit class organisations in 1884 and some firmer gains in trade unionism in the same decade that working people would next find the economic conditions, issues and ideological sustenance around which they could rally once again.[173] Modern Scotland had been born.

Notes

1 Meikle, *Scotland and the French Revolution*, 44–6.
2 J. Brims, 'From reformers to "jacobins": the Scottish Association of the Friends of the People', in Devine, *Conflict and Stability*, 36.
3 McFarland, *Ireland and Scotland*, 81.
4 *Ibid.*, 116–17.

5 Murray, *The Scottish Hand Loom Weavers*, 209–10; Fraser, *Conflict and Class*, 65–7.

6 Fraser, *Conflict and Class*, 68; NAS, RH 2/4 66, fos 254–7, Robert Dundas to Henry Dundas, n.d; fos 258–9, Alexander Riddoch to Henry Dundas, 8 December 1792. I am grateful to Dr Bob Harris for letting me see his transcripts of these documents.

7 DCA, Miscellaneous box of eighteenth-century burgh court papers, 'Warrant of Commitment, James Matthew', 1793.

8 See NAS, RH2/4, 209, fos 3–23, anonymous memoranda concerning Scottish radicalism.

9 PKCA, Perth Burgh Records, PE 51/25, 'Petition to the magistrates of Perth from James Miller', 1 March 1794, 'Petition of James Miller, procurator fiscal of Perth', 21 April 1794, 'Declarations of William Wedderspoon and David Buist', 28 April 1794, PE 51/279, 'Lybelled summons, procurator fiscal of Perth', 14 January 1795, B 59/32/104, Alexander Mackay to James Ramsay, provost of Perth, 20 August 1795, B 59/32/111/13, copy letter to Lord Adam Gordon, 31 October 1795.

10 PKCA, PE Mass (15) 338, Provost Robert Ross to Commanding Officer of Forces at Dundee, 27 June 1811.

11 NLS, Melville Papers, MS 1054, fo. 109, Robert Dundas to (?), 10 March 1796.

12 *Glasgow Mercury*, 6 September 1796; *Glasgow Courier*, 17 September 1796.

13 Lenman, *Integration, Enlightenment and Industrialisation*, 104; Fry, *The Dundas Despotism*, 201–4.

14 T. M. Devine, 'The failure of radical reform in Scotland in the late eighteenth century', in Devine, *Conflict and Stability*, 51–64.

15 Fry, *The Dundas Despotism*, 172; Young, *The Rousing of the Scottish Working Class*, 49–54; G. Mealmaker, *The Moral and Political Catechism of Man* (Edinburgh, 1797).

16 *Glasgow Mercury*, 18 March 1779; Fraser, *Conflict and Class*, 60–5.

17 Fraser, *Conflict and Class*, 65.

18 Colley, *Britons*, 285–308.

19 McFarland, *Ireland and Scotland*, 120.

20 Dickinson, *The Politics of the People*, 255–6; Colley, *Britons*, 310.

21 *Glasgow Mercury*, 22 June 1780.

22 Quoted in McFarland, *Ireland and Scotland*, 121.

23 *Glasgow Mercury*, 5 June 1795; see too Whatley, 'Royal day, people's day', 175.

24 ECA, CRB, Moses Collection, SL 30/244, 'Thanks to the committee of the Edinburgh Constitutional Association', 1794.

25 E. Vincent, 'The responses of Scottish churchmen to the French Revolution', *Scottish Historical Review*, LXXIII (October 1994), 191–215.

26 Murray, *The Scottish Hand Loom Weavers*, 165.

27 J. Brims, 'The covenanting tradition and Scottish radicalism in the 1790s', in T. Brotherstone (ed.), *Covenant, Charter and Party: Traditions of Revolt and Protest in Modern Scottish History* (Aberdeen, 1989), 52.

28 Vincent, 'The responses of Scottish churchmen', 206–11.

29 PKCA, Perth Burgh records, PE 51/25, 'Petition to magistrates of Perth from James Miller', 1 March 1794, precognitions.

30 Devon Record Office (DRO), Sidmouth Papers, OH 49, Alexander Boswell to Viscount Sidmouth, 4 February 1820.

31 McFarland, *Ireland and Scotland*, 140.

32 Meikle, *Scotland and the French Revolution*, 186–7; McFarlane, *Ireland and Scotland*, 144–5; Mitchell, *The Irish in the West of Scotland*, 9.

33 Meikle, *Scotland and the French Revolution*, 129–53.

34 E. P. Thompson, *The Making of the English Working Class* (London, 1963), 195; for reviews of the debate in the Scottish context see Clarke and Dickson, 'The birth of class?', 292–309; W. H. Fraser, 'Social class', in Cooke, *et al.*, *Modern Scottish History*, 216–19.

35 See Knox, *Industrial Nation*, 1–27.

36 Clarke and Dickson, 'Class and class consciousness', 16–33.

37 DRO, Sidmouth Papers, OH 46, Earl of Cassillis to Viscount Sidmouth, 29 December 1819.

38 *Glasgow Courier*, 4, 8 April 1820.

39 McFarland, *Ireland and Scotland*, 237–8.

40 Scone Palace, Mansfield Papers, Box 103/5, James Wood to the Earl of Mansfield, 13 April 1820.

41 P. Berresford Ellis and S. Mac A' Ghobbain, *The Scottish Insurrection of 1820* (London, 1989 ed.), 166–78; F. K. Donnelly, 'The Scottish rising of 1820: a re-interpretation', *Scottish Tradition*, VI (1976), 27–30.

42 Donnelly, 'The Scottish rising', 32; DRO, Sidmouth Papers, OH 55, Alexander Boswell to Viscount Sidmouth, 11 April 1820; *Glasgow Courier*, 8 April 1820.

43 Berresford Ellis and Mac A' Ghobbain, *The Scottish Insurrection*, 204–221; NAS, GD1/1147/1, Anonymous memorandum book (Kilmarnock), 1 January 1819–10 August 1820.

44 Young, *The Rousing of the Scottish Working Class*, 60.

45 M. I. Thomis and P. Holt, *Threats of Revolution in Britain, 1789–1848* (London, 1977), 76; Lenman, *Integration, Enlightenment and Industrialisation*, 152–3; Smout, *History of the Scottish People*, 446–8.

46 See W. M. Roach, 'Alexander Richmond and the radical reform movement in Glasgow, 1816–17', *Scottish Historical Review*, LI (1972).

47 Fraser, 'Patterns of protest', 286.

48 Somerville, *The Autobiography of a Working Man*, 15.

49 Scone Palace, Mansfield Papers, Box 103/4, James Wood to the Earl of Mansfield, 20 September 1819; A. W. Harding, *Pullars of Perth* (Perth, 1991), 20.

50 Public Record Office, Chatham Papers, PRO 30/8/190, fos 197–201, William Wilson to Mr McDowall, 29 March 1799; see too Whatley, 'Labour in the industrialising city', 386.

51 NAS, Lord Advocate's Papers, AD 14/16/58, Adam Duff, Sheriff of Forfar, to Hugh Warrender WS, Crown Agent, 22 December 1816.

52 E. King, 'Popular culture in Glasgow', in R. A. Cage (ed.) *The Working Class in Glasgow* (London, 1987), 157–8; Whatley, 'Labour in the industrialising city', 388.

53 NAS, Lord Advocate's Papers, AD 14/24/185, 'Information and Presentment of George Salmond to Sheriff-Depute of Lanarkshire', 12 July 1824.
54 NAS, Lord Advocate's Papers, AD 14/23/104, 'Information and Presentment, George Salmond v. Alexander McPhie and others', June 1823; *Glasgow Courier*, 24 June 1823.
55 *Ibid.*, 28 June 1823.
56 *Ibid.*, 27 August 1819.
57 NAS, Lord Advocate's Papers, AD 14/19/298, Precognitions in case of riot, Glasgow, September 1819, precognition of William Tait.
58 Alexander Richmond, quoted in Fraser, 'Social class', in A. Cooke, *et al.*, *Modern Scottish History*, 219.
59 Clark, *The Struggle for the Breeches*, 158–9; NAS, JC 45/12, Weavers' Committee Minute Book, 1810–11, 6 June 1810; see too Young, *Women and Popular Struggles*, 61–7.
60 *Glasgow Courier*, 28 October 1819; NAS, Paisley Sheriff Court, SC 58/55/24, Precognition v. John Fraser, schoolmaster, 12 April 1820.
61 Clark, *The Struggle for the Breeches*, 160; *Glasgow Courier*, 26 October 1819.
62 *Ibid.*, 2, 4 November 1819.
63 Treble, 'The standard of living of the working class', 204.
64 R. A. Cage, 'The standard of living debate: Glasgow, 1800–1850', *Journal of Economic History*, XLIII (1983), 178.
65 Fraser, *Conflict and Class*, 101.
66 NAS, Buccleuch Muniments, GD 224/30/15/17–24, Lord Advocate to the Duke of Buccleuch, 20 January 1817.
67 Fraser, *Conflict and Class*, 104.
68 Mitchell, *The Irish in the West of Scotland*, 88.
69 NAS, Sheriff Court Records, Paisley, SC 58/55/24, 1820 Treason Trials, 'Calendar of Prisoners Charged with High Treason, to be tried, Paisley, 1 July 1820'.
70 Clarke and Dickson, 'The birth of class?', 300.
71 NAS, Lord Advocate's Papers, AD 14/20/43, George Salmond to Hugh Warrender, 10 May 1820; (rather unconvincingly) on the disassociation of coal miners from radicalism, see Campbell, *The Lanarkshire Miners*, 74–5. On connections, see *Glasgow Courier*, 4 June 1820, and text which follows.
72 Whatley, 'The dark side of the Enlightenment?', 265–6; and for an example, see Strawhorn, *History of Irvine*, 120.
73 *Glasgow Courier*, 26 June 1819.
74 Whatley, 'Labour in the industrialising city', 386, 389; on seditious publications, see NAS, Lord Advocate's Papers, AD 14/21/213, George Salmond, Procurator-Fiscal v. David Potter, 1820.
75 On the Britishness of 1820 see Donnelly, 'The Scottish rising', 27–9; Clarke and Dickson, 'The birth of class?', 302.
76 McFarland, *Protestants First*, 53.
77 *Glasgow Courier*, 26 October 1819.
78 Aitken-MacKinnon Papers.
79 *Glasgow Courier*, 27 August 1819.
80 Scone Palace, Mansfield Papers, Box 103/4, James Wood to the Earl of

Mansfield, 4 December 1819; DRO, Sidmouth Papers, OH 46, Earl of Cassillis to Viscount Sidmouth, 29 December 1819.

81 NRA (S), Hamilton of Lennoxlove Papers, TD 94/57/797, Duke of Hamilton to the Earl of Liverpool, 16 December 1819.

82 NAS, Lord Advocate's Papers, AD 14/19/298, Precognitions in case of riots in Glasgow, September 1819; *Glasgow Courier*, 14 September 1819.

83 *Ibid.*, 16 September 1819.

84 DRO, Sidmouth Papers, OH 43, Lord Sidmouth to Lord Melville, 14 November 1819.

85 *Glasgow Courier*, 28 December 1819.

86 Berresford Ellis and Mac A' Ghobbain, *The Scottish Insurrection*, 138.

87 SRA, Lord Provost's Office, Monteith Correspondence, G.1.2 (25), Thomas Sharp to Henry Monteith, 20 March 1820.

88 NRA (S), Hamilton of Lennoxlove Papers, TD 94/57/1477, Anonymous letter to Duke of Hamilton, 16 December 1819.

89 SRA, Stirling-Maxwell Papers, T -PM 117/1/45, N. Patrick to J. Maxwell, 13 December 1819.

90 *Glasgow Courier*, 1 April 1820.

91 A. Richmond, *Narrative of the Condition of the Manufacturing Population and the Proceedings of Government which lead to the State Trials in Scotland* (London, 1824), 1.

92 Richards, *The Leviathan of Wealth*, 220–1; *A History of the Highland Clearances*, 331–9.

93 DRO, Sidmouth Papers, OH 39, Sir William Rae to Viscount Sidmouth, 19 October 1819.

94 DRO, Sidmouth Papers, OH 62, Kirkman Finlay to Viscount Sidmouth, 10 November 1820.

95 *Glasgow Courier*, 11, 14 December 1819; Scone Palace, Mansfield Papers, Box 106/2, Robert Jamieson to the Earl of Mansfield, 27 December 1819.

96 DRO, Sidmouth Papers, OH 68, Lord Sidmouth to the Duke of Wellington, 21 March 1821.

97 SRA, Lord Provost's Office, Monteith Correspondence, G.1.2. (25), Thomas Sharp to Henry Monteith, 20 March 1820; (27) Colonel Norcott to Henry Monteith, 20 March 1820; (28), H. Hobhouse to Henry Monteith, 22 March 1820; (30), H. Hobhouse to Henry Monteith, 24 March 1820; (32), Thomas Sharp to Henry Monteith, 1 April 1820.

98 Strawhorn, *The History of Irvine*, 108.

99 Fraser, *Conflict and Class*, 111–12; Donnachie, 'The darker side', 16–17.

100 Richmond, *Narrative of the Condition of the Manufacturing Population*, 185.

101 DRO, Sidmouth Papers, OH 50, Alexander Boswell to Viscount Sidmouth, 4 February 1820.

102 Scone Palace, Mansfield Papers, Box 103/5, J. Wood to Earl of Mansfield, 13 April 1820; *Glasgow Courier*, 8 April 1820.

103 NAS, Sheriff Court Records, Paisley, SC 58/55/24, 1820 Treason Trial Papers, 'Copy Memoranda by Sheriff touching those committed for High Treason'.

104 DRA, Sidmouth Papers, OH 49, Alexander Bosewell to Viscount Sidmouth, 4 February 1820.

105 SRA, Stirling-Maxwell Papers, T – PM 117/1/37, N. Patrick to J. Maxwell, 13 December 1819.
106 NAS, Lord Advocate's Papers, AD 14/19/298, Precognitions in case of Glasgow riot, September 1819, precognition of William Tait; Scone Palace, Mansfield Papers, Box 103/4, J. Wood to Earl of Mansfield, 20 September 1819.
107 DRO, Sidmouth Papers, OH 58, Lord Sidmouth to Alexander Boswell, 11 June 1821.
108 DRO, Sidmouth Papers, OH 59, John Hamilton to Alexander Boswell, 5 June 1820, HO 61, Alexander Boswell to Viscount Sidmouth, 8 November 1820.
109 *Glasgow Courier*, 14 September 1820.
110 W. H. Fraser, 'The Scottish context of Chartism', in Brotherstone, *Covenant, Charter and Party*, 73.
111 Fraser, *Conflict and Class*, 108–9.
112 SRA, Lord Provost's Office, Monteith Correspondence, G.1.2 (6), William Muir to Henry Monteith, 12 January 1820.
113 *Glasgow Courier*, 8 July 1819.
114 Brown, 'Religion', 73–4; 'Religion, class and church growth', in W. H. Fraser and R. J. Morris (eds), *People and Society in Scotland, Volume II, 1830–1914* (Edinburgh, 1990), 312–13.
115 Strawhorn, *History of Ayr*, 144.
116 Murray, The Scottish Hand Loom Weavers, 165.
117 Thom, *Rhymes and Recollections*, 72–6; see too Finlayson, *Simple Scottish Rhymes*; Leonard, *Radical Renfrew*.
118 *Perth Courier*, 19 August 1819.
119 Whatley, 'Labour in the industrialising city', 388–9.
120 Mitchell, *The Irish in the West of Scotland*, 103–4.
121 McFarland, *Ireland and Scotland*, 236.
122 Mitchell, *The Irish in the West of Scotland*, 90–1.
123 *Ibid.*, 92–3.
124 See Bartlett, 'The Irish militia disturbances', 44,
125 J. Smyth, *The Men of No Property: Irish Radicals and Popular Politics in the Late Eighteenth Century* (Dublin, 1992), 157–61; McFarland, *Ireland and Scotland*, 132.
126 C. G. Brown, 'Religion and social change', 158; Fraser and Maver, 'Tackling the problems', 397.
127 *Ibid.*, 395; I. Maver, 'The guardianship of the community', in Devine and Jackson, *Glasgow*, 244–6;
128 R. E. H. Mellor, 'Aberdeen – the Great Century', in Smith and Stevenson, *Aberdeen in the Nineteenth Century*, 8.
129 Nenadic, 'The middle ranks and modernisation', 297.
130 Nenadic, 'The rise of the urban middle classes', 122; for a recent study of Dundee see L. Walsh, 'The development of organised charity in the Scottish burgh: Dundee, 1790–1850' (unpublished Ph.D. thesis, University of Dundee, 1997).
131 Strawhorn, *History of Irvine*, 109.
132 Nenadic, 'The middle ranks and modernisation', 296; 'Political reform and

the "ordering" of middle-class protest', in Devine, *Conflict and Stability*, 73, 75–6.

133 *Glasgow Courier*, 27 April, 11 May 1820.

134 I. Maver, 'Glasgow's civic government', in Fraser and Maver, *Glasgow*, 447–8.

135 Strawhorn, *The History of Ayr*, 154.

136 Nenadic, 'Political reform', 77.

137 Fraser, *Conflict and Class*, 166.

138 *Glasgow Courier*, 13 April, 2 May 1820.

139 NAS, Lord Advocate's Papers, AD 14/22/175, Information in case of riot and destruction and robbing of house of Mr Provand, colour maker, West Clyde St, February 1822; *Glasgow Courier*, 19 February 1822.

140 *Scots Magazine*, IV (March 1742), 140–1; Strawhorn, *History of Irvine*, 113; *History of Ayr*, 151.

141 NAS, Lord Advocate's Papers, AD 14/23/104, Precognition of John West; AD 14/23/241, George Salmond to the Crown Agent, 23 April 1823.

142 *Glasgow Courier*, 29 June 1820; NAS, Lord Advocate's Papers, AD 14/20/225, James Peddie to the Lord Advocate, 3 July 1820.

143 Clark, *The Struggle for the Breeches*, 164–5.

144 Rogers, *Crowds, Culture and Politics*, 248–9.

145 On the view reported here see C. Calhoun, *The Question of Class Struggle* (Chicago, 1982), 105–15.

146 Scone Palace, Mansfield Papers, Box 103/5, J. Wood to Earl of Mansfield, 20 November 1820; *Glasgow Courier*, 18 November 1820.

147 Nenadic, 'The middle ranks and modernisation', 301.

148 Scone Palace, Mansfield Papers, Box 103/5, J. Wood to the Earl of Mansfield, 27 November 1820.

149 *Dundee, Perth and Cupar Advertiser*, 11 June 1819.

150 *Glasgow Courier*, 14, 16, 18 November 1820; Strawhorn, *History of Ayr*, 155.

151 *Glasgow Courier*, 21 December 1820.

152 *Ibid.*, 2 and 14 November 1822.

153 *Ibid.*, 11 September 1824.

154 *Ibid.*, 5 October 1820.

155 *Ibid.*, 14 September 1824.

156 *Ibid.*, 29 January 1825, 1 February 1825.

157 Fraser, *Conflict and Class*, 112–13.

158 A. A. Maclaren, 'Class formation and class fractions: the Aberdeen bourgeoisie 1830–1850', in G. Gordon and B. Dicks (eds), *Scottish Urban History* (Aberdeen, 1983), 116–17.

159 Brown, *Religion and Society*, 101–6.

160 J. McConechy, *Introductory Address on the Formation of a Literary and Scientific Institute Among the Workmen at the University Printing Office, Glasgow* (Glasgow, 1825), 15.

161 T. C. Smout, *A Century of the Scottish People, 1830–1950* (1986), 141–2; British Parliamentary Papers, Inquiry Into Drunkennness, III (1834), Evidence of William Murray, 238–40.

162 Clyde, *From Rebel to Hero*, 128–9; see too J. Prebble, *The King's Jaunt*.

George IV in Scotland, 1822 (London, 1988), for a version of a phenomenon which would justify more rigorous examination.
163 Cookson, 'The Napoleonic wars, military Scotland and tory highlandism', 73.
164 *Glasgow Courier*, 15 August 1822.
165 C. Kidd, 'The canon of patriotic landmarks in Scottish history', *Scotlands*, I (1994), 6–7; R. J. Finlay, 'The Burns cult and Scottish identity in the nineteenth and twentieth centuries', in Simpson, *Love & Liberty*, 73–4; Strawhorn, *History of Ayr*, 135; A. Noble, 'Burns and Scottish nationalism', in Simpson, *Burns Now*, 167–92.
166 Clark, *The Struggle for the Breeches*, 218–19.
167 University of Dundee Archives, MS 15/114/2, Diary of Thomas Handyside Baxter, 1829–30, 19 February 1829, 6 June 1830.
168 *Glasgow Courier*, 9, 13 July 1822.
169 Whatley, 'Labour in the industrialising city', 392–3.
170 F. A. Montgomery, 'Glasgow radicalism, 1830–1848' (unpublished Ph.D. thesis, University of Glasgow, 1974), 32–4.
171 *Glasgow Evening Post and Paisley Reformer*, 4 June 1831.
172 Fraser, 'The Scottish context of chartism', 70–1.
173 J. Hunter, *The Making of the Crofting Community* (Edinburgh, 1976), 131–45; J. Foster, 'Class', in A. Cooke, I. Donnachie, A. MacSween and C. A. Whatley (eds), *Modern Sottish History 1707 to the Present, Volume 2: The Modernisation of Scotland, 1850 to the Present* (East Linton, 1998), 220–1.

Select bibliography

Articles

Where the same or similar material appears elsewhere, in an essay collection or book, the article is not included in this short list.

Devine, T. M., 'The Union of 1707 and Scottish development', *Scottish Economic & Social History*, V (1985), 23–40.

Donnachie, I., 'Drink and society, 1750–1850: some aspects of the Scottish experience', *Journal of the Scottish Labour History Society*, XIII (1979), 5–22.

Elliot, J. H., 'A Europe of composite monarchies', *Past and Present*, CXXXVII (November 1992), 48–71.

Gibson, A. J. S., and Smout, T. C., 'Regional prices and market regions: the evolution of the early modern Scottish grain market', *Economic History Review*, XLVIII (May 1995), 258–82.

Graham E., 'In defence of the Scottish maritime interest, 1681–1713', *Scottish Historical Review*, LXXXI (October 1992), 88–109.

Harris, Bob, 'Patriotic commerce and national revival: the Free British Fishery Society and British politics, c. 1749–58', *English Historical Review*, CXIV (April 1999), 285–313.

Harris, Bob, and Whatley, C. A., '"To solemnise his majesty's birthday": new perspectives on loyalism in George II's Britain', *History*, LXXXIII (July 1998), 397–419.

Hunt, E. H., 'Industrialisation and regional inequality: wages in Britain, 1760–1914', *Journal of Economic History*, XLVI (1986), 935–61.

Kidd, C., 'North Britishness and the nature of eighteenth-century British patriotisms', *The Historical Journal*, XXXIX (1996), 361–82.

Nash, R. C., 'The English and Scottish tobacco trades in the seventeenth and eighteenth centuries: legal and illegal trade', *Economic History Review*, XXXV (1982), 354–72.

Smout, T. C., 'Peasant and lord in Scotland: institutions controlling Scottish society, 1500–1800', *Receuils de la Société Jean Bodin pour L'Histoire Comparative des Institutions*, XLIV (1987), 499–524.

Szechi, D., '"Cam ye o'er frae France?" Exile and the mind of Scottish Jacobitism,

1716–1727', *Journal of British Studies*, XXXVII, 4 (October 1998), 357–90.

Vincent, E., 'The response of Scottish churchmen to the French Revolution', *Scottish Historical Review*, LXXIII (October 1994), 191–215.

Whatley, C. A., 'Economic causes and consequences of the Union of 1707: a survey', *Scottish Historical Review*, LXVIII (October 1989), 150–81.

Whatley, C. A., 'Women and the economic transformation of Scotland, *c.* 1740–1830', *Scottish Economic & Social History*, XIV (1994), 19–40..

Young, C., 'Rural independent artisan production in the east-central lowlands of Scotland, *c.* 1600–1850', *Scottish Economic & Social History*, XVI (1996), 17–37.

Books and edited collections

As will be seen from the endnotes, much of the important work in Scottish history in the 1980s and 1990s has appeared in essay collections. The main volumes are included below. Place of publication is London unless otherwise indicated.

Allan, D., *Virtue, Learning and the Scottish Enlightenment* (Edinburgh, 1993).

Baldwin, J. R. (ed.), *Peoples & Settlement in North-West Ross* (Edinburgh, 1994).

Berg, M., *The Age of Manufactures, 1700–1820: Industry, Innovation and Work in Britain* (1994 ed.) .

Black, J. (ed.), *Britain in the Age of Walpole* (1994 ed.).

Brotherstone, T. (ed.), *Covenant, Charter and Party: Traditions of Revolt and Protest in Modern Scottish History* (Aberdeen, 1989).

Brown, C., *Religion and Society in Scotland Since 1707* (1987).

Butt, J., and Ponting, K. (eds), *Scottish Textile History* (Aberdeen, 1987).

Butt, J., and Ward, J. T. (eds), *Scottish Themes: Essays in Honour of S. G. E. Lythe* (Edinburgh, 1976).

Cage, R. A. (ed.), *The Scots Abroad: Labour, Capital and Enterprise, 1750–1914* (1985).

Campbell, A. B., *The Lanarkshire Miners: A Social History of their Trade Unions, 1775–1874* (Edinburgh, 1979).

Campbell, R. H., *Scotland Since 1707: The Rise of an Industrial Society* (Oxford, 1965).

Campbell, R. H., *The Rise and Fall of Scottish Industry, 1707–1939* (Edinburgh, 1980).

Campbell, R. H., and Skinner, A (eds), *The Origins and Nature of the Scottish Enlightenment* (Edinburgh, 1982) .

Canny, N. (ed.), *Europeans on the Move: Studies in European Migration, 1500–1800* (Oxford, 1994).

Clark, A., *The Struggle for the Breeches: Gender and the Making of the British Working Class* (Berkeley, California, 1997).

Clyde, R., *From Rebel to Hero: The Image of the Highlander, 1745–1830* (East Linton, 1995).

Cochran, L. E., *Scottish Trade with Ireland in the Eighteenth Century*

(Edinburgh, 1985).

Colley, L., *Britons: Forging the Nation, 1707–1837* (Yale, 1992).

Connolly, S. J., Houston, R. A., and Morris, R. J. (eds), *Conflict, Identity and Economic Development: Ireland and Scotland, 1600–1939* (Preston, 1995).

Cooke, A. J., Donnachie, I., MacSween, A., and Whatley, C. A. (eds), *Modern Scottish History, 1707 to the Present* (V vols, East Linton, 1998).

Crafts, N. F. R., *British Economic Growth during the Industrial Revolution* (Oxford, 1985).

Cummings, A. J. G., and Devine, T. M. (eds), *Industry, Business and Society in Scotland Since 1700: Essays Presented to John Butt* (Edinburgh, 1994).

Cullen, L. M., and Smout, T. C. (eds), *Comparative Aspects of Scottish & Irish Economic and Social History, 1600–1900* (Edinburgh, 1977).

Daiches, D., Jones, P. and Jones, J. (eds), *A Hotbed of Genius: The Scottish Enlightenment, 1730–1790* (Edinburgh, 1986).

Devine, T. M., *The Tobacco Lords: A Study of the ·Tobacco Merchants of Glasgow and their Trading Activities c. 1740–90* (Edinburgh, 1976).

Devine, T. M., *Clanship to Crofters' War: The Social Transformation of the Scottish Highlands* (Manchester, 1994).

Devine, T. M., *The Transformation of Rural Scotland: Social Change and the Agrarian Economy, 1660–1815* (Edinburgh, 1994).

Devine, T. M., *Exploring the Scottish Past: Themes in the History of Scottish Society* (East Linton, 1995).

Devine, T. M. (ed.), *Conflict and Stability in Scottish Society, 1700–1850* (Edinburgh, 1990).

Devine, T. M., and Dickson, D. (eds), *Ireland and Scotland, 1600–1850: Parallels and Contrasts in Economic and Social Development* (Edinburgh, 1983).

Devine, T. M., and Jackson, G. (eds), *Glasgow, Volume I: Beginnings to 1830* (Manchester, 1995).

Devine, T. M., and Mitchison, R. (eds), *People and Society in Scotland, Volume 1, 1760–1830* (Edinburgh, 1988).

Devine, T. M., and Young, J. R. (eds), *Eighteenth-Century Scotland: New Perspectives* (East Linton, 1999).

Dickinson, H. T., *The Politics of the People in Eighteenth-Century Britain* (1994).

Dickson, T. (ed.), *Scottish Capitalism: Class, State and Nation from the Union to the Present* (1980).

Dickson, T. (ed.), *Capital and Class in Scotland* (Edinburgh, 1982).

Dingwall, H. M., *Late 17th-Century Edinburgh: A Demographic Study* (Aldershot, 1994).

Dodgshon, R. A., *From Chiefs to Landlords: Social and Economic Change in the Western Highlands and Islands, c. 1493–1820* (Edinburgh, 1998).

Donaldson, W., *The Jacobite Song: Political Myth and National Identity* (Aberdeen, 1988) .

Donnachie, I., and Whatley, C. A. (eds), *The Manufacture of Scottish History* (Edinburgh, 1992).

Duckham, B. F., *A History of the Scottish Coal Industry, Volume 1: 1700–1815* (Newton Abbot, 1970).

Durie, A. J., *The Scottish Linen Industry in the Eighteenth Century* (Edinburgh, 1979).

Ellis, S. G., and Barber, S. (eds), *Conquest and Union: Fashioning a British State, 1485–1725* (1995).

Ferguson, W., *Scotland's Relations With England: A Survey to 1707* (Edinburgh, 1977).

Fitton, R. S., and Wadsworth, A. P., *The Strutts and the Arkwrights, 1758–1830: A Study of the Early Factory System* (Manchester, 1958).

Flinn, M. (ed.), *Scottish Population History from the Seventeenth Century to the 1930s* (Cambridge, 1977).

Fraser, W. H., *Conflict and Class: Scottish Workers, 1700–1838* (Edinburgh, 1988).

Fry, M., *The Dundas Despotism* (Edinburgh, 1992).

Gibson, A. J. S., and Smout, T. C., *Prices, Food and Wages in Scotland, 1550–1780* (Cambridge, 1995).

Glendinning, M., Macinnes, R., and Mackenzie, A., *A History of Scottish Architecture from the Renaissance to the Present Day* (Edinburgh, 1996).

Graham, H. G., *Social Life of Scotland in the Eighteenth Century* (1899).

Gray, M., *The Highland Economy, 1750–1850* (Edinburgh, 1957).

Hamilton, H., *The Industrial Revolution in Scotland* (Oxford, 1932).

Hamilton, H., *An Economic History of Scotland in the Eighteenth Century* (Oxford, 1963).

Hay, D., and Snyder, F. (eds), *Policing and Prosecution in Britain 1750–1850* (Oxford, 1989).

Holloway, J., *Patrons and Painters: Art in Scotland 1650–1760* (Edinburgh, 1989).

Hont, I., and Ignatieff, M. (eds), *Wealth and Virtue* (Cambridge, 1983).

Hook, A. (ed.), *The History of Scottish Literature, Volume 2, 1660–1800* (Aberdeen, 1987).

Houston, R. A., *Social Change in the Age of Enlightenment: Edinburgh, 1660–1760* (Oxford, 1994).

Houston, R. A., and Whyte, I. D. (eds), *Scottish Society, 1500–1800* (Cambridge, 1989).

Hudson, P. (ed.), *Regions and Industries: A Perspective on the Industrial Revolution in Britain* (Cambridge, 1989).

Hunter, J., *The Making of the Crofting Community* (Edinburgh, 1976).

Johnston, D., *Music and Society in Lowland Scotland in the Eighteenth Century* (Edinburgh, 1972).

Kidd, C., *Subverting Scotland's Past: Scottish Whig Historians and the Creation of an Anglo-British Identity, 1689–c. 1830* (Cambridge, 1993).

Knox, W. W., *Industrial Nation: Work, Culture and Society in Scotland, 1800–Present* (Edinburgh, 1999).

Langford, P., *A Polite and Commercial People: England, 1727–1783* (Oxford 1989).

Leneman, L. (ed.), *Perspectives in Scottish Social History: Essays in Honour of Rosalind Mitchison* (Aberdeen, 1988).

Lenman, B., *An Economic History of Modern Scotland, 1660–1976* (1977).

Lenman, B., *The Jacobite Risings in Britain, 1689–1746* (1980).

Lenman, B., *Integration, Enlightenment and Industrialisation: Scotland, 1746–1832* (1981).

Leonard, T., *Radical Renfrew: Poetry from the French Revolution to the First World War* (Edinburgh, 1990).

Logue, K. J., *Popular Disturbances in Scotland 1780–1815* (Edinburgh, 1979).

Lynch, M. (ed.), *The Early Modern Town in Scotland* (1987).

Lynch, M. (ed.), *Jacobitism and the '45* (1995).

Macinnes, A. I., *Clanship, Commerce and the House of Stuart, 1603–1788* (East Linton, 1996).

McFarland, E. W., *Ireland and Scotland in the Age of Revolution; Planting the Green Bough* (Edinburgh, 1994).

McLean, M., *The People of Glengarry: Highlanders in Transition, 1745–1820* (Montreal, 1991).

Marshall, P. J. (ed.), *The Oxford History of the British Empire, Volume II: The Eighteenth Century* (Oxford, 1998).

Mason, R., and MacDougall, N. (eds), *People and Power in Scotland: Essays in Honour of T. C. Smout* (Edinburgh, 1992).

Miller, J. A., *Mastering the Market: The State and the Grain Trade in Northern France, 1700–1860* (Cambridge, 1999).

Mitchell, M. J., *The Irish in the West of Scotland, 1797–1848: Trade Unions, Strikes and Political Movements* (Edinburgh, 1998).

Mitchison, R., *Lordship to Patronage: Scotland, 1603–1746* (1983).

Mitchison, R., and Roebuck, P. (eds), *Economy and Society in Scotland and Ireland, 1500–1939* (Edinburgh, 1988).

Mitchison, R. (ed.), *Why Scottish History Matters?* (Edinburgh, 1991).

Mitchison, R. and Leneman, L., *Sexuality and Social Control: Scotland, 1660–1780* (Oxford, 1989).

Mowat, I. R. M., *Easter Ross, 1750–1850: The Double Frontier* (Edinburgh, 1981).

Murdoch, A., *The People Above: Politics and Administration in Mid-Eighteenth Century Scotland* (Edinburgh, 1980).

Murray, N., *The Scottish Hand Loom Weavers, 1790–1850* (Edinburgh, 1978).

O'Brien, P., and Quinault, R. (eds), *The Industrial Revolution and British Society* (Cambridge, 1993).

Parker, A. W., *Scottish Highlanders in Colonial Georgia: The Recruitment, Emigration, and Settlement at Darien, 1735–1748* (Athens, Georgia, 1997).

Payne, P. L. (ed.), *Studies in Scottish Business History* (1967).

Phillipson, N. T., and Mitchison, R. (eds), *Scotland in the Age of Improvement* (Edinburgh, 1970).

Pittock, M. G. H., *Poetry and Jacobite Politics in Eighteenth-Century Britain and Ireland* (Cambridge, 1994).

Purser, J., *Scotland's Music* (Edinburgh, 1992).

Randall, A., and Charlesworth, A. (eds), *Markets, Market Culture and Popular Protest in Eighteenth-Century Britain and Ireland* (Liverpool, 1996).

Rae, T. I. (ed.), *The Union of 1707: Its Impact on Scotland* (Glasgow, 1974).

Richards, E., *The Leviathan of Wealth: The Sutherland Fortune in the Industrial Revolution* (1973).

Richards, E., *A History of the Highland Clearances: Agrarian Transformation and the Evictions, 1746–1886* (1982).

Riley, P. W. J., *The English Ministers and Scotland, 1707–1727* (1964).

Robertson, J., *The Scottish Enlightenment and the Militia Issue* (Edinburgh, 1985).

Robertson, J. (ed.), *A Union for Empire: Political Thought and the Union of 1707* (Cambridge, 1995).

Rogers, N., *Crowds, Culture, and Politics in Georgian Britain* (Oxford, 1998).

Sanderson, E. C., *Women and Work in Eighteenth-Century Edinburgh* (London, 1996).

Saville, R., *Bank of Scotland: A History, 1695–1995* (Edinburgh, 1996).

Shaw, J., *Water Power in Scotland, 1550–1870* (Edinburgh, 1984).

Shaw, J. S., *The Management of Scottish Society, 1707–1764* (Edinburgh, 1983).

Simpson, K. (ed.), *Burns Now* (Edinburgh, 1994).

Simpson, K. (ed.), *Love & Liberty. Robert Burns, A Bicentenary Celebration* (East Linton, 1997).

Smith, J. S., and Stevenson, D. (eds), *Fermfolk & Fisherfolk: Rural Life in Northern Scotland in the Eighteenth and Nineteenth Centuries* (Aberdeen, 1989).

Smout, T. C., *Scottish Trade on the Eve of the Union, 1660–1707* (Edinburgh, 1963) .

Smout, T. C., *A History of the Scottish People, 1560–1830* (1969).

Smout, T. C., *A Century of the Scottish People, 1830–1950* (1986).

Smout, T. C. (ed.), *Scotland and Europe, 1200–1850* (Edinburgh, 1986).

Smout, T. C. (ed.), *Scottish Woodland History* (Edinburgh, 1997).

Stevenson, D., *The Origins of Freemasonry: Scotland's Century, 1590–1710* (Cambridge, 1990 ed.).

Stevenson, D (ed.), *From Lairds to Louns: County and Burgh Life in Aberdeen, 1600–1800* (Aberdeen, 1986).

Stone, L. (ed.), *An Imperial State at War: Britain from 1689 to 1815* (1994).

Thomson, W. P. L., *Kelp-Making in Orkney* (Kirkwall, 1983).

Thompson, E. P., *The Making of the English Working Class* (1963).

Thompson, E. P., *Customs in Common* (1991).

Whatley, C. A., '*Bought and Sold for English Gold?' Explaining the Union of 1707* (Glasgow, 1994).

Whatley, C. A., *The Industrial Revolution in Scotland* (Cambridge, 1997).

Whyte, I. D., *Agriculture and Society in Seventeenth Century Scotland* (Edinburgh, 1979).

Withers, C. W. J., *Urban Highlanders: Highland–Lowland Migration and Urban Gaelic Culture, 1700–1900* (East Linton, 1998).

Wormald, J. (ed.), *Scotland Revisited* (1991).

Young, J. D., *The Rousing of the Scottish Working Class* (1979).

Index